# The Han

By Stewart Francis, F.R.S.A.

First Published 1961
Second Edition: Revised and Extended 1977
Third Edition: Extended 1991

# Fourth Edition

Edited, expanded and annotated
by Frank Andrew Lawler

PER ARDUA AD ALTA

Hanny of Sorbie

# Table of Contents

ix

# Preface to the Fourth Edition

There have been tremendous advances in publishing technology since *The Hannays of Sorbie* was first written over fifty years ago. This edition is the first version of the book to be transferred to a digital format for editing. New features have been added to make the text more accessible to family researchers. These include uniform typeface throughout, an index and greater use of diagrams, maps and illustrations.

In general, I have retained the variations in the spelling of proper names found in previous editions of the book. For example, "Balliol" may also be spelled as "Baliol", or "Sorbie" spelled as "Sourby" or "Sowerby". Spelling was not standardised even by the reign of James VI/I in the 17th century, which means that early Scottish documents may refer to the same name using varied spelling. Of course, it is possible that the variations were deliberate, and that, as in "Gilbert de Annethe" and "Gilbert de Hannethe", two distinct persons are meant. Unfortunately, from the vantage point of the 21st century, we have no way of knowing with absolute certainty the intent of an original transcriber in the 13th century.

The body of this edition has been expanded to incorporate the errata section and several appendices from the third edition, placing their information into relevant, existing chapters. Furthermore, extensive footnotes, additional images and tables have been added, as have a glossary, maps and an index. Finally, the text has been reviewed and revised with an eye to greater readability and relevance to a global Hannay community.

If you are reading this edition in an eBook format and have an internet connection, you will discover that underlined references to ancestors hyperlink to the corresponding record in the online family tree maintained by the Clan Hannay Society at www.clanhannay.org/fh/. This can prove to be helpful in navigating the many similar given names in Hanna/h/e/y history. It is not uncommon, for example, to find a father, son and grandson each named "John Hannay" in a particular town, all of whom are quite distinct from yet another "John Hannay" living in a nearby village. Confused as to whom you are reading about? Simply click on the name to see the context of the person in a web browser.

Sources of the new information include:

- Family history information provided by Dr. David Hannay, 2nd Chief of the Clan; Clan Genealogist Dr. Keith Hanna; and Clan Genealogist Emeritus Tony Lowe.

- The results of the 1983 dig conducted by the Archaeological Department of the University of Glasgow and a 1996 survey by Clan Archaeologist Packard Harrington.

- Input from Hannas, Hannahs, Hanneys and Hannays from around the world.

- A greatly expanded list of online and print sources which can be found at the end of the book.

Where it has been possible to identify the locations of places mentioned, I have tried to include them in maps.

I am indebted to Chief David Hannay and Keith Hanna of the Clan Hannay Society for checking historical information and to my extraordinarily patient wife Ann McCurdy for countless hours spent proof-reading.


Frank Andrew Lawler
Seattle, Washington
USA
October, 2019

# A Note on Dates

You may see the dating format

**OS/NS**, i.e. *Old Style/New Style*.

This is a standard way of representing a change that occurred in 1600 in the way years were numbered in Scotland. Up until then, New Year's Day was celebrated on the 25th of March, which meant that March 24th, 1598 would have been followed the next day by March 25th, 1599. Because of this, potentially ambiguous dates are written in an OS/NS designation. For example, 1587/88 means the year in which January 1 through March 24 would have been considered 1587, and the balance of the year, 1588.

The matter becomes more complicated when one realizes that the English did not realign their calendar to start on January 1st until 1752; thus for 152 years, England and Scotland started their years on different dates. As such, the OS/NS designation for *English* records applies to dates up until 1752.

Finally, to muddy the waters even further, British dates until 1752 were calculated according to the Julian calendar, which slightly overestimated the length of a year. The result caused the seasons to slip increasingly out of sync with dates. In 1582, Pope Gregory XIII decreed for all Catholic countries a new calendar, which more accurately calculated leap years. In addition, to make up for the lost time since the creation of the Julian calendar, that year was shortened by 11 days. Britain, however, a Protestant stronghold, stuck to the Julian calendar for another 170 years, and during that time was out of alignment with the rest of Europe by those 11 days.

A chart comparing old and new style Scottish and English dates is provided in Appendix E: Dates and Calendar Differences.

F. A. Lawler

# Preface to the 3rd Edition (1991)

This third edition is being launched by the Society with some generous anonymous help.

I should like to dedicate this edition to Alex Hannah who was our most excellent Secretary from the inception of the Society for many years until just recently.

Much of the success of the Society is due to his indefatigable efforts to place us on the map. He showed great skill and energy in getting the Society well recognized and we all owe him a very great debt.

For these reasons I feel that we should dedicate this edition to him for his great contribution.


S. Francis
Armathwaite Castle
Carlisle, UK
2 May 1990

# Foreword to the 2nd Edition (1977)

I am sure that we who are honoured to bear the name of Hannay will join me in offering a vote of thanks to Lt. Col. Stewart Francis for giving us this intensive history of our antecedents through the ages, and which is so admirably rendered.

My late husband, Sir Walter Fergusson Hannay[1], was one of the original members of the Committee for the restoration of the Tower of Sorbie, and I know he would have been grateful, as am I, for the painstaking research that has gone to the making of this memorable book.

It is of particular interest to me as a historian to read of the origin of the Clan even if, as Stewart Francis suggests, much has been lost in antiquity. But that the Hannay, or Hannach as he may have been known, fought under Richard Coeur de Lion during the third Crusade, has been floated into legend; yet is it legendary or is it fact?

We are told that the Hannach was knighted by King Richard, the Lion Heart, on the field of battle for conspicuous valour, and that he chose for his motto *Per Ardua ad Alta*. In some of the crests of the Crusaders we see the Saracen's crescent placed at the side of the coat of arms. Not so the crest of the Hannays. The crescent in our crest is placed under the cross crosslet indicating that Knights Templar in the third Crusade defeated the Saracen[2]. This book not only covers the families of Hannay right back to the thirteenth century, but also gives us invaluable information concerning Scottish social history. It must be of inestimable value to the descendants of those Hannays who figure in the many letters quoted by Stewart Francis in this second edition of the Hannays of Sorbie.

May we hope that a worldwide circulation among all of the Clan will go far toward the restoration of the Tower of Sorbie, stronghold of the Hannays whose roots are in the distant past.

DORIS LESLIE[3]

---

[1] Sir Walter Fergusson Hannay, MRCS, LRCP, 1904-1961, was a London doctor who was personal physician to British Prime Minister Clement Atlee.

[2] The crescent in our crest may or may not be related to the Crusades. There is now some dispute as to its meaning, as discussed in chapter XXIII: Tartan, Heraldry and the Clan Society.

[3] Lady Doris Leslie Fergusson Hannay, 1902-1982, wrote 14 novels and several biographies. Sir Walter was her second husband.

# Preface to the 2nd Edition (1977)

In undertaking a second edition of this book, I have endeavoured to expand the earlier chapters and to include the many amendments and corrections that have been sent to me by the subscribers and readers of the original work. I have also included a considerable amount of new material, which has come to hand and expanded on those of our name and Clan who spell their name Hanna, Hannah or Hanney. The formation of a Clan Society has helped greatly in this work and I should particularly like to thank Alex Hannah, our able Secretary, for all the help and encouragement he has given in getting this book to a second edition.

I trust I have cleared up any mistakes or omissions that were in the first edition. A family history is a living document and I trust that all of you who read it will from time to time make your new material available to the author so this document can be a true picture not only of the Hannays, Hannas and Hannahs of long ago but of today also.

Stewart Francis
Armathwaite Castle.
16th March 1974

# Preface to the 1<sup>st</sup> Edition (1961)

Family history is a subject that might be said by many to be produced rather out of pride, sometimes in itself no bad thing, than out of desire to produce history.

It might be that many books, such as this, started with that aim in view. But I can assure you that before long, the author becomes so absorbed in social history and, in particular, in the law, that the accent of his work shifts from motives of family pride to those of a serious historian.

It is only from family history that the various facets of everyday life can be discovered. From people's letters, from legal documents, from court cases, the historian begins to get an inside glimpse into the daily doings and actions of the average man of the period under review.

This book covers the whole of Scottish domestic history from the 13th Century onwards. It is by no means complete, and is lacking in many details—they were not always available—but most of the people in it were ordinary people of their time, and from them perhaps we shall be able to get a glimpse of the everyday life of our ancestors.

I must, before going further, thank the many members of the family who have been so kind as to put at my disposal a large number of most interesting documents and papers. In particular I must thank Mrs. Whitty who provided me with so much on David Hannay, the Consul at Barcelona, Mrs. Armour Hannay and her daughter for help with the chapter on Kingsmuir, Mr. Patrick Hannay for the diary of Margaret Hannay in India, Mrs. Helen Hannay of Sunnyside, Melrose, for much Ruscoe information, Mrs. Hannay Thompson of Drumaston for letters and documents, Col. Rainsford Hannay for the great help he has given me, and to many others.

I must not, however, forget the Universities of Glasgow and Edinburgh, the Bodleian Library and the British Museum, all of whom have given me much sympathetic understanding and a degree of help quite outside their statutory obligations.

To the Lord Lyon and to General Register House I also tender my thanks. In particular I must mention Mr. R. C. Reed of Cleughbrae, Dumfries, who has been a tower of strength and a constant help in the completion of this work. He has given me a great deal of his valuable time and placed at my disposal his extensive and scholarly translations and calendars of documents.

There are many others who have helped, and to whom I am grateful. I trust that this effort of mine will go some way towards repairing the gap in our social history that at present is so much in need of filling.

Finally, I want to thank particularly my father Col. A.N. Francis for making possible the production of this book by his indefatigable efforts and also Mr. Bernard Honess of the Independent Press for making publication possible at all.

Stewart Francis
Zaria
Kaduna State, Nigeria
20th February 1958

# I: Origins of the Family: 9th to 14th Century

**Figure 1: The Galloway Coast, Southwestern Scotland**

The origins of the Family of Hannay are lost in antiquity. Some authorities argue that they may be of Norse origin. During the ninth century, sea raiders from Denmark and Norway harassed and eventually settled along the west coast of Scotland. They are known to have used the bays and inlets on the coast of Galloway to raid ships in the narrow channel between Scotland and Ireland. The coast of Galloway (see Figure 1) lends itself to this sort of activity, and one can easily imagine a fleet of longships laden with armed raiders pushing up the creeks and inlets to plunder, establish a raiding base, and, eventually, to settle.

The Hannay name is found in various parts of Europe. In the Czech Republic region of Moravia[4], for instance, there is a district and a river

---

[4] Coincidentally in the 19th century, Moravians from the Hanna (or Hana) river valley emigrated to Pennsylvania (USA), where Scottish Hannas also settled.

1

named Hanna. The inhabitants are a Slavonian tribe called Hannako. In Poland, there is a town named Hannah on the river Bug. In Guernsey there is another island called Hannoys, and on the west coast of Ireland, near Rinveal Point, an island called Hannachrem.

Stewart Francis, in earlier editions of this book, suggested that the original home of the family was the island of Hanö, off the coast of Sweden in the Baltic Sea. The reasoning for this theory seems to be an etymological one: The ending 'ay' in 'Hannay' is likely of Norse origin; this is also the Icelandic ending for 'an island'. In Swedish, the ending for 'an island', however, is *ö*, as in *Hanö*. It is intriguing to speculate that the island is the birthplace of the first Hannays, but Hanö is very small and rocky. There are no cars, and its current population is roughly 60 full-time residents. Although there may be archaeological evidence of human activity in the region thousands of years ago[5], Hanö was likely uninhabited in modern times until the 19th century.

Villages named Hanney existed in both Lincolnshire and Berkshire before the Norman Conquest in 1066. As Lincolnshire was largely peopled by Northmen, it is a fair assumption that a Norse chieftain settled there, and possibly another chieftain from the same Norwegian village settled in Galloway. Another possibility is that the family first settled in Lincolnshire, and later came to Galloway either in the train of King Edward I during the late 13th century or as a part of the plantation of Anglo-Norman families in the 11th century. Tradition, however, has it that the Hannays were settled in Galloway in the ninth century.

There were a number of Anglo-Norman families, including Balliol, Veterpont and De Brus, who were settled by the eleventh century in Galloway; it is possible that the Hannays were among these.

Further suggestions have been made that the family might be of Irish origin. There were certainly Irish connections, but not until much later with the Scottish plantation of Ireland in the 17th century. Norsemen settled on both sides of the Irish Sea, and no doubt families have the same roots on both sides, but mostly likely the first settlement was on the Wigtownshire coast (see Figure 2).

---

[5] According to findings from the 2018 Haväng project, Lund University

2

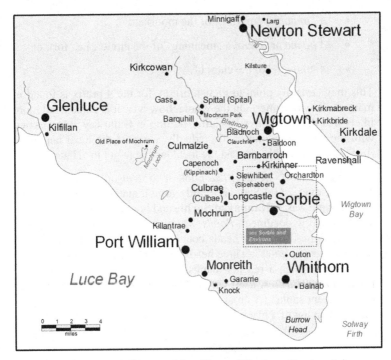

**Figure 2: The Wigtownshire Coast (Machars Peninsula)**

There are other possible origins of the Hannay name.

Watson (Dumfries and Galloway Archaeological Society, 1935)[6], states that the Hannay name may come from *Ap Sheanaigh* (son of Senanh), rather than *Ua Seanaigh*, as is sometimes proposed.

There is another suggestion that the name may be of Pictish[7] Gaelic origin from one of the following roots:

---

[6] It is unclear who **Watson** is. He is probably Prof. William J. Watson (1865–1948), who wrote *The Celts (British and Gael) in Dumfries and Galloway* (Dumfries, 1924), although it could possibly refer to the historian, architect and artist George Patrick Houston Watson (1887-1959). In either case, the "Dumfries and Galloway Archaeological Society" doesn't seem to have existed. Stewart Francis may be referring to the Dumfries and Galloway Natural History and Antiquarian Society, but a search of their proceedings from 1933 to 1935 has not turned up the source of this reference. Perhaps the research was originally related in the proceedings of the Ayrshire and Galloway Archaeological Society or its successors.

[7] **Pictish** refers to the language and culture of the Picts, an ancient Celtic people of the British Isles.

3

- *A'hannah*, signifying "of the moorland[8]";

- *A'hanne* or *A'hainne*, meaning "of the circle", i.e., fort; or

- *Ahannaid*, "of the church".

This may certainly point to Pictish origin, for the *A* prefix is found in many Galloway names. On the whole, however, it is considered more likely that the Norse invaders, after settling in Galloway, intermarried with the local population and gradually accepted the local language. *Ap Sheanaigh* was the nearest the local language got to "Hannay".

Alexander Nisbet, in his 1722 book *A System of Heraldry* (which describes over 2,600 Scottish family arms), states that the principal family name was **A'Hannay of Sorbie** and bore arms according to the 1624 heraldry document *Pont's Manuscript of Arms*[9] as follows: "Argent Three Roebucks heads couped azure collard or, with a bell pendant there-at gules" (Three heads of bucks, each wearing a yellow collar from which a red bell hangs, all on a white background; See Figure 114). The crest itself was a "Cross crosslet fitchcee issuing out of a crescent sable" (A cross whose arms themselves end in crosses, mounted on top of a black crescent, See Figure 3: The Clan Crest).

**Figure 3: The Clan Crest**

---

[8] A **moorland** is a field of peaty soil covered with moss, bracken and heather.

[9] **Pont's Manuscript of Arms** can be found at the Office of the Lord Lyon in Edinburgh.

There is a tradition that the progenitor of the family was Patrick A'Hannay living at Sorbie about 1150. Very little evidence can be found for him, but tradition is strong, and so he should be mentioned.

The original property of the family is not known, but a whole district of Wigtonshire was known as the "Machars[10] Hannay", so powerful were they.

The ancient property of Sorbie, which was the seat of the family for many years, is known to have belonged to a family named Sorby or de Sorby. According to Sorbie family history[11], there is a legend that the Sorbies were expelled from Galloway by King James VI in the late 16th century. It may well be that the Sorbie family were in fact Hannays, going under the same name as their property, for in *Acta Dominorum consilii* (Proceedings of the Council of Lords) for 1488, Odo Hannay is shown as Odo Sorbie, whilst his sons are clearly shown as Hannays.

## 1. The Veterponte Family

According to McKerlie, a 19th century researcher and author of the book *Lands and their Owners in Galloway*, there were two churches in the parish during the 12th and 13th centuries, one called Great Soureby (Sorbie) and the other Little Soureby. About the end of the 12th century, Great Soureby was granted by Ivo de Veterponte[12] to the Abbey of Dryburgh. This grant was confirmed by Roland, Lord of Galloway (under whom de Veterponte held the lands), and further confirmed by the bishop and prior of Whithorn. The abbey, founded in 1150, is located near Newtown St. Boswells, about 90 miles, as the crow flies, northeast of Sorbie. Abbey records inform us that in 1240 Robert de Veteriponte gave to the Abbey the church and lands of Lesser Sowerby (Sorbie), and that the Prior and Convent of Candida Casa (probably the first church in Scotland, established by St. Ninian in the 5th century on the site of what became the Priory of Whithorn) agreed to pay 20 merks (a Scottish silver coin worth 13 shillings, 4 pence) for the fruits, revenues and dues of Sowerby and Kirkgolan[13]. The Prior of Candida

---

[10] **Machars** are low-lying coastal land. In this case the term refers to the land between Newton Stewart and Burrow Head. - *Tony Lowe*

[11] See **sorbie.net**

[12] Variously spelled Veteriponte, Vetereponte, Veterpont, Vipont and several other variations. Prior to 1066, this ancient family of French origin was known as *Vieuxpont* (Old Bridge). The names William and Robert were very common in the family and as such it is difficult to ascertain the exact relationship between the various Veterponts.

[13] **Kirkgolan** – probably a now-vanished place in Sorbie parish, although it may refer to Kirkcolm, near Stranraer. It may also be a spelling variation of Kirkcowan, but this does not seem to be the case. – *Tony Lowe*

Casa was appointed as procurator[14] by the Abbot and Convent of Dryburgh, and in the register of Dryburgh, Sorbie appears in 1221, 1228 and 1280, when a rent of 12 merks is paid to the Prior of Candida Casa.

It may be that the Hannays even at this early date held Sorbie in fief from the Abbot, for it is unlikely that the Veterponts lived there after Robert's gift to the church in 1240. William of Veterponte had granted, in 1234, Lesser Sorbie to the Abbot of Dryburgh for the soul of his lord, Alan, son of Roland, Lord of Galloway. Whether these are the same grants is not certain; Robert was likely William's nephew, and probably a minor at this time. Robert's father may have been dead. His grandfather, Ivo, who started the Galloway branch of the family, had been granted Sorbie as early as 1165[15]. Ivo may have placed the guardianship of the estate in the hands of William, who seems to have headed the Midlothian branch of the family. Robert Veterponte headed the English branch, settling in Westmoreland.

In 1251 the Veterponts had the Manor[16] of Sorbie from John, 5th Baron of Balliol[17], and it is recorded that they gave wadset[18] half of it to Ivo's grandson, John le Fraunceys[19]. The first mention of Sorbie in the Register of the Great Seal of Scotland[20] is in 1325 when Robert I, the Bruce, confirmed the grant of various lands to the Abbey of Whithorn, among them being "that piece of land of Soreby which John McLachan gave them". In 1329 a charter confirmed one Richard McCuffok in the possession of various lands including "six Oxgangs[21] of land of

---

[14] Although in general a **procurator** means a legal proxy, a more archaic meaning is "tax collector", which may be a more appropriate definition in this case.

[15] **Ivo and Alan de Veteriponte** had a grant of lands at Great and Little Sorbie in Galloway from King William I (the Lion) of Scotland (1165 - 1214) -- *Tony Lowe*

[16] **Manor** in this sense refers to a parcel of land rather than a physical building.

[17] John, 5th Baron of Balliol, is not to be confused with his son, John Balliol, King of Scotland, 1292-1296

[18] A **wadset** was an early type of mortgage. See glossary for details.

[19] **John le Fraunceys** was the son of Hugh le Fraunceys (or le Fraunceis). His mother seems to have been Joan de Veteriponte, daughter of Ivo de Veteriponte. – French, Aaron Davis Weld, *Notes on the Surnames of Francus, Franceis, French, Etc.*, Boston,1893 and Harrison, George Henry, T*he History of Yorkshire*, London, 1885.

[20] **The Register of the Great Seal of Scotland** contained "information about recorded Commissions issued to Queen's [i.e., Monarch's] Counsel, persons receiving Royal Appointments, etc., authenticated with the Great Seal of Scotland" – *Registers of Scotland Executive Agency*

[21] An **oxgang** was a Scottish measurement of land approximately equivalent to 13 acres (on average, as the exact size varied from between 10 and 18 acres from region to region). It is supposed to be the amount of land ploughable by a single ox in one year.

6

Kelinsture and Cloentes in the parish of Soureby". In 1426 Robert II confirmed the gift that his father had made to Symon Lytil [Little] of lands in the Barony of Mallarynok, which included Sourbi.

At what date the Hannay family gained possession of the property is almost impossible to ascertain, as the records of the period are so sparse. Many historians consider that the Veterponts ceased to reside at Sorbie after 1240 and the Hannays followed them. Two Gilberts (Gilbert de Hannethe and a Gilbert de Annethe), possibly father and son, are not designated of Sorbie, but there are two facts which point to the Hannays succeeding the Viponts.

Firstly, "Gilbert de Sowerby" witnessed a charter by William de Cunynburg about 1268, according to the 1853 *Registrum Honoris de Morton: A Series of Ancient Charters of the Earldom of Morton with Other Original Papers in Two Volumes*. This was no doubt the same Gilbert de Annethe who signed the Ragman Roll in 1296.

The second fact is a heraldic one. The mottoes of the Hannays and Viponts are almost identical, namely:

> Hannay: *Per Ardua ad Alta*—Through Hardships to the Highest Places.
>
> Veterpont: *Per Aspera ad Alta*—Through Difficulties to the Highest Places.

This similarity in mottoes seems to point to a peaceable succession, possibly by marriage.

## 2. Earliest Mentions of the Hannays

In 1292, whilst Robert the Bruce was struggling to establish Scottish independence, Edward I of England succeeded in occupying the border regions of Scotland and setting up his nominee John Baliol as King. In order to secure his position in accordance with feudal custom, and to assert his rights as feudal overlord of Scotland[22], Edward arranged for the feudal lords and chieftains of Scotland to swear allegiance to him at Berwick, and their names were entered in a document called the

---

[22] This title originated not from conquest but from the Saxon heptarchy (seven kingdoms of Britain), when the Bretwalda of England was indeed the overlord of southern Scotland. **Bretwalda**, from the Anglo-Saxon *Bretanwealda*, means, roughly, "Lord of Britain". The Bretwalda was an (often unheld) honourary title conferred upon the single most powerful of the various kings ruling parts of Britain during the first millennium AD. This role implied a *de facto* overlordship rather than a legal one. The kings who held this title included Ethelbert of Kent (552-616), Ethelbad of Mercia (735-757) and Alfred the Great of Wessex (871-899).

Ragman Roll[23]. Among them on that day in 1296 were a Gilbert de Hannethe and a Gilbert de Annethe of County Wigtown, or as it appears in the roll, dated August 28th, 1296:

> "Item a tous ceaus qui cestes lettres verront ou orront / Dovenal Makachelson / Nichol le fiz Adam de Dunbertan.../ é Gilbert de Annethe / Fergus Askolo / Gilbert de Hannethe / é Thomas de Kithehilt / del counte de Wiggeton..."

Or

> "Likewise, to all those who read or hear these documents:/ Dovenal Makachelson / Nichol the son of Adam of Dunbertan.../ and Gilbert of Annethe / Fergus Askolo / Gilbert of Hannethe, and Thomas of Kithehilt / from the county of Wigtown..."

These two were probably father and son. Along with them were the other powerful chiefs of Galloway, the MacDowells and the MacCullachs.

The next entry concerning them is also in 1296, when Gilbert de Hannith (probably Hannethe) is mentioned as a juror in the inquest concerning the succession of Ela (also referred to as Eleanor or Elana) de la Zouche (*née* Longespée) in Scotland. Ela's son was claiming certain properties in five counties in southern Scotland. An inquisition assembled at Berwick with assessors from each of the districts. The register reads as follows:

> "Inquisition at Berwich on Saturday next after St. Bartholomews day 24th year before Sir Walter de Twynham Keeper of the Sheriff of Wigtoun by Sir John de Genilhiston, Sir Thomas de Thorthorold, Sir Henry de Mundewyl, Thomas McCulach, Michael his brother, Ralph de Campagnia, Roland Askeloch, Hector his son, William de Polmaloche, Elyas de Lehakis, Gilbert de Hannith, Dougal son of Gotrich and Fergus McDuhile who find on oath that Lady Eleonor la Zouche held in capite of the king the third part of the Vill of Manhinton in the County of Wigtoun by service due in the County of Dumfries. It was worth to her 27 merks yearly. Alan la Zouche is her next heir and 24 years of age or more.

> Inquisition on the succession of Elena de la Zouche in Scotland under six writs directed to the sheriffs of Fife, Dumfries, Ayr, Wigton, Berwick on Tweed and Edinburgh, dated at Haddington 20th August 1296."

Towards the end of 1296, trouble started up in Galloway. The rebellion was mostly likely due to the sympathy of the Galloway men for John Baliol, whose mother Devorgilla was a Gallovidian.[24] Compelled by

---

[23] Currently in The National Archives.

[24] **Gallovidian**: resident of Galloway

8

English indignities, Baliol withdrew his allegiance to Edward in March, 1297. The Hannays appear to have kept their oath of loyalty to Edward I, but the Gallovidians and Baliol himself are said to have taken an important part in the two great raids made into the rear of Edward's armies at Berwick, on Monday, March 26 and Sunday, April 8, with incredible cruelties. On June 12, 1297, Edward gave thanks to the Celts who had remained faithful. The uprising capitulated at Irvine in July 1297 and the Scots consigned 22 hostages into English hands. Robert Wishart, Archbishop of Glasgow, Sir James the Steward, John his brother (father of the first Stewart of Dalswinton), Robert Bruce, Earl of Carrich (later Robert I of Scotland), Sir William Douglas and Sir Robert Lindsey are mentioned in the "Covenant of Confession of Rebellion" at Irvine.

In 1298 between July 20 and August 7, the Galloway men besieged Carlisle castle. The Hannays do not appear in the list of names of those who aided John Balliol against England, who made submission to him by letters done at Wigtown, or who gave hostages on July 25.

In 1304 in the list of gifts conferred on various Scotsmen by Edward I, no doubt in return for some service in the Galloway rebellion, the following entry occurs:

> "...Fait a remembrer des .... Gaufrid .... monzr Renaud de Crauford et les authres les enemies le Roi... XLV merks. Gibon Hanechyn [Hannay] aura XXV merks / Dugal Macdowell aura XXV merks..."

Or

> "...Act to record .... Gaufrid .... monsieur Renaud de Crauford and the other enemies of the King...45 merks / Gibon Hanechyn (Hannay) will have 25 merks / Dugal Macdowell will have 25 merks..." [25]

The Hannays did not take part in Wallace's rising in 1297, nor in the subsequent successful efforts of Robert the Bruce in his struggle for Kingship in 1305. However, in 1308, Edward Bruce, brother of the king, invaded Galloway, took prisoners, destroyed much property, and drove out the English Keeper of the Marches. The Hannays who had been loyal to King Edward suffered heavily for their pains. After this, there is no direct evidence concerning the family till the middle of the fourteenth century. This is not at all unusual as, due to the wars of

---

[25] Palgrave, Sir Francis, *Documents and Records illustrating the History of Scotland and the Transactions between the Crowns of England and Scotland*, Vol. I, London, 1837.

independence and the generally disturbed state of the country, records were lost or deliberately destroyed.

## 3. Hannays in the 14<sup>th</sup> Century

In 1329, when David Bruce succeeded his father Robert to become King David II of Scotland, Edward Balliol the son of John Baliol disputed the succession. The dispute went to Edward III of England, and in 1333 an English Army was sent to Scotland to place Baliol on the Throne. The men of Galloway still loyal to the Baliols supported him, but after a few months the Barons of Scotland forced Baliol out and restored David II. The Hannays, having supported Baliol, again fell on hard times.

By this time the Hannays were likely in occupation of the Wigtown area and possibly holding Sorbie.

In 1346, King David II, to assist the French after their defeat at the disastrous Battle of Crécy, decided to invade England. He crossed the border of Cumberland at the head of a large army, and advanced towards Durham, laying waste to many places and burning the famous Abbey of Lanercost on the outskirts of Brampton, near Carlisle. He expected an easy march south into England as the English army was away overseas.

But Edward III had a plan to deal with just this contingency: in recruiting his army for Crécy, he had deliberately not included men from north of the Humber. William de la Zouche, the Archbishop of York and Warden of the Marches, collected an army and faced David II just outside the walls of Durham at Neville's Cross. On October 17, 1346, the Scots attacked and were decisively defeated, and King David II and many of his knights taken prisoner to London. There may well have been a Hannay among them on King David's side—in fact, in the list of prisoners taken at the battle is a David Annand; he may well be a member of the Annandale family, but it is possible that with the free spelling of the period that he might be of Sorbie's stock. Whoever he was, it was not until 1354 that the English Commissioners agreed to his release, together with Walter de Haliburton and Andrew Campbell, from Carlisle Castle without ransom.

Edward III was not satisfied yet. He sent an army into Scotland under Edward Baliol and Earl Percy in the spring of 1347. Baliol marched into Galloway and ravaged it.

Only eight years later, in 1355, Edward III entered Scotland once more, but the hostility of the people froze him out. He did, however, sack the southern part of the country.

10

The next Hannays that appear – and there are many in the Scottish records of the period, described as De Hannas, Hannays and A'Hannays – are two churchmen. Fynlaus A'Hanna on May 14, 1390 was granted by Antipope Clement VII[26], at Avignon, a benefice in the gift of the Bishop and Chapter of Whithorn. He is described as "Three years scolar of civil law and a Cannon of Whitherne". In 1394, Brice A'Hanna, also a priest, was put up in the Bishop of Dunblane's list for a benefice in the gift of the Abbot and Convent of Paisley. This was granted by Antipope Benedict XIII[27].

An Andrew Hannay of Sorbie is mentioned in 1416, when Archibald, Earl of Wigton, headed the Royal Archers of Scotland to France to fight the English. He remained for many years in the service of the King of France, probably as a member of the *Garde Ecossaise*, an elite Scottish military unit who were personal bodyguards to the French monarchy, and he likely fought alongside Archibald in the Battle of Baugé in 1421 when the *Garde Ecossaise* defeated the English. The regiment received precedence above all others in the French Army.

Some years later, we find members of the family in the Scottish Archer Guard of the French army. In 1448 David Lamne (probably Hannay) and James Han are mentioned. When Robert de Conygham was Captain in 1469 in the reign of Louis XI, we find Andro Hannay listed in the Muster roll as an *Homme d'Armes*. In 1498, Hannay Bar Bancor is mentioned.

Appearing in the Muster rolls of the King of France's Life Guards are Jehan Hanneste in 1452 and 1453, John Hannesle in 1453, and Andro Waneh in 1471. These are all probably variants of the family name.

## 4.  *John Hannay, Royal Shipmaster*

About this time also there is a John Hannay of Dundee who appears in 1424 as shipmaster to James I, King of Scots. He is thought to be of Sorbie stock.

There are two entries concerning John in the Calendar of Documents[28], and they show him as personal shipmaster to the king with special privileges, both from the Scottish and English Customs, as he is

---

[26] *Antipope* Clement *VII*, a rival claimant to the Holy See during the Great Schism of the Western Church, held office from 1378-1394. France, Naples, Scotland and Spain recognized Clement VII (ruling from Avignon, in France), while Bohemia, England, Flanders, Germany, Hungary, Italy, Poland, and Portugal supported Urban VI (ruling from Rome).

[27] Antipope Benedict XIII ruled from Avignon starting in 1394.

[28] **Calendar of Documents**: A collection of published abstracts of the affairs of state executed by the Secretary of State under the direction of the royal council.

11

permitted to import a number of items free of customs duty for the use of King James. The two entries, both on October 20th, read as follows, the first one:

> "Warrent for the safe conduct for John of Hanna, master of a ship of James King of Scotland and a crew of twenty men to trade to England for a year. Westminster."

> [Privy Seals (Tower), 3 Hen. VI. file 5]

and the second one:

> "Fiat for conduct for ... [John] Hanna, the master, to buy and ship at London in a vessel the 'Cristofer' of Aberdyn in Scotland, for the use of James King of Scotland free of custom, a 'pipa cum ollis de corio', another pipe with ... of leather, 1000 beams of wood, two pipes with stokfyssche ... called Standardes, a pair of coffers for the chapel, a pair of 'cofres' for wax, two buttes of Romeneye, four buttes of Malueseye, a barrel of Tyre ... ferdekyus of sturgeon, a 'pipa cum cellis', two pair of bouges for carrying water, a barrel of 'reysuns de corauntes', gabellos zingiberis viridis,' 2 bales of ..., 2 barrels of tin vessels, a trussell of canevas, 9 yards of purpill cloth, a piece of murrey cloth of 7 yards, a piece of green cloth ... 12 'scabellorum muttor', 4 lbs. copper, 2 barrels of pears called 'wardons,' 2 barrels of apples, 12 bows, 10 dozen of cords, ... crossbows with their fittings, viz. 12 takelys, 2 books of 'Chardequinte,' a phial of rose water, a certain purse (manticam) of Harald count of Danzhaw, 3 'getons', 2 books for the chapel, a bible (biblia), 12 menever skins 'pured', a worsted bed, 12 yards of worsted 'pro costeres,'5 groos of ligule, 12 skins of 'roo', ... 6 pulvinaria, 6 lanterns, 6 sconces, 50 lb. of seed for ' popynjayes', 10 pewter pots, 2 candelabra of 'laton', a bale of prunes, a chaufour of laton, and 6 ' fowy'. Westminster."

> [Chancery Miscellaneous Portfolios, No 41/188][29]

Legitimate piracy was a common sport of sailors, and perhaps the reason that John Hannay was given a safe conduct to trade with England, in these years when, to say the least, both countries were not on the friendliest terms. He was, in fact, the forerunner of the seadogs of Scotland, flourishing a century before Drake and Raleigh, in the person of Sir Andrew Wood[30] and those of his ilk.

At this period, the Navy, as such, did not exist. In time of war the merchant fleet were engaged as ships of war. The design of merchant ships was no different from that of warships, and in some cases the ships were property of the king, as probably in the case of Captain John

---

[29] This entry is noted as being "Much defaced in parts."

[30] **Sir Andrew Wood** (1455-1539) was a Scottish naval commander known for his victories against the English.

Hannay's ship, the *Christopher* of Aberdeen. His ship must have been similar to Sir Andrew Wood's famous *Yellow Carvel*, built in 1475 (See Figure 4). She would have been "carvel-built"—having flush (as opposed to overlapping) planks—with fore and stern castles to provide good fighting platforms for men at arms. Perhaps at this period they were temporary structures, but certainly by 1480 they had become a permanent part of ship's design. The stern castle also provided deck space for the commander, and headroom for the great cabin below. The mainmast carried a single square sail, with a laced bonnet which could be removed to shorten sail. The mizzen mast carried a small lateen sail, of the type frequently seen in the Mediterranean. This served to lighten the task of the helmsman. The original purpose of the small square foresail was to act as a headsail, and thus the foremast was placed as far forward as possible.

**Figure 4: The Yellow Caravel**

The ship's armament was intended to be used against the men of the enemy ship and not the ship herself. It consisted probably of small guns (about six or seven) besides culverins (medieval cannons) and crossbows. When the ship was grappled to the enemy ship, fire balls,

13

lime pots, and other missiles were thrown from the fighting top, and a battle was fought out to a bitter close, resulting in one side or other taking the enemy vessel home as a prize.

In 1426-27, John Hannay appears in the Burgess Roll[31] of Aberdeen, and in 1438, he is shown as master of the King's barge sailing to La Rochelle. It is supposed that his branch of the family settled near Dundee, since in 1575 "John Hannay of Dundee, Burgess[32] and Mariner", appears in the Edinburgh list of Testaments. His will is dated 1st March 1574/5.

## 5. The Hannays Gain Possession of Sorbie

In 1452, the virtual ruler of Galloway William Douglas, 8th Earl of Douglas, quarreled with James II. John Hannay[33], who tradition holds, came into possession of Sorbie around 1424, sided with his king against the Douglasses. The king summoned Douglas to Stirling Castle. There, the king, along with several other men, stabbed him to death and threw his body out the window. Parliament approved his action and sequestered the Douglas estates. The Douglasses resisted this order and raised an army in Galloway. The king marched on them, and in 1455, assisted by the Hannays, defeated the Douglasses at the Battle of Arkinholm. The rule of the Douglasses over Galloway was over and the Hannays were free to expand their influence.

During this time, the family extended its tentacles to many parts of Scotland. Apart from John Hannay, of whom we have just spoken, there are many others. Thomas Hannay, probably a relative of John's, settled in Perth, and was granted property there in 1480. A large family settled in Edinburgh, from whom the court tailor, baker, and commander of artillery to James V were descended (See IV: The Hannays in 16th Century Edinburgh). Branches established themselves in Ayr and Glasgow in the weaving business.

There appear in the early records a number of Hannays. Gilbert who was a bailie (a town functionary) of Wigtown in 1457, and also mentioned in 1448. In 1466 another Gilbert Hannay became chaplain

---

[31] **Burgess Roll**: a census list of sorts used for determining the civic duties of various townsmen (e.g. taxation and military service). In some cases, membership in a tradesman's guild required listing on a burgess roll.

[32] Free citizen of a town (i.e., not a serf).

[33] There appears to be no written record of this **John**, only traditional belief in his existence; the earliest documented Hannay owner of Sorbie was Odo, but as it is generally accepted that Sorbie was in the family's hands at least a generation prior to Odo, John may have been Odo's father or grandfather. Stewart Francis proposed (tentatively) that John was Odo's grandfather in Table II of earlier editions.

14

to the Parliament of Scotland. Other Hannays also appearing are William of Capenoch[34] (Kippinach) in 1484, Charles of Sorbie, 1484, and John in 1477. John, William of Capenoch and Gilbert were probably all brothers[35], but the relationship of these early members of the family it is almost impossible to guess.[36].

---

[34] **Capenoch** is just to the southwest of Penpont, and about two and a half miles southwest of Thornhill, in Dumfriesshire.

[35] In the 3rd edition, Francis' genealogy table and the text of his description of the early family are inconsistent, so for the 4th edition, the early Hannay tree in Figure 5 has been recreated from a combination of information from within the body of the text as well as from earlier versions of the table.

[36] It appears that William of Capenoch was a nephew of Odo's, based on a conjecture attempting to reconcile inconsistent information in Francis' tables and text of earlier editions. William is now listed in the genealogical charts as Odo's nephew, with his father added as Dougal of Culbrae, brother to Odo (See Figure 5: Early Hannays and Figure 8: Hannays of Culbrae and Capenoch).

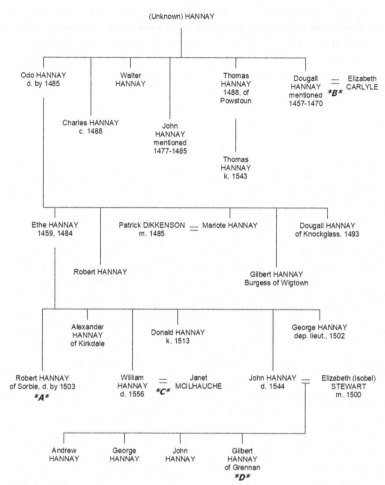

*A*: See Figure 7    *B*: See Figure 8    *C*: See Figure 20    *D*: See Figure 51

**Figure 5: Early Hannays**

The facts about these early Hannays are as follows: John appears in the Secret Seal Register[37] as a witness in a case in Glasgow: "The Register Episcopalis Glasguensis" confirms this, as on January 27, 1477/78 he was concerned in a burgh court case in the tolbooth[38] there. Gilbert, in the Exchequer Rolls on July 10, 1458, gave up the accounts of

---

[37] i.e., the **Privy Seal Register**, a record book of official commands written by the king or queen.

[38] A **tollbooth** (or tolbooth) was a building combining the local government offices and jail, the latter frequently consisting of cells under the town hall. The term comes from the stalls (booths) where taxes (tolls) were collected.

Wigtown. He was probably the provost (mayor) and may either have been the Laird of Sorbie, or perhaps a younger son who settled there as a merchant. He is mentioned as a member of an assize for the Abbott of *Dulce Cor* (Sweetheart Abbey)[39] in 1448.

Another Gilbert, a priest, is mentioned on December 8, 1467 as the Chaplain in Logan[40], and as being witness to a deed of Uthred McDowall. He was still alive in 1503. On August 10, 1471, Henry was cautioner[41] to a deed drawn up by John Makeriston, a burgess of Wigtown. Henry was a burgess and probably the son of Odo's son Gilbert. On February 19, 1466/67, a William Hannay, chaplain, and a Robert Hannay appear in the Register of the Great Seal as witnesses to a deed of John McClellane.

In the "Acts of the Lords in Council in Civil Causes" (*Acta Dominorum consili*) on January 22, 1484/85, the Lords ordered both Charles Hannay of Sorbie and William Hannay of Kippinach to appear before them at Wigtown "on pain of rebellion".

On March 1, 1489, Charles appeared again, when John Kennedy of Twynholm was appointed procurator[42] for Charles and John and Patrick Maxwell, who were summoned to appear before the Lords in some civil case. Yet another Gilbert is mentioned in a case concerning William Colvile of Cumerston[43] on February 13, 1492. There is also another entry concerning Gilbert and Robert as witnesses to a charter of Vedast Greyson, Lord of Lag[44] in 1459.

Another branch of the family were the Hannays of Knockglass, near Stranraer. The first listed member of that branch was Dougal, who was probably a brother of Ethe Hannay of Sorbie. On October 26, 1493, he was in a civil action against Robert Hannay of Sorbie. Dougal appears

---

[39] Located about 8 miles south of Dumfries, and now in ruins, the abbey was founded in 1275.

[40] This may refer either to Logan in Galloway (on the Rhinns, north of Port Logan) or to Logan in Ayrshire (east of Cumnock)

[41] One standing **caution** would act as either a 'backer' or 'character witness'.

[42] A **procurator** is a proxy, a person entrusted with the authorization to act on another's behalf.

[43] The village of Cumerston in Kirkcudbrightshire went under various names through the centuries including, Combistoun (1331) and Compstone (1504). It resides in the parish of Twynholm, which still exists today. -- *Tony Lowe*

[44] The ruins of Castle Lag now stand on Lagg farm in Dunscore, Dumfriesshire.

17

to have been succeeded by Odo, who was a witness to a Corswell[45] charter in 1514, and in 1534 Odo seemed to have been in a rather complicated civil case when he sued Henry Maxwell for obtaining "pretendit sentance" against him for the non-fulfillment of a contract. The extract in the "Acta Dominorium" reads:

> "Jan 20th 1534/5 Anent the letters purchased at the instance of Odo A'hannay and Alexander McDowell against Margaret Vaus spouses who had obtained a pretendit sentance against them as suretys for the deceased Uchtred McDowell of Garthland for nonfulfillment of a contract betwixt him and them for which sentence Odo and Alexander appealed to Glasgow; and because the official (of the Bishop of Glasgow) wrongfully hurt them therein, thus appealed from him and his sentence to the court at Rome and have instituted their appeal in due time and the same being dependant in plea as yet undecided, the said Henry and Margaret raised cursing, agreeing and reagreeing upon the said Odo and Alexander with Letters of caption theron and therwith tends to gar, tak put and hald the in prison wrongfully, considering the are under their appelation fra the said sentance and cursing and the plea dependent theron, nomination suld be made, and therefore the said letters of caption are purchased tanta et suppressa vitae, making no mention of their appelation and therfore the said Henry and Margaret to produce the said letters of caption to be seen and considered if they be ordourly, like as at mair length is contained in the summonds."

> "Odo Hannay and Alexander McDowell appeared personally and his wife failed to appear.

> "The Lords suspend the letters purchased by the spouses and decree their effect to cease until they be produced and the parties lawfully warned to the production therof."

This is quite a confusing entry, but as far as it can be interpreted, the story is this:

> A certain Uchtred McDowell of Garthland had signed a contract (the details of which are unknown) with a couple named Henry Maxwell and Margaret Vaus. They claimed that Odo Hannay and Alexander McDowell had guaranteed fulfillment of said contract. It seems that after signing the contract, Uchtred died before it was completed, and Henry and Margaret brought suit against Odo and Alexander as guarantors. In 1534, Odo and Alexander appealed to the Bishop of Glasgow, whose officer refused to address it satisfactorily. They escalated their appeal to the court at Rome. While waiting for a result, Henry and Margaret insisted on

---

[45] This may refer to a now-vanished village in Galloway. Corswell or Corsewell seems to refer to an area on the Wigtownshire coast near Stranraer now occupied by a lighthouse known as Carsewell. -- *Tony Lowe*

imprisoning Odo and Alexander, but as they could not provide the original letters of surety[46] regarding the contract, and as Margaret failed to appear in court with her husband, the case was suspended until Maxwell and Vaus were able to produce the documents. It's not clear whether they ever did.

Odo appeared again in 1537, and was apparently succeeded by Cuthbert, who in 1547 was a witness to a contract concerning Culmalzie[47]. Next in line in the Knockglass branch was Dougal, who witnessed a charter for Dom Robert Watson, the vicar of Claxheint.[48] Dougal seemed to have been the last, as the land reverted to Uchtred McDowell in 1593, according to a Monreith charter.[49] A genealogy of the branch is given in Figure 6.

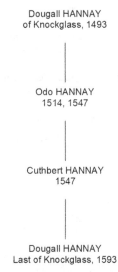

Dougall HANNAY
of Knockglass, 1493

Odo HANNAY
1514, 1547

Cuthbert HANNAY
1547

Dougall HANNAY
Last of Knockglass, 1593

**Figure 6: The Knockglass Family**

---

[46] A **surety** was a bond of obligation.

[47] **Culmalzie** is located in Kirkinner parish – from "Cul Malzie", meaning "the back of Malzie burn" -- *Tony Lowe*

[48] It is unclear where **Claxheint** is. Searches for this name have come up blank. Perhaps its current spelling is radically different. Possibly refers to Clachan near Newton Stewart. Keith Hanna suggests Claxheint may have been somewhere in Portpatrick Parish, which includes Knockglass.

[49] It is possible that the McDowells and Hannays, judging from Alexander and Odo's co-defendency as alleged guarantors of an earlier contract of Uchtred McDowell's, had some long-term agreement in sharing the land. Maybe it was a landlord/tenant relationship, or perhaps it was some sort of family arrangement through marriage which ended when the Knockglass line died out.

19

# 6. Early Hannays in England and Ireland

## 6.1. Lincolnshire

The Hannays or Hanneys in England are probably the descendants of Lincolnshire and Berkshire settlers, and no doubt distant relatives of the Scottish stock. They have many entries in the English records. The earliest, in 1211, appears in the *Curia Regia*[50] Roll:

> *"Berchsir;—Thomas de Hanny Gaufrius de Terburvill Robertus*
> *Maundit Sewalus de Osevill, quotuor milites summoniti ad*
> *elegendum XIj ad faciendum magnam assisam inter Thomam*
> *Malesmeins et Johannam uxorem suam petentes et Robertum le*
> *Bree tenentem de dimidia hida et ij acris terre cum pertinenxiis in*
> *Cumtun, unde Robertus, qui tenens est posuit se in magnam*
> *assisam et petit recogniciomen fieri utrum ipse majus jus habeat*
> *tenendi terram illam de ipsis Thoma et Johanna an ipsi tenendi*
> *illam in dominico, vererunt et elegerunt istos, Willelmum Hayard*
> *Halnatum de sifrewast Johannem Ridel Osmundum de Frilford*
> *Joannem filium Ricardi, Johannem Lemansel, Henricum de*
> *Ansevill Sewelum de Osevil, Thomam de Hany Ibertum de Grienvill*
> *Gaufrium de Hose Ilbertum de Bertun Robertum de Braden Robert*
> *de Port Randulfum de Makeneia Adam de Brinton."*

The above is a Berkshire record indicating that four knights, Thomas Hanny, Gaufrius Terburvill, Robert Maundit, Sewall Osevill, were elected to partake in the grand assize (great jury) to rule in a case between Thomas Malesmeins & his wife Johanna, plaintiffs, and Robert le Bree, tenant of some lands in Compton, to determine who has the greater claim on said lands.

## 6.2. Durham

In 1316 in the will of John Ovreby in Durham, a Symon and William Hannay are mentioned as witnesses. In 1377 William Hannay de Refhul, a burgess and alderman of Lincoln, was commissioned to provide stone and timber for the coronation of Richard II.

## 6.3. Ireland

Although the Hannay presence in Ireland seems to have begun during the plantation of Scots during the 17th century, the earliest mention of a possible Irish Hannay seems to be 1541, when William Hanne was attainted[51] for some political offence.

---

[50] *Curia Regia*: King's Court

[51] To **attaint** someone was to strip him or her of civil rights, title, and, in many cases, life.

# II: The Rise of Sorbie

Odo Hannay is the first known owner of Sorbie, and from him it is possible to trace the family in an unbroken line. If the early charters were available, it is tolerably certain that the family would be shown in possession of Sorbie at a much earlier date.

It is most difficult to ascertain exactly when Odo was in possession. In the records, the first quoted Laird of Sorbie was Ethe, in 1459/60. It was thought that this very peculiar name was an abbreviation for Cuthbert; however, from checking the original records in Edinburgh, it is quite clear that Ethe was his name.

In March 1459/60, Ethe Hannay of Sorbie witnessed an obligation of George Douglas of Leswalt in an assize with William Hannay of Kippinach (Capenoch) and others, as follows:

> "Obligation of George Douglas of Leswalt, Lord of Barquhane to his lovit friend Robert ye Vaus of Barnbarroch that when he and his heirs, shall quit the lands of Barquhane which Robert has of the granter in wadset for 200 merks Scots, that sum having been repaid the said Robert shall have the said lands in tack for six years. Witnesses, Andrew Agnew Sheriff of Wigtoun, Richard Syncler of Longester, **Ethe Ahanna** of Sorby, Alexander Ridal of Aryuling and **Geborne A'hanna** of Wigtoun."

In an entry in the *Acta Dominorum Concilii.* Robert Sorby [sic], son of the late Odo Sorbie[52] is stated to have leased four merkland[53] of Inglestoun of Sorby to Schir William Hannay, chaplain. In 1488/89, the lease was disputed by Robert Hannay of Sorby. Odo may have been the father of Ethe and Robert, and was dead some time before the land dispute occurred; the grant having been made some years previously. The entry reads:

> "The lords assign to William Hannay chaplain the fifth may next to come four merkland of Ingelstoun of Sorby at the tak of the same made to him be (by) [the] umquhile[54] Odo Sorbie said to Robert

---

[52] Note the apparent interchangeability in contemporary records of the Sorbie and Hannay names. Francis mentions Robert as being a son of Odo here, but in the relevant family tree (Table II) of the 1977 (2nd) edition, Robert is listed as a grandson of Odo. There may have been two Roberts, uncle and nephew, and the former should have been noted as a brother of Ethe. As Francis himself admits to guessing at the names of the sons of Odo and indeed of Ethe, Figure 5 in this edition contains an alternative view of the relationships, one which attempts to reconcile some discrepancies in the 1977 edition.

[53] **merkland**: a measure of land assessed as yielding a specified number of merks in annual rent. One merk was equivalent to 13s, 4d in Scots currency.

[54] **umquhile**: late, deceased

Sorbie quhile[55] his shewin (appearance) before the lords a (on) seizing of the lands the 5th may 1485. Witnesses, Walter, John and Thomas Hannay."

Walter, John, and Thomas, who appear in this grant of lands, were probably brothers of Odo[56]. Thomas is thought to have succeeded to a property at Powstoun, and had sasine[57] of property at Clounturk, Carsby and Capeltoun[58] in 1499. On March 19, 1490, he is mentioned in a case concerning Alexander Halyburton. And on May 2, 1543, either he, or more likely his son, came to a sticky end when Thomas of Powstoun was murdered by Gilbert McGown in a feud.

It is impossible to be certain who were the sons of Odo. They are thought to be Ethe, Gilbert (the Geborne A'Hanna of Wigtown mentioned above), and Dougal of Knockglass.

Odo definitely had a daughter, Mariote, who married Patrick Dikkenson of Clontis in 1485. In 1498 an entry in the "Great Seal Register" shows Patrick selling land at Kilsture "with the consent of his wyf Mariote Hannay to Symon McCristyn". In 1511 she was summoned for wrongful occupation of two merkland of Lubreck.

On February 5, 1484/5, Odo's son Ethe Hannay of Sorbie was baillie[59] in a crown precept[60], the charter being preserved amongst the Lochnaw papers. It is difficult to be absolutely certain of the names of Ethe's sons, but they most likely were Robert, who succeeded him to Sorbie; Alexander of Kirkdale; William, later Provost of Wigtoun; John; George; and Donald.

---

[55] **quhile**: during an earlier time

[56] Francis also lists Charles as a brother of Odo's, in Table II of the 1977 (2nd) edition, but not in the text.

[57] The act of taking of possession of land by an heir or transfer to a grantee is known as **sasine** or **seisin** (pronounced "SAY-SIN"). A notary recorded such an action in an Instrument of Sasine -- *Tony Lowe*

[58] These exact locations are unknown. Spelling may have changed radically since the 15th century. Keith Hanna suggests that **Clounturk** may refer to Glenturke in Wigtown Parish, and that **Capeltoun** may refer to Chapeltown in Wigtown.

[59] municipal officer or magistrate.

[60] order, command or mandate.

## 1. Robert Hannay and his many disputes

Ethe's son Robert (see Figure 7 for his family tree) first appears on February 26, 1482/3 as a witness in a Barnbarroch[61] charter, and again in 1491 as a witness to a deed of his uncle by marriage, Patrick Dikkenson of Clontis [Qulentis, in Wigtownshire].[62]

In 1493, the Lords Auditors

> "decreet that Robert Hannay of Sorbie dois no wrang in the occupying and manuring of the half of the land of Orchardtoun with the pertaineth and ordanis him to brouch and manure the same as assignes to Robert Hannay that by the time of Whitsunday next."

Robert appears to have been concerned in a number of land disputes about this time. On October 26, 1493, his uncle Dougal of Knockglass was summoned by Robert:

> "for the wrong delection and witholding from him of the some of 200 merks he fails to gif heritable steit sesing to be paid Robert of the Croft of St Johns and Ingletoun of Sorby at the time ordained."

In 1494, the boot was on the other foot:

> "Robert and others were summoned by the sheriff and baillies of Dumfries to appear before the king's councillors at Edinburgh on October 8th next to answer at the instance of George Grierson for unlawful occupation and labouring of lands of Rokkell and Haggis belonging to the said George."

Robert was a man of considerable influence in the county of Wigtoun. In 1498/99 he acted as curator[63] for the Sheriff of Wigtoun, Quentin Agnew, who at 37 was *non compos mentis*. He shared the curatorship with Nevin Agnew, the son of William Agnew of Creich.

---

[61] **Barnbarroch**: May refer to either an estate near Whauphill (five miles southwest of Wigtown; three miles west of Kirkinner), or to a village eight miles east of Kirkcudbright.

[62] Francis noted this as being in 1490, but a review of the Register of the Great Seal seems to list Robert as having been a witness on 9 September, 1491. –source: Balfour, James, editor, *The Register of The Great Seal of Scotland*, Volume II, Edinburgh, 1882.

[63] Legal guardian.

23

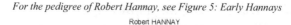

*For the pedigree of Robert Hannay, see Figure 5: Early Hannays*

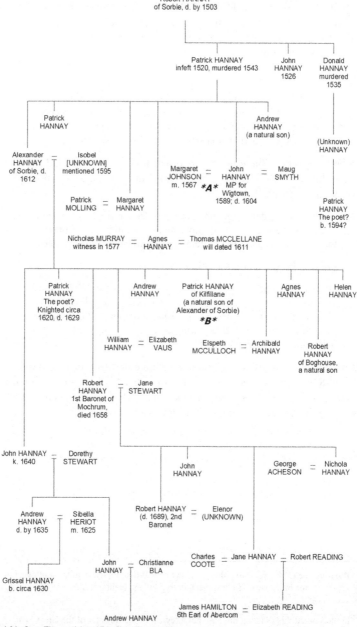

*A*: See Figure 14    *B*: See Figure 12

**Figure 7: The Descendants of Robert of Sorbie**

24

Robert was still alive in 1500, for he appears as a witness to a Saulset [Soulseat][64] charter. He was certainly dead by July 1503, when the ward of the lands of Sorby and of the marriage (i.e. the permission to marry) of his son and heir, Patrick, was granted to Robert's brother Alexander Hannay and the Parson of Powtoun, one William Stewart. Alexander was a burgess of Wigtoun. He subsequently acquired the Kirkdale property. Robert must have died fairly young, probably about 35 years of age, for his brothers all lived some considerable number of years longer.[65] The assignation reads:

> "1503 18th June. A lettre to Mr. William Stewart, Parson of Partoun and to Alexander Hannay and to their assigns and heirs ane (one) or mae (more) of the ward of all and sundry lands, rents and possessions pertaining to Robert Hannay of Sorby for all tyme of the ward etc., togidder with the marriage of Patrick Hannay son and heir to Robert failing that he dies unmarried to his heirs whomsoever."

## 2. Robert's brother Donald, and maybe more Donalds

In 1622, another Patrick Hannay published a collection of his poems in London (see Chapter XIX: The Hannay Poets), which included a dedicatory sonnet from a friend which stated that this Patrick's "father's father Donald was well known to the English by his sword."

It is not known for certain exactly who this Donald was, but there is a family tradition that Donald, brother of Robert and son of Ethe, was killed at the battle of Flodden Field in 1513. With a Donald appearing in the records as a witness in 1525, and again as the victim of a murder in 1535, Stewart Francis felt that there were two Donalds—perhaps father and son. The main problem is whether either Donald could be Patrick the Poet's grandfather. There is an 81-year gap between the death of the elder Donald in 1513 and Patrick the Poet's birth in, supposedly, 1594[66]. It is virtually impossible for the son of a man killed in 1531 to have fathered a child in 1594. It is slightly more probable that the Donald murdered in 1535[67] could have sired Patrick's father,

---

[64] Saulset or Soulseat was an ancient abbey, now vanished, located south of Castle Kennedy.

[65] This statement may support the alternate view that Robert was really one generation older than Francis thought, i.e. Ethe's brother, not his son.

[66] This year is given for Patrick's birth in notes left by historian George Chalmers (1742-1825), although no further source is cited, according to David Laing, in his 1875 preface to the reprint of Hannay's works.

[67] In the 1977 edition, Francis indicates 1543 as the date of the murder within genealogy table IIa. I have assumed from the quotation of the source material that the

25

who in turn would have had to be at least sixty years old at the time of the Poet's birth.[68]

It has been argued that the Donald mentioned in dedicatory sonnet was instead the son of Robert of Sorbie. Stewart Francis considered this unlikely, as in 1505/6, on 2nd February, Donald is "Sheriff in Hac Parte"[69] to a Carswell [Corswell] charter. Robert's son would have been too young, and so this is more likely to refer to Robert's brother Donald. If this elder Donald was killed at Flodden in 1513, a younger Donald—his nephew—could easily have been the Donald who was murdered in 1535. If the younger Donald is shown as 'of Sorbie' he must have been the son of the Laird, who at the time was Robert. Although we know of only two sons, Patrick, murdered in 1543, and John, Robert may have had more.

If he indeed existed, it seems that the younger Donald, the son of Robert, could also have been a thorn in the side of the English during skirmishes of his own generation, and thus have been the Donald referenced in the sonnet, *not* the elder Donald who fought at Flodden. If we take the younger Donald to be the granduncle of Patrick the Poet, we are at least within the realm of biological possibility. Figure 7: The Descendants of Robert of Sorbie reflects this relationship. Keep in mind, however, that it is still based on speculation.[70]

---

actual year was 1535, and that 1543 was a typographical error, as this is the same year that Patrick was murdered.

[68] The preceding paragraph replaces Francis' paragraphs on the Donald/Patrick relationship, which I include here from the 1977 (2nd) edition for reference:

> The whole of the question of Donald Hannay of Sorbie referred to as the grandfather of Patrick the Poet, and son of Ethe, is a difficult one. But there is no doubt that he fought at the disastrous battle of Flodden on 9th September 1513 in the army of King James IV, when Scotland's king and the flower of her nobility and gentry were killed. Tradition has it that Donald was killed in the battle. In the first edition it was said that this was unlikely. On reflection, and in the light of evidence subsequently produced, it would appear that there were two Donalds. The second Donald may well have been Donald the elder's son, and thus Patrick is his grandson. This ties up with Marshall's poem.

> The second Donald is shown in the Records as a witness in the case of Isabell Hepburn, Prioress of Haddington in 1525. And again there is a statement in the *Acta Dominorum* that he was murdered by John Lepreich whilst sleeping in his bed on 15th June 1535.

[69] *in hac parte*: (Legal Latin) in this matter.

[70] The preceding paragraphs modify Francis' (probably erroneous) conclusion that Donald the elder did indeed die at Flodden and was also the Patrick the Poet's grandfather. This would require Patrick the Poet's father to have been at least an

26

## 3. Robert's brothers John, George, and William

In addition to Donald, Robert Hannay had four additional brothers: John of Sorbie, Alexander, George, and William.

His brother John of Sorbie married the renowned daughter of Sir Alexander Stewart of the Garlies, and Elizabeth, daughter of Sir Archibald Douglas of Cavers[71]. Their daughter, named either Elizabeth or Isobel, married John in approximately 1500, having already had five husbands: Thomas MacDowell the son of Uchtred MacDowell of Garthland; Towers of Innerbith; Douglas of Pomperstoun; Moultry of Seafield; and Lundy of Balgony. Nothing daunted, she bore John four sons, Andrew, George, John, and Gilbert from whom the Grennan family descends.

John of Sorbie was a man of considerable consequence in Galloway and a baillie of Wigtoun.[72] He is reported to have died about 1544. He

---

octogenarian at the time of his birth. Here is Francis' text from 1977, which includes the sonnet from which the speculation has stemmed:

> The elder Donald would therefore fit into the pattern of the tradition as the son of Ethe — and the grandfather of Patrick the Poet. His death on the field of Flodden is thus confirmed. That he was a doughty fighter, and a soldier of some note is certain. His reputation was well known, for some years later John Marshall wrote a dedicatory Poem as a preface to one of Patrick's books of poems. I think it is worth quoting here, being the source of so much controversy:

> "To his much respected friend, Master Patrick Hannay.
> Hannay thy worth bewrays well whence thou'st Sprung.
> And that that honoured name thou dost not wrong;
> As if from Sorbies stock no branch could sprout,
> But should wish rep'ning time bear golden fruit.
> Thy ancestors were ever worthy found,
> Else Galdus' grave had grac'd no Hannay's ground.
> Thy fathers father Donald well was knowne
> To the English by his sword, but thou are shoune
> by pen (times changing) Hannays are
> Active in Acts of worth, be't peace or warre,
> Go on in virtue, After times will tell
> None but a Hannay could have done as well.

> *Note King Galdus (that worthie) who so bravly fought with the Romans lies buried in the lands of Patrick Hannay of Kirkdale in Galloway.*

> Jo Marshall."

[71] Earlier editions state "of Culrow".

[72] Stewart Francis also noted in earlier editions that John "was a signatory of the "Charter of Monuments [sic] of Holywood in Glasgow Diocese" on October 17, 1522. This appears to be an erroneous transcription of the Charter of the **Monastery** of Holywood, dated October 17, 1522, and witnessed by **Thomas** Hanna. Source: *The*

appears in several documents from 1504 to 1533, when he was baillie to the Abbot of Saulset.

A view has been advanced that John was the Laird of Sorby, but this is certainly inconsistent with the evidence available, although he used the title "of Sorbie". But this appears to have been a common practice, for Donald and Charles both did it.

William, the youngest brother, became Provost of Wigtown. In 1540, he rendered the accounts of the Baillies of Wigtown, and in 1543, as Customer (Customs Official) for the Burgh, he rendered the Customs accounts. Some dutiable items from those times include:

"Charge of 37/- custom for 37 woolen cloths for the year 1540.

46/8 of 360 woodfells

45/4 of 17 deerhides

38/- of 38 woolen clothes year 1544

34/3½ of 270 woodfalls year 1544

48/- of 18 deerhides year 1544

sum £39. 6. 2½d. the discharge to Comptroller of Customs years 1551 and 1552. £18.10. 4 ½ d."

In 1549, William, then burgess of Wigtoun, was licenced to "raise the roof of his house." In fact, to raise the roof to make a two storey house was a sign of wealth and position.

As Provost, William had sasine (inheritance) of four merkland of Kirkdale, and also of Killantreane [Killantrae[73]] about 1550. In 1556, he was again Provost. He also held the Clerkship of Langcastell till his death in that year. Upon his death, his widow Janet McIlhauche, married Patrick Blain. He was survived by his four children: John, Grizel, Isobel, and Patrick. His son, John, received the gift of nonentre[74] of Killantreane, Auchinree and Glenly, and John succeeded to Kirkdale. Grizel married William Gordon, son and heir to Alexander Gordon of Barquhill. Patrick went to France with the object of attending the schools (probably the University of Paris) and to carry

---

*Manuscripts of the Duke of Buccleuch and Queensberry*, Volume 15, Part 8, London, 1897. It is not known who this Thomas was. Some contemporary candidates are: Thomas Hannay (mentioned 1488), brother of Odo of Sorbie, Thomas Hannay (d. 1534) of Capenoch and Thomas Hannay (d. 1543) of Pouton.

[73] Killantrae is approximately 3 km North of Port William

[74] **nonentre**: the state into which a property falls when no heir has claimed possession after the previous owner has died. Until an heir claimed possession, the feudal lord to whom the owner was subject retained any income from the land.

out a trading mission for his late father's firm in Wigtown. Unlike in England, trade, for younger sons of landowners, was not considered unsuitable. What his successes were, or why and where, we do not know. Two years later, in 1570, he is reported dead. He wisely, before going abroad, made his will, dated June 30, 1568 and proved in Edinburgh on January 23, 1573 by his brother John. It would appear that he was a young man at the time of his death, and unmarried. The will states:

> "At Wigtoun the last day of Junii the yeir of God jm vic and thrie score aucht yeirs at the quhilk tym I Patrick Hannay sone lauchful to umquhile Williame Ahannay provost of Wigtoune intendis be the grace of God to pas to the pairtis of France to the scoles and tred of merchandice and believes in God be his grace and favour to return again to my native contrey navirthles mak my testament and constitutis Johne Hannay provost of Wigtoun my brother german, Janet McIlhauche my moder and Isobell Ahannay my sister germane my executirs"…

> Or

> At Wigtown the last day of June 1568 at the which time I, Patrick Hannay, lawful son to the late William Hannay, provost of Wigtown, intend by the grace of God to pass to the parts of France to the school and trade of merchandise, and believe in God by His grace and favor to return again to my native country. Nevertheless, I make my testament and appoint John Hannay, Provost of Wigtown and my full brother, Janet McIlhauche my mother, and Isobel Hanny my full sister, my executors…

He left to his executors all his moveable goods:

> "Testimentar and inventory of the goods and sums of money pertaining to the deceased Patrick Ahannay son lawful to the deceased William Ahannay provost of Wigtoun who died in October 1570, faithfully made and given up by his mother Janet McIlhauche with consent of Patrick Blain her spouse whom the said defunct by his will nominated one of his executores."

His mother and her husband Patrick Blain are shown as having "half mailes[75] and dues thereof." He leaves to William Ahannay, young son of his brother John,

> "the right and kindness of the ten merkland of Barnes with the miln thereof, after the decease of my said mother."

George, the fifth brother of Robert of Sorbie, was "Vice comite deputans de Wigtoun" (deputy lieutenant of Wigtown) in April 1502.

---

[75] **maile**: rent, lease payment

He appears as a witness to deeds written by Alexander Mure and John Dunbar of Mochrum between 1497 and 1500.

## 4. Robert's son Patrick

Robert had three sons, Patrick, John and Donald. Of John very little is known. Donald is mentioned earlier in this chapter as a possible candidate for the Donald mentioned in the preface to Patrick the Poet's collected works.

Robert's son Patrick succeeded his father on the latter's death in 1503, but as he was still a minor, his uncle Alexander became tutor for the estate. In 1509, a Patrick is recorded as procurator for Sir Alexander McCulloch; this probably was a kinsman, another Patrick. In 1520, Patrick of Sorbie had sasine of twenty merkland of Craigboy and the sixteen merkland of Sorbie, at this time worth £1260.[76]

In 1526, Patrick, along with George, Gilbert and John Hannay[77], and his brother John, as well as the Earl of Cassilis, and others of the Kennedys, were concerned in a feud with certain other Kennedys and the McIlwraiths. Gilbert McIlwraith and Martyn Kennedy were murdered in the feud, but it appears that the Crown respited the murderers, probably on the grounds of self-defence. Nothing more appears to have been heard of the case.

In 1528, Patrick was required to sell to Finlay Campbell, of Corswell, two and a half merkland of Kilantreane [Killantrae] and a merkland of Craigule [Craigley?], in repayment of a debt. Ninian Hannay, the Prior of Whithorn, summoned Patrick in 1527 for the alleged destruction of the mill there on October 26th 1526. Patrick did not come to the courts. It would seem that even at this time, some private feuding was going on, and the Hannays had their full share of it.

In May 1539, Patrick sold to Alexander of Kirkdale, his uncle, four and a half merkland of Kilantreane [Killantrae], the merkland of Craiginche[78] and the merkland of Auchinree in the parish of Inch[79].

In 1542, he acted as sheriff in "hac parte" for Wigtoun. In 1543, probably as a continuation of the feud, he was murdered by Patrick McClellane of Gelstoun [Gelston], William Mundwell and William

---

[76] Equivalent to approximately £200,000 in 2018.

[77] Presumably his uncle, cousin and uncle, respectively.

[78] Possibly refers to Craigcaffie – *Keith Hanna*

[79] The parish of Inch comprised the town of Stranraer and outlying areas, incorporating the Rhinns of Galloway.

McKennay. The murderers were eventually caught in 1545, and on October 28 sentenced to 19 years imprisonment.

His property was left as a

> "Gift of ward of all lands, rents, mills etc. within the Sheriffdom of Wigtoun to William Hannay[80] burgess there that belonged to Patrick Hannay of Sorbie and now through his decease in the hands of the Queen togedder with the marriage of Alexander his son and heir."

Patrick had six children[81]: Alexander who succeeded him, John, Patrick, Andrew (a natural[82] son) and two daughters, Margaret who married Patrick Molling before 1565, and is involved in a piracy case in that year, and Agnes who married Nicholas Murray. This last is a witness to a deed on October 25, 1577. She, probably, secondly married Thomas McClellane of Gelstoun, a relation of her father's murderer and a soldier. An entry in the "Register of the Great Seal" for November 21, 1609 shows, "Thos McClellane de Gelstoun milites et Lady Agnetis A'hannay his wife." On January 7, 1611, an Archibald (or perhaps it is a misprint for Alexander) Hannay is mentioned in the will of Thomas McClellane.

At the time of Patrick Hannay's death, the power of the Sorbie family was at its height. They held considerable sway over the Machars of Galloway, and the Burgh of Wigtoun marched to their tune.

---

[80] Presumably his uncle.

[81] In the 1977 edition, Francis listed John and Patrick in Table IIa but not in the body of the text.

[82] illegitimate.

# III: 16<sup>th</sup> Century Hannays

Late in the 15th, and early in the 16th centuries, Hannays appear in many records. It is not possible to join most of these on to any particular branch of the family; therefore, many of them do not appear in the family tree tables in this book. Branches of the family had established themselves all over Galloway, Ayr and Dumfriesshire, in the cities of Edinburgh and Glasgow, and as far afield as Dundee, Perth, and the Borders. In 1525, a John Hannay of Cumnoch is mentioned. In 1595 another John is ordered by the Sheriff of Ayr

> "to remove Lawrence Hannay and his son John tenants placed in
> the lands of Auchinleck by the rebels, fuirth thereof within ten days
> and suffer William Mathie peaceably to enter therm."

Mathie's father had been murdered by the rebels. In 1659 there were still Hannays there.

In 1535, a James Hannay was Chamberlain of the Barony of Trabeauch (likely Trabboch, about 5 km East of Ayr). In 1542, the Lord High Treasurer gave Damiane Hannay 40/ - for bringing a false coiner (counterfeiter) "fuirth de Wigtoun." In 1577, John Hannay of Knockdaw was summoned along with 50 others for

> "bodin in fear of weir with jak seil bonnet and instituted with all
> manner of wappynis invaisive accomplises of the said John Schaw
> of Halie forced their way in Hew Cathcarts lands at Aracrow
> stealing his sheep and pasturing theirs there by force."

## 1. The Hannays of Culbrae and Capenoch

Dougal Hannay of Culbrae and Capenoch received his lands from James II in 1457. He was in all probability the brother of Odo of Sorbie. In 1470/71, there is an entry dealing with Culbrae:

> "1470. March 13th. Instrument of sasine at the hand of John
> Murray notary public narrating that Dougal Hannay Laird of
> Capenoch and Slewhibert in the Sheriffdom of Wigtoun resigned
> those lands into the hands of the Crown in favour of his heir
> apparent William Hannay reserving life rent to the granter and
> Elizabeth Carlyle his spous. Done within the Kings chamber [*curia
> Regis*] in the Castle of Edinburgh."

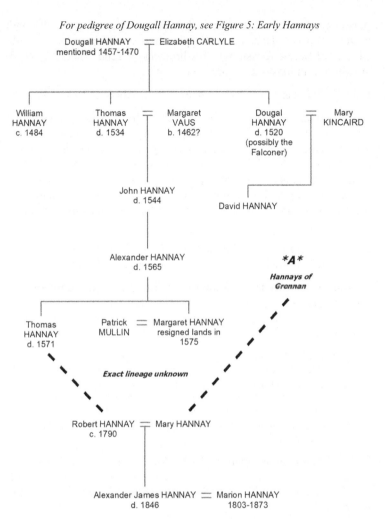

*For pedigree of Dougall Hannay, see Figure 5: Early Hannays*

*\*A\**: See Figure 51

**Figure 8: Hannays of Culbrae and Capenoch**

By 1498, Dougal's son Thomas Hannay had sasine of Capenoch. In 1501, Thomas and his brother Dougal (the younger) received the tenancy of the lands of Arboig[83] in Galloway "for three years from the feast of St. Martin for 25 merks." They were still in possession of their lands according to the *Rentalis Domini Regis*[84] in 1508. Thomas

---

[83] The location of **Arboig** is unknown.

[84] The register of rents due from a tenant to the crown.

33

A'hannay of Capenoch appears in the *Liber Glasguensis*[85] in 1498, and brother William Hannay of Kippinach (Capenoch) appears with Charles of Sorbie (possibly Odo's brother) on 22nd January 1484 to answer a summons of the Lords in Council.

In 1523, Thomas appears as a witness for the Abbot of Holyrood.

John, Thomas's son, succeeded him in 1534. In 1533, he appears in the *"Acta Dominorum"* as, "John Hannay young laird of Capenoch" in a summons for smuggling. He became a burgess of Wigtoun, and in 1542 gave wadset of Slewhibert to John Vaus of Barnbarroch. He died in 1544, for there is a crown precept as follows "crown gift of the ward of Capenoch to Andrew Hamilton since the death of John Hannay of Capenoch together withe the marriage of Alexander Hannay his son."

In 1544, Alexander was granted seven and a half merkland of Capenoch from Andrew Hamilton who had ward during his minority. In 1562, he invested Alexander Vaus into the "4 lands of Capenoch."

Alexander is succeeded by Thomas, who had sasine on 7th June 1565. Thomas does not appear to have lived long, or to have married, for his sister, Margaret, has sasine in 1572. The retour[86] regarding the lands reads as follows:

> "1572 Feb 17. Chancery retour narrating that Margaret Hannay was served heir to her brother Thomas A'hannay of Capennoch in the 24 merkland of Capenoch and a piece of land called the forty penny lands adjacent to Capenoch in the parish of Kirkinner now valued at £5. 10s. Scots held in chief of the Crown for ward and relief. The lands had been in the hands of the crown for five months since the death of Thomas."

By 1575 Margaret had married Patrick Mullin and with her husband's consent resigned the lands of Capenoch to Sir Patrick Vaus of Barnbarroch. A letter of Sir Patrick's concerning Capenoch exists, and it is quoted here:

> "Michael McCrechan to Patrick Vaus of Barnbarroch.
>
> "My Lord, efter heartie commendation of service I wraith of befoir. . . the quhilk concernit myself, to haif been resoulute of. . . of the quhilk I obtainit no answer as yitt; and now Margaret Hannay and Pate Mulin hes been at me shwanand that the seref would have poyindit thair goodes for the relief of the lands of Capenoch extending to xxij$^{lib}$ x$^s$ quhilk restis upon the scheriff. I post to the

---

[85] Literally "The Book of Glasgow". It is unclear to which book Francis was referring, but it could be the records of the City of Glasgow or those of the Diocese of Glasgow.

[86] **retour**: decision by a Scottish jury on who should be declared the rightful heir of an estate.

Sheriff and has gotten the same supercedit for xxi daus Theirfor ye pleas make the sum dues therefore and see if you can get the same discharged."

It would appear that after this the Capenoch family, who had fallen on hard times, sank into obscurity for we do not hear of them again until 1684, when Mary Hannay of Capenoch is mentioned in the Wigtown Parish Lists and is shown as taking the "Test."[87] Many years later Dr. Robert Hannay of Capenoch (Circa 1790) married another Hannay, Mary from Grennan, and from this union is descended the family of Alexander Patrick Cathcart Hannay, OBE, MC. This branch of the family is discussed in more detail in Chapter XII: The Hannays of Grennan.

## 2. *Hannays in Dumfries*

In Dumfries the first mention is in 1530, when a John Hannay is a servant to Nichol McBrae, an Alderman of Dumfries. A certain William Hannay had established himself as a merchant by April 28, 1598, when he appears as a witness in a bond. The next year he is bound "not to harm Herbert McKie for £500." The Dumfries Hannays seemed to have been a colourful lot. John Hannay of Dumfries was accused on January 14, 1601/2 of attending a Catholic service taken by Mr. Gilbert Browne, late Abbot of New Abbey, and Mr. William Hamilton. William, a burgess of Dumfries, on July 15, 1607, was charged with causing a tumult in Church, for as the "Register of the Scottish Privy Council" reads:

> "[he] came armed with swords quhiyiers acxis etc on 27th July last
> at the time of the morning Prayers to the kirk of Dumfries violently
> raisit and cast down the said stall and removed the same out of the
> yle upon the kirk flure."

> "He came armed with swords, quivers, axes, etc., on the 27th of
> July last year during morning prayers to the church in Dumfries,
> and violently raised and cast down the said stall and removed the
> same out of the aisle upon the church floor."

The "stall" mentioned above likely refers to a church pew. In 1608, William is bound not to harm John Dickson, a burgess of that town, for 300 merks.

Earlier in 1577, there is mentioned an Oswald Hannay, who was the Sheriff officer in Dumfries. Of later members of the family in Dumfries, there is little to note, except that in 1620, Hew Hannay, also a burgess, was accused of "communing with the rebel John Redik."

---

[87] This refers to the **Test Act of 1681**, in which each citizen had to acknowledge the religious supremacy of King Charles II, or else be labeled a rebel.

Hew again appears in a case concerning certain property in Ireland in 1618. An extract from the Kirkcudbright Hornings[88] reads as follows:

> "Horning at the instance of Hew Hannay and Thomas McMillan merchant burgesses in Dumfries Samuel Wilson of Clifton etc anent lands and castles in Ireland by Edward Johnson for annual rent of 560 merks for 21 years. The Wilsons had bound themselves to relieve the complainers of their caution for Johnson on the original contract."

Hew appears again in several other cases about this time, suing his various debtors. He seems to have had a very considerable number of financial irons in the fire.

In 1667 George and Robert are mentioned in the "Privy Seal Register" as weavers in Dumfries.

## 3. Wigtown Hannays

In Wigtown, the family was early established, for the younger sons in many cases went into business there. As early as 1459, there is an entry in the records concerning a Geborne Hanna, and a Robert Hannay (possibly Odo's son) regarding certain lands of Vedast Gryson, Lord of Lag. In 1467, a Master Gilbert Hannay, a Chaplain, is a witness of a McDowell charter. In the early 16th century, the Sorbie and Kirkdale families both had considerable interests there and were many times Provosts. In 1542, there is a David Hannay mentioned and many others are recorded during this time. In 1642, when a Patrick Hannay was Provost, there was considerable trouble over the possession of prohibited weapons. Together with John Hannay, a wright, Patrick was charged with this offence, and with the wrongful imprisonment of Robert McKie. He seems to have weathered the storm as in 1646 he is still the Provost. He lived in the Vennel[89]. And in 1656 there is a note that Barbara, his daughter, was owed £706. 3. 4d.[90] from John Hannay of Whitehills. In 1672, a George Hannay, a merchant burgess, receives notice. In later years the family is well represented, even up to the present day.

---

[88] **Hornings** refer to information gleaned from many sources -- wills, estates and court records -- which included names of individuals. These records were held in many places, and some have been indexed. The Kirkcudbrightshire Hornings are among those indexed, and they and relate to the period 1614-1621 -- *Tony Lowe.*

[89] The **High Vennel** is a lane in Wigtown which meets the town's High Street at a right angle, just east of where the latter splits into North Main Street and South Main Street. The **Low Vennel** is two blocks east.

[90] Roughly £10,000 in 2018.

In 1632, William Hannay of Wigtown was a witness to a somewhat extraordinary marriage settlement between William Mundwell and Janet Dunbar. William asked for Janet to be compelled to come to church to marry him. Janet was a "confirmed adultress with William Adair." She was ordered by the court to be married within 15 days, or to be excommunicated.

## 4. Hannays throughout Galloway and Beyond

In Glasgow, too, the family made a settlement, and in 1575 Thomas Hannay was made a burgess of that city, at the request of the Bishop. He carried on a business as a smith and wright.

In practically every town and village in Galloway the family had some representation by the end of the 16th century. Mostly they plied various trades and were merchant Burgesses of the towns and cities of Scotland. In fact, they even stretched over into the Borders, for we find Matthew A'hannay in 1565 having the Knaiffschieppes[91] of the Mills of Melrose, from the Convent there, with whom he always seems to have been falling out, as seen in this extract from the *Melrose Regality Records*:

> "ix Aprilis anno Domini 1558. We, Dene Ralph Hudsone, prior of Melrose, in presence of the Convent of Melrose being present, viz. Dene Johne Watsoun, supprior, Dene William Filp, guarden[92], Dene Thomas Meyn, Dene Bernard Boston, Dene Johne Hogart, Thomas Hallewell, Dene James Ramsay, James Arbothenot, John Watson, younger, George Weyr, and in presence of the parroschin of Melrose convenit for gud service the samyn day, viz, upoun Paische ewin[93], exponit the case how that he and the said convent had direckit ane precept to warne Robert Boustoun, **Matho Hanna**, George Downatson and certane utheris occupyaris of certane our yairdis houses and service of knaifschip of our abbay myllnis, and that [the] said Matho violentlie raef[94] the samyn precept furth of our handis within the gret kirk of Melrose at xj houris or thairby, quhilkis was clerlie prewit in presence of the auditour, and for the quhilk cause of violence be the auctorite of the kirk the said Matho was denuncit cursit and thairefter quhare Walter Chesholm of that Ilk allegeand him baillie deput tuyk defense with the said Matho and requyrit the said precept fra him, quhilk he grantit befor the said auditour, and efter the denunciatioun of cursing imput to the

---

[91] **Knaiffschieppes** : an ancient spelling of **knaveships**. Knaveships were dues paid (in grain) to the servants running a mill. **Knaiff** is an old spelling of **knave**, meaning (1) a boy or (2) a serving-man.

[92] warden

[93] **Paische ewin**: Easter evening

[94] ripped

said Matho for the said violence he remanit in the kirk with fortificatioun of the said Walter Chesholm, alleget bailie deput, and thairthrocht[95] be lang tym stopit God service and the parroschin to be servit of thair dewite and ministratioun of the sacrament; and als the said Walter Chesholm said gyf ony man or officer execute ony siclyk[96] precept at the said prior and brether command he suld stuw his luggis[97]; and quhair the said Walter Chesholm grantit the ressate of the said precept fra the said Matho, and being requyrit be us Dene Ralphe in our name and the said convent for delyverance of the samyn he wald nocht delyver it, upon the quhilkis we Dene Ralphe forsaid protestit for injuris within our said kirk and place, and remedy of law."

Matthew died without a son, for Thomas Mar of Newstead is given as his heir. To complete the picture of the omnipresence of the family, we find two young ladies being the cause of two divorce cases; the entry in the "Great Seal Register" on July 6, 1615, reads:

*"Rex dedit literas remisiois Gilberto Richeit in Drumblane pro adultero cum Joneta Hannay"*

(The king gives letters of pardon to Gilbert Richeit in Drumblane for adultery with Janet Hannay)

and on the same date:

*"Rex dedit literas remisionis Willelmo Ramsay in Largis pro adulterario Issobella Hannay."*

(The king gives letters of pardon for William Ramsay in Larg for adultery with Issobella Hannay)

---

[95] thereby

[96] such kind of

[97] **stuw his luggis**: cut off his ears

# IV: The Hannays in 16<sup>th</sup> Century Edinburgh

Very early on the family established a prosperous merchant branch in the Capital, which had many ramifications in many trades. They were mostly resident in the Canongate[98]. They should not be confused with the 17<sup>th</sup> century family of Dean of Edinburgh James Hannay (See Chapter VII: The Family of John Hannay, M.P.), who is of Sorbie stock, descended from John of Sorbie.

The relationships are almost impossible to work out, although some attempt has been made in Figure 9 and Figure 10. Much of the information must necessarily be conjecture, although trades are as sound a guide to relationships as anything.

The first mention is of Nicholas Hannay in 1463, almost as early as our first Wigtown entry. He was a man of some standing in the city, as he is mentioned in John Young's Protocol Book[99] as a judge in the case of John Walch on January 31, 1486, and as arbiter in a dispute regarding a will, for which task he was chosen by Issabella Foulis and William Froy at St. Giles's on January 31, 1489.

In John Foular's Protocol Book Nicholas is shown as having had two daughters, Jonet (or Janet) and Christine (or Cristina), who were his heirs, and received his property on January 12, 1502. Christine was thrice married: Maurice Flemyn, Patrick Murray and Edwin Purves are mentioned as her husbands. Jonet had two husbands, John Wilson of the Canongate and Thomas Swift.

In 1511, the following entry occurs in John Foular's book concerning Jonet:

> "18th November. William Lokkart, bailie, went to the tenement of the late Thomas Swift on the south side of the High Street, between the tenement of the late Thomas Levington on the east and the land of the late Sir Thomas Tod, knight, on the west and there Janet Hannay, daughter and one of the heirs of the late Nicholas Hannay burgess, resigned her half of the said tenement between the land of Earl of Eglynton on the north and the land of the late Thomas Swyft on the south. Sasine was given to Thomas McDowel in Sleichrik [Selkirk], his heirs and assignees."

---

[98] The **Canongate**, part of the Royal Mile, is a neighborhood in Edinburgh. It was originally its own Royal burgh.

[99] A **Protocol Book** or **Register** is where a notary (a clerk of a court) recorded details of transactions.

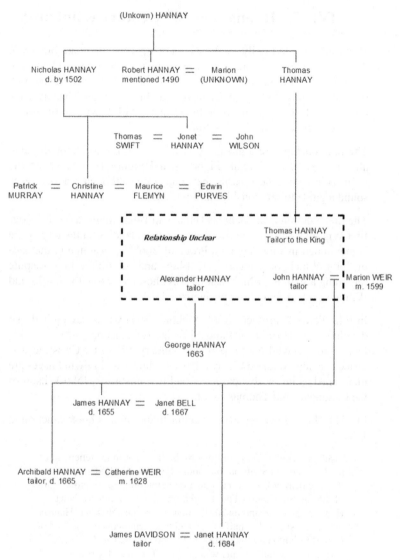

**Figure 9: Hannays in Edinburgh**

The property of Nicholas seems to have been very extensive, as there are numerous entries in the various books regarding transactions of land belonging to him, or that of other people whose land bordered his. William Lokkart, the bailey mentioned above, was married to an Elizabeth Hannay.

In 1490, a Robert Hannay and his wife Marion received sasine of the lands in "Heriggs, five particates[100] in length to north and two particates in length to south in the Barony of Dalry for 15/- annual rent."

In 1502, a William Hannay was a witness, as Serjeant of the Barony of Redhall[101], in a case of a sasine of land to William Craik by John Fischer. He also is described as "baillie of William Cunninghame Lord of Kilmaweris and Barony of Redhall." He appears again in 1504, 1505, 1507, and 1508. There is also a Thomas, who appears frequently in the protocol books.

Dougal Hannay is shown as owning property near the Netherbow and was living in 1508. This may well be the royal falconer (see later in this chapter). Dougal had a son, David, who enters into his property in 1520. Dougal is referred to as a burgess.

In 1504, John Hannay and Margaret "his spous" are mentioned in James Young[102]'s Protocol Book as being given sasine of certain property near Holyroodhouse. Others appear, including Andrew in 1491 and Alexander in 1513. There is a note of a Michael Hannay, who is known to have been dead by 1522, and amongst the witnesses in the records are Sir James and Sir Constantine Hannay, both chaplains.

## 1.  Hannays in the Royal Court

Sir Constantine was obviously connected with the Court and he appears frequently in the records between 1535 and 1537; one entry shows him to be: "sent to the King's grace with a dousane lute strings price 6 / -."

In Edinburgh, at this period, there were at least five other Hannays in the service of the Crown:

- Dougal, falconer to King James

- Thomas, the master tailor to the King,

- James the Culvener  (or commander of the artillery),

- John (probably the son of James) "the smyth and wright extra ordinary" and

- John A'hannay, baker to "the Kings grace."

---

[100] A **particate** is a measure of land, consisting of a quarter Scots acre -- *Tony Lowe*

[101] Just south of Edinburgh, near present-day Colinton.

[102] James Young produced a **protocol book** between 1485-1515 -- *Tony Lowe*

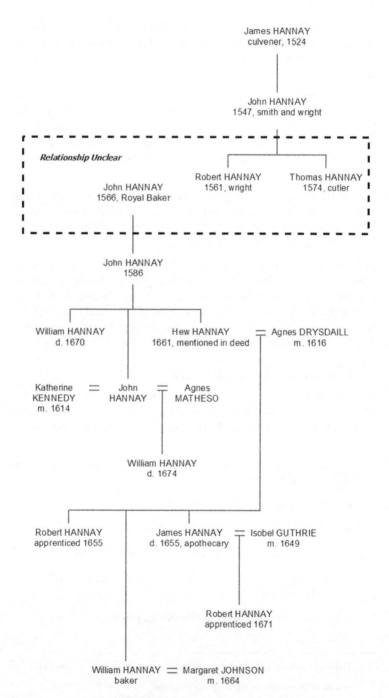

**Figure 10: More Hannays in Edinburgh**

42

## 1.1. Dougal Hannay, Falconer to the King

The Falconer to King James IV (see Figure 11) was named Dougal Hannay. He may have been the son of Dougal Hannay of Culbrae and Capenoch (see Chapter III: 16th Century Hannays), who was the brother of Odo of Sorbie.

**Figure 11: James IV with Falcon**

Dougal probably took over as the King's Falconer about 1490, for in the first available records of "The Accounts of the Lord High Treasurer of Scotland" in 1497, he is firmly established as the king's chief Falconer.

There are numerous entries showing payments to Dougal for wages, livery, and the purchase of hawks. He seems to have spent much time on the Island of Inchkieth[103], where the hawks were kept, and where breeding took place. He made several journeys to purchase birds for the king, to Orkney and Shetland. He visited Orkney in 1496, 1507 and in 1512, for which latter journey he received £40 in expenses from the crown.

Dougal received a wage of about £10[104] a quarter together with all his expenses, quite a considerable sum in those days. Dougal must have

---

[103] in the Firth of Forth, northeast of Edinburgh and south of Kirkcaldy

[104] Roughly £43,000 of relative income in 2018.

had a son, for there is an entry in 1501 concerning the provision of a livery for "young Hannay":

> "**6th September 1501**. 3 ells scottis tane to be ane coat to young Hannay falconer, ilk elne x 5/5. summa 26/6.
> Ane man doublet to him of fustian 8/9.
> ane pair of maid hos to him of Carsey 7/3."

The other entries are:

> **1496. 30 May**, giffen to Hannay to pass to the Isles for Hawkis £6. 0. 16.

> **1497. 13 November**. To Hannay to byd behind the King with ane seik hawk 9/-.

> **1498. 3 Jan**. The King was in Fintray, the Abbot of Lindores place giffen to Hannay at the kings command to help him with a horse. 31/-.

> **1498. 1 Mar**. A precept to Dougal Hannay falconer of the gift of £20 zerelie in his fee for the service to be done to the kings hens Zerale to be payit to him of his coffeis be the thesaurer being for the tyme for a! the days of the said Dougals life.

> **1501. 1 May**. To Hannay for fifteen days wages to remain on the Island of Inchkieth to help a halk to nest there and tua men with hem 42/-.

> **1501. 10 June**. To Hannay for two months expenses kepand hawkis at Inchkieth X owkis [weeks] and V daus ilk day XVJ pence. summa £4. 10. 8. for Hannay for coolis to them in Inchkieth and for Hannay fraucht divers times in and furth 14 / 4.

> **1501. 3 July**. Dougal A'hannay his fee of the Witsunday tenure bipast be command of a precept, £20.

> **1502. 5 Nov**. To Hannay to remained behind the King 14 pence.

> **1503. 25 July**. To Hannay quhen he brought a hawk of Inchkieth to the king 14/-.

> **1503. 25 Oct**. To Hannay for finding a heron be the kings command 5/-

> **1505. 28 Apr**. To pass to Athole for Hawkis 4 french crowns 41/-

> **1512**. Dougal A'hannay and David Drummond to pass to Shetland and Orknay for Hawks for the King for their expenses delivered to Sir John Dingwall £20 and 20 by the Lord Sinclair."

The King seems to have taken a very considerable interest in his hawks, and he visited Dougal at Inchkieth frequently.

In 1515, the king further rewarded him for his services by giving him life rent fee from the Customs of Edinburgh. In 1516 appears the entry, "payment of fee up to his demise Dougal Hannay £30."

## 1.2. Thomas Hannay, Royal Tailor

The accounts of Thomas Hannay the king's tailor, which are contained in those records of the Lord High Treasurer of Scotland between 1535 and 1541, give a very clear picture of the prices of the materials, and the glorious lushness of the clothing that the magnates of Scotland wore at this period. Recorded here are only the prices of the cloth delivered to Thomas and not his fees.[105] The frequency with which the King bought new clothes is indicative of the wealth and extravagance of his court:

"**5th Aug. 1535**. delivered to Thomas Hannay Tailor to the Kingis grace one galcoit[106] 3 quarters frenche broune price 24/-."

"**10th Sep. 1535**, to be the kinges grace ane doublet and ane pr of hos 3 ells and of gray stemmet[107] 43/-, to be ane uther pair of hos to the kingis grace 3 ¼ quarters white stemmet of myllane 35/-."

"**5th Oct 1535**, to the kingis grace a doublet 10 ½ quarters fine satin crammsey £10 10."

"**8th Oct 1535**. for the king a galcoit 7 quarteres of french gray 28/-."

"**1st Nov 1535**. a doublet for the king 10 ½ quarteres of fine satine blak £4. 10. 4."

"**22nd Nov 1535**. to be a cloak for the king 7 quarters of Paries browne £3. 18. 3. Another doublet 4 qyarters blak velvet £6. 16. 6. a raiding coat for the king 3 ells french gray £3. 4. 0., a night gown for the king 4 ½ rissalis blak £6."

"**July 1536**, A cloak for the king 3 ells 1 quarter Rowane russet £43. 6. 0."

"**31st July 1536**, doublet for the king 10 ½ quarters of fine blak satin £5. 5. 0. another doublet white fustian 26 6.'

"**23rd Oct 1536**, Coat for James of Alloway 2 ½ ells tanny granes £3. 15. 0."

---

[105] For comparison of prices: One shilling of goods purchased in 1535 would have been worth roughly six pounds sterling in 2018.

[106] A **galcoit** (also spelled **galcolt**) was a coat or jacket.

[107] **stemmett** was a woolen fabric used in the making of hose.

45

"**1st June 1537**. taken by Thomas Hannay fra Nicholas Carnecors at the kings gracis first departing to be his grace a doublet 10 ½ quarter blak satin £5. 5. 0."

"**May 1539**, Thomas Hannay sent to Thomas Arthur the materials delivered to them to Sanctandros [St. Andrew's] to be frenzies to the said journey the 17th day of May 6 double hanks of sewing gold and 3 double hanks of sewing silser £9. 10. 0."

"**10th April 1540**, to be schankis of hois for the king 6 quarteres of Lyminster blak £3. 12. 0."

"**10th April 1541**. 12 hanks of gold £8. 4. 0."

"**20th Dec 1541** a coat with tassels and two doublets for the king 10 ½ ells blak satin £18. 9. 0."

The entry of 24th July 1541 is quite amusing. Mary of Guise[108] clearly demanded the best, and the quality decreased as one went down the line:

"**24th July 1541**. for gartennis to his grace 1 ell[109] white taffites of cord £1 8. 0., for a pair of cloakes for the Queen 4 ½ ells of paris blak. £13. 10. 0., for five cloaks for the five ladies of honour 2 ½ ells french blak £40. 10. 0., 8 cloaks for other ladies 24 ells of french blak £35."

Thomas received his expenses on November 30th that year for taking the Queen's cloak to Perth; the sum was 11/-.

## 1.3.  James, Commander of the King's Artillery

James Hannay, the Master Gunner, was granted 22/- in 1529 for the "purchase of powder and lied at the kings command." He received a grant of livery in 1529 in the Lord High Treasurer's accounts and a "Christmas livery" in 1531. In the Exchequer Rolls he was granted lands in Leith on November 9, 1525. He would have been responsible for the guns in Edinburgh Castle and also probably those of the King's Army in the field. No doubt he was present at the battle of Pinkie[110] in 1547, and five years previously at James V's final battle at Solway Moss, after which James died of grief and wounds; and Mary, a child of 6 days, ascended her unhappy throne.

---

[108] **Mary of Guise** (1515-1560): Consort of King James V and mother of Mary, Queen of Scots.

[109] A Scots **ell** was a fabric measurement of roughly 37.2 inches, varying from the English **ell**, which was 45 inches..

[110] A great battle in which the Scots were bitterly defeated by the English. It prompted, the following year, a Scottish alliance with France, the cornerstone of which was the engagement of the child queen Mary to the heir to the French throne.

John, who was in all probability James Hannay's son, was employed by the Crown as "smyth extraordinary." His work concerned the maintenance of the Artillery in Edinburgh Castle, as the accounts of the Lord High Treasurer show:

> "August 1547, for meeting the artillery and conveying it to the castle of Edinburgh £3. 7. 6. John Hannay smyth extrodinary and his tua sevands for their labours upon the iron work of the said artillery to the space of one oulk (week) and a half, to himself in the oulk 20/- and ilk (each) ane of his tua servands oulklie 16/-."

In September he earned a further 42/-, and in November he is paid for his work the very large sum of £31. 10.[111]

In February 1549, there is another interesting entry in the accounts:

> "for wyrking of 12 stane of tua pounde and ane half of the said irne 32/-. Hyrit thre hors to take the wark lumes[112] of John Hannay smyth and Robert Hector wright and gunner to the Castell of Dunbar and given them for their wages 28/-."

By 1552 he was in regular employment in the Castle of Edinburgh on the Staff of the Artillery. The same guns he installed in Dunbar castle were to repel not long afterwards Gilbert Hannay (see Chapter XII: The Hannays of Grennan), the Sheriff of Wigton and the son of John Hannay of Sorbie; and Gilbert Earl of Cassilis, who laid siege to the castles of Dunbar and St. Andrews against Queen Mary of Guise. For which they were escheated[113] according to the Register of the Privy Council on October 31, 1546.

## 1.4.  John A'Hannay, Royal Baker

John A'hannay, the baker to Mary, Queen of Scots received payments of wheat in the "Great Seal Register" for 1566 and '67. He retained his post after Queen Mary took refuge in England and appears in the Accounts for 1569 and 1573. In the Protocol Book of Gilbert Grote[114] on March 14, 1558, John is shown as a "baker and burgess in Canongate" and is asked to relieve Mr. William Scott of certain actions pending against him. He was a man of some property, as the "Registers of the Ancient Priviledges of the Canongate" in 1569 give him as owing annual rents to the Baillies and Council of £2. 0. 0. and £1.10.

---

[111] £86,500 of relative income in 2018.

[112] **wark lumes** referred to tools or workbenches.

[113] **escheated**: had their property, possessions or goods taken from them by forfeiture or confiscation -- *Tony Lowe.*

[114] Gilbert Grote maintained a protocol book between 1552 and 1573 -- *Tony Lowe.*

4., also 13/4 owed to the hospital rate, and 40/- to the Convent for lands in the Canongate.

It is probable that he had two grandsons, John and Hew; both became burgesses and bakers. On April 14, 1608, John appears as the leader of the complainers in a case by the Town Council of the Canongate against the Magistrates and Baillies of Edinburgh for "troubling the bakers of Canongate in selling their bread in Edinburgh market." One suspects undercutting. However, on the May 27, 1617, the magistrates got their own back and proscribed John and Hew for "illegal trade combination." The Canongate outside the walls had long been jealous of its special privileges, and no doubt the City was interfering with them. The good burgesses of the Canongate resisted hotly.

Both John and Hew were married, John to Katherine Kennedy on May 26, 1614, and Hew to Agnes Drysdaill on July 18, 1616. Whether John had any children, history does not relate[115], but Hew is known to have had at least two[116] sons, James who was apprenticed to William Castlelaw, an apothecary, on November 12, 1634, and William who became a baker. There is also a Robert , shown as the son of "Hew A'hannay baxter in the Canongate" who is apprenticed to David Scott, also an apothecary on August 23, 1655. But the date seems to suggest another generation, although of course it is quite possible that he was Hew's son. Hew was a signatory of the Solemn League and Covenant at Greyfriars Churchyard in Edinburgh.

Hew's son William was a burgess by November 3, 1659, when he appears in the Roll of Burgesses of the Canongate. He was married on "fryday 1 july 1664" to Margaret Johnson in the "Kirk of Holyrood-house by Mr. Patrick Hepburn." As regards his death, it is somewhat confusing, as there are three Williams, all bakers, recorded as dying in the Canongate and Greyfriars registers, one on March 11, 1674, one on August 27, 1670, and "William the elder", who I suspect might be our William (one of the others probably being his son) on January 25, 1696.

In 1661, Hew Hannay, baker in the Canongate, is concerned in a deed with Francis Hannay, schoolmaster of Aberdour, William Hannay of Kirkdale and John Hannay of Whytehills [Whitehills].

---

[115] In the 1977 edition: *Table V (cont'd)* lists a William Hannay as the son of John Hannay and Agnes Mathesone, though neither William nor Agnes is mentioned in the body of the text.

[116] In the text of the 1977 edition, Francis lists **two** sons, but in the genealogy tables, he lists **three**, namely William, James and Robert.

## 1.5. Robert Hannay and the Robin Hood riot

Lastly there was in Edinburgh a Robert Hannay, a smith, probably the son of John the "smith and wright extrodinary" to the king. Robert's main claim to fame is his behaviour in a riot on July 20, 1561 which started as a sort of carnival and ended up little short of rebellion.

From the Middle Ages it had been the custom in England and Scotland to celebrate in May the "game of Robin Hood" (i.e., the re-enacting of some of the stories connected with him). Very often these pageants resulted in disturbances of various kinds. In 1555 the Scottish Parliament passed an act forbidding the game, but local magistrates found it very difficult to enforce. In 1561 the Edinburgh mob, enraged at being disappointed in "making a Robin Hood," rioted, seized the city gates and robbed strangers in the town. One of the ringleaders was condemned to be hanged by the magistrates, whereupon the mob broke into the jail, released all the inmates and destroyed the gallows. Then they besieged the magistrates in the Tolbooth, until they offered an indemnity to the rioters if they would lay down their arms. In spite of this assurance, it seems that some of the rioters were brought to trial, among them Robert Hannay. The historian Robert Pitcairn, in his 1833 *Criminal Trials, and other Proceedings before the High Court of Justice* includes this from the case:

**"Robin Hood—Abbot of Unreason, Lord of Disobedience.**

Jul. 20, 1561. Robert Hannay smith, James Cowper tailzeour, Thomas Johnson cordine, Andro Henderson swerdslipper, Andro Richmann cuke, William Clerk talburner, James Fawsyid talburner, John Cok tailzeour, Patrick Mow talvurner and Alexander Buffet talburner. The quhilk day James Cowper tailzeour come in will for arte and parte to be the chiefing (choosing) of George Durye in Robert Hude otherwayis culland and nammand him Lord of (In) obedience (misrule) amangis the craftismen and thair seruandis within the burgh of Edinburgh, in the moneth of April last by past foresaid and assistant to him in contrair be tennour of the act of Parliament and for breechin the said act. Item for breaking of the proclaimation of the Provost and Bailiees of Edinburgh maid for observing of the said act, forbidand all the inhabitants of the burgh that nane of thame suld take upon hand to chiefe ony sic persone in Robin Hude Abbot of Unreason, or any other name within the said burgh. Item for convocation of our souvrane Ladies leigis, in company with the said George Durye callit Lord of In obedience to the nowmer of... Persons bodin in fier with ane displayet handsense, halbrownis, jakkis, culveringis, morriounis, twa handit swerds, coatis of mailzie and other wepynnis invasive upon Sunday the xij day of May last by past in company with certain broken men were betuix thre and four houris eftir none cummand within the Burgh of Edinburgh entered at the East Porte thereof and passed by the Trone thereof, quhair they were met be ane parte of the Baihies,

council and officers of the Burgh and chargit be theme to pass
aback and devyid them to the said burgh, for eschewing trouble and
misorder in the samynn and notwithstanding the said charge
violently and contempnardlie pass and forward to the said
Castlehill and returned again to the Portis of the said burgh. Usand
the samyn be ische and entre, at their pleasure makend plane
rebbellion and inobedience against the Magistratis of the said
Burgh.

Thomas Johnson, in will for breaking act of Parliament and
proclaimarion made by the Magistratis, ut supra. Andro
Hendersoune, in will for breaking act of Parliament aforesaid- Item
the said Andro Hendesoune convict of the making of the said
Convocation and rebellion against the Magistratis in the manner
foresaid.

Thomas Cok. fflyit for breaking act of Parliament in chiefing the
said Lord of Inobedience and breaking the proclaimation made be
the Majestraris in manner foresaid aulauerhie (only), Andro
Richmann convict for assistance to the said lord of Inobedience and
his complices in breaking the said act and proclaimation and
furnessing them with meit and drink James Fowsyid, Patrick Mow,
Alexander Biffet convict of breaking the said act and
proclaimation, convocation and rebellion aforesaid conform to the
dittay."

Or, roughly:

**Robin Hood—Abbot of Unreason, Lord of Disobedience.**

July 20th, 1561. Robert Hannay smith, James Cooper tailor,
Thomas Johnson shoemaker, Andrew Henderson armourer,
Andrew Richmann cook, William Clerk drummer, James Fawsyid
drummer, John Cook tailor, Patrick Mow drummer and Alexander
Buffet drummer.

The which day James Cowper, tailor, willfully aided and abetted
the nomination of George Durye as Robin Hood, otherwise called
and named the Lord of Disobedience, among the craftsmen and
their servants within the burgh of Edinburgh, in April of the past
year, and assisted him in contravention of the wording of the act of
parliament and for breaching the said act.

Likewise, for breaking of the proclamation of the provost and
bailies of Edinburgh made for observing of the said act, forbidding
all the inhabitants of the burgh that none of them should honour
any such person as Robin Hood, Abbot of Unreason, or any other
name within the burgh.

Likewise for convocation of our sovereign lady's subjects, in
company with the said George Durye, called Lord of Misrule, to
the number of ... persons armed in fear with an open display of
banners, armored vests and jerkins, firearms, helmets, two-handed
swords, coats of mail and other offensive weapons upon Sunday the

50

12th of May last year, in company with certain lawless men of war between three and four o'clock in the afternoon, coming within the burgh of Edinburgh, entering at the East gate thereof and passed to the marketplace thereof, where they were met by a part of the bailies, council and officers of the said burgh, and charged by them to move back, and depart from the said burgh, eschewing trouble and misorder in the same:

And, notwithstanding the said charge, violently and contemptibly passing forward to the said Castle hill and returning again to the gate of the said burgh; using the same for exit and entry, at their pleasure, making plain rebellion and disobedience against the magistrates of the said burgh.

Thomas Johnstone, summoned for breaking of the said act of parliament and proclamation made by the magistrates, as above. Andrew Henderson summoned for breaking the said act and proclamation as mentioned above. Likewise, the said Andrew Henderson guilty of the making of the said convocation and rebellion against the magistrates in the aforementioned manner. John Cook, filed for breaking of the act of parliament in nomination of the said Lord of Disobedience, and breaking of the proclamation made to the magistrates, in the aforementioned manner, alone. Andrew Richman, guilty for assistance to the said Lord of Disobedience and his accomplices, in breaking of the said act and proclamation; and supplying the same with meat and drink. James Fawcett, Patrick Mow, Alexander Bissett, guilty of the breaking of the said act, proclamation, convocation, and aforementioned rebellion, corresponding to the indictment.

Robert's fate is not mentioned, but no doubt he was convicted, as he seems to have been fairly deeply concerned; however, he seems to have survived, as he appears as a member of the Hammermens Guild[117] in a decreet[118] of April 26, 1569.

From all this it is clear that the family had a position of some influence in the city during the 16th and 17th centuries. The Burgesses of the Canongate, which most of these Hannays were, held very considerable powers in the local government of their particular part of the capital.

---

[117] The **Hammermen's Guild** was the trade organization for any tradesman who worked with a hammer. In Scotland a Guild consisted of Burghers Supreme headed by a committee of 7 trades, e.g. Masons, Fleshers (i.e. butchers), etc… They set apprentice pay, number of years to be served, weights and measures and many other things, a bit like Trading standards nowadays -- *Tony Lowe.*

[118] A **decreet** was a judgment in a court of law.

51

# V: The Decline of Sorbie

"Opressors, sinflints and damned Usuary
for where these reign, my son we seldom see
descent of state until the third degree."

Patrick Hannay, 17th century poet

With the next three owners of Sorbie, the fortunes of the family go
from bad to worse, until in 1626 the greater part of Sorbie was sold to
Sir Patrick Agnew of Lochnaw. The reason seems to have been the
usual one, so common in Scotland at this period, of private war
between two landowners, causing them to have to sell property in order
to prosecute their enemies, either in the courts, or, if they could manage
it, on a private battle field. The relationship of many Hannays
mentioned in this chapter can be found in Figure 7.

## 1. *Alexander Hannay (d. 1612)*

Alexander Hannay of Sorbie succeeded his father, Patrick, after the
latter's murder in 1543. William Hannay, Patrick's uncle, the Provost
of Wigtoun, was made tutor to the estate. Alexander must have had
sasine about 1555 of part of the property. He is shown in the Exchequer
Rolls as having sasine of Sorbie at a value of about £1,505[119] in 1569.

Like many other Gallovidians, to whom it was a local "field sport,"
Alexander was concerned in a smuggling deal. For in 1565 he went
surety for Thomas McClellane (his sister Agnes's husband) in
Barfane[120], and Margaret Hannay, his sister, the wife of Patrick
Molling. Altogether three puncheons[121] of wine, value £45, and five
ells of kelt[122], value 40/-, were concerned. The case dragged on till
1577, and was eventually decided against Margaret and Agnes Hannay,
Alexander's sisters.

In 1573, Alexander summoned Sir John Dunbar concerning the murder
of Patrick Hannay. Since the murderers of the Alexander's father had
been caught and sentenced 28 years earlier, it is likely that this
concerns another Patrick, perhaps Alexander's brother. He was
possibly the father of "Patrick the Poet," (see chapter XIX: The Hannay
Poets) and may have had sasine or ward of the property after
Alexander's great-uncle William, the Provost, died in 1556. This

---

[119] Equivalent to £104,400 of purchasing power in 2018.

[120] Possibly **Barvane** in Dumfries Parish – *Keith Hanna*

[121] **puncheon** – a liquid measure equivalent to 84 gallons.

[122] **kelt** – a rough mixture of black and white wool in its natural state.

Patrick is shown as a tax defaulter on August 18 in the Privy Council Register, along with Andrew[123], John[124], William[125], and Thomas Hannay[126]. A letter from Sir John Dunbar of Mochrum[127] to the Laird of Barnbarroch, Patrick Vaus, gives some details:

> "1573/4 16th March. Brother, eftyr my verry heartie commendation, this sal be to advertis you that the Laird of Sorbie has summoned John Dunbar brother german to the quidnam of Ballidone my cowsing and youris with divers utheris of my kinsmen and surname to underlay the law at Edinburgh the fifth day of April next to come for the slaughter of one Patrick Hannay being at the kings house for the mutilation of the said John for the quhilk slaughter, I intend to advise and appear hence of men of law to cause my friends entry the said day and plan to abyd the law..."

Or:

> "16th March 1573. Brother, after my very hearty commendation (greetings), this shall be to inform you that the Lord of Sorbie has summoned John Dunbar, full brother to the head of the household of Balllidone (Baldoon, the seat of the Dunbars) my cousin and yours, with diverse others of my kinsmen and surname, to pursue a claim (of justice) at Edinburgh on fifth of April for the slaughter (i.e. the killing or murder) of one Patrick Hannay being (held?) at the king's house (Court of Justice/King and his Council) for the mutilation (accusation/trial/punishment) of the said John for the said slaughter (killing) I intend to advise and appear in defence of my friend on the said day and see justice done." - *modern English courtesy Tony Lowe*

An example of the wariness of the lairds in dealing with courts is shown in this letter from the Laird of Mochrum to the Laird of Sorbie:

> "I think it varry necessar to be accompanied at the same day with my loving freindis. I am forsid at this tyme to desyre you as ye luife the veill (weal) and honor of me, my house, and freindis that ye will kype the saidis day and place, accomponeit with your servanders, in sic manner as ever ye will desyre me my freinds and servanders to do for you when you lyffis or socht oures ar. March LXXIII, Mochrum."

Or:

---

[123] Probably Patrick's brother.

[124] Likely another brother of Patrick.

[125] Possibly Patrick's nephew.

[126] Possibly Thomas, son of Henry in Craigilton.

[127] **Mochrum** is located sixteen miles south of Newton Stewart and approximately six miles west of Sorbie.

I think it very necessary to be accompanied on that day by my loving friends. I am forced at this time to desire that you (as you love the well-being and honour of me, my house and friends) keep the said day and place, accompanied with your servants, in such manner as ever you would desire me, my friends and servants to do the same for you. March '73, Mochrum.

What happened at Edinburgh we do not know, but Dunbar's intention to "abyd the law" was certainly a rare thing.

In 1580 William of Grennan, Alexander's cousin, in his will appointed Alexander guardian to his children Marjory and Catherine, and also to two boys, John and James Hannay, who he insists are "to be held brother with my ane bairns."[128] Who they were is not certain, but they may well have been his bastards, who, in these days, were commonly supported in the same style as one's legitimate children.

In 1591, trouble seems to have started in earnest, and the eventual result was much ruin to the Sorbie family. Although at this time Alexander seems to have teamed up with the Murrays against the Kennedys[129]. Sir Alexander Stewart of Garlies went caution for Alexander of Sorbie, Dunbar of Baldoon and Murray of Broughton in 1,000 merks each, and for John McGown for £1,000, that James Kennedy, son of John Kennedy of Blairquhan, and his tenants living in Cruggleton Castle[130] should be harmless to the persons mentioned.

It appears that most of the Galloway families took part in this rather extensive and prolonged feud, which as far as one can see had nothing to do with the political situation in Scotland. The Kennedys, Hannays and Stewarts were on one side, and the Murrays and Dunbars on the other, with McDowells and McCullochs added for a little flavour.

Again in June 1591, Alexander is going surety for 5,000 merks that David Bogall should be harmless to him. He was, by this time, a Baillie of Wigtoun, along with John Hannay, a merchant there, William Hannay, Patrick in Killfilane, and Patrick Hannay of Kirkdale.

By 1595 Alexander was salting away some of his property by infefting[131] his sons in various of his lands. On December 19 there is an instrument of sasine as follows:

---

[128] i.e., "to be considered brothers of my own children"

[129] Instead of the typical alliance, which was vice-versa. It appears, as is later noted in this chapter, that the Hannays usually lined up with the Kennedys against the Murrays.

[130] Cruggleton Castle is about three miles South of Garlieston.

[131] investing with legal possession. "Infeft" is a verb used generally in Scots law. It is derived from the word "fief" (as in "fiefdom" or "held in fief").

"at the hand of Michael Cochrane narrating that Alexander
A'hannay of Sorbie as baillie of George Murray of Broughton on
precept dated at Broughton 19th Dec 1595 and witnessed by the
said Alexander, William Murray, brother to the said George.
Michael Cochrane notary and Andrew Hannay son of the said
Alexander—infeft William Hannay son of the said Alexander and
Isobel A'hannay his spous in an annual rent of £44 scots furth of
the 5 merkland of Little Owtoun and in another account of 22
merks furth of the same lands reserving liferent of Thomas
A'hannay[132] at the mill of Quhithills [Whitehills] and Elizabeth
McCleiland his spouse. — witnesses George Heroun of Cultis
[Cults], John Kieth in Orchilhern[133], John Rogers in Inglistoun,
John McCaichie in Broughton Skeoch [Skeog] and John and
Andrew A'hannay sons of the said Alexander."

And again in 1598:

"December. Andrew Hannay son of Alexander Hannay of Sorbie
and as his bailie infeft Robert Hannay son to the said Alexander as
nearest heir to his brother the deceased William Hannay in Inch in
half of the £44 scots furth of Balferne."

About this time the feud with the Murrays came to a head. Alexander
and the Hannay clan ranged themselves on the side of the Kennedys.
What was the reason behind the feud we do not know, but Alexander
certainly suffered badly, and a good part of his lands were escheated at
one time or another. The first notice of this comes in 1600 when he is
in a bond not to "reset" with the Master of Cassilis, the son of the chief
of the Kennedys. This family was extremely powerful in Galloway,
and a short rhyme written at the time gives some idea of the sway they
held:

"Twixt Wigtoun and the Town of Ayr
Portpatrick and the Cruives of Cree[134]
No man need think for to bide there
Unless he court with Kennedie."

That same year, Alexander was in trouble with the law again, but on a
different count. In the reign of James VI, owing to the unsettled state
of the country, it became the fashion for the country gentry to live in
taverns rather than in their own draughty and old-fashioned castles.
The Act of October 1581 had interposed "against the abuse of some
landed gentlemen and others forebearing to keep house at their own

---

[132] Possibly Alexander's nephew, i.e. the son of his brother John and sister-in-law
Margaret

[133] Possibly **Orchardton**, in Sorbie Parish – *Keith Hanna*

[134] The **Cruives of Cree** was a dyke across the River Cree, North of Newton Stewart. It
was constructed with several openings containing fish traps.

dwelling houses and boarding themselves in Ale houses." In March 1600, the Treasurer paid to James Crichton, Sheriff in "that part", i.e., Wigtoun, £5. 6. 8d. "for summoning a number of persons including Alexander of Sorby and Sir John Vaus of Barnbarroch to compair before the Lords of Session to hear themselves decernit[135] to have incurred the pains, contained in the Act of Parliament for burding themselves in Oisllar[136] houses."

In 1601 he was "put to the horn"[137] for not subscribing to a bond of assurance for George Murray of Broughton. The other defaulters were Alexander Stewart of Garlies, his own son John of Sorbie, and John of Kirkdale. The next year George Murray summoned Alexander , and the charges placed before the Privy Council best describe the trouble:

"29th June 1602.

1. John Hannay apparent of Sorbie, Robert in Boghous[138], Andrew and Archibald Hannay his brothers, Alexander Hannay son of Patrick Hannay of Kilfillan, John his son, John McMorie servant to John Hannay apparent of Sorbie, Quintin Mure of Auchinell[139] and Adam Boyd upon March... 1599 being Sunday appointed for divine service by in wart armed with hagbuts[140] and pistolets for the slaughter of the said Murray of Broughton Skeoch [Skeog], within half and a quarter miles of the dwelling place of Broughton and when they saw him coming to the parish kirk of Whithorn chased him to his said place, which they besieged attacking him and his company with pistolets and hagbuts for their slaughter.

2. In June 1599 Robert of Boghous Andrew and Archibald his brothers George and Gilbert the sons of Patrick of Killfilane, John of Gelston, Thomas Hannay son of Henry Hannay in Craigilton and John Rogerson with others shot at Patrick McCulloch of Owtoun [Outon] and William Gordon persuers servitors in the High Street beside. . . all but berieving them of their lives.

3. In July 1600 Alexander Cunninghame of Powton, Archibald Hannay of Sorbie, Patrick son of Gilbert in Crugilton to the number of 20 persons, treasonably under assurance pursued the complainer and his servants, while they were mowing his hay in the meadow of

---

[135] determined

[136] **oisllar** = oistellar, an innkeeper.

[137] **Put to the horn**: denounced as a rebel or outlaw, derived from a herald's horn blast preceding the announcement.

[138] **Boghous**: A place near the village of Mochrum.

[139] Possibly **Auchengallie**, five miles West of Sorbie or **Auchenclay**, a mile Northwest of Stoneykirk. – *Keith Hanna*

[140] A **hagbut** was an *arquebus*, i.e. an archaic rifle-like firearm.

Broughton shot hagbuts and pistolets at them hurting sundry and mutilating Adam McKenneth in the leg.

4. In July 1598 Andrew and Archibald Hannay Sons of Sorbie Patrick son of Gilbert in Crugilton are under assurance in the persuers lands at Broughton and cast down the meadow dyke and burnt a barn and the meadow.

5. August 1598 fired a haystack at Broughton.

6. Stole hay and chased Broughtons servants.

7. Stole six head of holt and a hors and cuttit his wyfs purse."

They were ordered to appear in court and denounced as rebels.

In October 1602, William Gordon, a burgess of Wigtoun, made a bond for Adam Hannay, also a burgess there:

"300 merks not to reset or intercommune with Alexander Hannay of Sorbie John Hannay his son and apparent heir John of Kirkdale Robert of Boghous Andro and Archibald sons of the Laird of Sorbie George Gilbert Alexander and John the sons of Patrick of Killfilane. Thomas and Symon Hannay sons of Henry Hannay of Craigilton John Hannay of Gelston and several others who are denouncit rebels at the instance of Sir George Home of Spot Treasurer and George Murray of Broughton."

These troubles had been costing Alexander a very considerable amount of money, for at one stage he had to go surety for £3,000[141] not to harm Murray of Broughton. In February 1603 he was called to answer before the King's courts, and the bond is repeated here:

"Bond of Alexander Hannay of Sorbie John his son, John of Kirkdale 300 merks each and for Robert and Archibald Sons of the Laird of Sorbie and Alexander son of Patrick Hannay of Kilfillan 200 merks each to answer before the King in Council upon 15th March next to a complaint made against them by the Treasurer and George Murray of Broughton touching hurting the said George and his men with Hagbuts and pistolets also not to harm the said George under powers contained in the Kings letters. 19th February 1603."

We unfortunately have no record of the final outcome of the case, but it is most probable that a very heavy fine was levied when they finally submitted to the King's justice, and no doubt much of Sorbie's property was escheated.

---

[141] Approximately £54,000 in 2018.

In 1608, there is a decree against him for non-payment of a debt to Gavin Dunbar of Baldoon[142]. Alexander had several children, all of whom are dealt with in Chapter VI: John, his heir; Sir Robert; William in Inch, who died in 1598; Sir Patrick; Andrew; Archibald; Helen; Agnes[143] and two natural (illegitimate) sons Patrick of Kilfillan [Kilfillan] and Robert of Boghouse. Patrick was a loyal supporter of his father throughout the troubles. He was granted the 20/ - Kirklands of Sorbie called Kilifihlane [Kilfillan] in 1589. Apart from much feuding in the time of Alexander and John of Sorbie, the Kilfillan have little claim to fame, except perhaps for the raid on Harie Gordon of Creich in 1624, led by Patrick, the great-grandson of Alexander, which is quite amusing: "Patrick Hannay son of Alexander of Kilifihlane and others armed with weapons came at night and stole 5 or 6 score threaves of beir[144] and took them to Mr. William Patterson minister of Sorbie." What the minister was doing mixed up in this is a mystery— but no doubt he was much like the rest. A genealogy of the Kilfillan family can be found in Figure 12.

Alexander died about 1612, and was succeeded by John his son. The retour is dated March 10, 1612 and reads:

> *"Joannes Hannay de Sorbie, heares masculus Alexandri Hannay de Sorbie Patris, in 10 libratis terram de Sorbie antiqui extensus, infra parochiam de Inche et gleba terrarum ecclesiasticarum ecclesiae parochahis de Sorbie, extendentibus ad 20 solidates terrarum vocatis Kilfillan, cum decimus inclusis infra parochiam de Sorbie."*

Or:

John Hannay of Sorbie, male heir to Alexander Hannay of Sorbie his father, [inheritor] of the 10 pounds worth of land of Sorbie earlier extended below the parish of Inch and the church lands of the parish of Sorbie, extending to 20 shillings of land called Kilfillan including ten more within the parish of Sorbie.

---

[142] **Baldoon**: An estate near Bladnoch.

[143] This Agnes was listed as being the wife of Thomas McClellane in the Second Edition, but there is also an Agnes in the previous generation (i.e. the aunt of this Agnes) who is listed elsewhere as being the wife of Thomas McClellane. It is possible that the younger Agnes was the wife of Thomas McClellane and that the elder Agnes, married to Nicholas Murray, was conflated with her niece.

[144] A **threave** was a measure of approximately 24 sheaves (bundles) of cut grain; **beir** is barley. A **score** being a group of 20 items, "5 or 6 score threaves of beir" means **2400 to 2880 bundles of barley.**

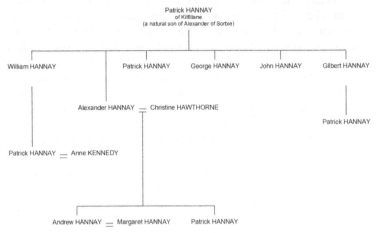

*For the pedigree of Patrick Hannay, see Figure 7: The Descendants of Robert of Sorbie*

Patrick HANNAY
of Kilfillane
(a natural son of Alexander of Sorbie)

William HANNAY — Patrick HANNAY — George HANNAY — John HANNAY — Gilbert HANNAY

Alexander HANNAY — Christine HAWTHORNE

Patrick HANNAY

Patrick HANNAY — Anne KENNEDY

Andrew HANNAY — Margaret HANNAY — Patrick HANNAY

**Figure 12: The Hannays of Kilfillane**

## 2. *John Hannay (d. 1640)*

John first appears as a baillie in a precept for Sir John Vaus of Barnbarroch in 1588, and by 1591 he was a burgess of Wigtoun. John of Sorbie married Dorethy Stewart, formerly the wife of Alexander Stewart of Tonderaghie near Whithorn, and a daughter of Stewart of Culcae [Culkae]. Alexander and Dorethy appear to have been divorced, as Alexander married Catherine Gordon as his second wife.

As if John's troubles were not enough—and he had plenty—Henry Cunningham appears to have forged his signature, and interfered with his handwriting in some executory papers.

John, with the usual stubbornness of Scottish lairds of his period, revived the feud with the Murrays, and as the inevitable result got himself into serious difficulties, resulting in the nearly complete loss of the family lands. In the Lochnaw Charter Chest[145], there is a contract entered into between Sir Patrick Agnew and John whereby John sold by way of wadset the lands of Creloch and Craigloch in Mochrum Parish to Sir Patrick on June 29, 1625. More misfortune followed, and on July 16, 1626, the main part of the lands of Sorbie were sold to Sir Patrick, and sasine given to him by Andrew Hannay the younger of Sorbie.

---

[145] A **charter chest** is a chest containing legal documents, minutes, letters, etc.

John still retained some property, and received a charter from John McDowell of Garthland, on July 18, 1627, for various lands for himself and his son and heir Andrew. But before long, misfortune overtook them again, and John was forced to sell more land to Sir Alexander Stewart of Garlies (a kinsman, a daughter of a previous Garlies, had married into the Hannay family). In a crown grant of February 6, 1630 to "James Stewart second son of Alexander Stewart Earl of Galloway of ten merkland of Ingleston of Sorbie, Revelloch and Langlands, three merkland of Inche, Kilfillan in the parish of Sorbie apprised for £3,130.[146]" There is a further grant referring to an escheat, which probably the grant to Alexander Stewart was as well, also in the same year:

> "Crown grant to Hugh Viscount Montgomerie of 2½ merkland of
> Killantreangane [Killantringan], lands of Craiginlee etc. in the
> parish of Inch resigned by John Hannay of Sorbie with consent of
> Archibald Dunbar of Baldoon duration of his escheat."

Eventually, most of the lands of Sorbie found their way into the hands of the Earls of Galloway, in whose hands they are today. Mostly they were lost by rebellion and feuding, and the subsequent fines and escheats. Andrew, the eldest son, was charged with carrying out most of the distasteful sales, but his younger son John had problems as well.

Andrew married Sybella Heriot on May 20, 1626 in Edinburgh. His brother, John, got married the next day to Sybella's mother, Christine Bla (or Blow), also in Edinburgh. The marriage was performed by James Hannay, future Dean of Edinburgh. George Heriot, Sybella's half-brother, was the founder of the magnificent hospital in Edinburgh which bears his name, and also of George Heriot's School. He had been Goldsmith to King James VI and was an extremely wealthy man.

Andrew had sasine of lands at Killantreane [Killantrae] in 1622, and later certain other lands on his marriage, as the marriage contract shows:

> "May 20th 1626. . . They [Andrew and Sybella] are infeft of his
> father in 3 merkland of Craigboy [Inch] 2½ merkland of
> Killantreane 2½ merkland of Knockglass and the £10 lands of
> Sorbie."

The will of George Heriot is worthy of quotation, as it shows the rather tortuous relationships of Sybella and Christine better than any table:

> "…[To] Sybella wife of Andrew Hannay the younger of Sorbie
> daughter of George Heriots mother in law (i.e. stepmother) 200
> merks English."

---

[146] Approximately £33,000 in 2019.

To Sybella's children he left 500 merks to be paid after the death of their parents:

> "...[To] Cristian Blaw my mother in law (stepmother) late wife of my father, Sybella Heriot my half-sister, I give and bequeath unto the said Sybella Heriot the sum of 500 merks of like money to be employed for the best benefit and profit of her and to be paid to her at the age of 21. If she happen to die befoir that age, that I will bequeath the sum unto such lawfull children as she may happen to have, and for want of such issue that I give and devise the said sum to the Provost and Baillies of Edinburgh for further foundation of the said hospital."

Of Andrew's later life we know little. He had a daughter Grissel, who is shown as his "heir generall and of provision" in 1652, which would put her birth at about 1630 and make her his only child. Andrew was dead by 1635, when there is a complaint concerning by the Earl of Cassilis concerning a bond which reads:

> "Caution by John of Sorbie and Andrew his son (who is shewn as the deceased Andrew Hannay apparent of Sorbie) became cautioners for 1,000 merks that Sir Patrick Agnew of Lochnaw Sheriff of Wigtoun would keep the peace with the Earl of Cassilis on 30th July 1628. The bond had been broken."

John, the second son of John of Sorbie, received a charter from his father for 3½ merkland of Inch in 1633. He succeeded to what was left of the family property on the death of his father in 1640, reported to have been killed in a quarrel. Afterwards, in 1644, he is a witness in a reversion of James McCulloch of Myretoun, and is still referred to as John Hannay of Sorbie, signifying that he was still in possession of at least part of the Sorbie estate. In 1677 there is an entry showing the final sale of Sorbie lands, and John the younger by this time appears to be resident in Edinburgh:

> "Sasine at Edinburgh the 2nd March 1677 John Hannay of Sorbie with the consent of Christine Bla his spous and Andrew Hannay his oldest lawfull son and of John Murray of Broughton as cautioner for them on the ane pairt and Master Archibald Lindsay Doctor of Physic and Christine Heriot his spous on the other for lands lying in the parish of Sorbie 3,000 merks[147]."

The remainder of the property was sold to Alexander, Earl of Galloway, for 2,700 merks[148]. In 1689 there is a document in the Calendar of Culvennan[149] writs which is of considerable interest,

---

[147] Approximately £22,000 in 2018.

[148] Approximately £20,000 in 2018.

[149] Culvennan lies approximately 1 km northwest of Castle Douglas.

particularly in regard to the mention of a certain Abraham Henderson:

> "At Monygoff [Minnigaff]. Minuite of a contract between Mr.
> Abraham Henderson minister of Whithorn and Rosina McClellane
> spouses on the one part and Mr. Alexander Hamilton minister of
> Monygoff and Margaret Henderson spouses on the other part. Mr.
> Abraham Henderson is to deliver a perfect assignation to Mr.
> Alexander of the sums owed to him by John Hannay of Sorbie for
> which the lands of Tathe are wadset for 3,000 merk and the other
> writs including a bankbond to be destroyed. In return Mr.
> Alexander is to obtain further crown confirmation of the lands of
> Polbae and Dirloskin, to be infeft there in and there to dispose the
> same without reversion to Mr. Abraham and his spous. Mr.
> Alexander to dispose to Mr. Abraham the tack[150] he has of
> Barnbarroch of the teinds[151]."

An Abraham Henderson is known to have been married to a sister of
William Hannay of Kirkdale. She may have been this Abraham's
second wife, but he is shown as a merchant, and resident in London in
1730 approximately: still this does not rule him out altogether.

The close connection with the Hannays seems to point to these
Abrahams being one and the same. While John Hannay (the younger)
of Sorbie was known to have had a son Andrew, there may have been
other children, including Robert and Ann of Kingsmuir. One theory is
that Robert was John's heir, for his sister Ann left her property to
Abraham Henderson as the fourth substitute in her will, after William
of Kirkdale.

We know little else of John Hannay the younger, but if his direct line
died out, it is quite possible that the succession passed to the family of
Dean James Hannay, a view which is advanced elsewhere in this book
(see Chapter VII: The Family of John Hannay, M.P.).

This ends an era in the fortunes of the Hannay family. From now on
their connections with Galloway are centred around Kirkdale. But all
over the rest of Scotland, in England, in Ireland, in the colonies,
members of the family are carving out an honoured name in the law,
as soldiers, in shipping, in industry and colonial settlement and
establishing the branches which are still alive today.

---

[150] lease

[151] tithes

# VI: The Sons of Alexander of Sorbie

The sons of Alexander of Sorbie, John's brothers, in most cases are well documented, and there is much of interest concerning them. They were William, Sir Patrick, Robert, Andrew and Archibald. There was also Patrick of Kilfillane, and Robert Hannay of Boghouse in Mochrum, natural (illegitimate) half-brothers to those listed, and sisters Agnes and Helen. William is mentioned in the sasine of December 29, 1598, but further information about him, Andrew and Archibald is confined to the charters, deeds and bonds, and their activities in the feud with the Murrays, explained in the previous chapter.

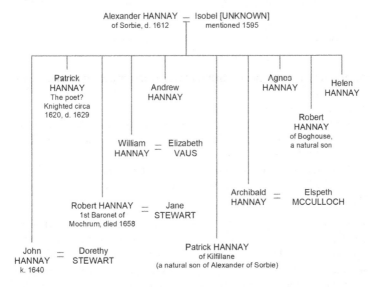

**Figure 13: Alexander Hannay's family**

In 1603, James VI came into his long-awaited inheritance, England at last was in his grasp, and such wealth as poor Scotland could never provide was his. No sooner had the Earl Marshal's message been received than the King of Scots left for his southern capital—and that in indecent haste. To add insult to injury, although James promised his Scottish subjects that he would return frequently to Edinburgh, his first and only return visit to Scotland did not occur until 14 years after he had ascended the throne in London.

Two of the brothers, Robert and Patrick, along with many other far-seeing and ambitious Scotsmen, joined the King and accompanied him to London. These two young men found favour with Queen Anne[152].

## 1. Robert Hannay, 1st Baronet Mochrum (d. 1658)

Robert is first mentioned in the will of Alexander Maxwell of Wigtown as "Son to the Laird of Sorbie" in August 1597. Robert is shown as having a son, John, in the Great Seal Register for July 12, 1616. This John certainly did not succeed to the baronetcy and must have died without issue, as no further mention of him can be found anywhere.

Robert seems to have become popular with James VI, for in 1628 he is mentioned in a letter from the King to the Lord Deputy of Ireland:

> "Robert Hannay, one of the squires of our body has been at pains to discover our title to the lands of Glencapp which are now possessed by some mere Irish without title[153]."

A trial was to take place forthwith as to the ownership, and Robert Hannay and his heirs were to be deemed free denizens of Ireland[154] in return for their services. A year later Robert was granted Glencapp [Glencap][155] for sixty-one years for thirty pounds Irish. In 1629 he was further granted by King Charles the lands and barony of Mochrum Park, which belonged to the deceased Sir John Dunbar of Mochrum Park, knight, or to the deceased Alexander Dunbar, his son. By this time he had accepted a Nova Scotia baronetcy in the style of Sir Robert Hannay of Mochrum.

The Nova Scotia baronetcies were developed by the British crown in 1624 as a way of raising money; i.e., candidates paid the King a certain amount (ostensibly for seeding the new colony with people and supplies) in exchange for being granted the title of *baronet*, which, in the social hierarchy, ranks between *knight* and *baron*. Although in theory the title came with some territory in Nova Scotia (Canada), the land itself was, at the time, in dispute with the French. The grants of

---

[152] Stewart Francis suggested that favour may have been gained through the influence of Patrick Hannay the Poet (see XIX: The Hannay Poets), if Patrick the Poet was not Patrick the son of Alexander. If they were indeed two different people, it is possible that influence went in the other direction, as Patrick the Poet is said in some sources to have been born in 1594, and so would have been only nine years old when James came to the united throne – Perhaps his cousins later introduced *him* to the court.

[153] King James was certainly not known for his empathy for the common man, be he Irish or of any other nationality.

[154] "free denizen": a state of citizenship involving the granting of certain legal and customs rights.

[155] **Glencap**: Near Bray in County Wicklow, Ireland.

land ceased in 1638 (whilst the titles themselves continued to be granted), and the land was not completely conquered by the British until over a century later.

On October 19, 1629, he was appointed Clerk of the Nichells[156] in Ireland. An extract from the Patent Rolls gives some idea of the meaning of this appointment. The Crown for many years had been trying to organize the government and courts of Ireland on the English model. This appointment was one of those designed for the more orderly government of the courts. The extract reads:

"The King to Viscount Loftus of Ely[157], Chancellor, and Richard Earl of Cork, Justices, directing the appointment of Robert Hannay to the Office of Clerk of the Nichells with a fee of £30 a year, it being his Majesty's royall care and the care of his late dear father in all things to reduce the government of that Kingdom unto the very same order and form as in England, but especially the Order and Course of the Exchequer, as near as maybe by the very same model to the end that no officer there shall execute two offices in any one of the Courts out of which he is to certify his proceedings with any other officer there."

In 1629 he was also granted lands in the Longford Plantation in Ireland of some 500 acres.

During the civil war, Robert was stationed in Ireland as Quartermaster-General and Paymaster-General to Sir Charles Coote, the Lord President of Connaught who eventually married Robert's daughter Jane.

The State Papers of the period have a considerable quantity of correspondence to, from, and concerning Sir Robert; there is a rather amusing story contained in a letter to Sir Francis Willoughby concerning the views of a certain Major Piesly on the Scottish Nation and Sir Robert's reactions:

"1644 May 20th. Sir Robert Hannay to Sir Francis Willoughby. By your letter unto me of the 19th of this instant month, His

---

[156] Or Clerk of the **Nihils**, literally, Clerk of the **Nothings**. A Clerk of the Nihils would record instances of writs that were unable to be served by sheriffs or constables, presumably creating a record of persons of interest who could not be found – or at least, who had no known address/location. Source: Scargill-Bird, S. R., *A Guide to the Principal Classes of Documents Preserved in the Public Records Office, Her Majesty's Stationery Office*, London, 1891.

[157] History sometimes revisits itself unexpectedly. The title of Viscount Loftus eventually was merged with that of the Marquesses of Ely when the family was further ennobled in 1801. The 8th Marquess of Ely, Charles Tottenham, was headmaster at the school attended by the future Major General James Hanna, a clan councilor and longtime member of the Clan Hannay Society; the two maintained a friendship for many years before the former's death in 2006.

Excellency's pleasure in these ensuing words expressed. 'Sir, my Lord Lieutenant is informed lately that some unbeseeming words hath been spoken by Major Piesly, to the prejudice of the Scots nation, which his Excellancy having understood to have been uttered in your presence, Lt Gilbert being also by, his pleasure is that I should examine the business and so to inform my lord of the truth thereof. Sir, in your letter you desire me and Lt. Gilbert to collect our memory and send unto you in writing by eight of the clock this morning what the words were and to set it down under our hand. Sir, in obedience to which I, Sir Robert Hannay, together with Lt. Henry Gilbert do according to our best remembrance herein truly set down those words spoken of the Scots nation as followeth.

That upon Friday last the 17th of this instant month, in the shop of Mrs. Rochford, Seamster, near the castle gate of Dublin Major Piesly in the presence of us, in great passion uttered these words: 'That the Scots in the town of Belfast had betrayed the town to Munro.' Major Piesly swore by the Lord, that for aught he did know, that if the Scots did advance, they of that nation which were here would also betray this town unto them. Withall Major Piesly swore 'God damn him but if every man were of his mind and do as he would they of that nation here, wherever he could meet them he would despatch them.' All which we do certify to your honour under our hand."

In 1643 he was appointed custodian of the town and lands of Drumcondraght, near Dublin, and the towns of Clonturk and Balgriffin, part of the estate of James Bath of Athcarne and Robert Bath of Clonturk, two rebels against the King. He received a grant of £200 from the property for which he had to give no account to the crown.

By this time, he had completely severed his connection with Mochrum, having resigned the place to John Dunbar "together with all the removal of all his instruments."[158]

In 1645, Sir Robert left for England to attend the Joint Irish Committee of both Houses of Parliament. He was present at the meeting of the committee on August 30. By September 22 he appears to have been made a prisoner of war, as in the committee's minutes it is noted that they agreed to exchange Lt. Brabazon, Sir Henry Tichborne and Sir James Ware, prisoners in the Tower, for Lady Moore, Sir Peter

---

[158] There were two baronetcies of Mochrum, corresponding to two settlements of the same name in neighbouring shires. The baronetcy of Mochrum, Kirkcudbrightshire (established in 1630), was held by the Hannays and became dormant in 1842. The baronetcy of Mochrum, Wigtownshire (established in 1694), was conferred on a branch of the Dunbar family and continues to this day, being represented by the 14th Baronet. To confuse matters further, Dunbars resided in both Mochrums. Robert apparently relinquished the land (in Kircudbrightshire) to a Dunbar several decades before the Dunbar baronetcy was created (in Wigtownshire).

Weymes, Sir Robert Hannay, Captain Ponsonby, Captain Warkwith, Lt. Draper, Mr. Baten, etc. At all events he was back in Ireland at the end of the year, and in 1646 was again in London as his son-in-law Sir Charles Coote's agent. On June 5, 1646, Sir Charles wrote to Sir Phillip Persival in London from Belfast of the condition of the army in Ireland, which in spite of Coote's successes does not seem to have been administratively sound. His letter is typical of the troubles of a soldier dealing with a parsimonious government:

> "I will not trouble you with the sad storeis of our wants but refer
> you to Sir Robert Hannay's relative thereof but in short let me tell
> you that if I be not speedily relieved, all the service which has been
> done will be lost which were great prejudice to the public service.
> You will from the other men more particularly receave
> informations of what I have done since coming to the kingdom.
> And the Lord be praised he had blesed my endeavour, to Him be
> the glory. I pray you offord Sir Robert Hannay your best advice in
> my business."

There next follows a letter from one Joseph Davis to Sir Phillip saying, "The Lord President depends on Sir Phillip to advise Sir Robert Hanna as Major Ormesby is now going over to solicit supporters." This appears ominous; Sir Robert had gone to London to acquaint the Government of the situation in Ireland, and it appears that the Lord President was changing his allegiance from Crown to parliament. Perhaps Major Ormesby was going to Ireland to try and influence the administration in this direction.

On July 27, there is another letter from Sir Phillip in which he says, "Sir Robert Hannay is very affectionate and vigilent but can do no great good untill God's time comes." The Treasury apparently did not respond adequately, so officers like Sir Robert spent their private fortunes in keeping the army in the field.

Sir Robert visited England again in 1648. On his arrival he was arrested for debt, the debt being incurred by his ordering stores for the army on his personal account. The government was not disbursing his arrears of pay.

However, he petitioned the House as follows:

> "Petition of Sir Robert Hannay—The petitioner has been affronted,
> while entrusted by Sir Charles Coote, Lord President of Connaught
> to negotiate with Parliament, what may conduce to carrying on the
> work against the rebels in Ireland, and this though about £3,000 are
> due to him in arrears. He is ready to satisfy all his creditors as soon
> as it shall be in his power to do so and prays to be protected that he
> may prosecute the public affiares entrusted to him."

67

On November 15, there is a further petition in which he thanks the House for granting him a protection, which it appears the Commons would not deliver until he had assigned to his creditors the money owing to them out of his arrears. This petition reads as follows, and clearly shows Robert to have been very hard done by:

"He thanks the house for granting him a protection which however Mr Browne will not deliver untill he has made assignment to his creditors out of his arrears, he is ready to do so though a great part of the debt was contracted as surety with Sir Charles Coote Lord President of Connaught for provisioning the soldiery there, but no part of his arrears is yet settled to be payed at any place and no assignment thereof would be valid. He prays the House to order Mr Browne to deliver his protection that he may be able to follow the business of the Province of Connaught which is suffering greatly by his restraint and he promises to make the assignment to his creditors as soon as his arrears are settled."

One wonders if and when these arrears were settled. On July 4, 1650, the Council of State discussed the report of the Irish Committee of the House concerning Sir Robert, and on August 22, the following minute appears in their proceedings:

"The Council of State having ordered the buying of certain provisions for the Army, viz.: Kettles, Mugs, and beds for married soldiers, handmills, etc., the payment for which cannot be placed on the soldiers' entertainment, that the Council be moved to appoint £1,300 for this… having received the report of Robert Hanna Bart they find last November certain sums due to the state. Committee report that £297-2-0 should be paid to him as part of his arrears to help him delay his long attendance here as agent of Sir Charles Coote, the sum otherwise disposed of. Order was given to the Commissioners of Goldsmiths Hall to pay Sir Robert out of revenue £150."

In 1649, things seemed to have quietened down somewhat in Ireland, and the army was about to suffer one of its periodic reductions. Twenty-nine field officers were called upon to stand down and the army reduced to 108 companies. Robert, however, was not one of these, and retained his company and his commission. It is interesting to note that in this entry in the State Papers Domestic the army is referred to as "His Majesty's Army in Ireland." King Charles I having by this time been deposed and executed, it would appear therefore that the Irish army did not recognise the Protectorate.

Sir Robert married Jane Stewart, but no more is known of her except that her death is recorded in the register of the Ulster Herald. She was buried at Christchurch, Dublin, on March 27, 1662. Her arms shown in Ulster's record are: "First and fourth quarters argent, three bucks' heads crazed azure, horned and second and third argent three cross crosslets fitchee issuing from as many crescents sable with the motto 'Per ardua ad alta." These arms were presumably matriculated by Sir Robert as the third son, both bucks' heads and cross crosslets fitchee being family charges.

They had two sons, Robert, who followed his father as a soldier in Ireland, and John, as well as two daughters. The first, Nichola, is reported to have married Sir George Acheson of Market Hill County Armagh, third baronet in 1654. The other daughter Jane married firstly, before May 1645, Sir Charles Coote, afterwards first Earl of Mountrath. Coote must have fallen for the daughter of his Quartermaster General during the periods he returned from the field to his headquarters in Dublin. They lived together till Charles' death on December 18, 1661. Jane, according to the custom of the period, married again with a certain Sir Robert Reading, Baronet, who died on the March 26, 1689. Their daughter Elizabeth married James Hamilton, 6th Earl of Abercorn, and thus the Hannay blood was transmitted to the noble houses of Abercorn and Hamilton. An acquittance[159] is in existence as follows:

> "To discharge Sir Robert Reading and Jane Countess of
> Mountreath from £500 quit rents for lands in Ireland, in lieu of a
> similar sum granted them from the King by concordatum under
> patent of 19th July, 24th year of his reign, for faithful services
> performed by Countess of Mountreath and other considerations."

In an instrument dated December 26, 1642, Sir Robert resigned the property of Mochrum Park. The reason is not clear, except that his interest now lay entirely in Ireland. The property seems to have returned to the Dunbar family:

> "Compeared personally Mr John Henrysone procurator for Mr
> Francis Hay of Balhoussie W.S with consent of Commissioners in
> the contract dated 25th of December 1642 between the said Mr.
> Francis Hay with the consent of the said commissioners on the one
> part and John Dunbar of Pinkhill on the other part quoting contracts
> dated 4 may 1640 between Sir Robert Ahanna of Mochrum knicht
> on the one part and John Flemyng some time of Carwoode anent a
> disposition therebye made by the said Sir Robert (in cais of the
> failzie therin mentioned) to the said John Flemyng of the lands and
> barrony of Mochrum therein designed Mochrum Park, with
> pertinents quhilk John Fiemyng by his letters of resignation dated
> 27th october 1631 assigned the said John Dunbar and to the said
> John Henderson procurator resigned all and haill the said lands and
> barrony of Mochrum with all the pertinants lying within the Parish

---

[159] receipt indicating the fulfilment of a debt.

of Mochrum also the lands of Barquhannie and Knockerfrick parish of Kirkinner etc in favour of the said John Dunber."

The estate now forms part of the property of the Marquis of Bute, and was one of his favourite residences in Scotland.

Sir Robert died and was buried in Dublin on January 8, 1657/58. His will was administered at Dublin on November 29, 1658. He would probably have been about 70 years old.

His son, Robert, succeeded him as second baronet. At the time of the Restoration he was commanding a company of foot as a captain, and received the general pardon from the King along with Charles Coote and others, by the act of April 28, 1660. The Irish army was, however, to be reduced to sixty-one companies and the supernumerary companies disbanded. Sir Robert was one of those whose company was to go, and he himself was to be axed. His father's old friend Charles Coote interfered and wrote to George Monck, Duke of Albermarle, requesting a company for "Sir Robert Hannay my wifes only brother, there still being some vacant." By February 12, 1661 it had been decided to retain four further companies, and Sir Robert's bacon was saved.

On the March 17, 1661, no doubt due to past services, he was made a member of the Council of Connaught.

In May 1661, his company was stationed at Bellaghy160. The strength return for May 1662 is still extant and given below:

### Sir Robert Hannay's Company

| | |
|---|---|
| Capt: 1 (Sir Robert) | Sgts: 2 |
| Lieut: 1 (Mathias Tubman) | Cpls: 3 |
| Ensign: 1 (Edw Price) | Drummers: 2 |
| | Privates: 93 |

In September the situation in Ireland was such that further companies were disbanded, and amongst them Sir Robert's.

---

[160] This probably refers to Bellahy or Bellaghy in Co. Sligo near the Mayo border; although there is also a Bellaghy in Co. Londonderry. The latter is worth consideration because it was the site of the 1641 rebellion of Irish landowners, which was brutally put down by troops under the command of Sir Charles Coote, who was Sir Robert's brother-in-law.

In 1663, there is a claim for payment of "Disbanded soldiers lately under Sir Robert Hannay's command." His pay roll for the seven months ending in August 1661 was £832 / 10 / 8.

In 1669, he appears to be in command of another company, and a letter on June 10 exists from Lieut. Edward Price, lately ensign in Sir Robert's company, to Major John Beversham concerning ten months' arrears of pay due to Sir Robert's Company.

By 1680 he had become involved in Irish politics, and was hauled before the courts in October to answer charges regarding plots together along with Francis Edgecombe, John Cooper, John Hawkins and Niall O'Molligin. An extract from the Ormond papers[161] gives some information regarding the case:

> "1681 October 12th. Dublin. In the case of a certain Father St. Lawrence, Sir Robert Hannay depones; 'that he saw St Lawrence about four months since go into William Smiths chambers in the Marshailsea and that Smith and St Lawrence were locked up together at that time about two hours, the cause of his [Sir Robert Hannay's] knowledge being that he continued walking near Smiths chambers until he saw St Lawrence go out.'"

What this case is all about is difficult to ascertain, but it may well have some connection with the anti-Catholic feeling roused by the Titus Oates denunciations[162]. At the siege of Londonderry in 1689 a Captain Hanna is mentioned. This might be Sir Robert. He is mentioned for gallant conduct in a poem of the time.

Sir Robert died in Dublin and was buried in St. Michael's on April 30, 1689. The *Memorials of the Dead of Ireland, volume VIII*, say that he was married, and had a daughter Elizabeth, who married Sir George St. George, of Smithfield, who was buried in Christ Church on December 3, 1711. She is referred to as his second wife. There is mention of Lady Elenor Hannay, who was, buried at Reading on January 4, 1674, who was probably the second Sir Robert Hannay's wife.

## 2. Patrick Hannay (d. 1629)

It is now necessary to return to Robert's brother, Patrick. It was he who probably started Robert off in his career in Ireland. Patrick came to court early in the century and entered the legal profession. He served

---

[161] A collection of writings concerning the administration of Ireland under the Duke of Ormond.

[162] Titus Oates led a paranoid frenzy to purge England of Catholics involved in a non-existent plot to overthrow the king. Between 1678 and 1681, many innocent men were executed for treason before Oates himself was arrested for having fabricated the conspiracy and implicating anyone who was his political opponent.

the Crown well, for in 1620 he received a grant of land in County Longford, Ireland. It appears that at this period English and Scottish expansion in Ireland was proceeding with much pressure and encouragement from the State. Several great Scottish families at this time established a branch in Ireland. The reason may well have been connected with the desire of the Government to establish a non-Catholic and actively Protestant ruling class in Ireland and thus displace its native Catholic nobility. While the Recusancy Laws[163] were never enforced in Ireland with the same rigidity as they were in England, Patrick Hannay's lands might well have been the property of some recalcitrant Irish gentleman.

Sir Patrick was knighted by King James, what for we do not know. But probably, like so many others at this period, he was offered a knighthood at a price, and virtually forced to accept it. James had hit upon an ingenious method of raising money by selling knighthoods in exchange for considerable sums of money, a cash-for-title arrangement similar to the Nova Scotia baronetcy of Sir Robert, Patrick's brother (see earlier in this chapter).

In 1621 Patrick was sent to Sweden on a diplomatic mission for King James. Patrick returned from his visit to Sweden the same year, and was granted the Clerkship of the Irish Privy Council in Dublin. Here he would be concerned with the maintenance of law and order in that turbulent country assisting the Viceroy of Ireland, and in fact being virtually head of the Irish Civil Service. In *The Scots In Early Stuart Ireland: Union and separation in two kingdoms* (Egan and Edwards, 2016), it is proposed that Sir William Usher, the Clerk at the time, refused to vacate the position right up to Patrick's death, even when ordered to do so by Kings James and Charles. Thus, Sir Patrick may have never actually officially received the title of Clerk of the Privy Council. The book goes on to describe Irish politics of the era, which tended to favour the Anglo-Irish over the Scots, much to the frustration of the latter.

On the death of King James in 1625, however, King Charles I had reinstated Patrick on the grounds that he had "done good and acceptable service and being recommended to us by our dear mother." Queen Anne had long been friendly to Patrick and was largely responsible for his good fortune. In regranting the Clerkship, King

---

[163] Laws passed against Catholics after the establishment of the Church of England. Heavy fines were levied on anyone partaking in masses or other Catholic rituals. Although the goal of these laws was to eradicate Catholicism from English soil, they had a side-effect of generating income for the government (from wealthy Catholics; Papists who were less financially secure either abandoned their faith in favour of Protestantism or took it underground).

Charles I also noted that Patrick had "done our Late dear Father good and acceptable service beyond the seas with great charge and danger to his life."

After Usher's removal by the king, he endeavoured to keep the post, and bickering went on certainly as late as 1628, when Patrick got a

"new grant absolute of the post to the prejudice of William Usher. Hannay never had had the post and Sir William has it yet. Sir William is considered incompetent."

Patrick certainly all this period exercised the duties of the post, although thanks to Sir William he did not always receive the revenues. Patrick was clearly an able and determined administrator, anxious to get things done and impatient of administrative delay. His 1626 memorial to Lord Conway on Irish Affairs gives some indication of his duties and of his ruthlessness in affairs of state:

"In Ulster rebels abound in the Church College servants and Londoners lands this must exist as long as they are allowed to have recusant tenants, they should compell them to conform.

The delay in getting Irish business done and waiting for decision of the Irish Committee here, bring many of the petitioners unto poverty and discontent. The case of the recusant magistrates should be considered.

A priest, privy to the murder of Mr Pont a minister and Justice of the Peace is in Dublin Castle. If he were racked the intentions of the discontented papists might be got out of him. The Lord Deputy would like to know what is to be done with him. The new companies should be paid. Lower Ormonde should be planted with a reserve to the Natives. Sir Richard Aldworth as commander of the Army should have a seat on the Council, and the Council should be reformed both in number and quality especially residentaries in Dublin."

In 1627 he was appointed one of the Masters in Chancery in Ireland, "in consideration of the surrender of a former patent thereof granted to Sir Archibald Aichison with a fee of £20—to hold during good behaviour in as ample a manner as that office was held by Thomas Rogers or Sir Archibald Achison."

Thus, he was head of the civil administration of the country. Two years later in 1629, when journeying on the king's business, he died at sea. He never seems to have married. His will was confirmed at Edinburgh on March 31, 1636, and given up by his sister, Helen. On November 2, 1641, the following entry appears in the Register of Retours naming his brother Robert Hannay his heir:

*"Robertus Ahannay in Thorntounloch, haeres Magistri Patricii Ahannay aliquando clerici secreti concilii infra regnum Hiberniae fratris natu minimi."*

There was a contemporaneous Patrick Hannay who was a court poet. It is quite possible that Sir Patrick and Patrick the Poet were one and the same. For more details on this theory, see Chapter XIX: The Hannay Poets.

## 3. *Alexander's Children in Ireland*

Both Robert and Patrick must have brought other members of the family to Ireland to assist them in their administrative work. In 1628 we find reference to David Hannay in enlisting soldiers in Ireland for service in Sweden, in the service of Gustavus Adolphus[164], which is detailed in Chapter VIII.

There is also mention of a Captain Richard Hannay in 1658 as a Company Commander in Ireland; it is probable that this is a misprint in the records for Robert.

The family has left a permanent mark on Ireland, and there are many Hannays in Ulster today. The Hannas, the Irish spelling[165], have produced many contributions to Ulster's prosperity. For more information on Hannas in Ireland, see Chapter XX: Irish Hannas.

---

[164] King of Sweden, born 1594; reigned from 1611 until his death in 1632. His reign was marked by the country's involvement in multiple wars (some inherited from his predecessor), including the Thirty Year's War.

[165] Although there were also a few Hannas in Scotland. The initial cause of spelling variation may be related to inconsistent transcriptions of the spoken name. For example, a clerk in one parish may have written down a phonetically identical family name in a completely different way from a clerk in the neighboring parish. In such a way, a simple clerical act may have inadvertently sealed the spelling of a family name for generations. Alternatively, with the inconsistency of spelling at the time, we also see examples of relatives spelling their own last names differently within the same family. Of course, both practices may have been coexisted, muddying the waters even further when trying to use spelling to isolate specific branches of the family.

# VII: The Family of John Hannay, M.P.

John Hannay, the younger brother of Alexander, moved into Edinburgh, no doubt in search of more lucrative employment than the Galloway countryside afforded a second son. In 1567 he married an Edinburgh girl, Margaret Johnson, in the Canongate, where he settled.

The family tree of John Hannay can be found in Figure 14.

There are several mentions of him as owning land in the Canongate during 1569. He was clearly building up a valuable estate for himself in the city. His second wife was Maug Smyth, the daughter of John Smyth, a merchant burgess of the Canongate.

He, no doubt, frequently visited Wigtown. In 1589 he became Wigtown's member in the Scottish Parliament. In 1590 he represented the Wigtown Presbytery along with Sir Alexander Stewart of Garlies and Mr. James Adamson at the General Assembly of the Kirk in Edinburgh.

He was a bailie burgess of the Canongate, then a Burgh independent of Edinburgh. He died on March 8, 1604, leaving five sons, James (afterwards Dean Hannay), George, Francis, and Thomas, and a natural son John.

Of Francis and Thomas, we know little. John, apart from appearing in the Edinburgh register of Apprentices in 1586, and in the register of sasines in 1618, leaves little mark on history. He appears to have died unmarried on March 28, 1628, and left his brothers, "Mr. James and Mr. George his executors the ministers of Holyroodhouse and Torphin [Torphichen] respectively." James and George, however, both have important histories, recorded below.

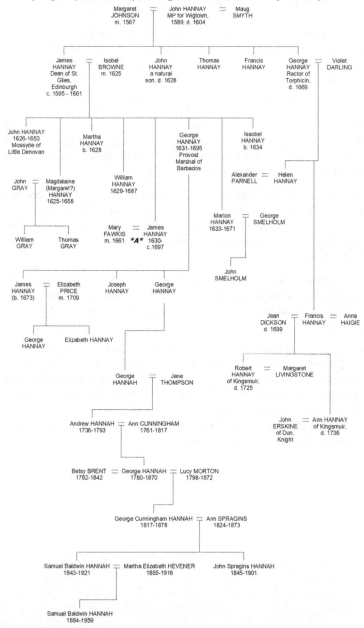

*A*: See Figure 44

**Figure 14: Descendants of John Hannay, MP for Wigtown**

## 1. Dean James Hannay (c. 1595 – c. 1661)

James, the future Dean of Edinburgh, was the eldest son of John Hannay and Margaret Johnson and a minor at the time of his father John's death in 1604. He was brought up by his stepmother Maug Smyth's father, John Smyth, who had been appointed by his father as "tutor to the said bairns."

James graduated Master of Arts in 1615 at Edinburgh University and was appointed Minister to Kilmaur Parish in Ayrshire in 1620. During his term there he must have attracted the favourable notice of King James VI, perhaps through his cousins Robert, 1st Baronet of Mochrum, and Robert's brother Patrick, for on December 5, 1623, King James VI appointed him minister of the Kirk of Holyroodhouse, which did duty as the Chapel Royal and also the parish church for the Canongate.

It is likely that he married Isobel Brown the following year, as their first child Magdalaine was born on November 18, 1625.

Isobel Brown was the daughter of William Brown, "Clerk to ye chekker", who witnessed the births of their children Magdalaine, John and William. Her brothers were "Mr John Broune, ane of ye Regents of College of Edinburgh" who witnessed Marion's birth; and Patrick and Hew Braune who witnessed Issobel's birth in 1634.

There is an interesting letter dated April 2,1635, from King Charles I to Isobel's father the clerk to the Exchequer:

> "Right etc. Having bene informed of the long and faythfull service done unto our dear late father for many yeres togidder by his and our old servand Mr. William Broun, in his charge of presenting the signature and making the Counsell dispatches, we wer pleased in regard thereof, and of the abilities and sufficiencie of Mr. Patrick Broun, his sone, for dischargeing the office, to confer the same upon him; whairof, being will that he enjoy such priviledges as doe properlie belong thereunto, our pleasur is that you suffer none to encroach upon same etc."

In October 1625, in the list of rents for the month, James is shown as being taxed a fairly large sum of money in those days: for a tenement value £50 at 11/6, for another "tenement and lands" value £50, another at 11/6 and for one other at £20 value at 4/7.

In 1627, James acted for his cousin Captain Alexander Hanna, an officer in Jacob Ramsay's regiment serving in Sweden under King Gustavus Adolphus. James was suing a certain Patrick Christie, a burgess of Dysart who was denounced as a rebel for withholding cash entrusted to him by Captain Alexander Hanna (see Chapter VIII: The Hannays of Kirkdale).

There are several entries in the *Book of the Ancient Priviledges of the Canongate* relevant to James, such as this one on October 11, 1629:

> "Letter from the same (the Bailies and Council of the
> Cannongate) to Mr. James Hannay as to the drawing up of the
> signature of their priviledges for which they have delivered all
> their evidents to Mr. James Law. We besiek you therfoir for
> the love of god as ye tend the welfair of our burgh and as ye ar
> ane boirne bairne therof to sett your briest to the busines and
> concurre with our said guid friend Alexander Peiris thereintil
> ye evin to the saitling of our bissiness to the uthermost for we
> understand that my lady dryburgh hes written to my lord of
> Roxburgh quhilk we suspect will caus my lord stay perhapis to
> our prejudice dated 11 October 1629 signed by Adam
> Bothwell, James Aytoun, Bailliees Henry Bellenden, Walter
> Logan, Thomas Glen."

James was a great favourite of Charles I, as will be seen from the Earl of Stirling's Register of Royal letters from 1615-1635. In the register we find that Charles I was constantly pleading on his behalf. In 1628, the King requested that James should be provided with a manse and glebe, and that his church be repaired. On December 8, 1629, King Charles I wrote to the Earl of Mar that two old cannons in the castle might be converted into a bell for use in his parish:

> "Whitehall, Charles R.
>
> Right trusty and well-beloved cousin and councillour. We greet you
> well whereas for the providing of a peale of bells for the Church of
> Holyroodhouse fitt to be hung there against our coming to that
> kingdom we have given directions to Sir Henerie Bruce Master of
> our Artillery to deliver unto Mr. James Hannay, minister of that
> church, these two broken canons in our castle in Edinburgh. Our
> pleasure is that no lett or hindrance be made herin by you but that
> they be forthwith deliver'd to the said Mr. James Hannay for the
> use aforesaid and if need be we are futher willing that you be futher
> secured by act of council. For these presents shall be unto you a
> sufficient warrent: —given at Whitehall the eighth day of
> December 1629."

In 1630, Charles I requested James's stipend be increased. In 1631, he got himself a new manse, the money raised by a tax on the people of the Canongate, each property owner subscribing towards the cost. James himself had to subscribe on account of two properties, one value 300 merks and taxed at £11.5.0 and the other 100 merks and taxed at £3.15.0. The entry in the record reads:

"1 March 1630. Inventar of the stent[166] roll of the land of the burgh
of the cannongait stentit in maner underwritten be the stent maisters
undersubscryvers sworne and admittet to that effect be the baillie
and councile in the cannongait for thair parte of my lord
holierudhous releiff of thrie thowsand merks modifet be the lords
of… and appoyntit to be pay it be him to Mr. James A'Hannay
minister at halierudhous for building of ane mans within the said
burgh for him self and his successoris ministers at holidrudhous."

In 1631 he asked for an assistant minister for his church at
Holyroodhouse. The Records of the Canongate read as follows:

"The whole council of the Canongate being present, Mr. James
Hannay Minister of Holyroodhouse, desired them to appoint an
assistant for him, especially since the King has recommended to his
Commissioners the said Church and that Lord Holyroodhouse was
selling the tiends (tithe) of the whole Abbacy and that was the time
to provide for the maintainance of anothere minister. Dated 4th
February 1631."

The next entry still on the same subject reads:

"Letter by Mr. James Hannay, the Bailiees and Council of
seventeen members to the Archbishop of St Andrews, shewing the
need for a second minister and that, should one actually be settled
among them Lord Holyroodhouse might be urged to contribute for
his support before all the tiends were disponed[167]. They reccomend
to him the bearer, Mr. Mathew Wemyss, for the charge, and beg the
Archibishop to approve and give warrent to some of their 'brethren
of Edinburgh' to come to their church and admit him. Dated 7th
February 1631."

He got his assistant, but the Book of the Records shows that the Bailees
were not going to be out of pocket over the deal if they could help it:

"The minister of Holyroodhouse, Mr. James Hannay and the
Bailees and Concil of the Canongate chose Mr. Mathew Wemyss as
second minister, but conditionally that he should use all diligence
to obtain a stipend from Lord Holyroodhouse and that he should
not seek a stipend from the burgh of the Canongate. In the event of
Hannay's obtaining an increase of his present stipend from the
King or Lord Holyroodhouse or any other way, he would give over
the 300 merks paid to him by the Session in favour of Mr. Mathew.
Dated 7th February 1631."

As minister at Holyroodhouse, James duly repaired the peal of bells
and continued to make constructional repairs to the church. On May
14, 1633, the following warrant was issued:

---

[166] tax assessment, in this case, for parochial use.

[167] granted or conveyed.

79

"Warrent to the treasurer to pay Mr. James Hannay Minister of the church of Holyroodhouse his disbursements for repairing that church with allowences as the charges expended were his own means and the attendance of a minister during the Kings residence would be necessary, signed the King. Theobalds 14th May 1633."

However, by October, as usual, the money had not been paid, and another letter in similar terms was written to the Lord Treasurer, dated October 11.

In 1633, Charles I requested that new bells for his church be brought from London. In 1634, James was appointed a member of the High Commissioners Court. In January 1636, there is a letter from Archbishop Laud to John Stewart, 1st Earl of Traquair, which "thanks his lordship for favours shewn to Mr. James Hannay Dean of Edinburgh in paying principle and interest of the moneys laid out on Holyrood Chapel."

James remained minister until 1635, when he was elected Minister of the High Kirk of St. Giles, Edinburgh. He has a prominent place in Scottish history. Like his kinsmen Sir Robert Hannay, 1st Baronet of Mochrum, Sir Patrick Hannay, and the Kirkdale family, he was a Royalist and an ardent supporter of Charles I.

In 1633 the long-awaited Scottish Coronation of Charles I was drawing close. In the Register of Royal letters there are many communications between Whitehall and the Scottish Capital—the place, the music, the preparations, the robes, medals for issue, the book and offices of the coronation were all thoroughly discussed.

King Charles I, accompanied by William Laud, Bishop of London (soon to be Archbishop), the Bishop of Ely, and a great number of nobles arrived on June 15 at Holyrood with much pomp and ceremony, to be greatly acclaimed by the Scottish people. The next day brought Sunday morning service in the Abbey. Bishop Bellenden preached the sermon and the Rev. James Hannay assisted.

The Coronation was fixed for Tuesday and The Reverend Charles Rogers (1825-1890) in his 1882 *History of the Chapel Royal of Scotland* gives us the following excellent description of the proceedings:

"On Monday evening Charles proceeded to the Castle, where he remained for the night. Next morning at eight o'clock he, in the great hall of the Castle, seated on a chair of slate received a congratulatory address from the nobility and barons, presented by the Lord Chancellor. A procession was formed, in which, proceeded by trumpeters, the nobility, clergy and officers of state took their places each according to their degree. Next came the

King, attired gorgeously in crimson velvet, his train borne by four noblemen.

Dismounting at Holyroodhouse, he walked to the Abbey Church, having borne over him a canopy of crimson velvet fringed with gold. The Archbishop of Glasgow [James Law, whose elder son, James, Keeper of H.M. Signet had been witness to the birth of Rev. James's son, James Hannay, on December 26, 1630] rode with the procession, but the Archbishop of St. Andrews [John Spottiswood] waited at the western door of the Church to receive His Majesty.

The king, as he entered the building, knelt upon the floor. When he rose up, Bishop Bellenden, as dean, conducted him to a seat, and then presented to him Mr. James Hannay, Minister of the Abbey Church.

Preceded by the choristers, discoursing appropriate music, His Majesty now moved forward to the dais, while the crown, sceptre, sword, and anointing oil were placed near the communion table."

When the King sat down James gave a short address. Afterwards, Rogers continues,

"Dr. David Lindsay, Bishop of Brechin, preached from the passage in the first Book of Kings relating to the anointing of Solomon as the King of Israel. At the close of the discourse the King re-ascended the dais, where the Primate presented him to the people."

To mark the occasion, silver coronation medals were executed at the Edinburgh Mint by the famous French engraver, Nicholas Briot, and a specimen is in the possession of the family of Hannah of Leith.

When Charles I returned to England, Archbishop Laud remained in Scotland for a short time and visited Stirling where, along with James, he was made a burgess and guild brother:

"8th July 1633. The saidis provest, baillies, and counsell, frelie ressavit and admitted the persones following, to the libertie and fredome of burgessis and gild brother of the said burgh, quha maid faithe as use is: -

The reverend father in God, William (Laud) Bishop of London. The reverend father in God, William, Lord Bishop Electe of Holyrood. Johnne (Maxwell) Bishop of Ross. Maister James Aynslie, chaplain to the Lord Bishop of Ross. Maister James Hanny, preicher at Holyrudhous. James Kirk, his servitour." (Burgh Records of Stirling)

John Maxwell, the new Bishop of Ross, was confidential adviser to Laud and a personal friend of James. He witnessed the birth of two of James's children: John on December 17, 1626; and Martha on January 29, 1628; at that time Ross was minister of St. Giles.

This was neither James's first nor last connection with Stirling, as in his youth he had applied unsuccessfully for the Mastership of the High School of Stirling; and during his later persecution he and his son John are believed to have fled to Denoven close by.

The same year James and his younger brother, George, the Rector of Torphichen, were appointed to the "Supreme Commission in Scotland for the punishment of Scandelous and Abnoxious Persons and the remaining Jesuits and Seminary Priests still in Scotland."

James was still maintaining his connections with Galloway as we learn from the Register of the Privy Seal August 6, 1633 that he was taxed £52:18:4[168] for lands and the Mill at Poltown, Whithorn. One would hope that he had no difficulty in meeting the payments as only three months previously, King Charles I was writing to the Treasurer that "we will that such speedie payment be made to him." This, however, did not bring the desired result, as Charles wrote a letter in similar vein on October 11.

There is no doubt that Dean James was a great favourite of the King. On October 19, 1634, we have Charles I writing the Bishop of Edinburgh that Dean James should reside at Holyroodhouse, "Being willing that our trustie and weil beloved Mr. James Hannay, Deane of Edinburgh, reside at Holyrudhous till he hath performed some service there to us etc." The Dean's house was at the rear of the palace and is marked on an old map in possession of the family of Alexander Hannah of Hook Heath.

At the same time, he wrote to the Edinburgh Town Council, that as far as stipends were concerned, they should have a "speciall care of the Principall Minister of St Geillis."

James seemed to always need to meet the cost of the King's projects out of his own pocket; in a letter on October 20, 1634, the King requested the Treasurer to reimburse the Dean for the outlays of maintaining the organ at Holyrood; further on we learn that James was still waiting settlement of his account for repairing the Chapel Royal.

James was a keen advocate of the King's policy for Anglification of the Scottish Church, and in 1636 he accompanied his friend, John Maxwell, Bishop of Ross, to the Court in London to discuss with the King and Archbishop Laud the new Services Book. His support of the Episcopal regime is shown by the fact that he went specially to Durham, "to take a draught of the choir of the cathedral in that city, in order to fit up and beautify the inside of the choir of St. Giles Church

---

[168] Roughly £600 in 2019.

in the same manner." This, of course, would make him most unpopular with the Presbyterian faction in his congregation.

On May 13, 1637, James received from the King a grant of lands near Kelso. James's future seemed assured; Dean of Edinburgh and high in the King's favour. Then fate took a hand in the destinies of James and his Sovereign; but before we write of the Jenny Geddes affair let us consider the effect of Charles's policy of Episcopacy on Scotland.

King James VI/I, his father, had fully understood the feelings of his native Scotland and had ensured that Episcopacy was consistent with Calvinist doctrine, ritual and the democratic government of the Scots Kirk. The King also knew Laud and shrewdly declared to him that he "knew not the stomach of that people, if he hoped to make that stubborn Kirk stoop more to the English platform." Unfortunately, Charles I was quite ignorant of the Scots temperament and with Laud as his adviser he decided that the Scots Kirk would adopt a Prayer Book based on that of the English Church in place of Knox's Book of Common Order. Charles had had little firsthand knowledge of the Scots. Brought up in England, he did not realise the difference between the English Peasantry and the Scots Commons: The English peasant was unarmed, while all Scots carried weapons. Also, he failed to appreciate the difference in the Scots and English social structures. Duncan Harald MacNeill in his 1947 history *The Scottish Realm* states that the social divisions of the Scots nation were vertical as between groups or clans, instead of horizontal, as in England, between castes.

British historian Professor G.M. Trevelyan states in his 1922 volume *England Under the Stuarts*:

> "England knew neither democracy nor feudalism; Scotland
> presented a formidable interfusion of both these fighting spirits.
> The English peasant took his religion from his betters and knew
> neither learning nor politics; Scottish peasant, nominally less free,
> actually worse fed and housed, had yet acquired an active spirit of
> equality in thought, religion, and even social practice."

Such was the essential difference in the two peoples: King James knew his Scots because he was one; his son King Charles, in many ways a much more honest man, lacked his father's shrewdness. Thus, Charles decided to impose the new Service Book on the Scots Kirk.

Archbishop Laud had long been trying to bring the Scottish Church into line with that south of the border. This policy finally led to his downfall, and also unfortunately Dean James's. Laud had been working on the Bishop of Edinburgh, and on March 5, 1634, that Bishop wrote to the Presbytery of Edinburgh:

"Requiring them to give the Sacrament at the next Easter Day (i.e. 6 April), and to 'take it upon your knees, giving a good example to the people, and lykewyse that ye minister the elements out of your awin hands to everie on of your flock.'

He asked for a written consent to this within fourteen days. He also desired no one to be admitted to the Sacrament except those of "those of your awin parochin' for want of which there has been great profanation of that holy mysterie."

He also required "you to preach of Jesus Christ his passion, for our redemption, upon Fryday before Pasch according to the canon of our church."

A reply signed by Dean James and others and sent to Bishop William states:

"The within written letter [that above] being produced from the Right Reverend Father in God William Bishop of Edinburgh, we the bretheren of the Presbetary those of the underscribe and obliges and promises to obey the whole contents of the letter by their presents subscribed with our hands, day year and place above written.

Thos Sydserf, Andro Ramsay, Alex Thompson, Harie Rofloch, David Mitchell, James Farlie, Wm Wishart, James Hanna, Wm Myretoun, John Adamson. Two members Wm Arthur of St Cuthberts and James Thompson of Colinton refuse to sign."

Shortly after, on May 13, came James's reward—he was appointed Dean of Edinburgh by King Charles I, in succession to Thomas Sydserff, who had been made Bishop of Brechin. The King's letter to the Town of Edinburgh reads:

"Trustee etc - Whereas upon yere good consideration of the habilities and sufficiencie of our trusty and wellbeloved Mr. James Hanny, Minister at Holyrudhous, we have recommended to be Deane of that our citie of Edinburgh, wherein our zeall and princelie care being for the service of God and for provydeing of your with qualifeid ministeris, we have heirby thought fitt to recommend to you in spetiall manner that your present to him to the reverend father in God the Bishop of Edinburgh, to be elected to the place of principall Minister of St. Geillie, waiking by the removing and promotion of Mr. Thomas Sydserff to the bishoprik of Brechin which we shall tak as acceptable service done unto us.

Grenvitch"

About this time also, the Bishop of Rosse, John Maxwell, came from the Court in London and with him Dean James. With them was the draft of the new "Booke of Common Prayer for the use of the Church of Scotland" which as Woodrow puts it:

"was to be enjoyned to all ministers and readers by virtue of the vast perogative Royall. The bussie bishop presented to the Kings council that they might approve the same whilk was done by proclamation."

In July 1637, Archbishop Laud ordered it to be read in all Scots Kirks.It was arranged that it would receive its first reading in the High Kirk of St. Giles in Edinburgh and the reader was James Hannay, Dean of Edinburgh.

July 23, 1637 was a memorable day in the annals of St. Giles. An eagerly expectant crowd assembled early, and on the opening of the doors at once occupied the Mid Kirk or what had formerly been the Great Kirk. After the congregation had settled, Mr. Henderson, the reader of the church, read the usual prayers from the Old Scottish Book of Common Order, and when he was done, added a few words, in which he said goodbye to those present with tears in his eyes, "Adieu, good people, for I think this is the last tyme of my reading prayers in this place."

Just as James Hannay was a staunch Episcopalian, Henderson was a staunch Presbyterian. About ten o'clock David Lindsay, Bishop of Edinburgh and James entered the church, the latter taking his seat in the reader's desk (now preserved in the Antiquarian Museum in Queen Street, Edinburgh) and Bishop Lindsay proceeding to the pulpit above him. Standing at the reading desk, Dean James began to read from the new service book. The scene which followed has had many narrators. They differ in small detail but are at one as to the tumult which ensured. As Dean James went on reading, on every side arose murmurs of discontent. The women in the congregation were loudest in their protests. They are often referred to as maidservants, and it has been supposed that they had been sent to keep places for their mistresses at the sermon which followed the prayers.

Scottish historian Robert Wodrow (1679-1734) says that they were apprentice lads dressed up in women's clothes. The Bishop from the pulpit asked the audience to be calm and allow the service to proceed, and turning to Dean James told him to go on to the Collect for the day. At this the famous Jenny Geddes, a herbwoman or kail-wife who kept a stall near where the Tron Kirk now stands, jumped up and shouted, "Deil colic the wane of thee, out, thou false theif! - dost thou say Mass at my lug?" or "Devil cause you colic in your stomach, false thief: dare you say the Mass in my ear?" Then she picked up her stool and threw it at Dean James, intending to have given him a ticket of remembrance. Confusion reigned, others followed Jenny's example, and after a vain attempt to restore order the magistrates were called in and the mob cleared from the church. This was the first and last time that the Service Book was read.

**Figure 15: The uproar at St. Giles**

What happened is best told in John Spalding's (fl. 1650) book *Memorials of the Troubles in Scotland and In England V2: A.D. 1624-1645*:

> "Upon Sunday the … July, doctor Hannay began to reid the buke of Common Prayer in Sanct Geilles Churche of Edinburgh, the nobillis being foriseen of this novaltie, nevei hard before sen the reformation in Edinburgh devyses a number of rascall servin women to threw stoolis at the reidger and perturb the Kirk quhile they did vehementtlie. The marestatis being in churche (no doubt upon the councill of this disorder) commandit the officers to hurl thir rasccallis to the kirk dur and bk them out. But then they became moir furious ano made (as they were directet) crying and shouting saying popery was now broucht in amongis them dang at the doors with stanes and break down the glass wyndois with sic noyss that there was no more reading."

Dr. J. Cameron Lees (1835-1913) in his book *St. Giles, Edinburgh* states, "Seldom has there been a popular tumult that led to greater results than this one within St. Giles. It not only suppressed the English Liturgy almost until the 19th Century, but it gave an impulse to the Civil War of England, which ended in the overthrow of the Church and Monarchy."

There is a most descriptive woodcut (see Figure 15) of the Jenny Geddes incident in Nathaniel Crouch's 1681 *The Wars in England, Scotland and Ireland*. John Leslie, 6th Earl of Rothes, a prominent Covenanter, gives an eyewitness account in his *A Relation of Proceedings Concerning the Affairs of the Kirk of Scotland from August 1637 to July 1638*.

Jenny's stool (See Figure 16) is now in the National Museum of Scotland, Edinburgh.

**Figure 16: 18<sup>th</sup> C. engraving of the famous stool**

Popular opinion was against the King and Episcopacy, but Dean James was nothing if not steadfast in his beliefs. The National Covenant was signed in the Churchyard of Greyfriars on February 28, 1638, many subscribing with their pens dipped in their own blood. Dean James was also a man of courage, for, in the face of such violent opposition to the Episcopacy and the King, a week after the signing on March 8, he rebuked his congregation for subscribing and was attacked in his church. Scottish clergyman and historian Robert Baillie (1602-1662) in his *Letters and Journals*, wrote:

> "Mr. Hannay has been in hott water with his people since his entrye, so the Sunday after his people had subscribed against his command, they sett on him in the church, ryves his goune, gives him dry cuffes, and so without further harme dismisses him."

Needless to say such a spirited defence of the Service Book finished Dean James with the Covenanting Party. A committee sitting in Edinburgh composed of Covenanters, who had now taken over the Kirk affairs of Scotland, removed Dean James, Dr. Elliot, Mr. Alec Thomsone, and Mr. David Mitchell from their offices as ministers in the capital for not subscribing to the Solemn League and Covenant: "This was the first act of the committee of the General Assembly ordainit in Edinburgh for Kirk affairs as is formerlie said." James was deposed by the General Assembly which met at Glasgow on January 1,1639.

As a result of this riot in St. Giles, the King ordered all strangers to leave Edinburgh within twenty four hours, and he transferred the government to Linlithgow where no doubt Dean James took refuge. Linlithgow would suit James as his friends the Spottiswoodes, Primrose and Livingstones all held land round Linlithgow, Falkirk and Stirling. This was the natural retreat for the Dean—in addition, he was a Burgess of Stirling. The tradition handed down by the Stirlingshire Hannahs has always been that he and his family fled to the Falkirk Denny area to avoid the persecution of the Covenanters.

The star of the Covenant was on the ascent and that of the King waning. Civil war was close at hand. Dean James went down with his King and little is known about his life after 1639. But it is tolerably certain that his allegiance never wavered from his monarch. Even after the execution of King Charles I in 1649, one of Dean James' sons is found on the Royalist side at Worcester. James died in impoverished circumstances sometime before June 21, 1661, when his children (then quite adult) had £100 a year allowed by the restored Royalist government out of vacant stipends, on account of their father's sufferings. Also, the City of Edinburgh was ordered to pay his stipend up to the date of his dismissal by the General Assembly and had to borrow money to do it.

Many years of strife and discord followed the outbreak of the Civil War; families were split. Two Hannays at least are known to have been Covenanters:

- Patrick Hannay, son of Hew Hannay of Grennan, who became a Colonel of Horse in the Civil War in the Scottish army under David Leslie, 1st Lord Newark (1600-1682) and was also M.P. for Wigtown.

- Hew Hannay, a baker in the Canongate.

Dean James Hannay's wife Isobel Brown died in July 1674, many years after her husband, and was buried in the Abbey Church of Holyrood.

Dean James Hannay and Isobel Brown had eight children, and their births are recorded in the old parochial records of the Canongate. They were Magdalaine, John, Martha, William, James, George, Marion and Issobel, and they are described in detail at the end of this chapter.

## 2. George Hannay, Rector of Torphichen (d. 1669)

George, brother to Dean James, was also a clergyman, being admitted in late 1627 and appointed to Torphichen parish. He became a J.P. for Linlithgow, and married at Holyroodhouse, Violet Darling on January 28, 1630. Presumably his brother Dean James conducted the ceremony. Whilst at Torphichen he was appointed to the Supreme Commission

88

for the Punishment of Jesuits, etc., together with his brother. He had also the distinction, whilst in charge of that Parish, of being beaten by his parishioners for standing out for Archbishop Laud's ecclesiastical Settlement. As a result, in May 1637, he was suspended. His troubles then began. By 1640 he had successfully petitioned the Assembly to restore him to the Ministry, and he was transferred to Alves in Morayshire.

At the visitation of 1642, he was found to be satisfactory. The Presbytery records give the following account:

"Mr. Geo Hannay their minister being removed the gentlemen and elders of the paroche did witness and testine that he gave full content in all things and on both lyf and doctrine he was unblamable. The so Mr. George Hannay regraited that in the remotest parts of the parish to wit Killosand Findhorne did not keep the kirk wherefore he was advised be the bretheren to process them before the Presbetary. The roof and Thack [thatch] of the Queir [choir] being found ruinous therefor the session was appointed to see to the repairing of it and to speak to the Eail of Murray and rest of the tiend menters for their concurrance. Archibald Forsyth raider and schoolmaster was approved."

Two years later the "cuir is still found ruinous" and it is again decided to repair it.

At the end of 1644, George seems to have got himself into really serious trouble. Sir Ludovick Gordon wished to marry the daughter of Lady Grant, and forced George, at pistol point, to carry out the ceremony. The presbytery was not so sure of George's story and charged him and Sir Ludovick before the General Assembly in 1645.

George originally complained to the Presbytery in November 1644, perhaps with intention of covering himself in the event of further trouble. His complaint and subsequent statement to the Presbytery of Alves gives some information about the affair:

"Mr George Hannay complained of 'violence and injuries' done to him by Lord Ludovick Gordon who 'in the midst of the night sent for him in the name of Lady Grant elder pretending that the common enemy was approaching. He coming on his journey from his own house was surprised by the said Ludovick and charged him under pain of his life or he would pistol him, yea draw him in a horse taile if he went not with goodwill, and after the said Mr George had escaped, he violently shot pistols at him, and brought him back, and caused him to marry the said Ludovick with the Lady Grant her daughter the same night."

And again, in the depositions before the Assembly:

"17th May 1647 Deposition of Mr. George Hannay, sometyme minister at Alves (Alvie, Presbetary of Abernathy), before Mr. Walter Grey concerning the references for the Provinciall of Murray touching Mr. George Hannay , the said Mr. George being personally present and at length heard in the matter and the particulars in the said references considered whereupon the said Mr. George was suspended being seriously considered, the Commission of Assembly finding the said Mr. George  by his own confession guilty of subscribing of that perfidious and rebell bond and that sometym he drunk the said sometym Marquess of Huntly's[169] health and of other particular messages contained in the reference of the said Provinciall do judge him worthy of deprivation. And now therefore depose him from the said ministry and all exercise thereof, declaring the Kirk at Alves now to be vacking and appoynts Mr. Alexander Symer minister of Dumfries to intimat this sentence upon the Sabbath come 15 days according to the accustomed order.

"The Commission of Assembly considering the hard condition of the wyf and children of Mr. George Hannay  now deposed from his ministry do therefore recommend to the Presbetary and Patron and all others interested that for their maintainance and entertainment the stipend of the Kirk at Alves as long as the same shall be vacate shall be given to him.

"The Commission of Assembly reccomends the Presbetary of Elgin to see Mr. George Hannay  complaitly satisfied of the charges he has bestowed on the repartion of the Manse in respect of his necessitious condition."

Poor George, he was now without any form of employment and little prospect of getting any. During 1648 he was called to the Kirk to make public repentance of his actions, which he did first at Alves and after at the Presbytery church at Elgin. He did however manage to remain in the manse until July 1649, despite repeated attempts to evict him by the Kirk Session.

He petitioned the General Assembly for reinstatement in 1650 but the Assembly would "not medall with the samen (same) they not having seen the testimonial of his Presbetary." In June he asked for a testimonial from the Presbytery and they "being much affected with his most humble expression and his verie submissive suplication" granted him one.

He seems to have had little luck, for by 1652 his funds were very short and he petitioned the Presbytery of Strathbogie as follows:

---

[169] During the English Civil War, the Marquess of Huntly was a supporter of King Charles I.

"The said day Mr. George Hannay sometime minister of Alves presented a supplication earnestly desiring the presbetary would tak to heart his poor and distressed condition for the tyme and give some supply out of the vacent stipend of Batriffay. The Presbetary being assured of his necessity by a letter from the Presbetary of Elgin in quhilch he lives for the present disposed to him and for the supply of his poor family the just half of the stipend of the foresaid place anno 1652 and give the whole power to uplift the samen."

In May 1656 his case again came before the Presbytery of Elgin and the following year he was admitted to the rectorship of Inveraven. His star began to rise again, for after the 1660 Restoration he was allotted on June 21, 1661, £100 by Parliament for "his sufferings." He was finally transferred on July 4, 1664, to Auldern and became Dean of Moray and Chancellor of the Diocese. He died on July 7, 1669, leaving a widow who is still shown as claiming a stipend in 1673. His children's names are not all known. He had a daughter Helen, who was married to Alexander Parnell, a merchant in Elgin. He almost certainly had a son Francis.

## 3.  Francis Hannay (d. c. 1705), son of George

Francis Hannay, the son of the Reverend George Hannay, graduated at Edinburgh University in 1647, and according to the Dumfries Commissary records was a student there, probably of the law, in 1655. In 1661 he became the schoolmaster at Aberdour and in 1680 was appointed Precentor of the College Kirk of Edinburgh, which must have been a fairly lucrative post. Francis married Jean Dickson who predeceased him on March 9, 1699. In 1702, he appears to have married again, by this time he must have been a very old man, a certain Anna Haigie, the daughter of James Haigie former minister of St. Andrews, Deerness, Orkney. Francis was living at the time in North Parish, Edinburgh. Francis died c. 1705.

All this makes him a very likely candidate the father of Robert (and Ann) of Kingsmuir (See Chapter IX: The Hannays of Kingsmuir). If Robert was an advocate, as tradition avers, then his father's early experience in the law, and his subsequent employment as a "writing Master" (i.e. teacher of the Law) in Edinburgh at the University, would all point to this being the case.

## 4.  Francis Hannay and The Kingsmuir Connection

The origins of the present Kingsmuir family (described in more detail in Chapter IX: The Hannays of Kingsmuir) are obscure. According to

Mr. James Hannay of Barcelona (d. 1873)[170] and George Francis Hannay of Kingsmuir (circa 1780-1867), the Reverend George Hannay's son Francis was the father of Robert and Ann Hannay of Kingsmuir. Thus, Dean James Hannay, the Dean of St. Giles, would have been Robert and Ann's great uncle. Dean James's ring is in the possession of the present Kingsmuir family, and it might therefore have come from Dean James's son, also called James, through a cousin, to its current owners.

George Francis Hannay's father (George Hannay of Kingsmuir, great-great-grandson of Dean James) lost all the family papers during the American War of Independence. So, it is reasonable that the oral tradition passed on to his son might well have been substantiated if those documents were still in existence. This explanation seems the correct one, particularly as the names Francis and George (rarely found outside of this branch), continue to appear in the Kingsmuir line from early times when the parentage of Robert and Ann would be well known. The Morpeth Hannays in England, from which the present Kingsmuir family descend, must have been also been either of the family of the Reverend George or Dean James, and thus cousins of Robert and Ann of Kingsmuir.

After the death of Ann Hannay in 1736, the succession to Kingsmuir would appear to have been granted to the second, third and fourth substitutes by the descent from Sorbie, of whom Robert of Kingsmuir was considered chief, certainly by the herald Alexander Nisbet who was living at the time (1710). The first beneficiary, Captain William Hannay, was not in the direct succession, but was a scion of the Kirkdale family, and succeeded as a personal friend of Lady Ann. (For more on their friendship, see Chapter X: William and Ann Hannay of Kingsmuir). The second and third substitutes were probably the sons of Dean James or his brother Rev George. Their cousin – i.e., Alexander Hannay (d. 1612)'s grandson – Sir Robert Hannay, 2nd Baronet of Mochrum, was considered Chief, for in one of the letters from Ann to Captain William is the remark: "Your chief Sir Robert Hannay was just so treat."

Thus, with Sir Robert's death in Dublin without sons, some (including Stewart Francis) believed the succession of the baronetcy and chieftainship passed to the present Kingsmuir family. The Lord Lyon (The Scottish government official responsible for issues of Heraldry),

---

[170] James Hannay (1827-1873) was an author and diplomat who eventually became the British consul to Barcelona. He is discussed in further detail in Chapter XIII: The Hannays of Knock and Gararrie.

however, has identified the Kirkdale branch as the Chief line of the Name and Arms of Hannay.

## 5. The Children of Dean James Hannay

Dean James married Isobel Brown, who is buried in the Kirk at Holyroodhouse; she died in July 1674. They had several children: Magdalaine, John, Martha, William, James, George, Marion and Issobel.

Information about Dean James Hannay's children is listed below, except for son John, who is described, along with his descendants, in Chapter XXII: Stirlingshire Hannas).

### 5.1. Magdalaine Hannay (b. 1625), daughter of James

Magdalaine was born on November 18, 1625. The witnesses to her birth were her grandfather William Brown, Clerk to the Exchequer and James Primrose, Clerk to the Privy Council of Scotland—both very influential men of their times. James Primrose was the progenitor of the Earls of Rosebery, and there are many entries concerning him in the Register of Royal Letters 1615-1635. His second wife was Catherine Lawson, daughter of Richard Lawson, burgess of Edinburgh.

In 1641 James Primrose was succeeded by his son, Sir Archibald Primrose, who like the Hannays was an enthusiastic Royalist. After the Battle of Kilsyth in August 1645, he joined the Marquis of Montrose and was captured at Philiphaugh in September. In 1646 he was tried by Parliament at St. Andrews, the same which condemned Sir Robert Spottiswoode, Archbishop of St. Andrews and Chancellor of Scotland. Both the Spottiswoodes and the Primroses held lands in Dunipace between Falkirk and Stirling, and it was no doubt as a result that Dean James Hannay and some of his family after their persecution sought refuge in the pro-Royalist area of Linlithgow, Falkirk and Stirling.

Dean James Hannay was of course a Burgess of Stirling. It is interesting to note that Robert Hannay who was first Laird of Kingsmuir married Margaret Livingstone of Baldamy[171] and the Livingstones were Earls of Callendar near Falkirk, while another branch held Dunipace before the Spottiswoodes.

Little is known for certain of Magdalaine, but she might possibly be the same as the Margaret Hannay whose Testament is recorded in the

---

[171] This is a typographical error; no location named "Baldamy" has been found. It may refer to Balhary (14 miles west of Kingsmuir) or Balbinny (6 miles northeast of Kingsmuir).

Commissariat of Stirling on December 6, 1661. She died in January 1658. Her husband was John Gray, indweller in Stirling, and their children are given as William and Thomas Gray. It is interesting to note that the name Gray appears on the following Hannay Testaments, and we wonder if it is just coincidence or is it indirect proof of a connection between the father of Dean James, Margaret Hannay and Robert Hannay of Kingsmuir:

(i)     Testament of John Hannay, Baillie Burgess of Canongate, died January 11, 1604. Debtors include Mr. Gray, Edinburgh, XIII Pounds.

(ii)    Testament of Margaret Hannay died January 1568. Wife of John Gray, sons William and Thomas.

(iii)   Testament of Robert Hannay of Kingsmuir died March 27, 1725. Commissariat of Edinburgh Record of Testaments Vol 90. Debtors include William Gray tenant, Lands of Dechmont. This is contained in a decreetal obtained before the Sheriff of Linlithgow at instance of mistress Margaret Livingstone formerly relict of the deceased Colonel William Borthwick of Dechmont, thereafter spouse of the said umquhile Robert Hanna.

Could the above-mentioned William Gray be Margaret Hannay's son?

## 5.2.  Martha Hannay (b. 1628), daughter of James

Dean James' daughter Martha was born January 29, 1628. The witnesses were Mr. John Maxwell, Bishop of Ross and Ludovick Keir.

## 5.3.  William Hannay (1629-1687), son of James

Dean James' son William was born on June 26, 1629. The witnesses cannot be read in view of age of record and all that is legible is William, and possibly his grandfather William Brown. No more is known of William although there are two marriages recorded in Edinburgh Parish Registers:

- William Hanna, Glover, and Alison Gray proclaimed November 16, 1677. Here again is a connection with the Gray family. This William died August 29, 1687, when he was described as a skinner, and was buried in Greyfriars East End Kirk, Edinburgh.

- Another William Hannay, weaver, and Janet Job were married April 26, 1649 in Edinburgh.

94

## 5.4. James Hannay (b. 1630), son of James

James, was born on the Sabbath, December 26, 1630, and was baptised in the Church of Holyroodhouse by Mr. John Maxwell, Minister of Edinburgh, (future Bishop of Ross). The record reads: "to Mr. James Hannay, Minister of Holyroodhouse and Issobell Broun a son named James." There were six witnesses, all with the Christian name of James, and they are a very distinguished company:

(a)  James Graham, son of the Earl of Menteith,

(b)  James Murray, Master of His Majesty's Works,

(c)  James Primrose, Clerk of Privy Council,

(d)  James Kinninmonth, The Chamberlain of Fife,

(e)  James Law, Keeper of His Majesty's Signet, also one of the King's Heralds,

(f)  James Campbell, Writer to His Majesty's Signet.

Dean James's son James appears in the Master Roll of Lieutenant General Drummond Troop when it was disbanded at Stirling on September 18, 1667.

He was in the Cornet Squadron along with Thomas Dawling (or Darling), no doubt a relative of Violet Darling who married James's uncle, the Reverend George Hannay, Dean of Moray. This Troop of Horse was raised in 1666, they were composed mostly of old officers, few under the rank of Captain of Horse. Drummonds Troop fought at Rullion Green against the Covenanters, where they formed part of the night wing.

We next hear of James as a Gentleman of Kings Life Guard of Horse. At a muster at Linlithgow on June 5, 1678, he is a member of the Captains Squadron, the commander being the Marquess of Atholl. In the Muster Roll which is preserved in Register House Edinburgh, he is mentioned as "James Hannay, sane to Mr. James Hannay, Dean of Edinburgh, has been long in the troop".

Military historian Andrew Ross, in his 1908 book, *A Military History of Perthshire, 1660-1902*, tells us that the rank and file consisted entirely of the sons of noblemen and gentlemen; they were denominated "the private gentlemen of the Kings Life Guard" and they received pay at the rate of two shillings and sixpence sterling per diem. Considering the value of money in the time of Charles II, the pay was high.

James may have been the first Morpeth Hannay, whose family tree can be found in Figure 45, and who is discussed in further detail later in chapter IX: The Hannays of Kingsmuir.

We do not know with certainty when died, but there is a record of a James Hanna, Castle Soldier, being buried in Greyfriars Enterkin Tomb on May 30, 1697.

## 5.5.  Marion Hannay (1633-1671), daughter of James

Marion was born April 10, 1633, and married on March 10, 1663, to George Smelholm, a merchant of Edinburgh and described a "Servitor to the Earl of Tweedale." Witnesses to her baptism were: James Law, Keeper of His Majesty's Signet; John Whyte; and John Broun, an uncle.

They had a numerous family, most of whom died young with the exception of John, who became a doctor in Edinburgh. Marion died in December 1671. She was buried in Greyfriars.

## 5.6.  Issobel Hannay (b. 1634), daughter of James

Issobel was born July 3, 1634. Witnesses to her baptism were: James Primrose, Clerk to the Privy Council; Patrick Broun, an uncle; and Hew Broun, an uncle.

## 5.7.  George Hannay (1631-1695), son of James

Dean James' son George Hannay was born December 12, 1631. The witness was Dean James's younger brother George Hannay, Minister at Torphichen.  George fought, possibly along with his brother James, with King Charles II in the ill-fated Worcester campaign of 1650 and was taken prisoner by the Commonwealth forces after the battle. He did not receive the death sentence which might reasonably have been expected, but instead was transported as a slave to Barbados. However at the Restoration his fortunes improved and by 1672 he was "Deputy Provost Marshal (head of military police) of the Barbados to a certain Edwyn Steed."

In 1673 he is ordered to "search the ships and places in St. Michaels town and seize and deliver the provisions necessary to the Master of the Garland as she is at present retarded for want provisions."

In 1682 Colonel Edwyn Steed recommended that his appointment of Provost Marshal be transferred to Hannay, whom he described as follows:

> "The Marshal is much troubled by his fortune. I can call it by no
> other name for he is an honest man, who was sold out here as a
> slave for helping the King at Worcester and is resolved to make a
> vigorous protest of his position to England though it was a great

risk for one who lived so long in a hot climate to expose himself to the extremity of the winter and the expense of the voyage must needs be great."

The trouble was that Colonel Steed "was so much affected with the Gout that he cannot perform his duties without the help of his deputy that he prays that he may surrender the patent and that it be granted to George Hannay."

In 1683 George left for England on leave, and on October 31 the Crown Law officers were ordered to prepare a bill constituting him Provost Marshal of the Barbados.

During his absence there was some trouble over the case of Samuel Hanson whom George had arrested in 1682. And as the common jail had been destroyed by the hurricane of 1675, he was forced to confine him in George's house. This form of custody seems to have been pretty lax for persons of quality. But George seems to have been stricter than most, for when Hanson escaped on November 27, 1682, after giving his parole "the Lords find no blame in Hannay for Hansons escape for Mr. Hannay had refused to let him go and drink with his friends in town whilst in custody."

Samuel Hanson and an accomplice, Richard Piers, tried to sue George for wrongful imprisonment in 1684, but the King in Council ordered the Attorney General, Sir Robert Sanger, to defend him from "Urgent and vexatious suits" brought against him by these two.

In Hanson's statement he also appears to have tried to set the Governor Sir Richard Dutton against George for he complains: "That Dutton had ousted George Hannay out of the Clerkship of Bridgetown and put in Rawlins, one of the musicians he brought from England, in his place," and continues that "no man who can leave the Island will stay while Sir Richard Dutton remains Governor."

Dutton's answer was that "he knew nothing of Hannay and the appointment took place a month after Dutton's arrival, in any case Rawlins was not a 'common fiddler' but had been educated in the Law at the Temple."

In spite of these tribulations, George maintained his position except for a short period, for in 1689 Sir George Eyles and Colonel Kendall petitioned for his continuance in the appointment and on June 11, 1690, the Council agreed to restore him to his appointment.

A curious insight into the West Indies in general, and the position of the aristocracy before the law is shown in a memorandum from George on June 28, 1690, in the case of Sir Thomas Montgomerie:

"Sir Thomas Montgomerie was committed by order of 28th Feb 1690 and delivered to my custody on March 1st having been caught trying to escape in a boat to the French. I gave him three rooms in my house for respect to his dignity and all good usage but such was his strange lewd behaviour that I could not enjoy quiet in my own house and was obliged to keep a guard over him at my own expense, while his behaviour was so bad that the court passed several orders to prohibit him from receiving visitors, news ink or paper. On Governor Kendall's account he had great hopes of release but has remained to my house until his departure when he refuses to pay my fees whereupon I distrained on his property. On my return he attacked me with a sword. I am ready to release him on payment of my just fees."

In 1691 he went on leave to England again, and returned the next year. He was now a fairly old man, for in 1694 Lord Willoughby wrote to Sir John Trenchard begging the office of Provost Marshal for Captain Finney as Mr. George Hannay "the present holder is very infirm and aged." He however seems to have held his post till his death in 1695, when on December 31 a warrant was issued to his son, James Hannay, as Provost Marshal of Barbados.

James took on where his father left off and was at once sued by one Ralph Lane regarding his imprisonment. His petition makes interesting reading:

"Petition to the Council of Trade and Plantations—I omitted to tell you in my last address that after the death of George Hannay I was released from jail and since December 1695 have been living in my own house though under restraint that I am liable upon any humour to be confined again in the common jail. This is such an awe to me that I have not ventured to seek for proofs of the wrongs I have sustained.

"I sent a petition to Governor Russell for copies of papers I required, but no answer was returned and I was told that if I made another attempt to attend you James Hannay will confine me with severity in the loathsome common jail. I am obliged therefore to remove my grievances to royall determination (i.e. London) dated April 29th, 1697."

In 1701, James is also described as Marshal of the Court of Vice Admiralty, which dealt with the arrest of privateers. In 1709, there is an entry in the State Papers referring to George holding certain appointments. This might be a misprint for James as the appointments appear under James's name elsewhere. They are the Marshal of Assembly, Marshal of Council of Court of Errors, Marshal of Court of Admiralty and Serjeant at Arms of the Court of Chancery.

There may have been another George as both James and George appear in 1709, together with a George Hays, as executing the office of

Marshal of the Admiralty Court. So perhaps George was the younger son also holding a legal benefice due to his late father's influence.[172]

James subscribed to the Loyal address to Queen Anne on May 18, 1702 when she was proclaimed at Bridgetown:

> "We pray your Majesty may preserve the balance of Empire against the overgrowing and exhorbitant power of the French King and all other that shall attempt to disturb the peace thereof of any of your Kingdoms, especially on the score of the supposed Prince of Wales[173] whose pretention we abhor and renounce from the bottom of our hearts being ready to offer up the last drop of our blood and the utmost penny of our fourtunes in defence of yr majesty's right."

In 1705, James petitioned and was granted leave for one year by the Queen. On May 10, 1707, the Queen wrote to the Attorney General stating, "you are to prepare a warrent for George Gordon to be Provost Marshal of the Barbadoes and thereby revoking the patent whereby James Hannay was so constituted."

James thus resigned his post and became a private gentleman. In 1709, James married Elizabeth Price. They had a daughter Elizabeth and a son George. James is described in 1714 in the list of Gentlemen proposed by President Sharpe for vacancies on the Council of Barbados on June 1 as "a worthy gent of good parts improved by a liberal education at Oxford, of great prudence, resolution and integrety and of very good estate." He appears to have continued to serve on the Council until 1728. In this year he could not serve on the Grand Jury of Session on December 10, but it is stated that he was a "proper person to do so" as he owned a large number of slaves. The seventeen Gentlemen listed as "proper persons" owned 339 slaves between them.

---

[172] Stewart Francis, in previous editions of *The Hannays of Sorbie*, added:

> "Supporting this theory, the Reverend James A.M. Hanna [1924-2007] of Oak Hill, Ohio, asserted that the second George was the younger son of George Hannay, the Provost Marshal General".

The Reverend James, however, in his 1959 work *Hanna of Castle Sorbie, Scotland and Descendants,* also believed that Provost Marshall George was the son of John Hannay of Sorbie (d. 1640). James wrote that the younger George Hannay (or Hannah as spelled in the Rev. Hanna's book), the Provost's son, died in Lunenberg County, Virginia, in 1783. This implies a 143-year gap between the death of George and his grandfather. There is likely either one or more missing generations between Barbados and Virginia or a case of mistaken identity in conflating two different George Hannays. As noted later in this chapter, Stewart Francis believed that the George Hannay in Virginia was the grandson of Provost Marshall George.

[173] James Francis Edward Stuart (1688-1766), Prince of Wales until his father James II was deposed. James Francis Edward was known as The Old Pretender and was the father of "Bonnie" Prince Charlie, the Young Pretender.

The Provost Marshal General's second son George may in turn have had a son, also George, for one is recorded as living from 1700 to 1783[174]. He married Jane Thompson and lived in Lunenburg County, Virginia. His son Andrew married Ann Cunningham and died in 1793. Andrew's son, Captain George Hannah, served in the War of 1812 against the British, and in 1806 married first Betsy Brent by whom he had three children. Later after they had moved to Arkansas, his wife died and he married Lucy Morton and had a further three children. His son, also a Captain in the U.S. Army, George Cunningham Hannah, was born in 1817 and died in 1878. He married Ann Spragins in 1842; they had eleven children. His son Samuel Baldwin also served in the Army, and married, in 1874, Martha Elizabeth Hevener[175]. They had also eleven children, the most notable of whom is the Revd. Samuel Baldwin Hannah, who died in 1959 and was a noted Presbyterian divine in Virginia and also in Arizona.

## 6. Hannays in the West Indies

There was a George Hannay (1702-1776) who was born in the Barbados and married Anna Maria Blackman (1711-1790). Both George and Anna eventually moved to the United Kingdom and apparently died in London. It is possible that *this* George was a grandson of George Hannay, the Provost Marshal General, and that the aforementioned George Hannay (d. 1783) in Virginia was a completely different individual. There is today an area of Christ Church parish, Barbados, called "Hannays", in which the Hannay & Blackman families ran a plantation.

Only one other member of the family appears on the pages of Barbadian history, a certain Joseph Hannis (Hannay) who in 1707 signed a document expressing satisfaction at the appointment of Governor Mitford Crowe (1669-1719). Joseph's identity cannot be ascertained.

In addition to the family of George Hannay, there are other Hannays, Hannahs and Hannas of note in the history of the West Indies. For example, the merchant firm of Hannay and Coltart, which was founded in St. John's, Antigua, in 1836, is today primarily known in numismatic

---

[174] although as noted later in this chapter, there was a contemporaneous George Hannay (1702-1776) born in the Barbados, who subsequently emigrated to the United Kingdom.

[175] In previous editions, Stewart Francis stated that Samuel's wife was incorrectly listed as Elizabeth Andrew Stevenson. This is possibly due to some records being improperly transcribed. For example, one census entry lists Samuel's wife as "Elizabeth A. Hannah", and it is plausible that "Hevener" was at one point misheard as "Stevenson".

circles for issuing one of the few Antiguan coins prior to the late 20th Century. In the 1850s, labourers collected baskets of salt from ponds and lagoons where the seawater had evaporated. They in turn sold the salt to Hannay and Coltart, who paid them with privately minted copper farthings (see Figure 17: The Hannay and Coltart Farthing).

**Figure 17: The Hannay and Coltart Farthing**

In the late 18th century, John Hanna, thought to be from Aberdeen, emigrated with his family to the Bahamas, where they settled on the islands around the Bight of Acklins. The Hanna name can be found throughout the history of the local population. Arthur Dion Hanna (b. 1928, see Figure 18: Arthur Dion Hanna), likely a descendant of this family, was Deputy Prime Minister of the Bahamas from 1967 to 1984, and Governor-General from 2006 to 2010. In 2014, the Royal Bahamian Defence Force christened a new law enforcement vessel, the HMBS *Arthur Dion Hanna*, in his honour.

**Figure 18: Arthur Dion Hanna**

# VIII: The Hannays of Kirkdale

*For the pedigree of Ethe Hannay, see Figure 5: Early Hannays*

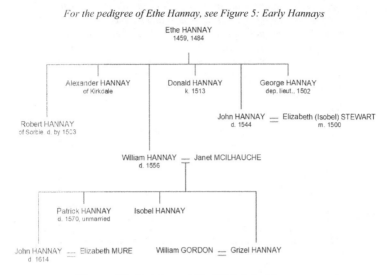

**Figure 19: Origins of the Kirkdale Hannays**

On November 1, 1532, the estate of Kirkdale, in the parish of Kirkmabreck, was bought by Alexander, the second son of Ethe Hannay of Sorbie from Duncan Murray of Whithorn He went, as many younger sons of the landed gentry did at the period, into business in his local town, in this case Wigtown. As a result of his assiduous efforts, he made a tolerable fortune. He became a burgess in 1501 and in 1505 delivered up the accounts as treasurer of the Burgh. He appears with Marion (or Mariote) Hannay, his aunt, in a case of wrongful occupation of certain lands in Lubreck in 1519.

He seems to have acted in the usual highhanded manner of his time, for in 1513 there is recorded in Pitcairn's Criminal Trials the following case — "Alexander Hannay the brother of the Laird of Sorbie and Ucthred McDowell" are hauled before the courts "for raiding forth of the burgh of Wigtoun in a warlike manner in rioting and thereby breaking acts of Parliament." What was the result of the case is not known, but Alexander's future prospects do not appear to have suffered for it.

The lands in Kirkdale purchased in 1532 consisted of 4 merkland and 2 merkland of Browich. Alexander supplemented these with lands in Killantringan (possibly Killantrae, near Port William) for which there is a charter extant, dated 1539, giving sasine of these lands to Alexander by Patrick of Sorbie son of his brother Robert:

> "*Carta confirmationis Alexandro Ahannay burgensi burgi de Wigtoun heredibus suis et assignatis super Cartam venditionis fibi factam per Patricium Ahannay de Sorby de data apud Wigtown 6 die Maii 1539. De omnibus et singulis quatuor mercatis et dimidia mercata terrarum subscript antiqui extensus viz. duabus mercatis et dimidia mercata terrarum de Killantrenane mercata terrarum de Craiginlee et mercata terrarum de Auchinree cum omnibus suis pertinentis jacentibus in parochia de Inche et infra vice comitatum de Wigtoun...*"

Roughly,

Charter confirming Alexander A'hannay burgess of the burgh of Wigtown as heir and assignee of Patrick A'hannay of Sorbie, dated May 6, 1539, to four and a half merkland, namely, two merkland of Killantrenane, one merkland of Craiginlee and one merkland of Auchinree lying in the parish of Inch within the county of Wigtown...

Alexander apparently did not marry, or at least had no children, as his property passed to his brother William, for a time. In 1550 William had sasine of some land of Kirkdale. In 1554 he is shown as purchasing land in the following charter –

> "Alexander Vaus of Barnbarroch by which he sells to William Hannay burgess of Wigton, '*totas et integras illas meas sex merkland terras antique extensus cum pertinet de Kirkdale et Bronach aucupet jacet in par Kirkdale etc et hoc summa tricenterum mercatum...*' [The entirety of six merkland of mine extending from Kirkdale as well as the part of Bronach that lies in Kirkdale, etc., for the sum of three hundred merks]"

On William's death two years later, Kirkdale passed to his son (Alexander's nephew) John.

The relationship between Ethe, Alexander, William and John is shown more clearly in Figure 19: Origins of the Kirkdale Hannays. The family tree tracing William (d. 1556) to the present-day chief can be found in Figure 20: The Hannays of Kirkdale.

*For the pedigree of William Hannay (d. 1556), see Figure 5: Early Hannays*

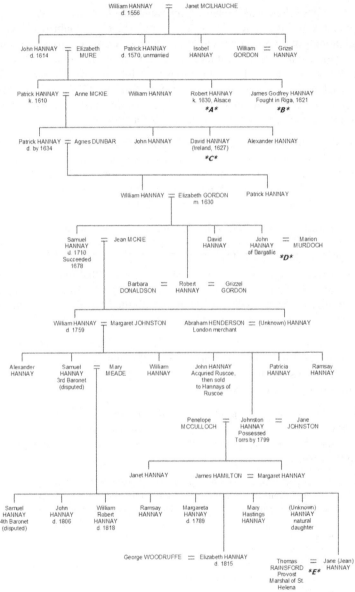

*A*: See Figure 68   *B*: See Figure 88   *C*: See Figure 47   *D*: See Figure 77
*E*: See Figure 33

**Figure 20: The Hannays of Kirkdale**

105

## 1. *John Hannay of Kirkdale (d. 1614)*

Alexander's heir and nephew John went into business in Wigtown, probably in his Uncle Alexander's firm, which no doubt dealt with shipments of Scottish goods to France and the Low Countries. He later became a burgess. His brother Patrick, who died in October 1570 (his will is dated 30 June 1560), mentions both John and their sister Isobel. Patrick's will was proved in Edinburgh on June 28, 1573 by his brother John, so it is fair to assume that Patrick died unmarried. John had sasine to part of Kirkdale in 1561 and to the rest in 1563.

In May 1568 he followed his uncle Alexander's footsteps and found himself in trouble with the law for causing a riot against John Schaw of Halie. In 1565 he became Provost of Wigtown and held the post again in 1587 and 1588 when he gave up the burgh's accounts. He was "sheriff deputy" in 1587/8 and again in 1592/3.

On February 17, 1598, John Hannay witnessed a deed for John Kennedy, 5th Earl of Cassilis. About this time Helen Kennedy, the Earl's daughter, married Hew Hannay of Grennan (See Chapter XII for more about the Hannays of Grennan). It appears that this connection was the beginning of the disastrous feud in which the Hannays and the Kennedys became so deeply involved with the Murrays of Broughton to the detriment of the former.

John married a daughter of the Mure family, probably the daughter of Alexander Mure of Casincarrie. It is thought that her name was Elizabeth, as a Dame Elizabeth is referred to in a document of 1602 concerning John of Kirkdale.

In 1609 John was still going strong, but it appears he had mortgaged certain of his properties, probably due to the quarrel with the Murrays in which he was deeply involved, or because of the steep rise in prices in the early 17th century:

> "9th July. 51 James VI. –by contract of 11 August 1609 John
> Hannay of Kirkdale grandfather of Patrick bound himself in fief to
> said Hugh Gordon in Merkland of Barnes in Kirkinner Wigtoun
> redeemable for 4,000 merks. Hugh gave John tak of the lands as
> long as he paid 400 merks a year by a bond dated 1610, 4
> December, Patrick bound himself to implement the contract. By a
> contract of 27 December 1615 his grandson Patrick undertook the
> same obligations further binding himself to pay 80 bolls of oats if
> the 400 merks were unpaid by the 30th of November any year.
> Hugh demands the payment of 400 merks and arrears of interest on
> 17th March 1618."

John had four sons, William, Patrick , Robert and James.

## 1.1. Patrick Hannay (d. 1610), son of John

John's son Patrick married Anne, the daughter of Patrick MacKie of Larg, by his wife Margaret Stewart, the daughter of Alexander Stewart, Fifth Laird of Garlies.

The Provostship of Wigtown was kept in the family during this period, for in 1598 Patrick was executing this duty, when a complaint was raised on December 21 by the Baillies of Dumfries. The town of Dumfries was suffering from famine and pestilence, and James Scharpe and John Martine were sent to buy cattle about the area, despite not having a grant for any cattle they bought to cross the Water of Cree. Coming to Wigtown, the Magistrates gave them permission to buy what they could. They bought 38 head of cattle. At Minnigaff they were met by an armed party under the command of Patrick Hannay, the Provost of Wigtoun, and two baillies who escorted them back to the town. They were allowed to go after paying a fine of 100 merks. The Burgh exacted dues for all cattle crossing the Water of Cree long before the grant of that privilege in 1662.

In 1610 the Earl of Cassilis, to whom Patrick was much attached, took the field against Kennedy of Blairquhan and on the December 16 in an action at the Curves of Cree, Patrick was killed by John Baird, the brother of the Laird of Kilquhinzie. The slaughter of Patrick is well documented and an extract from Pitcairn shows something of the legal processes of the time:

"May 21st before Sir William Heast Justice deput John Kennedy of Blairquhan and John Bairdis brother german to the laird of Kilquhinzie.

"Dilaitit of airt and pairt of the felloun and cruel slauchter of Umquhile Patrick A'hannay of Kirkdaill provost of Wigtoune; committit be thame and their complices with schottis and hagbuts and pistolets at the cruves [cruives, i.e. a fish pen] of the Watter of Crie in the month of December imvjc yearis upon set purpois. provision and forthought felonie. And forbeiring wairing and shoitting of hagbuts and pistoletts contrair the tenno of the Acts of Parliament.

"Persewairs Patrick A'hannay of Kirkdail as son of umquhile Patrick A'hannay, Sir Thomas Hamilton of Byris Kt advocate of our Sovereign Loard for his Majesties interests.

"Predocutouris for the pannell-My lady of Cassius My lord Uchilrie, Gilbert Roise. Mr. John Russell Mr Thomas Hope and Mr Lawrence Mr Gill Advocates.

"The panel accepts the summonds and speeches and part thereof quhair the deceast was shot with peisks or droppis [small shot]. It is alleged, that the matter cannocht pass to an assize. because his majesty of his special grace has given to the persons on the pannel one remission, quhilk thar producet to the justice of the dait at Edinburgh the xviij day of may instant. And offers caution to satisfy the partie—it is a suruit that this remission cannot stay the matter to pass to an asize because of an act of parliament of 1593, it is providit that all remissions are null that are purchased after one party passis to the home for the tyme.

"The parties were bound to keep the law of the realm and obliged to leave their cautioners and the cautioners also abliged themselves to free each other pro rata."

Patrick had four sons, Patrick, David, Alexander and John.

## 2. Patrick Hannay of Kirkdale (d. by 1634)

Patrick the younger succeeded to the property in 1614 on the death of his grandfather John. He married in 1606 Agnes, the daughter of Gavin Dunbar of Baldoon (near Bladnoch), a house which subsequently passed into Hannay hands. The house is the one in which the title character of Sir Walter Scott's 1819 novel The *Bride of Lammermuir* is supposed to have lived.

Patrick seems to have had strong views on clerical matters, for in 1617 he was charged with "carrying arms," then a pretty serious offence in Galloway, although nothing the law could do seemed to be able to stop it, "and destroying a kirk desk." On November 27 he broke into church and threw out the kirk desk, representative of the English ecclesiastical settlement so hated in Scotland. The desk was restored by Alexander Gordon; the church was locked, and the key given to the minister. But Patrick was not having any of this; he broke into the church again, removed the offending desk, and threw it outside into the kirkyard; as a result of this rather violent action he was duly fined 1,000 merks and appears, surprisingly, to have paid.

The estate by this time consisted of five merkland of Balmurrie, four merkland of Broche, eight merkland of Kirkdale, also two merkland of Braidfield, six merkland of Clachaire [Clauchrie] held from the Provost and Burgesses of Wigtown, ten merkland of Barnes and three merkland of Balnab held from the Earl of Cassilis. The four merkland of Torhouse Muir are also mentioned, when in 1619 with the consent of his wife, he sold them to Hew Gordon of Grange, with whom his grandfather, John, had entered into a bond granting the lands of Barnes in exchange for a loan of cash: possibly to pay some of the fines or sureties called for by the courts as a result of the feud with the Murrays. The ten merkland was redeemable for four thousand merks and let to Patrick for four hundred merks a year.

In 1618 Patrick was forced to sell some land to Alexander McKie of Ferrietoun. This was probably in the form of a fine for some disturbance he had created as part of the family feud which was then at its height. The extract reads: —

"13 May Edinburgh. *Rex pro se et tanquam administrator etc cum consensa... concessit Alex McKie in Ferrietoun de Crie heredibus ejus assignatus quibusquamque 2 mercat terrarum de proache antiqui extensus in parocchia Kirkdail senesc de Kirkcudbright guus Patrick Hannay de Kirkdail resignavit.*"

Or, approximately:

13 May, Edinburgh: On the King's behalf and as an administrator, etc...Agreement to assign to Alex McKie of Ferrytown of Cree the 2 merkland extended into the ancient parish of Kirkdale in Kirkcudbright resigned by Patrick Hannay of Kirkdale.

Patrick was a Justice of the Peace and served on the bench at Wigtown. In 1621 one of his tenants, John Turner, who occupied the farm at Barnes, no doubt much in debt to Patrick, sued him in the Wigtown Sheriff Court for "Having conceived a deadlie malace, hatred and envy against the complainer." There is unfortunately no document now in existence giving the details of what might have been an amusing case.

Patrick died in 1634 when a will lists William Hannay, "the eldest son of the deceased Patrick Hannay of Kirkdale along with Agnes Dunbar relict (widow) of the said deceased Patrick and Anne McKie mother of said defunct."

It seems that Patrick succeeded in dying quietly in his own bed, in itself quite a remarkable feat for a Hannay at this time. He had two sons whose names have come down to us: William, who succeeded him, and Patrick.

## 2.1. Alexander and David, Brothers of Patrick

Of Patrick's brothers there is some interesting information. Alexander was an officer serving in the Scottish forces in the army of Gustavus Adolphus in Sweden. He probably went over originally in the train of his third cousin[176], Sir Patrick, who visited Sweden in 1621 in the service of King James VI, and of whom mention is made in Chapter VI: The Sons of Alexander of Sorbie. In 1624 Alexander first appears in contract of a certain William Forester as a witness, when he is described as a brother of Patrick Hannay of Kirkdale.

---

[176] Sir Patrick's great-grandfather Robert was the brother of Alexander's great-grandfather William.

His brother David Hannay in 1627 was working in a junior post in Dublin Castle, whence he had gone in the service of either Sir Robert, or perhaps more likely Sir Patrick to an appointment in the Irish Government. David was acting for his brother Alexander in enlisting soldiers in Ireland for service in Captain Alexander Hannay's Company in Sweden. In 1628 David wrote a letter recommending "Mr Dawson as a likely person to be of use to the King in raising the revenues from the plantations." He seems to have met with the usual problems of administration, for he goes on to say, "the writer had been very careful in the addresses business, but not without meeting ill will in high places."

An interesting sidelight into the method of recruiting soldiers in the early seventeenth century is to be seen in a case recorded in 1628 when Thomas Sankey, described as an "Englishman, keeper of His Majesty's Jail at Durham" complained to the courts regarding one Samuel Sayer. Sayer, it seems, was originally recruited in Ireland, by David, for Captain Alexander's Company in Sweden. But at some time during his journey to join he succeeded in deserting. Sayer then either borrowed money or bought goods and did not pay for them, to the extent of £100 from the citizens of London and York, who promptly hounded him into Durham jail for debt. Prison walls were not for Sayer, and probably by bribery he managed to escape and went hurriedly north taking the road for Galloway, in order to pass over to his native Ireland; however, on his arrival in Wigtown he was spotted by Patrick Hannay of Kirkdale, who recognized him as one of his brother Alexander's deserters and arrested him. It appears that Kirkdale was used as a collecting centre for recruits sent by David from Ireland, from whence they were despatched to Leith and thus to Sweden. Patrick naturally did not want to produce Sayer to the English authorities, and held on to him. As the Register of the Scottish Privy Council puts it, Sayer was "a deserter from Captain Alexander's Company in Sweden who had been enlisted by David Hannay brother to Alexander the defender's [defendant's?] brother (Patrick)". History does not relate the outcome; no doubt such a strong force of Hannays must have succeeded in spiriting the body off to Sweden. From David, the family of Hannays of Kelso are descended and of whom the author Stewart Francis's father was the male representative (For more details, see Chapter XI: The Hannays of Kelso).

At this time also a most interesting piece of information has come to light. Serving in the Army of Gustavus Adolphus was a certain James A'Hannay, who for services rendered to the Swedish King received a gold medal about two and a half inches in diameter with an inscription to this effect around the edge. James was probably an uncle of Captain Alexander of Kirkdale (who was known to have fought in Riga, Latvia, in 1621) or a brother of Patrick Hannay the poet, who served in the Bohemian Army[177]. The medal eventually passed into possession of the family of Colonel Walter Hanna of Speen in Berkshire, one of James' descendants.

There were a number of Hannas, including Ensign David Hanna, in Captain Alexander Hanna's company.

### 3. William Hannay (d. before 1679) of Kirkdale

Patrick of Kirkdale had two sons: William, who succeeded him to Kirkdale, and William's younger brother Patrick.

In 1637, when the religious issue again raised its head with the reading in St. Giles of the English service book (see Chapter VII: The Family of John Hannay, M.P.), families were split and sides taken. William's younger brother  came out strongly against the service book and together with Richard Hannay of Kirkmabreck, William Hannay of Kirkmabreck, Gilbert in Aichie, and John Hannay in Kirkmabreck, all members of the Presbytery of Kirkcudbright, forwarded to the General Assembly in Edinburgh a strongly worded protest against the use of the book in Scottish churches. The relationship of these Hannays to the overall family tree is unknown.

In 1630 William married Elizabeth Gordon, daughter and heir of Alexander Gordon of Castramont; her mother was Euphemia Maxwell. By 1642 his lands, according to the Kirkcudbright valuation roll, were worth £120 a year in taxes. He appears to have still been the feudal superior of the ten merkland of Barnes, for in the same year Gilbert Brown acted as his bailie at the infeftment there of David Dunbar of Baldoon.

William was a Justice of the Peace. By 1662 the estate had grown, and consisted of Kirkdale, Barholm, Broagh, Baglie, Clanchied, Cambrer, Bargallie, Carsluith inherited from his wife, Strewans, Kirkbridge, Kirkmuir, Cairnholy, Duffin, Hallcroft, Ravenshall, and certain other

---

[177] Although Patrick the poet served in some capacity in the Thirty Years' War, Francis erroneously stated in the 3rd and prior editions of this book that Patrick had been a Lieutenant General in the Bohemian Army. This assertion appears to be derived from an error in Peter McKerlie's *The History of the Lands and their Owners in Galloway* (Patterson, Edinburgh, 1877). In that work, it is noted that Patrick "attained the rank of General of Artillery under the King of Bohemia." The biographical information on Patrick Hannay that precedes the Hunterian Club edition of his collected works quotes McKerlie but adds a footnote that the rank applies to **Sir Andrew Gray**, under whom Patrick served in Bohemia, and **not** to Patrick himself. This is supported by Patrick's own dedication to Gray in the 1622 edition of his sonnets: "To the Right Honorable Sir Andrew Gray Knight, Colonell of a foot regiment, and Generall of the Artillerie to the high and mightie Prince Fredericke King of Bohemia."

lands. In 1669 William let half the Kirkdale estate to John Brown of Carsluith for three years for a yearly take of 190 merks.

William died in or before 1678, leaving four sons, Samuel, who succeeded him, Robert, David, and John of Bargallie the founder of the Drumaston family (see Chapter n).

Of David, little is known except that he appears in the parish list of Kirkmabreck in October 1684.

Robert is concerned in several legal matters mostly about debts. In 1673 he is cautioned for three thousand merks not to molest Sir David Dunbar of Baldoon. In 1678 he married Grizzel Gordon the daughter of James Gordon, a notary burgess of Kirkcudbright. The marriage contract reads as follows, and is dated April 16,1678:

> "Marriage contract between Robert Hannay, lawful son of the deceased William Hannay of Kirkdale on the one part and Jean Thompson widow of James Gordon Notary burgess of Kirkcudbright, taking burden upon her for Grizzel Gordon her lawful daughter on the other part and the said Robert and Grizzel are to marry in a certain time in contemplation of which Robert Hannay promised to infeft the said Grizzel in whatever lands and goods or heritage he may acquire during his marriage in life rent and their heirs in heritage forever and in an annual rent of £1,000 to be laid out in heritable bonds or upon lands; and the said Jean Thompson promises to pay the said spouses 1,000 merks for fuilfillment of which she assigns to them 500 merks contained in a bond by Roger Gordon of Troquhain and another 500 merks contained in a bond by John Ingles of Kirkcudbright, which sum the said Grizzel accepts in satisfaction of her bairnes portion, and should the said Grizzel decease within a year and a day of the said marriage the said Robert is to make payment of 600 merks to her children or nearest kin and if there are not children alive 500 merks to her nearest of kin."

Grizzel apparently did not live very long, and Robert is, by 1680, married to Barbara Donaldson. He was still alive in 1702, for in this year he was concerned in a case of debt to a William Charteris, the schoolmaster at Kirkwinzean.

## 3.1. Patrick Hannay, brother of William

William's brother Patrick became Member for Wigtown in the Scottish Parliament in 1639, and between 1643 and 1646 he was on the Commission of War of Kirkcudbright and became a colonel of horse in General David Leslie's army and finally in 1646 Provost of Wigtown. No more is known of him, which is rather a pity as he would have been the typical example of a Lowland Laird of his period. The work of the Commission of War was mainly concerned with the supply

112

and administration of the army, or that part of it stationed in Kirkcudbright. Their minutes are in existence and have been published.

As regards Patrick's service in the army, he was probably present at the Battle of Philiphaugh September 13, 1645, when David Leslie's Covenanter cavalry destroyed the remnants of the Marquis of Montrose's Royalist army, thereby restoring the secular power of the Kirk in Scotland. This was during the Wars of the Three Kingdoms (1639-1651), and no doubt there were Hannays on both sides, for by this time the family was firmly split between King and Covenant.

### 4. Samuel Hannay of Kirkdale (d. 1716)

Samuel, William's eldest son, succeeded to the Kirkdale property about 1678. In 1695 he married Jean McKie of Larg. She was the widow of William Ramsay of Boghouse. In the troubles of 1684-1689, when Dundee and Sir Robert Grierson of Lag were ranging the Galloway hills persecuting Covenanters, and many Covenanters had fled for refuge to the mountains, the Kirkdale family were out on the side of the Government. In the list of Heritors[178] of Galloway, who took the Test before the Justices at Dumfries, are "Samuel Hannay of Kirkdale and Robert Hannay, a portioner[179], there."

Samuel lived the life of an ordinary country gentleman of the period, keeping out of trouble and improving his property and estate. In 1704 he became a Commissioner of Supply for the Stewartry, together with Samuel McDowell of Glen and Robert Brown of Carsluith.

As far as we know, Samuel only had one son, William, who succeeded him, and one daughter, who married Abraham Henderson, a merchant in London, who was the fourth beneficiary in the entail of Lady Ann Hannay of Kingsmuir (see Chapter IX: The Hannays of Kingsmuir).

---

[178] **Heritors** were major landowners; most farmers leased land from Heritors. Heritors also paid, through levying taxes, for community resources such as justices, roads, ministers and teachers.

[179] A **portioner** was the owner of a small part of an original, larger estate which had been subdivided, perhaps among the original owner's heirs.

**Figure 21: William Hannay of Kirkdale (died 1759)**

## 5. *William Hannay of Kirkdale (d. 1759)*

William succeeded about 1716, having served, according to the letters of Captain James Gordon, as an ensign in General George Lauder's Regiment in Flanders in 1702 in the War of the Spanish Succession. He married, in 1740, Margaret, the daughter of the Reverend Patrick Johnston of Girthon.

114

**Figure 22: Margaret Johnston (married William Hannay in 1740)**

They had six sons, Samuel (William's heir), Alexander, afterwards a soldier of note in the Indian Army, William, John of Ruscoe, Johnston of Torrs, and Ramsay. William also had a daughter Patricia. He died in 1759.

## 5.1. John Hannay of Ruscoe

John of Ruscoe (see Figure 23) served in the Indian Civil Service, and in 1786 bought the Rusko (Ruscoe) estate[180]. He died in 1797.

---

[180] **Ruscoe** is an estate outside Gatehouse-of-Fleet. Its tower house was restored in modern times by the Carson family, whose ancestors may have built the original

**Figure 23: John Hannay of Ruscoe (died 1797)**

## 5.2. Ramsay Hannay

Ramsay (see Figure 24) was engaged in trade with India and China. In 1800 he purchased the Carsluith property from the Browns.

---

structure, which, during an intervening period, was owned by Hannays. - *Dr. David Hannay, 2nd Chief*

**Figure 24: Ramsay Hannay**

## 5.3. William Hannay of Bargallie (d. c. 1830)

William's son William of Bargallie lived in Kirkdale, and acted as agent and factor (business representative) for his brother Samuel, who spent most of his time in London. He assisted in the construction of the military road to Portpatrick[181] , being responsible for the section from Borland of Anworth to Skyreburn Bridge[182]. William remained as of the estate after his nephew Samuel had succeeded, and two of his letters are extant. They give an interesting line on 18th century estate management:

"To Charles Stewart Esq W.S. [183] Edinburgh.

Kirkdale 13 March 1802

---

[181] Clan Hannay genealogist Keith Hanna notes "Portpatrick was the main port to Ulster in the 16th-18th century from Scotland. It was always liable to explode militarily as it had in 1798 in the Irish Rebellion."

[182] West of Gatehouse of Fleet.

[183] **W.S.**: Member of the Society of Writers to Her/His Majesty's Signet, a Scottish professional society for solicitors.

Dear Sir,

Yours of the 9<sup>th</sup> instant I received, since which I have been busy with one thing and another, so as to defer replying till now. That cursed receipt of Mr. Kellys, I cannot lay my hands on and therefore suspect that I must have given it to Torrs[184]; however I shall make sure by a general search as soon as convenience will permit. I have wrote to Mr John Thompson respecting the state of his namesake's factorage[185] and application of the Ardwell[186] rents, and very pressing for immediate information which I trust will be readily complied with, but from which I can learn from Mr. Sym the deposit is not above £1,200. If so, the funds have been shamefully wasted and nobody has ever taken the trouble to examine the factor's accounts till now. I am a good deal surprised at your mode of establishing the rent of Craignook[187] and still more so at your listening to such proof, had she shown him one or two of my discharges that must have been satisfactory and proof positive, but that was not in her power as her husband never paid me more than £20 per annum and the state of our settlement fell into my hands when looking for other papers which will shew the fallacy of this woman's assertions, and in my opinion must be more convincing than any recollection from memory or any other voucher except a discharge which this woman can produce if she chooses, but I perceive a considerable degree of readiness in some people to serve a certain purpose by departing from the truth, a copy of the totting[188] have given you below—

I observe that the Kirkdale business stands over to the summer session. I am sorry for the delay but I flatter myself that Mr. Kir will be found ... in all expenses I am sure that he deserves to pay for his breach of faith and dishonorable conduct.

I observe what you say as to the Ardwell process and will answer your queries as to the tenants new lease in a few days, however the rent is sixty guineas; but what dykes or houses the landlord is bound to build at present cannot inform you. I am sorry to see you have not got expenses of Macfarlane [;] the court has leaned much to the side of a great scandal and I wish his cautioners may be sufficient, but don't know who they are.

---

[184] Torrs lies to the east of Castle Douglas.

[185] factorage is the commission paid to an agent or business representative.

[186] Ardwell is located on the Rhinns of Galloway, on the western shore of Luce Bay.

[187] Craignook may refer to a property Southeast of Glasgow.

[188] sum, total.

Dear Sir, your obedient servant

William Hannay

| Wm Muir to Wm Hannay Dr | | By 2 stoth | £5.5.0. |
|---|---|---|---|
| To one year's rent due | | By cash | £3.2.0. |
| Martinmass | 1785: £20 | By supply | 17.4. |
| " | 1786: £20 | By balance of 1 years rent | £8.13.8. |

Martinmass 1785

---

£20.0.0.

and the second one:

Kirkdale 28 June 1801.

Dear Sir,

Since my arrival here after meeting with you at Balcarry[189] I
understand that Mrs. Janet Muir who is. entitled to receive the £40
annuity remitted from India by her daughter Mrs. Grant, is in great
need of money at present, and as you carried the bill with you to
Edinburgh I trust the proceeds will be sent to her as soon as
convenient. She tells me she has not received above a hundred
pounds of that annuity from the beginning, which was in 1793, so
that the balance, whatever it may be, is a debt against my brother's
estate and I presume that the present draft should be paid to her
without delay. Or even so much as being reckoned owning my
brother's funds further than negotiating the draft or bill for the
intended purpose by you in conjunction with Mrs. Hannay and me,
a quorum of trustees. I was obliged to lend her ten pounds to pay
her pressing demands and when her daughter comes home it will be
very unpleasant for her to find that her mother should be in want or
that the annuity has not been regularly paid her. For want of the
charter of Kilbride[190] nothing has been done as to the fishing which
I had a right to. I have now given directions for my servant in
Kilbride to occupy a stand in the Ford when they catch salmon in
the Water of Cree opposite to the minister's glebe near to the march
of Kilbride, and I beg to know how I should proceed to establish
my right.

At present the minister makes every person that stands in the ford
pay the "tiendfish[191]", but I am determined to make the fishers pay
me, as the minister cannot establish any other right but use and

---

[189] located south of Glenluce

[190] Possibly a misprint or misstatement of "Kirkbride", as there doesn't appear to be a
Kilbride on the shores of the Cree.

[191] a **tiend** or **teind** is a tenth, so tiendfish likely refers to a tithe of the fishermen's
catch.

119

wont, a right acquired by old Mr. Samuel Brown when minister of Kirkmabreck and tenant of Kirkbride at the same time at which period he assumed the right of fishing by having the Farm of Kirkbride in tak and has continued it for glebe, ever since by his successors in office.

I therefore request you will give me proper instructions how to proceed and the charter if necessary to substantiate my claim may be sent out with Mr Kelly when he leaves town—this is a matter of some importance. Should I defeat Mr. McKie's intentions and present prospects, which I trust will be the case, I flatter myself you will soon be in this county to attend McCulloch's proof which certainly should not be delayed a single moment in order to expedite the disgraceful process and bring it to a conclusion. Shall be happy to learn that you got safe to town, my daughter joins me in kindest compliments—believe me most truly yours,

William Hannay.

William is supposed to have served for some time in the Indian Infantry—he had a daughter who predeceased him. He died about 1830.

## 5.4. Johnston Hannay of Torrs (d. 1801)

Another of William Hannay of Kirkdale's sons, Johnston of Torrs, had sasine of Ruscoe [Rusko] for some time in 1779 but sold it to Robert Hannay from Jamaica, who founded the present Ruscoe branch now represented by the Hannays of Sunnyside, Melrose.

Johnston was in possession of Torrs by 1799, and married Penelope, the daughter of David McCulloch of Ardwell. Johnston had two daughters: Janet (who married James Gordon of Culvennan , who had no children and who succeeded to the Balcarry property) and Margaret (who married the Reverend James Hamilton of St. Stephens, Kent, who succeeded to Torrs). After Penelope's death, Johnston Hannay married Jane Johnston.

Jane was the daughter of Peter Johnston of Carnsalloch[192] He is pictured in Figure 27. Johnston died in 1801.

---

[192] About five miles North of Dumfries.

**Figure 25: Johnston Hannay**

**Figure 26: Jane Johnston (2nd wife of Johnston Hannay of Torrs)**

**Figure 27: Peter Johnston (father-in-law of Johnston Hannay)**

## 5.5. Alexander Hannay (d. c. 1788)

Another son of William Hannay of Kirkdale, Alexander, like so many sons of Scottish lairds, went to seek his fortune as a soldier. He joined the cavalry, and during the Seven Years' War (1756–1763) served in Flanders, taking part in the Battles of Minden (1759) and Warburg (1760) under John Manners, the Marquess of Granby.

**Figure 28: Lieutenant-Colonel Alexander Hannay**

At the end of the war he was a lieutenant and had gained for himself the high opinion of the Commander in Chief. However, with the inevitable reductions in the Army which follow a war's resolution, Alexander opted for service in the East India Company's Army, and finally became Adjutant General of the Army in India, and Commander of the King of Oudh[193]'s Army.

His journey to India was not without its troubles. He was shipwrecked and lost most of his newly formed military unit. This constituted a very considerable financial loss to him. He started his service in India on a very slim purse.

---

[193] Also known as the **Nawal** (provincial governor) of **Awadh** (alternative spelling of Oudh, which is a Britishism)

Like most officers of the Company's army, he served both in military and administrative posts. And he climbed slowly to the top of his profession. In 1775 there was trouble over his appointment as Adjutant General with the Directors of the East India Company. It shows something of his brother Sir Samuel of Kirkdale's sterling qualities, that he campaigned on behalf of Alexander with the Company at home, and wrote to the shareholders of the Company after he failed in his suit for his brother with the directors. The letter gives a very clear picture of the system by which appointments were given:

"March 7th, 1775. To the proprietors of the East India Stock:

Having given already so much trouble to the Proprietors it is with the utmost unwillingness and regret that I find myself obliged to appeal to their justice on behalf of my absent brother.

The memorial following, presented to your Court of Directors on the 14th of February, will explain what has happened concerning the office of Adjutant General to the Company's Forces in Bengal, since the last ballot:

To the Honourable the Court of Directors of the Honourable Company of Merchants of England trading in the East Indies:

The memorial of Samuel Hannay on behalf of his brother Alexander Hannay Esq Adjutant General of the Companys Forces in Bengal sheweth —

That your memorialist is informed that the committee of correspondence has under consideration, a resolution for a paragraph in the General letter to Bengal, which directs that the office of Adjutant General to the troops in that settlement, shall be executed as heretofore and with a salary of £100 a year, in lieu of perquisites etc.

That the paragraph, if agreed to by the Honourable Court, will deprive the Company of all the advantages which the President and Council had in view, when (after mature deliberation) they in substance resolved that the manner in which the duties of the office had heretofore been done, was insufficient for the public service and that the appointment of a field officer of experience and capacity, to be Adjutant General was necessary.

That it will at the same time deprive Major Hannay of an office confered on him by force of merit only, and of which he is in possession by the complete act of the Company, no law or order to the contrary existing in India, at the time of his appointment, for your memorialist humbly submits that it makes no difference to Major Hannay, whether he is dismissed from the office, or if the office is ordered to be annihilated and his duties executed as heretofore, they having

125

never been executed by any other officer above the rank of Captain.

That your memorialist humbly apprehends, that the late resolution of the general court respecting the office of Adjutant General over all India, has no relation to the same office in Bengal, but was evidently grounded upon the impossibility of one man's executing the office in all the settlements at once, whilst the necessity of such an officer in Bengal is established by the concurrent resolutions of the whole executive power of the Company, viz the President and Council at Fort William[194] upon the representation of the C-in-C [Commander in Chief] under the strong impression arising from daily expenses in the actual service, and by the Hon. Court of Directors in their resolution that the office is necessary to all the forces in India.

Your Memorialist therefore humbly prays, that no order be given inconsistent with Major Hannay's continuing to exercise an office so effectual to your military service, and to which he has been appointed under circumstance so honorable to himself, by the President of the Council at Fort William who were at the time fully authorised to make such appointment.

Samuel Hannay.

Philpot Lane[195], Feb 14th, 1775.

The Court of Directors gave no answer to the above memorial. On the contrary, the paragraph complained of has been confirmed without material alteration. Application was made, in form, for a copy of the paragraph, but this was also peremptorily refused by the court. This conduct in the Directors left me without any recourse for redress, but in the justice of the proprietors.

If this measure complained of is founded on personal resentment against Major Hannay, because he finds, without either his knowledge or participation, he opposed the wishes of the Court of Directors in a former appointment, I trust the illiberality of the motive will defeat the intention. If it is grounded on inexpediency of the office in Bengal, it stands in direct contradiction to former resolutions of the Govt in India and the Directors at home. If it is alleged to be taken in consequence of the resolution of the General Court, against the appointment of one Adjutant General over all India, it is humbly submitted, that a resolution does in no respect apply to the present case, and that the General Court has never debated the expediency of an Adjutant General in Bengal only, if ever therefore, it was fit, and even necessary to appeal from the decision of the Directors to the supreme authority of the Company,

---

[194] in Calcutta (now Kolkata).

[195] in London, located a couple of blocks northeast of the Monument to the Great Fire.

I hope it will be deemed so in his present instance and trust, that I shall be pardoned for soliciting the attendance of the independent proprietors at the General Court on Thursday 9th instant, when the business is appointed be taken into consideration.

I have the Honour to be with great deference and respect your most obedient and humble servant.

Philpot Lane,
March 7th, 1775

Samuel Hannay."

The Appeal seems to have been successful. Warren Hastings, the Governor General of Bengal, held Col. Alexander Hannay in high regard. In the State Papers, India is a report by Warren Hastings on the Insurrection of Chait Singh, Faizabad, in 1781:

"Two battalions of Regular Seypoys in the Vizeers service (of Barnaris) under the command of Lt-Col Hannay who had been entrusted with the charge of that district were attacked and surrounded by enemy forces. Many of them were cut to pieces, and Col Hannay himself encompassed by many, narrowly escaped the same fate. On 8 Oct Major Naylor with the 23rd Regiment was sent to the relief of Lt-Col Hannay, arrived on the Northern bank of the Dewa and defeated a large force which had assembled round Col Hannay and entirely dispersed them."

A letter, written in 1782, to Sir Elijah Impey, one of the Directors of the East India Company resident in India, shows the sort of negotiations in which Col. Alexander Hannay was involved:

"I have delayed replying to your last favour of 28th until I could inform you of the effect of your friendly support of my claim on the estate of the late Nabob Nidjiff Khan for between the time of my first writeing to you on that subject and the receipt of your answer, the agent of the Begum[196], Nidjiff Khan's sister, had so widely changed his conduct and attuned his conversation, that I had great reason to suspect my obtaining possession would have been disipated prior to my first advising you on that subject. He had repeatedly, both privately and in the presence of Mr. Middleton, [attempted] to take possession without waiting [for] Mr. Hastings' assent to the measure; And in order as he pretended to unmake all difficulties pressed me to receive a letter from him, to the Begum's agent; on the lands to yield me possession, or to agree to his sending him to Lucknow for that purpose, these proposals I declined complying with; on account of the motives I have already written to you in a former letter, however on the arrival of Mr. Hastings' assent he flatly refused to write the letter to the Admiral, which he had formerly voluntarily prepared; and proposed the

---

[196] **Begum**: female royal title; roughly, queen or princess.

renewal of negotiations at Delhy. This conduct was evidently intended to give time. And he knew I was under a necessity of immediately leaving Lucknow contrived to disappoint my hopes of obtaining an equivalent from the debt due to me, under these circumstances I had no alternative but to express my intention of taking possession on the authority I already had, which happily has answered my expectations, for rather than that the matter should be settled without his purturbation he has this morning sent me the Begum's sunnad[197] to the Aumil[198], in virtue of which I have about an hour ago obtained peaceable possession—I will not pretend my dear Sir, to express the sense I entertain of your goodness and, friendship on occasion, it is to the zeal with which YOU interested your alone, I owe my success, for had Mr. Hastings consent been delayed even but a few days longer, I had irretreavably lost with the object of my business—from the inquiries I have been able to make I am apprehensive the produce of the lashkar[199] will not exceed the sum I mentioned in my former letter but every rupee I do get, is so much saved out of fire, as there was no other means of recovering an anna[200]—enclosed I return you a letter which by mistake enclosed with Mr. Hastings note, or rather your note to him with his reply. It was lucky it was your letter was exchanged and not the note, for without it I could have done nothing—I have the pleasure to inform you that with the assistance of my worthy friend Murchisan[201] I have recovered most wonderfully and consider myself altogether out of danger. I have had little or no return of my fever at the last full or change of the moon and I have recovered more strength than I would possibly have hoped in so short a time, a circumstance which is particularly happy for me in every point of view for had my health been ever so bad it was out of my power to return to Europe for want of money there and I should have also found much upset at being under a necessity of returning while the war lasted. I shall proceed to Calcutta on the 1st of July and trust I shall have the pleasure of seeing you there by the end of the month—I beg you will do me the honour to present my most respectful complements to Lady Impey and believe me I am with most unalterable attachment and grateful sense of obligations I owe you.

---

[197] **Sunnad**: grant or bequest.

[198] **Aumil**: revenue agent; superintendent of a district or region.

[199] **Lashkar**: likely *lascar*, a local (Indian) sailor employed by the British Navy. Lascars were notoriously underpaid and ill-treated.

[200] **Anna**: coin equivalent to 1/16 of a Rupee.

[201] This probably refers to Dr. Kenneth Murchison (d. 1796), a surgeon with the East India Company, who was the father of Sir Roderick Murchison, the noted Scottish geologist of the 19th century.

My dear Sir,

Your afft friend and most duetiful humble servant,

Alexander Hannay"

He returned to England in 1786 as a witness for Warren Hastings, for whom he had a great attachment, during the former's impeachment trial. Hastings had been impeached by Burke, Fox and Sheridan in Westminster Hall, largely on information supplied by Philip Francis, a personal enemy of Hastings and a member of his council. Hastings had retained India for the British Crown with most inadequate means during the American War of Independence, but not without the mistakes a strong man makes under these conditions and actions which soldiers believe to be necessary at the time; afterwards, many civilians viewed his time in India as being rife with corruption and mismanagement, a perception encouraged by politicians who took advantage of the tremendous public interest in the trial to suit their own political aims.

The trial lasted seven years, but Hastings was acquitted, and in no small measure was this due to Alexander. His actions in the Rohilla[202] War of 1781, and in the case of Begums of Oudh, all of which are well documented in the State Papers of the Governor General of India, published by Her Majesty's Record Office, resulted in his being one of the principal witnesses for Hastings' defence.

An extract of the evidence from the State Papers India are illustrative of Col. Alexander Hannay's part in the business:

"The first charge brought by Burke concerned the Rohilla War. The house divided at 7.30 am 2 June 1786, for the motion 67, against it 119.

The house therefore decided that there was not sufficient grounds to impeach Hastings upon the matter of the Rohilla War."

Evidence of Col. Hannay:

"Major [at the time] Hannay was the next witness—In answer to the first question regarding the oppression stated to be exercised by the Vizeer[203] he said 'to the best of my knowledge I saw no signs of oppression to the inhabitants of newly conquered country. But from particular enquiries which I had the opportunities of making of the country people, they said they had met with no treatment that they could complain of; and from the treatment they had met with they

---

[202] **Rohillas**: Pashtun tribesmen from the north. They were invaded by the Nawal of Oudh in a series of punitive campaigns for non-payment of a military debt.

[203] i.e. **Shuja-ud-Daula**, Nawab of Awadh (Oudh), who led the invasion of Rohilkhand on the Nepali border in 1773-1774, supported by soldiers provided by Hastings.

had no reason to fear greater severity from the Vizeer than from their former masters[204]."

This is a very different picture from that painted by Macaulay[205], who describes Hastings folding his arms and looking on while villages were burnt.

Col. Hannay went on:

> "I have learned from many people that it is only within fifty years that the Rohillas have become masters of the country north of the Ganges, that they were originally Afghans, come to Hindostan and since that time they have followed no other profession but that of arms and the ancient Hindoos have cultivated the country.
>
> I was informed that some days before our arrival at Shawbad, the Rohillas had burned some villages towards Maraby in the Vizeers ancient domains."

As regards reducing the country to a desert, Col. Hannay said:

> "At the time that I went upon the expedition from Bessonly to Sumbad, Merababad and Nampore, the country appeared to be in good cultivation, the inhabitants were employed in tilling it. It is in general one of the best cultivated countries I have seen in Indostan and very well inhabited. And the people appeared to be busy at the time as if there had been a profound peace and order and no kind of apprehension from the conquerers."

In the course of his cross-examination by Sir Philip Francis, when asked the question "Do you know or believe that the Vizeer entered the Zennanas [Zenanas—women's quarters] of the wives of any of the Rohilla chiefs?" Col. Alexander Hannay answered:

> "It is impossible for me to answer with any degree of precision for the Zennanas being spacious places, consisting of many apartments, many of which are occupied by women. I never knew of his going into any of them at Pelleybeet. I can positively say he did not, for he never went into the town of Pelleybeet. At Bassouly I have heard that he went frequently to the womens zennana there, but to the best of my remembrance it was after the women were removed to the camp and that he 'was fitting up the Zennanas for the reception of his own family during the time he was going to Puttegur."

Later regarding the Rohillas he says:

---

[204] i.e., the hereditary ruler, **Hafiz Rahmat Khan Barech** (killed in the Rohilla war) and his followers, who subsequently fled into the jungle to wage a guerilla campaign against the occupying forces from Oudh.

[205] **Thomas Babington Macaulay**, First Baron Macauley, a member of the Governor-General's council in India and, later in life, an historian.

"Their manner of making war is much the same as practised all over Indoostan – Towards conquered enemies they have generally been bloody; those whom they have saved they have commonly made captive of; and in the late campaign I have been very well assured by many of the prisoners that their intention towards us were very bloody, that they had orders to give us no quarter"

In the second document there is a reference to the insurrection of the Zamindari of Benares, in mid-August 1781:

"On August 16th, 1781 two Companys of Sepoys with English officers were massacred almost to a man in Benares. Warren Hastings left on the 22nd August after repeated warnings that he would be slaughtered with only 30 Sepoys to Chunar where Hannay was still holding out."

Col. Alexander Hannay seems to have returned to India and predeceased his brother Samuel Hannay of Kirkdale, to whom he left his not inconsiderable fortune, probably about 1788.

## 6. Samuel Hannay of Kirkdale (d. 1790)

Samuel went to London and into business. He became a druggist, and eventually a very wealthy manufacturer of chemicals and drugs. An advertising token for one of his more successful products – a liquid "to prevent the venereal disease"[206] – can be seen in Figure 109: Sir Samuel Hannay's Token.

A typical eighteenth-century character, Samuel made several fortunes and lost them gambling. He lived in great style and magnificence in London and was sometime M.P. for Westminster. He got Robert Adam, a Scottish architect and designer who led the revival of classical architecture in Britain, to design a new mansion house below the family farmhouse, overlooking the sea. The new structure was built of local granite and completed in 1787 (see Figure 29: Kirkdale House). There was an internal fire in 1893 which destroyed some family papers, but the exterior is largely unaltered. The house was subsequently divided up and is still occupied by the family. But Samuel's interest did not really lie in Scotland.

---

[206] UK Patent 1078, granted Sept 1, 1774.

**Figure 29: Kirkdale House**

He had considerable irons in the fire in the Americas, and in 1764 requested a grant of 20,000 acres in West Florida—two years later he received the grant, but only for 500 acres. He did receive, however, in addition, the office of Provost Marshal of East and West Florida at a salary of £100 per annum, which he no doubt executed through some other person, reserving to himself the very considerable revenues from the appointment. In 1779 he was reporting to the Commissioners for Trade and Plantations in London on the state of those Provinces. Again in 1782, he was agent for a certain Adam Christie who was complaining to the Commissioners against Peter Chester, the Governor of West Florida.

## 6.1. Samuel Hannay as 3rd Bt of Mochrum

In 1783, after much research, Samuel had himself served heir to Sir Robert Hannay of Mochrum the second baronet, who died in 1689. How Samuel managed to achieve his title is difficult to understand. His claim is based on descent from Ethe Hannay of Sorbie, a valid claim, but the Kirkdale branch left the main tree when William, Ethe's son, founded the Kirkdale family in 1532.

Samuel had no conceivable right to the title—it was granted originally on March 1st 1630 by letters patent under the hand of Charles I. Robert Hannay, described as "one of the esquires of our body" was created a Knight Baronet of Nova Scotia, and a grant of the Lands and Barony of Mochrum in the County of Wigtown was conferred upon him.

The patent is addressed to '*Domino Roberto*' *Hannay de Mochrum militi hearedibus masculie quibuscunque* [Sir Robert Hannay, whose knighthood is inheritable by the male heir, i.e. a baronetcy], and it confers the usual arms in these words: '*Et quod dictus Dominus Robertus Hannay suique haeredes masculiante dicti habebunt insignia procedente manu armata et nuda conjunctis cum hoc dicto (muni) haec et altera (Vincit)* '[and the aforementioned Sir Robert Hannay and his male heirs shall have the following coat of arms].

Figure 30: Samuel Hannay, 3rd Baronet (died 1790)

That the grant was made to Sir Robert's heirs male and that Samuel was a cousin to Sir Robert (Sir Robert was Ethe's great-great-great grandson, while Samuel was Ethe's great-great-great-great-great-great grandson in a completely different branch) are both quite clear, but without a common ancestor holding the Baronet of Mochrum title, it could not have lawfully passed to Samuel. However, John Grieve, the Lord Provost of Edinburgh before whom the case was tried, served Samuel heir to Sir Robert. The Kingsmuir family asserted they had a better right to the title as the senior descendants of the Sorbie family,

133

which indeed they had. But George Hannay of Kingsmuir would not file a claim, as he had not sufficient funds to support it. In 1860, George Francis Hannay of Kingsmuir placed a Caveat on the Title with the Lord Lyon. Subsequently Charles Graham Hannay (1861-1946), great-great grandson of James Hannay of Creetown (1725-1810), claimed the baronetcy, and provided the proofs referred to above. He proposed to assume the title, and though he sued a document to that effect, he never appears to have in fact done so. More information on the Kingsmuir family can be found in Chapter IX: The Hannays of Kingsmuir.

## 6.2. The Children of Samuel Hannay of Kirkdale

Samuel married Mary, the daughter of Dr. Robert Meade. He had several children: Samuel, who succeeded his father; John (d. 1806); William Robert (d. 1818); Ramsay (d. without issue); Margareta, who is mentioned in the Universal Magazine's obituary for July 1789; Elizabeth, who married George Woodroffe and died without issue in 1815; Mary Hastings, named after her uncle Alexander's commander and friend Warren Hastings; and Jane, from whom are descended the Rainsford-Hannays of Kirkdale. Samuel also had a natural daughter for whom he built the house at Ravenshall, about 2 km southeast of Kirkdale.

On December 11, 1790 he died, leaving vast debts. He had dissipated not only his own fortunes (for he had made many), but also the very considerable sum left to him by his brother Alexander. He was in fact in debt to the extent of £200,000[207]. Fortunately for the family, Scottish law is wise: one third of the property could not be sequestered but was reserved for the use of his widow. So, Lady Hannay had something to pass on to her eldest son, Samuel. It appears that Samuel's brother Ramsay bought the rest of his Scottish estates.

## 7. Samuel Hannay, 4th Bt of Mochrum (1772-1841)

Samuel's eldest son, a second Samuel, does not seem to have been very interested in Scotland, probably on account of the impecunious condition in which his father had left him. A portrait of Samuel by an unknown artist is shown in Figure 31.

Stephen Wood, former curator of the National War Museum in Edinburgh, tells us that Samuel's dire financial situation likely led him to join the military. Posted to Ireland in 1791, he returned by 1797 to

---

[207] £23,500,000 in 2018.

Scotland. Wood goes on to provide a vivid description of the "pay-to-play" nature of military rank at the time:

> On 24th August 1797, he sold his lieutenancy in the unfashionable 61st Foot and bought the rank of cornet and sub-lieutenant in 2nd Life Guards, a regiment of which his fellow-Scot, Lord Cathcart, had recently become colonel. On 17th January 1799, he purchased promotion to lieutenant and adjutant and acquired command of a troop, in the rank of captain and without purchase, on 3rd June 1801.

Samuel left for the continent sometime in 1802; he was reported in the *Times* as having fought a duel near Hamburg on September 11 of that year. After the Napoleonic wars resumed in 1803, he became a prisoner of war in France (along with his sister and brother-in-law, see below), where he likely remained until 1814[208]. Samuel eventually went into the service of the Emperor of Austria as an officer in the Imperial Guard in Vienna. He does not seem to have married, and he died of tuberculosis in Vienna in December 1841, leaving his few belongings to a Baroness Schaffalitzky *née* Lubeck.

**Figure 31: Samuel Hannay, 4ᵗʰ Baronet of Mochrum (d. 1841)**

---

[208] Wood cites the following source: Bulloch. J.M., 'British Prisoners of War in France', Notes & Queries, Vols. 175 & 176 (1938 & 1939), pp. 77 & 194 and *passim*.

On his death, the estate passed to his sister Mary Hastings Hannay by a deed of entail made by her uncle [earlier editions incorrectly stated her brother] Ramsay. Whether Ramsay was ever in possession is in doubt, but it would appear that he did hold the property for a short period. Mary died at Kirkdale on November 20, 1850, and the estate passed to her nephew William Henry Rainsford, the son of her sister Jane.

**Figure 32: Mary Hastings Hannay (died 1850)**

Of Jane, there is a charming if somewhat whimsical story to tell. Jane was in London doing the season, when she met a dashing young $2^{nd}$ Life Guards officer, Captain Thomas Rainsford. Any talk of marriage was frowned on so Jane eloped with the handsome captain. They were married and had a large family (see Figure 33), from whom descends the chiefly line. At the time, Jane's family practically disowned her, and for some time they were none too wealthy.

*For a pedigree of Jane Hannay, see Figure 20*

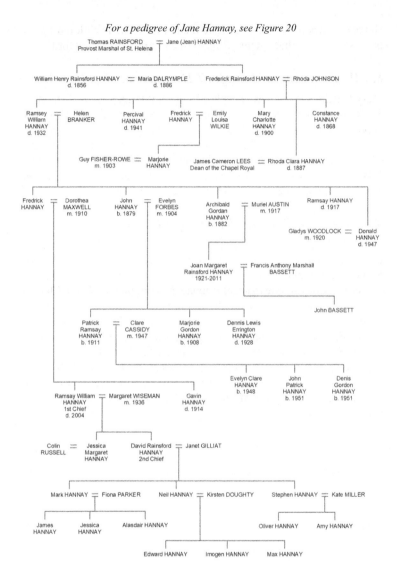

**Figure 33: The Rainsford Hannays of Kirkdale**

Jane accompanied Thomas to France for the early campaigns and remained there after the Treaty of Amiens in 1801. When Napoleon broke the treaty and reopened the war, they were both taken prisoner and interned in France for the duration.

Eventually Captain Thomas Rainsford took the post of Harbour Master and was some time Provost Marshal under Sir Hudson Lowe on St.

Helena[209], where both he and Jane died. Two of their children are of interest to us, William Henry Rainsford and Frederick Rainsford.

## 8. William Henry Rainsford-Hannay (d. 1856)

Mary Hastings Hannay was the last living child of Sir Samuel Hannay, 3rd Baronet, and when she died in 1850, she was succeeded by her nephew William Henry Rainsford. William was an advocate in Edinburgh, and adopted the surname of Rainsford-Hannay. On August 21, 1851 he married Maria, the daughter of Col. Samuel Dalrymple, C.B.[210], and widow of Robert Stewart of Alderson, M.P. She died on May 9, 1886, and he in 1856. There were no children.

## 9. Frederick Rainsford-Hannay (d. 1884)

After William Henry Rainsford's death, his brother Frederick Rainsford succeeded him. He was a Deputy Lieutenant[211] of Kirkcudbright and a Justice of the Peace for the Stewartry. On November 26, 1840 he married Rhoda , the daughter of Oliver Charles Johnson. They had several children: Ramsay William (who succeeded Frederick), Percival (who was born in August 1851 and who died in 1941), Frederick (of whom more anon), Mary Charlotte (who died in 1900), Rhoda Clara (who in 1872 married the Very Rev. Sir James Cameron Lees, K.C.V.O., D.D., LL.D., Dean of the Chapel Royal of Scotland, and died in 1887), and Constance (who died as a child in 1868). Frederick Rainsford died in 1884, and was succeeded by his son, Ramsay William.

---

[209] Sir Hudson Lowe was the Governor of St. Helena, where Napoleon was exiled from 1815 until his death in 1821.

[210] Companion of the Most Honourable Order of the Bath

[211] The King or Queen's representative in the area – *Keith Hanna*

**Figure 34: Frederick Rainsford Hannay (died 1884)**

## 10. Ramsay William Rainsford-Hannay (1844-1932)

Ramsay William Rainsford-Hannay was born on September 9, 1844 and educated at Windermere College and the Royal Military Academy, Woolwich. He entered the Royal Artillery, and in 1874 married Helen Lane Branker, the daughter of John Branker, who was Lord Mayor of Liverpool. Ramsay rose to the rank of Colonel and was finally Chairman of the Kirkcudbright Territorial Force Association from 1908-1920. He was a Deputy Lieutenant and Justice of the Peace for the Stewartry. He died in November 1932.

**Figure 35: Ramsay William Rainsford-Hannay (1844-1932)**

Ramsay had a five children: Frederick, John, Archibald Gordon, Ramsay, and Donald. Frederick, the eldest, succeeded his father.

## 10.1. Frederick Rainsford-Hannay (1854-1950)

Ramsay's brother Frederick, born ten years after Ramsay on September 7, 1854, was also educated at the Royal Military Academy (R.M.A.) and entered the Royal Engineers. He became Commandant of the School of Military Engineering from 1907-08, and Director of Fortifications and Works as a Brigadier General at an Army Headquarters overseas in World War I from 1914-17. He was appointed a C.B.[212] in 1911 and a C. M. G.[213] in 1918. In 1891, he married Emily Louisa , the daughter of David Elliot Wilkie of Midlothian and Melbourne. They had a daughter, Marjorie, who married, in 1903, Guy Fisher-Rowe, the son of Edward Rowe Fisher-Rowe of Thorncombe. Frederick died in 1950.

**Figure 36: Helen Branker**

---

[212] Companion of the Order of the Bath.

[213] C. M. G. refers to Companion of the Order of St. Michael and St. George. "The Most Distinguished Order of St Michael and St George (1818) honours service overseas or in connection with foreign or Commonwealth affairs. Ranks in the Order are Knight or Dame Grand Cross (GCMG), Knight or Dame Commander (KCMG or DCMG) and Companion (CMG)." – *Keith Hanna.*

## 10.2. John Rainsford-Hannay (1879-1951)

Ramsay's second son John, born on September 4, 1879, and educated at Wellington and the R.M.A., served in the Queen's Regiment (2nd Foot) in the South African and First World Wars. In 1904 he married Evelyn Gordon, the daughter of Stephen Forbes. There were three children: Patrick Ramsay, Dennis Lewis Errington who died in 1928, and Marjorie Gordon. John died in 1951. A sketch of John can be seen in Figure 37.

**Figure 37: John (Jack) Rainsford-Hannay**

John's son Patrick , born in 1911, went to Wellington and thence, a new venture of that time, to the Imperial College of Science and Technology gaining a B.Sc. in 1935. He served in the Second World War as an officer of the Royal Army Ordnance Corps and became a Field Chemist for the Iraq Petroleum Company. He was a Fellow of the Zoological Society and a member of the Marylebone Cricket Club. In 1947 he married Clare Catherine Maude Cassidy, the daughter of the late John Cassidy of Newcastle. They had three children: John Patrick and Denis Gordon , twins born in 1951, and a daughter Evelyn Clare born in 1948.

## 10.3. Archibald Gordon Rainsford-Hannay (b. 1882)

Ramsay's third son Archibald Gordon, born in 1882, also went to Wellington and the R.M.A. He served in the Royal Engineers and

142

became a Lt.-Colonel. He fought in World War I and took part in the Darfur Expedition[214] in 1916 for which he was awarded the Order of the Nile. He was also a recipient of the Distinguished Service Order (D.S.O.) and the Order of the British Empire (O.B.E.) In 1917 he married Muriel, the daughter of William Austin of Rye Hill, Luton. They had a daughter, Joan Margaret (1921-2011), who married Francis Anthony Marshall Bassett of Dormers, Illford, Illminster, Somerset. They had two children, John and Sally.

## 10.4. Ramsay Rainsford-Hannay (1884-1917)

Ramsay's fourth son Ramsay, born in 1884, was also at Wellington and the R.M.A. and joined the Indian Army, serving in the 1908 campaign on the North West Frontier, now the border area between Pakistan and Afghanistan. He was killed in action with his Regiment, the 45th Sikhs, at the siege of Kut in Mesopotamia (now Iraq) on February 1, 1917 as a Captain.

**Figure 38: Ramsay Rainsford-Hannay**

---

[214] In which Britain annexed Darfur (then allied with the Ottoman Empire) into the Sudan.

## 10.5. Donald Rainsford-Hannay (1886-1947)

Ramsay's fifth and youngest son Donald was born in 1886, and was at Wellington and the R.M.C. He also went into the Indian Army and in 1908 served on the Frontier in the Mohmand and Afridi Campaigns. He served in World War I and was wounded at Loos in 1915. After the war he retired from the 53rd Sikhs and entered the service of the Maharajas of Jhind and Jhodpur. In 1920, he married Gladys, the elder daughter of John Woodcock, and died in 1947; there were no children.

**Figure 39: Frederick Rainsford-Hannay**

## *11. Frederick Rainsford Hannay (1878-1959)*

To return to the main branch, Ramsay's eldest son Colonel Frederick Rainsford Hannay was educated like his brothers at Wellington and the R.M.A. He entered the Royal Artillery and served in the South African War, where he was both wounded and mentioned in despatches. He received the Queen's Medal and six clasps, and the King's Medal with two. In World War I he served in France, and was awarded a D.S.O. in 1917. From 1924 to 1928 he commanded the 52$^{nd}$ Lowland Divisional Artillery and in World War II served in the Observer Corps and Home Guard.

He was much interested in the affairs of the Stewartry and was the County Commissioner for Boy Scouts, a Justice of the Peace and a County Councilor. He was also a member of the Marlyebone Cricket Club He received a CMG (Companion of the Order of St. Michael and St. George) in 1919. On August 16, 1910 he married Dorothea Letitia May , the younger daughter, and later heiress, of Sir William Francis Maxwell, the fourth and last Baronet of Cardoness. They had two sons, Ramsay William and Gavin (d. 1914). Frederick died in 1959.

**Figure 40: Dorothea Maxwell**

145

## 12. *Ramsay William Rainsford Hannay (1911-2004)*

Ramsay William Rainsford Hannay was born on June 15, 1911, in Conoor, India, where his father Frederick was serving in the army, but returned as a child to Edinburgh during World War I. He was subsequently educated at Winchester College where he rowed for his school, as he did for Trinity College, Cambridge, where he read law.

**Figure 41: Ramsay William Rainsford Hannay**

At the outbreak of World War II he joined the Highland Light Infantry, but was seconded to Special Operations where he trained personnel in Canada and the UK for action behind enemy lines in Europe. He was in Paris for the liberation of France, and in Berlin before the Russian Army arrived. After the war he worked in the legal department of the Board of Trade under Harold Wilson and Edward Heath, before taking early retirement to manage the family estate in Galloway, where he established a successful caravan holiday park.

Ramsay was a founding member of the Clan Hannay Society in 1960 and subsequently became its first Chief. In 1980, he legally changed his last name from Rainsford-Hannay to Hannay. He was a member of the Council of Chiefs and travelled widely to Clan functions, especially in North America. He took a great interest in Clan Members, who were always made welcome when they visited Galloway.

**Figure 42: Margaret Wiseman**

A man of integrity with a strong sense of humour and a natural concern for others, his advice was widely sought. He was an Honorary Sheriff, President of the Galloway Area Scout Council, and a founder member of the Dry Stone Walling Association of Great Britain (and, at one time, its president). He was also a founding chairman of the South West Holiday Parks Association, President of the Gatehouse Festival Group, and a Trustee of Carsluith Village Hall.

In 1936 he married Margaret , the second daughter of Sir William George Eden Wiseman, 10th Baronet of Canfield Hall, Essex. They had two children, David and Jessica Margaret , born in 1939 and 1937

147

respectively. Ramsay died in on January 10, 2004 and was buried in the old churchyard above Kirkdale House, his family home.

## 13. *David Rainsford Hannay (born 1939)*

Ramsay was succeeded by his son David, who became the second Convenor of the Clan Society and second Chief of Clan Hannay. David Hannay is a retired family doctor and academic who trained at Cambridge University and St. George's Hospital in London. He became a senior lecturer in General Practice at the University of Glasgow. In the 1970s, he stood as Liberal candidate for Galloway. After a period of family practice in Wigtownshire, he became Professor of General Practice in Sheffield before returning to Galloway as a partner in a local practice and Director of a Regional Research Network. In 1997, David was a Visiting Professor at the University of Western Australia. In 1999, he stood for a candidate in the first elections of the Scottish Parliament. In 2004, he retired as a partner in the Galloway practice but continued as a research adviser for the Royal College of General Practitioners and was elected to the Regional Health Board. He was also a Justice of the Peace and Deputy Lord Lieutenant for Wigtownshire. He plays bagpipes, both Highland and Scottish smallpipes, and enjoys sailing. David is married to Janet, the daughter of the Reverend Patrick Nevile Gilliat, M.A., who was vicar of Holy Trinity Church, Brompton, London, and Prebendary of St Paul's Cathedral. She is a teacher and environmentalist with a special interest in garden history. They have three sons and eight grandchildren. The eldest son lives at Cardoness, seat of the baronets Maxwell, and the second son at Kirkdale.

Though the story of Kirkdale is long and sometimes troubled, it remains the leading branch of the family still resident in Galloway. Through 400 years of vicissitudes, the Kirkdale property has been in Hannay hands; let us pray that such a condition will endure for as many more.

# IX: The Hannays of Kingsmuir

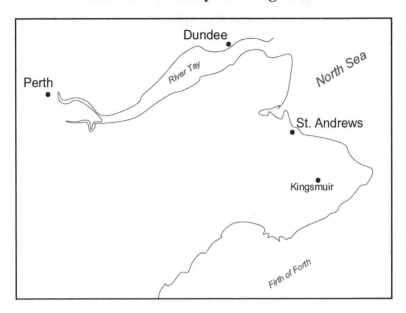

**Figure 43: Kingsmuir in Fife**

Kingsmuir, moorland and wild as it was, originally belonged to the Crown: hence its name. Subsequently it was given to the Thanes of Fife, with whom it remained until the second Duke of Albany was executed at Stirling and his estates forfeited to the Crown. In 1542, James V bestowed the estate of Kingsmuir on one Charles Murray because of his services in purchasing "large war horses for the King." Horse traders today are not so lucky. Years after, the property returned to the Crown, and, after the Restoration, Charles II gave it to Colonel William Borthwick, who had been a faithful follower of his in the days of his misfortune and troubles, and was in exile with him. On Col. Borthwick's death, not having any children, it passed to his wife Margaret Livingstone, and thus to her second husband Robert Hannay.

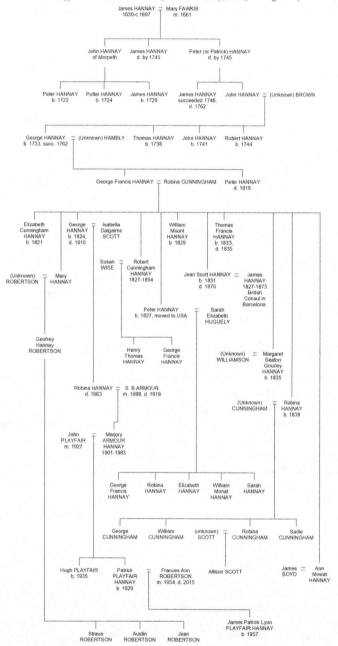

*(For James Hannay (1630-1697)'s pedigree,*
*see Figure 14: Descendants of John Hannay, MP for Wigtown)*

**Figure 44: The Hannays of Kingsmuir**

150

## 1. *Robert Hannay of Kingsmuir (d. 1725)*

There is a very strong tradition that Robert was an advocate in Edinburgh, although no proof of this exists. It has been also said that he was an apothecary, and there seems to have been in Edinburgh, at the time, a family of apothecaries bearing his name. In any case, Robert would have been a Merchant Burgess and a man of considerable standing.

Robert's pedigree is unclear, but there are several possibilities:

- There were two apothecaries named Robert Hannay in Edinburgh during this era, and both were apprenticed to the same guild brother, according to the burgess rolls. The elder Robert was probably the son of Hew Hannay, who in turn was the grandson of John, the baker to Mary Queen of Scots. This Robert was apprenticed to David Scott, burgess and apothecary, on August 23,1655. Robert's brother James (1610? - May 8, 1655) was also an apothecary, apprenticed to William Castlelaw in 1634. On November 1, 1649, James married a certain Isobel Guthrie with whom he had a son, Robert. This younger Robert was apprenticed to David Scott on February 1, 1671. Either of these Roberts, uncle and nephew, may have been Robert of Kingsmuir.

- Another possibility is that Robert of Kingsmuir was the grandson of James Hannay, Dean of St. Giles. It may be that James the apothecary (listed above) and James the son of Dean James Hannay were one and the same. Robert of Kingsmuir is described by Alexander Nisbet, writing about 1700, as the representative of the Sorbie line, which appears to support this theory. James, son of Dean James Hannay, does not, however, seem to have had a son named Robert.

- Mr. James Hannay of Barcelona (1827-1873) believed quite clearly that Robert was the son of Francis Hannay, who in turn was a son of the Reverend George Hannay. This seems the likeliest possibility, and the one that is pursued below.

Robert had considerable trouble on the Kingsmuir estate about "the coal sinks"—coal mines, but possibly also referring to sinkholes caused by illegal coal mining on the Kingsmuir property . These troubles continued into his sister Ann's time, and of which she wrote voluminously to Captain William Hannay, later of Kingsmuir. Robert had a house in Edinburgh, and is referred to in his will as "Residentor in Edinburgh."

Among other things, Robert was an artist of some talent, and Ann refers in her letters to Captain William to the pictures drawn by her brother

151

that hang in the house of Kingsmuir. Sadly, all efforts have failed to trace these pictures, together with those pictures presented in turn to Ann by Captain William Hannay and his wife Mary Hathaway. Robert died on March 27, 1725 in Edinburgh. His will gives some idea of a Scottish town house at the period:

> "Imprimis, two old feather beds at £3 apiece, item two stouped beds with hangings old fashioned and a dozen old fashioned broken chairs, two tables, two old trunks, two old little chimminys and an old Kitchen chiminy all at £21, item some old hangings £1, item 10 pairs of old sheets £12, item 9 pair of old blankets £9, item an old chist of drawers £1, item 12 items silverplate £331, item a looking glass 2, item a house clock £24, item three dozen old napkins £4, item one dozen more and a table cloth £3, item three old table cloths £1, item 20 old pewter £3, item a pot a pan and three old candlesticks £3, item some old timber of broken furnishings £4, item another house clock old £9, all Scots Money."[215]

There follows then a list of debts, etc., owing to him. One entry is interesting as it shows his wife Margaret Livingstone to have been an astute landowner:

> "Alexander Clarkson for the said crop the sum of £13/10 all scots money and contained in the decreetal obtained before the Sheriff of Linlithgow at the instance of Mistress Margaret Livingstone formerly relict of the deceased Colonel William Brothwick of Diehmond thereafter spouse of the said Umquhile Robert Hannay .... "

There is a further piece of interest referring to Alexander Livingstone of Baldamy[216], who was Margaret's brother. Ann Hannay refers to the Lady Baldamy in her correspondence with Captain William Hannay on a number of occasions. Robert's will was witnessed by "Sir James Smollet, Master Henry Walker, Minister of the Gospel sometime at Mochrum in Galloway." So it would appear that Robert's connections with Sorbie – which is quite close to Mochrum – were fairly recent. Since, as noted above, his exact lineage is conjecture, there is always the possibility that Robert was descended from John, the last known laird of Sorbie.

## 2. Ann Hannay of Kingsmuir (1685? – 1736)

On Robert's death, his sister Ann succeeded him in the estate of Kingsmuir. Her correspondence with William Hannay of the Kelso branch of the family, from whom the author Stewart Francis is

---

[215] £1 from 1725 would be approximately equivalent to £145 in 2018,

[216] Likely Balhary (14 miles west of Kingsmuir) or Balbinny (6 miles northeast of Kingsmuir).

descended, is of great interest and very charming. Ann and Captain William, their letters, and their story, are treated at much greater length in Chapter X: William and Ann Hannay of Kingsmuir.

Upon her death in 1736, Ann left the Kingsmuir property to Captain William Hannay and his male heirs.

William had several children, but unfortunately, none of them lived to succeed him. After his death in 1743, his personal estate went to his nephew Edmund. Kingsmuir, however, went according to Lady Ann's entail, which is quoted here:

> "1734 Entail made by Ann Hannay of Kingsmuir 23rd May.
>
> By the said Ann Hannay widow of Captain John Erskine, Kingsmuir was limited to the use of William Hannay of Rotherhithe [who succeeded] and his heirs male, with remainder to Peter Hannay of Morpeth, Northumberland, son of the deceased James Hannay residenter there and his heirs, male; remainder to the spous of Abraham Henderson merchant in London sister german to the said William Hannay of Kirkdale."

Mary Hathaway, Captain William's widow, lived at Kingsmuir until her death in 1777.

## 3. James Hannay of Kingsmuir (1693-1762)

The next in succession at Kingsmuir, after Captain William, was James, the son of Peter (or Patrick) of Morpeth, who had sasine in 1745. The origins of this branch of the family are not clearly known, but this family of Hannays who were resident in Morpeth, County Northumberland, at the time Lady Ann wrote the entail, were in all probability descended from Dean James. A tree here may help readers to understand the relationships of this branch:

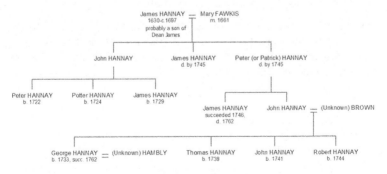

**Figure 45: The Hannays of Morpeth**

153

The earliest references to the Hannay family in Northumberland and Durham are in 1630 and 1641. In 1630 a certain Peter Hannay was Bailiff of Bedlington, a small village about 5 miles from Morpeth, when the State Papers Domestic record of him:

> "that 11 Hollanders in the street of that place armed with muskets and pursuing a Dunkirker, he proceeded to take them into custody."

The second entry refers to two John Hannays who are included as householders of Darlington, and who submitted to the Protestation of 1641[217]. The Protestation read:

> "We the knights, Citizens and burgesses of the Commons House of Parliament finding to the grief of our hearts, that the designs of the Priests and Jesuits and other adherants of the See of Rome of late boldly and frequently put into practice, this formerly, to the undermining and danger of the ruin of the true reformed religion in his Majesties dominions established etc.... "

There is a note in Chapter I of a certain Symon and John Hannay in Durham in 1316, but Stewart Francis did not think they had any connection with this branch of the family.

## 4. The Morpeth Connection

Of James, the first known Morpeth Hannay, unfortunately we know nothing except that he was (possibly) dead by 1697 or (certainly) by 1734, and the fact that he had three sons: John , James and Peter or Patrick. He may have been a son of Peter Hannay the Bailiff of Bedlington, mentioned on the previous page, or perhaps a son of Dean James, the latter being more likely.

This family must not be confused with the Kelso Hannays, of whom Captain William Hannay was one, who came first to Bothal and later to Blyth, both near Morpeth, after the troubles of 1685[218].

Of James' younger sons James and Patrick (or Peter) little is known, except that both were dead by 1745. Patrick (or Peter) was apparently more favoured by Ann, as he (or, as it turns out, his male heir James) was second beneficiary after Captain William.

---

[217] This was an oath of allegiance to King Charles I and the Anglican Church, required, by an act of parliament, for anyone holding a government or church office.

[218] In 1685, after Charles II's death, general displeasure with the ascent to the throne of Catholic King James II (James VII of Scotland) led to a rather chaotic environment in Britain. Archibald Campbell, the 9th Earl of Argyll, led a Scottish rebellion against the king, while James Scott, 1st Duke of Monmouth, rose up with his troops in England, and declared himself to be the true heir of Charles II. Both uprisings were quelled.

## 4.1. John Hannay of Morpeth

James' eldest son John had three known sons of his own, Peter, Potter[219], and James, born respectively 1722, 1724, and 1729, and from this family descends the Hannays who are resident in Morpeth today. One of them, George, became a baillie and Alderman of Morpeth in 1797.

## 4.2. James, John and Kingsmuir

Although Patrick (or Peter) of Morpeth did not live to succeed to Kingsmuir, Patrick's eldest son James inherited the property on Captain William's death in 1743, a third of it being left in liferent to Captain William's widow Mary Hathaway until her death in 1777.

James does not appear to have married and died in 1764. The property passed through his brother John and his wife, a certain Miss Brown, to their son George. George had sasine in 1765. John, it appears, was resident at Morpeth at the time of his death.

## 5. *George Hannay of Kingsmuir (1733-1800?)*

In the handwriting of George Francis Hannay, a son of George, is a list of birth dates. George Hannay was born in 1733. His brothers were Thomas (born in 1738), John (born in 1741) and Robert (born in 1744).

A copy of the Retour dated January 12, 1764 which clearly shows this much disputed succession is reprinted below:

> The Inquisition which has been carried out in the court of the Shire of Fife held in the Council Hall of the Burgh of Cupar on 12th January 1764 in the presence of James Dagliesh of Scotscraig. advocate, Sheriff deput of the above shire with the following honorable and loyall citizens as Jury viz :*(15 names follow)* who declare on oath that whereas James Hannay deceased of Kingsmuir paternal uncle of George Hannay now of Kingsmuir the proposer of these presents, eldest legitimate son of John Hannay deceased residing in Morpeth, who was full blood brother to the said James Hannay of Kingsmuir eldest son of Patrick Hannay of Morpeth in the county of Northumberland died vest and seized as a loyall and peacefull vassel of our most Excellent Majesty in all and whole of the honourable office of keeper of the Mora[220] commonly known as

---

[219] Potter cannot be found in any other source but Francis' book. He is indicated as having been born in 1724 in the body of the text of the 2nd edition, but as having died that year in the genealogical tables of the same edition. Likely he died in infancy.

[220] Mora" has two definitions, either (a) "moor" or "heath", or (b) delay in fulfilling a contract or in filing a claim. If the title meant the latter, "Keeper of the Mora" may have implied some notarial position that kept records of such infractions.

Kingsmuir of Craill with the three undernoted tofts[221] and the acres respectively mentioned hereafter and lying in the said more, viz:

1. That toft or croft known as Swine Cow Hill, with 15 acres of arable land.

2. The toft and pasturage of the same lying on the north side of the said more and locally known as Scotsfaulds with 6 acres of arable land and' the things pertaining thereto.

3. That locally known as Greenwells with 8 acres of arable land and the things pertaining thereto and whereas vest in all and the whole of the lands of more itself known as Kingsmuir

... and also in all and the whole the aforesaid *mores ins communitatis*[222], a right formally belonging to the Bailiffs, Council and Community of Craill by whom it was transferred to James Spence of Wolmerston and by him to Mr Jerimiah Linsay in Lieth and by him to Mr Borthwick of Dunino, with all the privileges attaching to the same ... As this by virtue of a charter in his favour given under the Great Seal by the late George II dated 12th February 1747 and sealed 10th April thereafter, and in accordance with his, infeftment following thereon dated 23rd June and registered in the Particular Register of Sasines kept at Cupar for the shir of Fife 28th July 1747.

By the aforesaid charter the aforesaid lands etc were granted and disposed to and in favour of the said James Hannay deceased of Kingsmuir paternal uncle of the said George Hannay the proposer of these presents and the heirs male of his body and the heirs male of their bodies when failing to William Hannay of Kirkdale in the Stewartry of Kirkcudbright and the heirs male of his body and their heirs male, who in failing to *[illegible]* Hannay full blood sister of the said William Hannay of Kirkdale, wife of Abraham Henderson trader in London and to the heirs male of their bodies whom failing to the heirs whomsoever of the said *[illegible]* Hannay, a female heir always succeeding without division and excluding heirs portioner and under the conditions therein and afterwards mentioned to the heirs and assignes of the late Ann Hannay superior of Kingsmuir heritably and iredeemably without any reversion redemption or return, And with and under the disposition and deed of tail of the same made by the said Ann Hannay to and in favour of Captain William Hannay formerly of Rotherhithe, Shipowner, later Captain of the ship Adriatick in the service of

---

[221] homesteads

[222] Likely a transcription error, as this doesn't neatly translate in context to English (the closest being *mores in communitatis* = "behaviour in the community", which doesn't seem to fit). It may have intended to mean something along the lines of "moors held in common".

Messers Gibbs and Clay Traders in Lisbon, and to the heirs male of his body and the heirs male of their bodies whom failzing to Patrick Hannay of Morpeth in the county of Northumberland and the heirs male of their bodies, whom failzing to the heirs male of tail and provision given above dated 23rd May 1734 and duly recorded in the Particular Register of Tails[223] 24th December 1736 and registered in the books of the Council and session on 26th November 1737 to which deposition the said James Hannay in the presence of the Sheriff of Fife in accordance with the service dated 30th July 1745 and as the closest lawful male heir of tail and provision to Captain William Hannay who died without lawful heirs and in the presence of the Sheriff of Edinburgh in accordance with a second service dated 28th July 1745 for which services assurances were duly given to chancery as follows:

1. Throughout the whole time of the succession eldest female heir will succeed without division and will exclude heirs portioner.

2. All heirs of tail succeeding to the said lands and others mentioned above and the husbands of the said heirs will be obliged and bound to take and keep the name, arms and designation of Hannay of Kingsmuir as their own names, arms and designation in all time coming.

3. In the same charter there is provision that it will not be permissable for the said James Hannay or for any heirs of tail to sell or pledge the lands etc or any part of the same, or to contact debts or borrow money from them as security, so as to make it possible for the same to be taken from them, or made subject to judges award, nor shall it be permissable to do any other act or deed civil or communal which would affect the said lands or deprive the heirs of their right, it being laid down that all such debts or acts will be void ... and it being laid down also that if James Hannay and other heirs and husbands of female heirs do not take and keep the name etc of Hannay of Kingsmuir or if they sell, pledge etc the lands etc or if they do anything to deprive themselves of the lands, then in any of these eventualities the person in breech of the provision will lose his right for himself alone and the same will *ipso facto* pass to the nearest male heir of tail even if his own descendant who is to succeed as if on death. And it will be lawful for the nearest heir of tail to complete such title to the said lands in his

---

[223] Tails, or entails: inheritance restrictions that ensure property remains in the family and cannot be sold.

own name in compliance with the law of the Kingdom for the time being.

4.    Nothing in Tail or Charter is meant to hinder or prevent the various heirs mentioned from letting the said lands as to hinder or prevent the various heirs abovementioned or the female heirs above mentioned from giving their wives or husbands as the case may be a life rent out of the said lands, provided that the liferent does not exceed one third of the free income of the same and provided the said liferent is in lieu of all terce[224] and courtesy and other provisions in favour of the wife or husband failing to be made out of the said lands, from which they are excluded by the said charter, it being laid down that such liferent shall not begin until the expiry of any former liferent so that in all time coming there can only be one liferent of the said lands at one and the same time.

5.    If James Hannay, or any of his substitutes, should not accept the said Tail within the period of a year and a day after being duly required to by the next substitute willing to accept or by any other authorized person, then the person who was required so to do and refused or delayed to accept will lose all benefits which he or she or the heirs of their bodies would otherwise have been entitled to claim by virtue of the said tail unless one or other of the said heirs accept in the prescribed manner.

6.    The said Tail and charter lays down that the right of succession will go to the person willing to accept it and to his or her substitutes as if the persons who had been required to accept and the heirs of their bodies were dead with and under the provisions of the aforesaid disposition and Right of Tail is declared to be granted by the said Ann Hannay, with and under them it must be accepted by the said Captain William Hannay and other heirs and these provisions must be set forth in charters and deeds in all time coming.

And further whereas the said Ann Hannay, by an additional deed executed by her on 4th June 1734 relative to the aforesaid disposition and right of tail, bound Captain William Hannay and other heirs to accept the condition that it would not be permissable for the said Captain William Hannay or his heirs to let the mansion house of Kingsmuir, servants quarters, gardens, parks, and lands to

---

[224] life-rent to widows.

the extent of 60 acres of land lying near the mansion house of Kingsmuir bounded on the west by Mr John Loch's lands of Over Carnerbie, at first on the north by the Kingsbarns road running to the east in a straight line by the said road to the disused mine, then to the east in a straight line through the mine to the stream on whose bank is the boundary stone seperating Mr John Lumsdains lands of Drumrack from those of Ann Hannay, then in a straight line SSE to the boundary stone on the north side of the public road leading from *[illegible]* to Crail, and then running in a straight line to the SW to the boundary stone *[illegible]* towards the south away from the mansion house of Kingsmuir, then in a straight line towards the west boundary stone on the furthest western boundary of Ann Hannays lands *[illegible]* together with all coal mines of gold and all other minerals which are or may be found below the said lands of Kingsmuir.

Also laid down that it will not be permissable for Captain William Hannay etc after Ann Hannay's death to let the said lands and coalsinks as are or might be found under the lands of Kingsmuir all such lets of land and coal to be void.

With and under which provisions the additional deed is declared to be granted, and with and under them it is accepted by Captain William Hannay and other heirs and these provisions must be set forth in future charters etc...

And further whereas the substitution in the aforesaid charter is wrong and charter failing male heirs, the lands and other mentioned are to go to William Hannay of Kirkdale and the heirs male of his body and the heirs of their bodies are called in succession before the said William Hannay, as the said James Hannay and their male heirs the lands and others mentioned are to go to William Hannay of Kirkdale and the heirs male of his body and their heirs male are called in succession before the said William Hannay, as the said John Hannay father of the said George Hannay the proposer of these presents, is the second son of the said Patrick Hannay deceased, the said George Hannay proposer of the presents is by the death of the said James Hannay, his paternal uncle without male heirs to his body entitled to succeed him in the lands of Kingsmuir and others as male heir of tail and provision by virtue of the said tail and additional relevant deed, and whereas George Hannay is lawful and nearest male heir of tail and provision to James Hannay his paternal uncle he should be as from the death of his paternal uncle possess the title and the lands, as male heir apparent of tail and provision to him, and whereas he is of age and whereas the aforesaid honourable office of keeper of the Mora with its tofts and acres is of the annual value of 8 Scots Denarii[225] and whereas the

---

[225] **denarii**: plural of denarius, from which comes the "d" used to denote pence. This would imply that the value of the land was 8 pennies a year, which seems rather low –

159

aforesaid lands of the moor called Kingsmuir and "Ins Communitatis" of the same are of the annual value of £5 of Scotch money and whereas the honourable office of Keeper of the Mora the lands and others mentioned before are held from Our Most Excellent Majesty and his immediate lawful Royal Successors as superiors in feu and heritage for ever for the payment of the following sums; -for the said lands of the moor the sum of £5 of Scotch money, and for the honourable office, tofts, crofts and acres 8 denarii of silver at Pentecost if asked for.

And whereas the honourable office of Keeper of the Kingsmuir and the lands etc are, as they were before, in the hands of the King as the immediate lawful superior of them and have been from James Hannays death which took place 22nd July 1762, a period of 1 year and five months."

The property, unfortunately for George, did not come in its entirety into his hands until 1777 when Mary Hathaway, Captain William's wife, died, she having had liferent under the entail of one third of the property. George left Scotland in 1764 for the American Colonies, where he was a civil servant and intended to settle. His son, George Francis Hannay, wrote to James Hannay of Barcelona on the subject of the origins of the Kingsmuir family and an extract from that letter will explain his father's early life and the reasons for the paucity of information on the lineage of the Kingsmuir branch:

"My father left Scotland in the year 1764 for the U.S. of America and remained there for about twenty years, in the Government's civil service, and at the time of the American Independence he along with other Royalists were driven out, and my father was robbed by two of his servants of the trunk which contained his money and Family papers: he returned to Scotland and shortly afterwards, both my parents died at Kingsmuir leaving me an orphan at the age of ten years, having no relations to give me the History of my family along with the fact of the papers being lost in America, has left me almost ignorent of these points.

But to my certain knowledge Robert Hannay, an Advocate in Edinburgh, was the first possessor of Kingsmuir by his own conquest. He married a Margaret Livingstone, widow of Colonel Borthwick the former possessor of it, this Robert Hannay had an only sister Ann Hannay she was married to Sir John Erskine of Dun and died without issue.

---

in 2018, it would be worth a mere £5. The Dictionary of the Scots Language, however, states that the term "denarius" could be applied to a coin in general. The actual denomination (merk, chilling, pound) would be determined from context. The only explicit denomination in this paragraph is the pound, so it is likely that £8 was implied, worth £1,200 in 2018.

I am also aware that this same Robert Hannay prevented Sir Samuel's father or grandfather from assuming the baronetcy[226] by proving his preferable claim, but about fifty years after the decease of the said Robert Hannay, Samuel Hannay Esq of Kirkdale claimed and obtained the Title in the absence of my father at that time in the U.S. and being expelled from thence and losing all his property there on his return to Kingsmuir found (owing to an unjust steward) that the whole of the rental he received from the lands of Kingsmuir for the space of about twenty years was only twenty pounds, the House in ruins and the land lying waste, consequently he was in no position to dispute the assumption of the title; however I believe that by making proper application I might still prove my right to the same, which I have no intention of doing at the present, as it would require as many thousands as I have hundreds to support it with dignity."

In this extract from a letter written on November 25, 1851, James Hannay of Barcelona echoed George Francis Hannay's belief of the Kingsmuir primacy as the senior descendants of Sorbie:

"I write to thank you for your very courteous communication. The John Hannay W.S. whom you met, is an uncle of mine. He has since then acquired, by marriage, a very good fortune, and now lives on land of his own in Galloway — which is fair enough, considering our name have had land there, since Edward 1st: No wish for titles – no vanity of any sort – makes me curious about family details; it is simply with me a sentimental feeling that makes me love and honour the memory of brave and good men - for Power was not got in the old days by any other people. I got from the Register Office the other day at Edinburgh the Retour of Service of James [sic] Hannay of Kirdale [sic] — He acquired the baronetcy in 1783[227], but the document gives no details of his proof, asserts simply that he proved himself consanguineous of Robert Hannay of Mochrum. Of course, he was of the blood, but how near or who was nearer — these are matters of detail only to be settled by pedigrees. My present wish is to ascertain the exact branching from 'Sorbie' of all extant Hannays - I have always looked and do look upon Kingsmuir (the fact being explicitly stated by Nisbet in his Heraldry) as the eldest or head of the family - I am now corresponding with various relatives in Scotland and gathering information, which I shall use either when reprinting Patrick Hannay's Poems, or possibly by inducing Burke of the Peerage and

---

[226] For details on Samuel Hannay, 3rd baronet, see Chapter VIII: The Hannays of Kirkdale

[227] Undoubtedly he mistakenly remembered the name on the Retour, because it was Samuel Hannay of Kirkdale (not James Hannay) who was served heir to the baronetcy in 1783.

Baronetage whom I know to insert 'Hannay' among the abeyant baronetcies with a brief notice."

George Hannay , served heir in 1764, was born in 1733 and married Miss Hambly of Exeter. They had two sons: George Francis, who succeeded him, and Peter, who entered the Royal Navy and served in several actions including Trafalgar, when he served on HMS *Defiance*. Peter died unmarried in 1819.

## 6. *George Francis Hannay of Kingsmuir (d. 1867)*

George Francis Hannay did great things on his succession to Kingsmuir by draining the land adequately and turning it into the fine agricultural property it is today.

He married Robina, the daughter of Robert Cunningham of Pitarthie. They had a large family, five sons and six daughters: George, the eldest son, born in 1824 of whom more anon; Elizabeth Cunningham, the eldest daughter who, born in August 1821, died unmarried; Mary, born in September 1822 who married a Mr. Robertson; Robert Cunningham, who married Susan Wise and was drowned in 1854 and whose story is told later; Peter, born in August 1827, who married Sarah Elizabeth Huguely and became Hannay Cunningham of Pitarthie. Peter moved to America where he founded a large family. He became a patent attorney in Washington, D.C. Of William Mount, born in 1829, nothing is known. Jean Scott, born in 1831, married distant cousin James Hannay, consul to Barcelona in 1868, a story which is told in Chapter XIII: The Hannays of Knock and Gararrie. Thomas Francis died young. Margaret Seaton Gourley, born in April 1835, married a Mr. Williamson. Robina, born in 1838, married a Mr. Cunningham, and Ann Mowat, the youngest, married James Boyd.

George Francis died in 1867.

## 6.1. The Letters of Jean Hannay (1831-1870)

George Francis's daughter Jean Scott Hannay wrote several letters which enlighten her relationship with James Hannay, whom she would later marry.

First of all, here is one from 24-year-old Jean to John Hannay W.S., the grandfather of Janet Hannay Schofield (see Chapter XIII: The Hannays of Knock and Gararrie):

Kingsmuir 17 July 1855

My Dear Mr. Hannay,

My father has been wearying for a letter from you for some time, and so yours of the 9th last afforded him great pleasure. So that it gave him an early prospect of seeing you at Kingsmuir, in his pleasure we all participate as we also do with you in this happy event, the prospect of which has obtained for you a 'months leave of absence' we hope that by this time it is over and that nothing will occur to prevent the long looked for visit.

The route you propose is excellent and I can safely assure you that railway, steamboat and coaches all conveniently combine to bring you within a very little distance of Kingsmuir. You will probably proceed from Dundee straight to St. Andrews, which is the most direct route, when if we know of your coming some of us will meet you.

It was very unsatisfactory that Mrs. Hannay should catch cold again; we trust now she has quite recovered her usual health.

My brother George's health is now quite restored. Indeed, on seeing him you will find it hard to believe he was ever ill. He has taken well to the military life – it has quite revivified him, I may say.

He is in excellent spirits, and high favour with his superiors. He is already all but gazetted Captain, which speedy promotion he has gained from among many applicants of high families, partly through the kind influence of a friend; but more so on account of his own excellent conduct since he has joined (I trust you will not think we say this through vanity) – true – he is only a soldier of a few months, but then, his heart has been with them since boyhood, though not by any means a clever scholar, he is yet a quick observer, and very soon became master of at least the practical part of his new profession and obtained a most flattering encomium from his commanding officer, both verbally and by letter.

He was with us last week, on a few days leave, and as his regiment is still at Cupar, he looks forward with as much pleasure as any of us to seeing you here.

We are all busily engaged with *Eustace Conyers*. I have as yet read only the first and second volumes and 1 fear must acknowledge them too clever for me. I do not think our friend Mr. James is sufficiently impressed with the importance of securing the good opinions of young lady readers, who can enjoy a genuine love story without being able to philosophise on the subject. And then what he himself designates his harmless and dilletante taste for genealogical enquiries shine so conspicuous throughout that one never loses sight of the author in the book. Politicians, genealogists and sailors he appears to hold in especial reverence, and I should fancy that these parties will read with keen relish *Eustace Conyers*.

Of one thing, however, I am sure: that the author cannot retain more friendly or warmer recollections of Kingsmuir than the family there entertain for him. All his kindness in dedicating the book to my father, while it pleased and flattered him, was justly appreciated by us all.

My father and Mother desire to be very kindly remembered to you and Mrs. Hannay. George and my sisters beg to join me in kindest regards and hoping to have the pleasure of seeing you soon, I remain very sincerely yours,

Jean S Hannay."

*Eustace Conyers* was a novel just published that year by James Hannay of Barcelona, whom Jean eventually married in 1868.

The second letter was written after the long-awaited visit:

Kingsmuir 13th November 1855.

Dear Mr. Hannay, I received your last kind letter just as I was setting off for Dumbarton to visit George and on my return when I had just commenced to answer it, my father got a letter from Mr. James mentioning that you had left London for the seaside and stating his intention of being down to see us in the autumn, so I have waited in vain, and so long that I now am almost ashamed to address you, but I need not assure you that it was not from want of interest or inclination on our part, as we have been very anxious to learn whether the change of air has benefited Mrs. Hannay. We hope Mr. and Mrs. James (your son) are well and that little Marion continues to thrive and 1 have the pleasure in acquainting you that my brother Peter's wife (in America) has a son, such also my sister in Dundee who has been married for six years has had a son about three weeks ago–all are well.

George is still at Dumbarton and expects to be there for the winter; he had a month's leave lately and still expresses his great disappointment at not seeing you.

We were highly amused at your description of St. Andrews; briefly our ancient city is not overthronged with inhabitants at any time but now the schools and Universities now open – There will be an addition of fourteen or fifteen hundred youths and children – our girls are to be in Edinburgh this session for a change. They have been so long at St Andrews that it thought a change might prove beneficial to them.

My father still complains of rheumatism, but the doctors have pronounced it gout; he says however that it is impossible as he is no winebibber, whereupon they declare it constitutional, at which insinuation he is thoroughly indignant.

Your kind visit afforded him great pleasure and he desires me to thank you for coming so far to see him. We have almost despaired of seeing Mr. James this autumn goes, as we presume he will have difficulty in getting away. So, I will enclose this letter to him, when perhaps he may be able to forward it. We all write our kindest regards to you and Mrs. Hannay and beloved son.

Yours very sincerely,

164

Jean S. Hannay.

One further letter referring to her mother's health from Jean to John is, I think, of interest:

Kingsmuir 7th June 1866.

My Dear Mr. Hannay.

We have been waiting to hear from you for a long time and I would have written long ere this had I been sure you would have still been at Inverness Terrace-however thought to put off no longer. I trust this will take its chance of finding you there for I think I may say we are sure of your kind sympathy when I tell you that my dearest Mama has been and is still very ill.

She has for a long time been suffering from a very severe internal disease-but none of us were aware of it till the end of February last when she went to Edinburgh and consulted the first physician there. Since then all has been done that human skill could to arrest the progress of the disease – but in vain, and while I write my dear mother lies in a very mournful state indeed.

Need I tell you how very heavily this blow has fallen on us all – My dear father feels it most acutely. And to add to all, my poor brother George, who, upon the disembodiment of the Militia, which took place on the 27th last, had occasion to visit the hospital in Cupar and unfortunately, but do not murmur, caught smallpox and was laid up a very few days after his return home. I am very thankful to say however that his case proves to be a very mild one and he is rapidly improving. Anxiety on his account has done our dear mama much harm-but she may rally for a time when she finds him getting over it so easily, etc

Most sincerely yours,

Jean S. Hannay."

## 6.2. The Tragedy of Dr. Robert Hannay (1827-1854)

Robert Cunningham, George Francis' second son, was born at Kingsmuir in 1827 and educated at Anstruther and later at St. Andrew's University. He attended medical classes at Edinburgh and qualified as a doctor. He assumed the name of Hannay Cunningham of Pittathie (which his brother subsequently took on his death).

In 1854 he embarked as a ship's surgeon in the ship *Tayleur* for Australia with his wife and children. In the course of the voyage they met with very heavy storms. On January 21, about noon, James

Nicholson, a mason of Pittenweem[228] and a passenger, went below and reported that the ship was in danger being not far from land and drifting ashore. Many rushed on deck to see the tempestuous seas and the ship driving fast on a lee shore. About one o'clock in the afternoon the ship struck Lambay Island in Dublin Bay. A rope was got ashore from the vessel and many reached land by this means, among others a James Watson from Callerdyke, who was a passenger. Just as he reached land the rope parted as the ship lurched and those on it were thrown into the sea and perished. When the ship struck, she was within thirty yards of the Island but the waves were running 20 or 30 feet high; only the strong and able-bodied could reach the land.

The passengers and crew totaled 574, of which 344 were drowned and 230 saved. A private letter from one of the survivors, alluding to Robert, says:

"The ship's surgeon was a noble fellow; he struggled hard to save his wife and child; he succeeded in getting half way to the shore on a rope, holding the child by its clothes in his teeth when again the ship lurched dragging the rope from the hands of those who held it on the rocks, when the poor fellow, with his child were buried in the waves. He again appeared above the water, however without the child, and in place of swimming ashore to save his own life, he swam back to the ship, and got upon the ladder suspended from its deck. He climbed aboard, and the Captain assisted him in strapping the remaining child, the elder boy, on his back and thus burdened he made another desperate attempt to gain the shore, but failed, the particulars of the second attempt can only be imperfectly gleaned. He regained the vessel however, once more, but without his boy who in some inexplicable manner was torn from him and perished notwithstanding the precaution which had been taken to secure him to his father's person. His wife, who had undergone the anguish of witnessing in succession the destruction of her children, and the fearful danger of her husband, was now on her knees on the deck, apparently in a slate of frantic desperation. Her husband endeavoured to rouse her, parted her hair from before her face, and fastened it in a knot behind and led her over the side of the vessel, and for the third time, heavily burdened, attempted to gain the shore. He had reached the rocks and was almost safe, when a heavy surge carried them both into the water. He, still retaining hold of his wife, again succeeded in catching hold of a rope hanging from the ship's side. He caused her likewise to take hold of the rope, and they held themselves suspended for a considerable time. At length Mrs. Cunningham dropped from her hold, while he at the same instant grasped her: both went down and were swept under the vessel. He was once seen to rise, but only to throw his arms high in the air and then he sank for the last time. Thus perished in the 27th

---

[228] a village in Fife.

year of his age, Robert Hannay Cunningham, Susan his wife (who was the third daughter of Dr. Wise, R.N. of Cupar) in her 26th year, Henry Thomas Hannay aged 4 years and 6 months and George Francis Hannay aged 14 months and Elizabeth Sheppard their attached servant."

## 7. George Hannay of Kingsmuir (1824-1910)

George, the eldest son of George Francis Hannay, succeeded to the estate and married Isabella Dalgairns Scott, the daughter of William Scott of Dalgairn near Cupar. George joined the Militia and finally became Colonel of the Fife Militia Artillery and a noted local landowner.

Colonel George erected the tablet to Dean James Hannay in St. Giles' Cathedral in Edinburgh, which reads as follows:

To James Hannay, D.D.
Dean of this Cathedral
1634-1639

He was the first and the last who read the
Service Book in this Church.

———

This Memorial is erected in happier times
by his descendant.

George and his wife had a daughter Robina who succeeded to both the estates of Kingsmuir and Dalgairn on the death of her father in 1910.

## 8. Robina Hannay (1877-1963)

Robina Ann Marjory Hannay, born in 1877, married in 1899 Sheriff S.B. Armour (who died in 1919). He took, under the ruling of the entail, the name of Armour Hannay on Robina's succession. She was extremely helpful in the production of the first edition of this book, and one of the foremost in encouraging the author Stewart Francis. She resided at Dalgairn, the house at Kingsmuir itself having been sold, the estate however remaining in its entirety in the hands of the family. She died on August 7, 1963.

## 9. Marjory Jean Armour Hannay (1901-1983)

Mrs. Robina Armour Hannay had a daughter, Marjory, 1901-1983, who married John Playfair in 1927 and resided in Fife where both were much engaged in local government work, John Playfair being sometime Provost of Elie.

They had two sons: Patrick, born in 1929 and Hugh, born in 1935. Patrick married Frances Ann Robertson (d. 2015), the eldest daughter of R.S. Roberton of Morebattle of Kelso in May 1954 and has a son James Patrick Lyon born in April 1957. They assumed the name of Playfair Hannay under the provision of the entail.

# X: William and Ann Hannay of Kingsmuir

The story of Ann Hannay and Captain William Hannay is a fascinating one, and has been extracted largely from a collection of old letters. These letters must have been collected by Captain William's wife, Mary Hathaway Hannay, for no letters written by her are contained in the correspondence, although the collection includes letters addressed to her. William's nephew Edmund Hannay (son of his brother David) and Edmund's daughter Margaret went to Kingsmuir in 1777 on the death of Mary Hannay to take over her personal estate, and also that of Captain William. These letters were found by Margaret, probably tucked away in a desk or drawer, and obviously very much treasured.

Margaret took them home and fortunately preserved them. They are remarkably fresh and modern in their outlook and give a very illuminating glimpse into the thoughts and preoccupations of two eighteenth century Scots people, very conscious of their nationality and full of family pride.

Ann Hannay, Lady Kingsmuir, was a sister of Robert Hannay of Kingsmuir. At the time of writing these letters, she must have been between sixty and seventy years old, a generation older than Captain William.

Ann must have been a most attractive young lady, judging by the havoc she played amongst the young bloods of Fifeshire. The only allusion to her affairs that can be found is bland and dry, but a great deal of grief can be read into it, for John Erskine, the son of the Laird of Dun, fell into her coils and the blast of the Laird's displeasure was overwhelming. The poor freemen of Aberdeen went down with all hands before it. The document is dated 1690, and Ann at this time must have been between twenty and twenty-five:

"I, Johne Erskine, lawful sane to David Erskine off Dune
forassmutch as my gud father att my earnest desyre and request has
condescendit for my going abroad. Therforwit ye me to be bund
and obleigit lykes under the conditions. provisions etc.... written I
bind and obleis me that I shal never promise or presume any
marriage to no persons withoutt consent of my said father, he being
on lyffe and particularlie ffor the satisfaction to my father I do
declare that I have not any such base intentione with Anna Hannay
nor shall heirinafter correspande with her or any of her relations
and I further bind and oblies my selfe when ever my said father
shall recall me to return home for the good off his familie I shall
obay his commands and this under paine of losing all benefitt I can
expect or all right or title and interest I can expect as his eldest sone
to the estate of Dune and this in the sincerity of my heart I
subscribe."

This paper, duly witnessed, was signed perhaps in the sincerity of the young man's heart, perhaps not. But he married Ann in spite of it. His father died at some date before July 23, 1710 and his mother Jean in 1702. John joined the 2nd Battalion of the Royal Regiment of Foot (now the Royal Scots).The paper speaks of his intention of going abroad, and the regiment was just about to embark when it was signed; but whether he joined at once or later is uncertain, for there is no record of his serving with it until June 1695, when he was appointed 1st Lieutenant to its Grenadier Company. Yet it must be supposed that he had some previous service or he would have joined as an ensign. He fought at Blenheim and was not in the regiment in 1708, his name not being found on the "Commissions Renewed" list for that date. He was killed in Spanish Brabant, the date of which is unknown but it must have been about 1708, for in 1710 there is a charter of resignation received by his brother David, described as the second surviving son of his father. Lady Ann's letter to Mary Hathaway Hannay describes her feelings as a soldier's wife. She seems, however, to have been present on the campaign in which her husband was killed. In her letter written to Mary commiserating with her over Captain William's absence is the following:

> "I cannot but sympathize with you in your griefe for his absence thar fourtune has trysted you with and the more by reflecting how that it was my own case whilst I was married my husband being a soldier and yours, a saler. I cannot say ther wifes hes much pleasur when ansent I had the misfortune my husband deed abroad at the Buse of Brabon I being with him at the time and is intered in the great church in the Bush. he was an officer in the Royall Regiment commanded by Earl of Orknay who was absent from me some years which made my married life a kind of [widowhood]."

This letter is dated September 16, 1732.

The correspondence between Captain William and Ann opens with a letter from Ann, written as a result of a casual conversation with a certain Charles Loch of Anstruther, who apparently knew Captain William, presumably through his business connections. Charles Loch was the son of John Loch, who is described in 1726 as a merchant in Anstruther Easter. John purchased the estate of Over Carnerbie; another son David became a master in the Merchant service, and it is through him that Charles would have heard of William. David became a shipowner at Leith and was engaged in the Greenland Fisheries, and introduced woolen manufacture into Scotland.

The first letter of Ann's shows, written in 1731, the store she sets by the family name:

"Sir,

There came to my house ane nebouring heritors son to see me which it simes he's the honor of your aquarantens he inquarerd at you if you knew me your answer was you did not he asked if I knew you I told him no so we are both strangers to on another but perhaps of no family but in this place of the Kingdom of Fife is none of oure name here but in Gallaway abundance the good character that young man Charles Loch gave me of you made me presume to give you the trouble of this and a ship lying at Anstruther bund to the pleas wher you are as he told me if I pleased to wreat he wold get it to you so I have wroate on adventor. Sir I hear you went away from your native countrie very young so I hope you will returnen to the honor of it againe which I long wish for I shall live in the good hopes to see you but my time cannot be long here for I am old, I think by what I hear you are a right Hannay for all I knew of them ther word wold ben taken sooner then ane others bond I heard but four days agoe you see I doo not stand on cerimonies, but semes you doo if you please favour me with a line from you and will take it very kindly pray give my humble duty to your lady on aquanted I hope you wil pardon this freedom but name goes a great length with me."

William received this letter when he was at Danzig on October 20, 1731 and wrote directly back to her giving as she requested an account of his family. A detailed account of the family is given in Chapter XI: The Hannays of Kelso, but suffice it to say here that William was the great grandson of David Hannay, a brother of Patrick Hannay of Kirkdale. After his father, also named William, had left Kelso in a rather precipitate manner about 1690 owing to, as it is so nicely put, "a political offence", he fled to Northumberland for shelter to the little village of Bothal near Morpeth. William left home when about fourteen and was apprenticed to sea. In the letter "Three gentlemen that have provided for me in the station I am now in" are referred to. Who they were we do not know. No doubt they were influential friends of William's father in Edinburgh, who succeeded in getting him set up as a sailor. By 1732 he was Master of a ship, the *Adriatick*. His first letter to Ann reads as follows:

"Honoured madam,

Yesterday, I had the honor of receiving your most esteemed lines of the 15th ult[229] under cover of Mr. Charles Loch. I am very much obliged to your Ladyship, for the notice you have taken of me and the trouble you have given yourself to write to me, who am unworthy of any esteem.

I confess Madam I came out of my native country very young. I was born at Kelso, on the south of Scotland at which place was an estate formerly beloning to our family but now in the hands of the

---

[229] past, i.e., of the previous month.

Duke of Roxburgh and as far as I am told unjustly detained, our family lived at Kelso a great many years and I think there is none left except three brothers of us and one sister, my father being by misfortune obliged to move into Northumberland and there dyed about two years agoe at Eighty nine years of age. His name was William and my grandfather's name David; my grandfather was one of the family of the Grays. This madam is all the account I can give at present of my family and self, except that they were always remarkable for their great honesty and other virtues the name was always endowed with..."

He wrote again on October 14, following up his first letter as indeed Ann had done to him sending out a copy of her seal of which he says: "the impression of the seal came safe and I believe is the same or near what I had formerly seen in our family." He goes on to say he has met "with several in my travels, whose name ends with an *a*, but none with *ay*, as myne does, except your Ladyships."

He was at sea at the time of his receipt of Ann's first letter, or, as he says:

"If I had been honored with your ladyships letter sooner, if I had time to write my owner in London for leave, then should have left the ship with my brother, who is my first mate to proceed the voyage and then, my wife and selfe by this opportunity would have had the honor to wait on your ladyship."

He goes on to say that he has sent:

"to your ladyships acceptance, myne and my wifes pictures, newly drawn, att fourty two years each, with six bottles of Tockay hungaria wine, and two halfe pounds of picobohea tea, they were put aboard Capt Alexander Reed, to be delivered to Mr Charles Loch who is desired to forward them to your Ladyship ..."

Ann replied to him on November 16, 1731 saying "Pray forgive me for not writing sooner" and signing herself "your cousin and very humble servant." The letter which follows makes mention of the troubles she was having with her neighbours, in regard to the "coal sinks" on the Kingsmuir estate (Captain William Hannay wrote on the bottom of the letter "I am sorry you have such wicked people to deal with but hopes you will overcome them.") :

"Sir,

I receaved yours of the 5th instant a most creasten and kind letter what I heard of you and what you wreat makes me admier you and everyone who knows you will estiem you and regard you, I read yours with pleasur. I am fond to hear you and your Lady are in good health I coming from the countrie to the citie cached cold and has ben a littel indisposed but now am better that made me be so long a time in returning yours I hope you will forgive me.

172

Sir, I think all should notice such a wirthie person as you ar to lay yourself out to serve the nedie there is few of such good dispision but you are lick to the families you are come of for all I know a them are tenderhearted simpathising with every ons condition. Sir, your good behaveour shews what ansient families you are come of you have gone from your native countrie very young and the Lord has preserved and winderfully provided for you which is more to your honor then you had been left ten thousand a year for many of our youth is left good fertons and deboches themselves and breings them to miserie.

I hope the Lord will hear your prayer and myne and bles your endevours god grant you a prosperous voige to Spaine and a safe retouren to your Ladyfriends and releytions which I will mightily long for. Sir I am very weel pleased of the acompt you give of your familie for you chief Sir Robert Hannay of Sorbie was just so treat and I think it is inherent in the name. For I am mutch oprest by all the heritors about the Kingsmuir as anybody can be but I will give non to them I have left all of them somened before the Lords for I plede only justice and I hope I will defet them all this winter it has ben along plie. I think you ar very much in the right in livieng of that troublesome way of life since it has pleased God to provide so largely for you and devote yourself to god is a good thought you and your Lady ar both young I am told but hop in got to see you here which all I desayer you have past a very prettie compliement on me as your picktors which I will be very proud of when come to hand you wreat they ar to come with Captain Alexander Reed and I know not what port he comes to that I may inquayer for them if it please god to send you to your oune netive countrie, I will let you see some of our Familie pictures and several of litel dun by my brothers own hand I intend to give your Lady the trouble but I know not the direcktion but however I will wreat. Direck your letter thus to me, to the Lady Kingsmuir att her lodging in Givens land in the Lawnmarket, Edinburgh."

It appears from this letter that Ann's brother Robert Hannay was something of an artist. These pictures unfortunately now cannot be traced and seem to have completely disappeared.

The presents sent by William duly arrived and Ann wrote again to him on February 24, 1732, addressing him as the "Commander of the *New Granada*, Frigatt, and in his absence to his Lady to the care of Mr Gibson and Mr Hage both factors in Danzig."

She refers again to the matter of the "coal sinks" where things seemed to have improved, for she says that: "I think a litel time will end it now." Apparently her brother Robert had some trouble with this matter earlier as is shown in this extract from the case before the Lords of Session in 1729:

"... By which ordinance of your Lords the said John Corstorphine knowing that he himself is expressly forbidden from any further encroachments of that kind hath sold the said piece of ground adjoint and marching with my lands of Kingsmuir and ... whereof he pretended the said priviledge to the said John Loch who of purpose to erect a new vexarion and trouble to me as his predessor did to my said brother does just now set down this his coal sink near the very same spot where the said John Corstorphine had put down his discharged sink ..."

Then correspondence proceeds on an even more cordial basis. In September 1732, Captain William Hannay returns safely from the Spanish expedition to Oran, in which his ship had been employed as a transport. Ann also, at this time, opens a correspondence with Mary Hathaway Hannay, William's wife. Sending her the coat of arms of the Hannays she says:

"I this return that I am joyfull and heartily weel pleased of having the pleasure and satisfaction of send the coat armorial of the once Honourable and antient family of Sorbie unto one of our name worthy by merites, and in all respects knowingly accomplished to use and wear the arms of the family and when I consider of the large and good character I have of my good friend and namesake from all who have had the honour of his acquaintance."

Her views on the General Assembly are attached at the bottom of the letter and read: "I give you a littel pise of news our General Assembly is to sit the fourth of May wher they think will be a great deal of confusion at it."

Ann soon became very fond of William, and asked him and Mary to stay in Edinburgh with her during the Spring. William went off on a voyage to Lisbon, Cadiz and Italy in February 1733, and was thus unable to do so. He, however, returned to England in the following year and visited Kingsmuir.

William's views on religion, particularly that of Spain, are interesting:

"I cannot forbear giving your Ladyship a smale acct of the naturall temper of these people with their blind and ignorant zeal for the Romish Religion their actions and manners seem to me a piece with the Scribes, pharasies and hypicrites against whom our Saviour denounced soo many woes I shall only instance one in particular touching their compassing sea and land to make one prosolite and the Gospell expresses they make them ten times more the child of the devil an example we have lately had here, please do observe we have here a Roman Catholick English College the members of which takes great deal of paines to make new christeans of our drunken sailors who very often are prevailed with when they have spent their money to incourage them they keep them in the College for a month to instruct them, gives them a new suit of clothes and

174

some money and then dismisses them, the fathers take great care how many new christians they have made of heriticks. About eight dayes agoe for or five of these new Irish and English converts their money beng spent were guilty of robbery and murder and are noe in prision and will be executed soe you see Madam that the Romish Religion has made those was bad before, to be worse.

Their auricular confession with the priests, absolution gives them the loose of conscience cannot check as because they think it is only confess and the priests pardons."

William was clearly a religious man, as in a later letter, he has this to say:

"I have often reflected on the disadvantages we seafaring people labor under to those that has the happiness to be fext in their native country, we have few examples of piety, no churches to frequent in these parts, but such as are contradictory to our faith, and even those we converse with in the same condition of life (if they do think) seems to think religion only a name and lives without fear of God in this world, notwithstanding the many awakening, and those snatches of holy violence from the very brinks of destruction which we often must meet are such examples of mercy that ought to awaken the most stupid. I pray God I may in time withdraw from such a way of living, and from such conversation to take up my staff of rest and end my days in the land I received my first breath."

By October 1733, Mary was living permanently at Kingsmuir with Ann, their visit having been a great success. William returned to the sea and in a short letter to Ann –on the reverse is one to his wife – he writes from Lisbon, saying:

"I arrived at this port in safety the 6th instant and in my passage was chased by a Salle[230] pryate [pirate] who fired severall shot but fell short, and bless God we out sailed him and got clear in two hours time. They have taken several English ships, some of them has been retaken by the portugeese and brought to this port. I have orders to provide this ship with guns and fit for defence, but our greatest benefit is we have a good pair of heels."

And in his letter to his wife on the reverse the following:

"I am going to put in ten guns into the ship. and fix her for defence but am not afraid since the ship sailes exceeding well."

---

[230] The Salle Rovers were Moroccan pirates in the 17th century. Since they were long gone by the 18th century, William may be using the phrase as a term for pirates in general.

A rather attractive little postscript is added. "The carpenter is well; remember him to his wife." One wonders where he lived – perhaps on the estate at Kingsmuir.

A year later, in September 1734, he again is in trouble at sea, presumably from a serious storm. He writes from the Downs to say:

> "I wrote twice to my wife from hence but none to your Ladyship, I hope you'll pardon me. My time has been throughly taken up in providing what was necessary and am now getting up anchor for sea soe begs you'll pardon me both the shortness of this letter and the manner in which it is wrote.
>
> It was a mellancolly condition I was in on Sunday ye 27th last past where God was soe mercifull as to take no more of us away nor suffer more damage to be done than what of us was left with his blessing might extricate ourselves for which my tongue shall never depart his praise, nor my heart most gratefull acknowledgements due to his mercies and goodness."

William's letter to his wife of July 29, 1734 written "off Beachy Head with a fair wind this will be sent ashore at Dover where I hope to be in the afternoon" gives a very accurate picture of his business. His method of address to his, wife "My dear Mally" is a rather pleasant homely touch characteristic of these letters.

> "I have yours of the 27th March last in which you give me all account of the things of Captain William Rowland to whome I am obliged for his care. I had another from you at the same time but without a date forwarded by Mr. Smith both came to me at Gibralter-in the latter you mention letters from my late father. I have here inclosed one of them of the year 1725, I have severall others aboard.
>
> I am now loaded with wine and salt and am concerned a quarter part as last voyage and believes as Dantzig has been besieged will be no place for me, especially to load at, but I expect advyses in the South if not shall try Copenhagen.
>
> Mr Gibbs has given me leave to act as think fit both with the ship and the cargoa but under my own command soe that I can meet any good frieght for England etc shall accept of it.
>
> I have three pounds of Naples soap which I will send you as soon as I can I have a piece' of spanish snuff coulour paradosoi for two suites, and a suit of black. Let me know which you'll have, the former I bought for you and the Lady. I have a fan likewise. Write me directly to Elsinore and cover your letter and direct it to Mr Hans Peterson Merchant in Elsinore because I have lost severall letters directed to me at that place. I shall write you the needful from at that place as I expect you'll write me I shall be able there to give you account how I may proceed.

The war in Danzig has doubtless made those goods scare that I should have bought soe if I go there shall not load on our own account but if any freight offers to England, Scotland, anywhere shall accept if none offers then must go to Norway and load for Lisbon. My duty to the Lady and service to Messers. Loch and Graham I have wrote to Mr William Hog to know if any good freights offers to Spain Portugall or the Medditeranean for such a ship as ours I would come and accept of it. I likewise told him if any of my wines would doe with him I would send him a few pipes.

I bless God we are in good health the carpenter sends his love to his wife. I send myne to you because I am my Dear

your affectionate loving husband

Wm Hannay

July 29th aboard the *Adriatick*."

The final letters in the correspondence are from William to his wife in 1735. Both are short and worth quoting in full:

New York October 25th, 1735.

My Dear,

Six dayes agoe I received your kind letter of the sixth of May last and am glad to see by it you were, and they Lady well, I wrote you last week by way of Lisbon but this by way of London in which I advised you that was dissapointed here and am now ready to sail for Charles Town, S. Carolina where hopes shall load for Holland or London if soe please God shall make it my happiness to see you as soon as possible.

Mr. Gibbs sent me a power of attorney to recover of Peter Bayard and Mr Henry Wileman about two thousand pounds but they are both gone off soc cannot recover anything

which has put us by the schemme designed. My duty to her Ladyship. I wish you both your health and God send us a happy meeting."

And the second one:

CharlesTown, South Carolina
Sunday 7th November 1735

My Dear

I wrote you the last of October at the same time wrote Mr Samuel Smith in case they come not to your dear hands these are to advise you that I shall be loaded in all next week and sail God willing the beginning of next, I am to be loaded with rice for Rotterdam and to call at Cows or Portmouth to unload it and the reload it again for Holland. I shall be glad this might find you in London that I might be the sooner in your dear company if not must bear it with patience. I bless God we are all well at present and hopes the Lady and you enjoys the same blessing. I shall be glad to see her Ladyship and if I can get any frieght from Holland to the Firth shall accept of it ..."

On Lady Ann's advice, William applied to the "Herald Office" in Edinburgh for a grant of arms. One of the letters reads:

"The impression of the seale came safe and I believe is the same or near what I had formerly seen in our family, and have had severall times thought to send to the Heraldry in Scotland for Armes, but bemg a transient person and no correspondance there prevented me, I have desired Mr Loch to get my coat of armes, ingraved and send it me, and ye scutcheon imblazoned, from ye Herald Office."

This was forwarded by the Lord Lyon to Ann, who sent it on with the following remarks:

"that I am joyfull and heartily weel plesed of having the satisfaction of sending the coat armorial of the once honourable and antient family of Hannay."

The arms were collared or Crest a cross crosslet fitchee issuing out a crescent; the motto was "Per ardua ad alta." The grant bears the name Captain William Hannay and the style "Defender of Sorbie." The arms are the same as those of Kingsmuir, and differenced from the Sorbie arms by the lack of a bell pendant gules.

There is one other letter that gives some idea of the doings of polite society in eighteenth century Scotland, and here is part of it:

"I have received ... the sex bottles of Tockay hungaria wine and two half pounds of picobohea tea the best of our qualitie in this kingdom hes, both drunk of your fine wine and tea and we have ben very mery with it and drounk your health and your Ladys very heartily. Such wine as this comes seldom to this kingdom so it is prayessed such a fine thing the Ladys ar fond to test it becas they have heard of it but never sae it. A lady of very great qualitie told me she had been at the greatest entertainments, in Scotland but never tasted Tockay wine she has heard of the taste of it that it had a sharpnes and a fineness in it. The lady wold not let me say it was Tockay becas it was such fine wine ther were several! other Ladyes, by, well Madam seeing is believing and testing to, so I will both let your La; see it and test it I will knoe it so soon as I test it so when her La; tested it she sade it is indeed Tockay they were all fond of it ..."

William was married on April 17, 1712 to Mary Hathaway at All Hallows, Barking Church in the City of London. They had numerous children, all of whom died in infancy. The only names that have come down to us are from the Rotherhithe Parish Register. These are a "stillborne" on August 11, 1722, William buried on November 9, 1718 "two days old," and George, baptized on August 12, 1722. Ann refers to this in one of her letters:

> "I think your Lady hapie in such a comfortable husband and you in such a loving and good and kind wife the Lord bles you both and bles you with mo cheldren ther is non of you so old but hops of more which I pray God grant you them and make the name stronger."

Captain William's company was based on the river Thames. William took his brother to sea with him as his first mate, and eventually as a result of William's training, he became a captain for William's owners, Messrs Gibbs and Clay. It also appears that his nephew William was also at sea; the captain took him on as an apprentice, a story which is more fully told in Chapter XI: The Hannays of Kelso.

Ann died in 1736, and in her will she left the estate to William and his heirs male. In the event William had no heirs and the property passed to the second substitute in her entail. The will was drawn up in 1734 and proved in 1747.

William retired from the sea in 1736 and settled down as the Laird of Kingsmuir, as he had so long wished to do. And no doubt he spent his declining years in comfort, and the company of his beloved Mally. In 1743 he died, still not an old man and left his whole personal estate to his wife, the estate passing to James Hannay, as noted in Chapter IX: The Hannays of Kingsmuir.

Mary lived on at Kingsmuir, with life rent of one third of the property, till her death in 1776. Her will was proved on May 26, 1777, and some extracts of interest are reproduced here:

> "to Edmund Hannay [her nephew] ... sixty pounds sterling, the said Captain William Hannay's diamond ring, two pictures [Perhaps these were the pictures given to Ann so many years before] and to his wife a Damask orange colloured suit of clothes...to Margaret Hannay [her niece], daughter of the said David Hannay [another brother-in-law] her heirs and assigns Thirty pounds sterling. To Dorethy Hannay [her sister-in-law]'s children thirty pounds sterling."

To Janet Dickson, probably one of her servants, she left:

> "Ten pounds sterling, a blue and orange silk sluff gown, a white twilled pettycoat, a copper pot two copper saucepans an oval cedar table a cask with iron hoops lid and padlock six hard metal pewter trenchers never used, six china soup trenchers, two pewter plates, and six pounds to buy mourning."

To her servant Janet Gardiner she also left most generously including "a little oval table standing in the kitchen" and the spinning wheel, amongst other things.

So, we come to the end of the story of three rather charming people to whom the name of Hannay meant so much.

# XI: The Hannays of Kelso

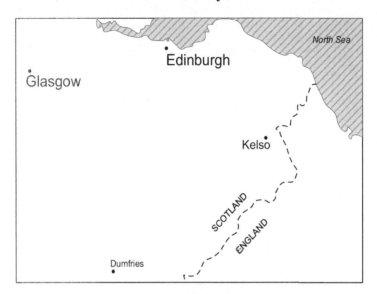

**Figure 46: Kelso**

This branch of the family, of which the author Stewart Francis was representative, has partly been discussed in the chapter on William and Ann Hannay of Kingsmuir.

The family breaks off from the Kirkdale line in 1628 with David Hannay , the brother of Patrick Hannay of Kirkdale. David was employed in Ireland as a civil servant and has been fully dealt with elsewhere in the chapters on Kirkdale and Sir Robert Hannay. David Hannay had a son, David Hannay of Kelso.

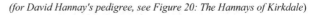

*(for David Hannay's pedigree, see Figure 20: The Hannays of Kirkdale)*

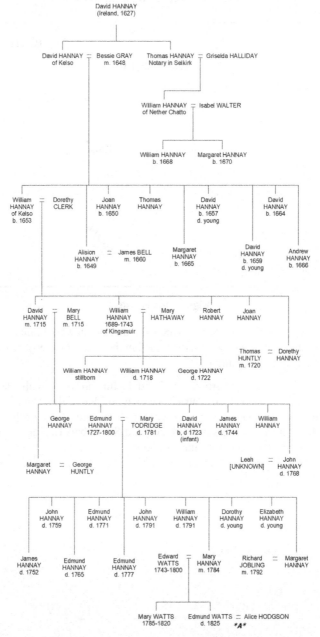

*A*: See Figure 49

**Figure 47: The Hannays of Kelso**

182

## 1. *David Hannay of Kelso (1630? – 1700?)*

David Hannay, who, according to Captain William Hannay (of Kingsmuir), bore the motto "Per Ardua ad Alta," lived in Kelso where he had a civil service appointment as "comditorensi"[231] which can be translated in several ways–Laing[232] puts it as a jailor. It more correctly means keeper. It is probably a similar thing to the Kingsmuir family's appointment of "Keeper of the Mora." He is a witness to a charter by Alexander Ker of Littlesdean in 1667. He was married in 1648 to Bessie Gray, one of the cautioners being Thomas Hannay, probably his brother and a notary in Selkirk, who was the husband of Griselda Halliday. Again, in 1667, David appears as cautioner at the baptism of a John Liermont. He had a large family: William, who succeeded him to the estate in Kelso, born in 1653; Thomas, born in 1663; three Davids, the first two dying young; Andrew, born in 1666; Margaret; Joan; and Alision. There was an Alision Hannay married to James Bell in 1660; she was probably David's sister.

In 1684, the Test Act was rigorously applied to the South of Scotland, with the object of diverting all Covenanters from their religion to the approved form of the Church of Scotland. The result was a scar that perhaps has not yet been quite removed from Scottish hearts – the "Killing Times." Galloway and the Borders were racked with dissention. Robert Grierson, 1st Baronet of Lag (aka "Cruel Lag") and John Graham of Claverhouse, 1st Viscount Dundee (aka "Bluidy Dundee" or "Bonnie Dundee"), both known for their persecution of Covenanters, ranged to and fro, shooting or arresting all who would not take the Test. The Kelso Hannays were concerned in this. They included David of Kelso's nephew William of Nether Chatto (near Kelso), John of Traquair, John and James in Ryslaw in Fogo Parish in Roxburghshire, William of Foulaw and William of Tundergarth.

David Hannay's son, William Hannay of Kelso, himself was concerned, and whether he was arrested or not it is impossible to say, although it is considered extremely likely that he was one of the Williams mentioned, probably as "William Hannay from the Borders, of England." He certainly however had to leave Kelso on account of some "political offence." He fled to Bothal in Northumberland, near to Morpeth, whence the Kingsmuir Hannays came. The estate near Kelso was purloined by the Duke of Roxburgh, and as far as is known, is in

---

[231] This is assuredly a typographical error. It is unsure what Stewart meant when he wrote this. Perhaps "conditorens" (founder/creator)? The source document of this phrase is unknown.

[232] David Laing, F.R.S., 1793-1838, wrote many articles and books. It is unclear which one is the source of this definition.

his hands today. As noted in the previous chapter, Captain William Hannay referred to it as being "unjustly detained."

## 1.1. William of Tundergarth and his Bible

The bible of William of Tundergarth currently resides in the National Museum of Scotland, in Edinburgh, on loan from the Hannay family. He had to abandon it while fleeing from government forces. When later retrieving it, he discovered it had been damaged by a sword thrust, as seen in Figure 48). The bible's first proprietor was John Hannay of Sorbie, MP for Wigtown (d. 1604), who acquired it in 1579. The book was passed on down through the Hannay generations. Its front pages and margins record births, marriages and deaths of the Morpeth branch of the family over the course of four centuries.

**Figure 48 – The Bible of William Hannay of Tundergarth**

## 1.2. William Hannay of Nether Chatto

William of Nether Chatto, who was probably a son of Thomas of Selkirk (and thus a nephew of David Hannay of Kelso), married Isabel Walter. They had a son, William, and a daughter, Margaret. He was cited to appear at Jedburgh to take the Test, along with his wife and children, but they failed to appear, no doubt taking to the hills, as did so many Covenanters. He was eventually taken, and in May 1685 when the Test was put to him, refused it. William was brought to Edinburgh with 120 men and 42 women mostly from the Borders, and a further

14 men and 8 women from Dumfries. They were confined in the Tolbooth at Leith. William was one of the 19 men who attempted to escape, and was accordingly brought to Edinburgh for closer confinement. The Tolbooth records on the subject read as follows:

> "30th October 1685, at Edinburgh. The Lords of the Committee of H.M. Privy Council for Public Affairs having received information from the Baillies of Lieth that several of the persons in their prison upon the public account had been attempting to escape and in order thereto had gott instruments and towes carry'd in to them do therefore heirby give order to the Lord Provost of Edinburgh to causs a pairty of the town guard to transport the said prisioners from the Tolbuith of Leith to the Tolbuith of Edinburgh and to causs putt them in the iron houss and in irons till further order."

As a result, he, and his son William were confined for nine days in a dark pit under the prison. Young William, a lad of sixteen, was tortured with the thumbikins (thumbscrews) and loaded with irons. They were confined for a further eighteen months when William the elder was banished to the East New Jersey Plantations. But on August 27, an order came from General Drummond and Graham of Claverhouse, ordering him to be held in prison. On the news of Argyle's invasion, many Covenanters from the South and West, who at different times had been made prisoners for conventicles, were removed from Edinburgh to Dunnottar Castle. The Governor, George Keith of Whiteriggs, ordered them to be confined in a long narrow room which is still to be seen, and is known locally as the "Whigs vault." Whether or not William was finally banished is not certain, although it is, always thought traditionally that he was, for on March 12, 1687, a William Hannay was ordered to be transported. After the Revolution of 1688[233] he is supposed to have returned to England and become a Minister in Scarborough.

The others all suffered similar fates; some being transported. Another William was released, as "an old and decrepit man," little wonder after the treatment he had probably received.

## 2. *William Hannay of Kelso (b. 1653), son of David*

To return to the Kelso family, William of Kelso lived quietly in Bothal, presumably assisted by the Hannays of Morpeth, or on funds he had brought with him. He became the Parish Clerk amongst other activities, and there is an early 18th century Parish Register with the following on the flyleaf in his writing: "bound by William Hannay Sept 10th, 1724."

---

[233] When King James II was deposed.

He was interested in family history, and an extract from Sir Henry A. Ogle's "Ogle and Bothal" says

> "There was on the South wall of the Chancel of Bothal Church a pedigree of the Ogle family but when the Church was cruelly mutilated during the Scotch occupation of Northumberland during the commonwealth it was nearly obliterated, but the best possible copy was made and after the year 1664/5 the new copy in the Additions was placed up. This was copied in 1725 for John Craster, Esquire, and sent to him by the Clerk of Bothall who signed himself William Hannay. This transcript has since been found at Craster Tower by Mr Cadwaller Bates."

William married Dorethy Clerk and had five children, three sons— David, William and Robert – and two daughters – Dorethy (who married Thomas Huntly of Morpeth in 1720) and Joan (born in 1684 and died whilst a child).

Captain William Hannay, born in 1689, his second son, has already been spoken of at length in Chapter X: William and Ann Hannay of Kingsmuir.

Robert, the third son, went to sea as mate to his brother William, and became subsequently a Master in the employ of Messrs. Gibbs and Clay. It is not known when he died, but he cannot have been of great age, and, as far as can be ascertained, was not married.

## 3. David Hannay (m. 1715), son of William of Kelso

David, the eldest son of William of Kelso, remained at Bothal, and subsequently moved to North Blyth Nook, then a quiet stretch of seashore with no hint of the port that is there today, and for whose construction and development his son, Edmund, was largely responsible.

There is a rather delightful entry in the Bothal Parish Register when he married Mary Bell of Wellheads (sometimes known as Bell of Bothal Barns), on "October 13th 1715, the day the rebels entered and lodged in Morpeth." One wonders what happened to the wedding festivities.

David and Mary had five sons—David, James, William, John, and Edmund—and a daughter, Margaret, who married George Huntly of South Blyth, and is mentioned in her brother Edmund's will.

Of the others, David died in infancy, and was buried at Bothal on October 17, 1723. James died at Bothal on April 8, 1744. William and John both lived longer and went to sea, the former with his uncle, Captain William Hannay of Kingsmuir. He apparently started his naval career on his own account, and had met with his uncle Captain William, who applied to his owners and took him as one of his officers, training him in navigation and seamanship. Captain William wrote:

> "I have met my nephew William son of brother David and shall agree with his Master to spare him to me in order to teach him Navigation and qualifie him for a better post he by his Masters character is a good sailor. I will endevour to make the rest he is a sturdy boy and what I find does not want naturall sence which can be improved with some of my direction."

This was written about 1733, and no doubt in time he became a Master of a ship, probably in Captain William's firm. He died unmarried.

John also went to sea and became a Master Mariner. He subsequently settled in America at New Bern, North Carolina. He died there in September 1768 and was outlived by his wife Leah to whom he left his estate. They had no children. His will proved at the County Inferior Court in 1768 before His Majesty's Justices continues after the usual opening as follows:

> "I give and bequeath unto Leah my beloved wife all my whole estate be it of what kind or nature soever within the Province of North Carolina or elsewhere in America to her and her assigns forever.
>
> Item. Wheras, I am entitled to the sum of Forty pounds sterling after the death of my mother in England I do therefore hereby give and bequeath the same to my brother Edmund Hannay's eldest son and his assigns and my will and desire is that if he should die before the death of my said mother that then I give the said .sum of forty pounds to my said brothers next eldest son and if he should die before the said sum be due to the next heir of my brother Edmund Hannay.
>
> Lastly I appoint by beloved wife Leah my whole and sale executrix of this my last will and testament."

## 4. Edmund Hannay (1727-1800), Shipbuilder

Edmund, the fifth son, was the only one to have any children to survive him. He was born in 1727, and it appears that by 1742 or 1743 he was living at Kingsmuir with his uncle Captain William Hannay, learning the shipbuilding business at Leith. He would then have been about 15. He was still there when Bonnie Prince Charlie landed in the West at Moidart in 1745, trying to restore the Stuart line to the British throne during the Jacobite Uprising[234]. That young Edmund joined his forces there is little doubt, for although John Wallace's *History of Blyth from the Norman Conquest to the Present Day* (1869) refers to Edmund's

---

[234] The attempt by Charles Edward Stuart to regain the British throne in 1745.

actions on his return to Bothal rather as if he were sent south on account of the derangement of trade in Scotland, this reason seems most unlikely. If his aim was to avoid any disruption due to the uprising, he would surely have gone from Leith to his aunt in the country at Kingsmuir rather than follow the Prince's army south.

He was quite young when he returned to Northumberland at the end of Uprising in 1746, and found it necessary to secrete himself in the ruins of Bothal Castle. England at this time was full of Scottish refugees from the Prince's army. After being in concealment for some days, he ventured some distance down the River Wansbeck, where he encountered Justice Watson of North Seaton who, thinking him to be a rebel (which he probably was), made an attempt to apprehend him. Edmund fled across the river. The Justice, who was mounted on a pony, attempted to follow him and stuck fast in the mud.

Watson shouted to the fugitive to stop and help him out of the river. Edmund, seeing his pursuer incapable of following him, ceased to flee, and after some parley helped to extricate the horseman. This act won the good opinion of Watson, who, instead of arresting him, helped him to get established. He set him to work to build a boat; his ability as a shipwright pleased Watson, who then employed him to build a sloop. Watson was then a young man, and had for some time begun those commercial enterprises, which he successfully continued for the remainder of his long life. Edmund, however, had an eye towards Blyth, as a rising place and where he would have a fairer prospect of succeeding as a shipbuilder. We find him settled there in 1750. There is no reason to believe that any ships were built in Blyth before the middle of the 18$^{th}$ century. The first person to carry on shipwright's work is a Henry Clarke, who from time to time received certain sums from the Plessy Coal Company for repairing *keels*, the name given to the local small trading craft. In the Raff yard ledger for 1739, Henry Clarke and James Knox, carpenters, each have an account for wood, but to a very trifling amount. In Knox's account are "twelve hand spokes 5/-." In October 1765, there is an entry in the Plessy accounts: "Paid Henry Clark's funeral expenses to his wife Barbara one pound one shilling." Whether this was an act of respect to an old servant, or he had lost his life in their employ by some mischance, does not appear, but we may gather from this fact that his worldly position was not an elevated one. The number of ships then using the port would need the services of Clark and Knox to effect the little repairs that would from time to time be needed, and they may have built craft of the class of the "Woodcock", a small trader, but nothing that deserved the name of a ship. Edmund Hannay was the first person to carry on the trade of shipbuilding in the port. He was in the town in 1750 and we find in August of that year his name in the Custom House as bondsman for the

"Constant Ann," of Scarborough for London, with 79 chaldrons[235] of coals and 3 tons, 13 quarters[236], 13 lbs. of British stripped tobacco stalks. From very small beginnings he rose to considerable eminence as a builder of fine vessels. He continued in business for about 50 years. The vessels he built were highly prized; their seagoing qualities were excellent; the materials used were of the best description; and the workmanship was attended to with the utmost care. One man did all the caulking, another drove down all the treenails (Wooden pegs or dowels), and marvellous were the tales about the length of time some of his crack ships went without needing to be pumped. In some cases, as much as seven years elapsed before they required re-caulking.

Edmund must have acquired wealth very rapidly, as by the year 1780, he was not only the owner of several ships, but had purchased the estate known as Hannay's farm from an old family named Preston, whose property it had been for a very long period.

Edmund had several children, none of whom, save two daughters, survived him.

His wife, Mary, was the daughter of James Todridge of South Blyth; she died in Blyth in 1781; the Newcastle Journal of February that year referring to her as a "gentlewoman greatly respected by all her friends..." Edmund also owned the Cowpen Town farm and a portion of what is now Cowpen High House farm. His building yard was at the end of Low Quay and was flanked by those of Edward Watts and Mark Watson whose yards were situated at the Flanker or mouth of the Gut in the neighbourhood of Cowpen Square. Of the ships owned by Edmund Hannay, two lists from 1700 and 1789 show some of them (A John Hannay was a master of one of them in 1770. Who he was is not known, but he was probably a relative, although as far as one can work out, not from this immediate family):

"**1770**. John and Martha, 61 chaldrons. Mary, 109 chaldrons. Master John Hannay James and Mary, 95 chaldrons. –Master Richard Wheatly.

**1789**. Hope, 116 Chaldrons, Master Mathew Watson Chancellor ,106 Chaldrons. Master William Cillier Holderness 137 Chaldrons, Master William Rusell John 36 Chaldrons, Master William Taylor"

On the death of Mary Hathaway (Captain William Hannay's widow), Edmund, accompanied by his daughter Margaret, went north to Fife,

---

[235] A Newcastle **chaldron** was a measurement of coal equal to **53 imperial hundredweights** (5936 pounds or 2692.5 kilograms)

[236] A **quarter** was a measurement of weight equal to **one quarter of a hundredweight** (112/4 = 28 pounds or 12.7 kilograms)

and as executor settled his aunt's business. During that visit, he, or perhaps more likely his daughter, must have found tucked away in a drawer the letters from Captain William and Ann Hannay of Kingsmuir on which so much of this history has been founded, and indeed the correspondence that sparked off the author's Stewart Francis' enquiries into the family history.

In 1791, Edmund had a very severe blow in the death of first his son William in June and then his other surviving son John in December the same year.

In 1795, the Napoleonic wars were in full swing, and many sailors were needed for the fleet. Mathew White Ridley, a member of Parliament and a friend of Edmund's, wrote to ask his assistance on a committee forming in Newcastle to provide seamen. Ridley's letter follows here as it is considered that not only has its family interest, but it is also of historical value:

Portland Place March 12th, 1795.

Dear Mr Hannay

Mr Milburn forwarded to me your letter of March 1st I think you have in some measure misunderstood the effect of the Bill, it differs materially as I apprehend from the former by two particulars; By the former Bill not only the expense of the men fell on the shipowner, but he was called upon to provide a larger sum of seamen than this demands, the men to be provided by the Port of Newcastle although somewhat increased in number are to be understood not as actual seamen, but as landsmen, I hope also that a clause may be received in the Bill, to count one seaman equal to two of these men wherby the number will be considerably reduc'd. The Bounty you will also observe is to be from the revenue from the Government and not as, in the former Bill by the shipowner; your exertions are required to procure these men, the necessity of which I am afraid you are too sensible of. From the situation of the coast between Hartley and Blyth that spot is thought to be particularly liable to attack, you and your neighbours will not be surprised therefore at the preparations made for the defence there, Captain Shand who has been sent down to inspect the coast will be at Blyth and may probably suggest something in which the inhabitants may afford him as instance which I doubt not but you will all readily do. The Ballot for seamen, it was thought (although much approved by the Government) would not be sufficiently efficatious but may hereinafter be resorted to. The idea of limiting the wages has been talked of and will be attended to I believe, with proper security in future to the apprentices and three years servants, Governments are aware I believe, how much the service has suffered by the violation of their protections,

I am, Mr Hannay, your most obedt Servant

Mathew White Ridley.

PS. As the trade of the Port of Newcastle will be called together as soon as the Bill is, passed, I hope yourself and the others concerned at Blyth will attend the meeting, probably committees will be appointed at Blyth, Hartley etc in this business I trust and hope you will take an active part."

Edmund was active right up to his death in 1800 at the age of 73 and much engaged in the Local Shipping Committees in Blyth and Newcastle.

Edmund Hannay's eldest daughter Mary married Edward Watts of Blyth at Earsden, on May 16, 1784. They had two children, Edmund and Mary, baptized at Earsden on October 10, 1784 and October 24, 1784, respectively. Mary died at the age of 66 on 15th April 1820 at Malvin's Close, the Blyth estate which Edmund Hannay had purchased in 1780.

Edmund Hannay's second daughter, Margaret, married Richard Jobling of Newton Hall, Northumberland in 1792. Jobling was a wine merchant in Newcastle and a Deputy Lieutenant of the County. She wrote a brief account of the family, which was referred to in Edmund Watts' claim to the Baronetcy of Mochrum as "Mrs. Jobling's Letter." It in fact gives very little information that is not in the letters of Captain William and Ann Hannay of Kingsmuir.

*For pedigree of Edmund Watts (d. 1825), see Figure 47: The Hannays of Kelso*

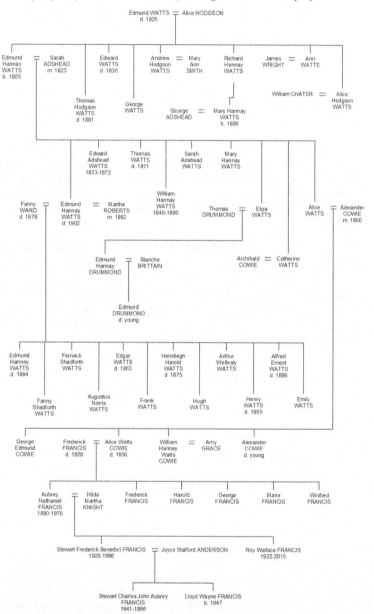

**Figure 49: The Watts Family**

## 4.1. Edmund Watts (born 1784)

Edmund Watts succeeded his grandfather Edmund Hannay in the shipbuilding business. Edmund was baptized at Earsden on October 10, 1784. He continued to expand the Hannay Watts shipping and coal interests in Blyth.

He married in 1804, at Horton, Alice the eldest daughter of Richard Hodgson of Cowpen and Bedlington, by his wife the daughter of Andrew Watson, the justice of North Seaton who, decades earlier, had gotten stuck in the mud and had been rescued by Edmund's grandfather. Her nephew John Crawford Hodgson was a celebrated Northumbrian Historian and author of the Northumberland Volume of the Victoria County History and several other works, and also sometime honorary librarian to the Duke of Northumberland. He carried out much research into the family history, and in fact produced the tree that led to the compilation of this work.

Edmund and Alice had six sons and three daughters:

- Edmund Hannay Watts, born in 1805, who succeeded his father;

- Thomas Hodgson Watts, who died in 1881 without children and was a doctor of some note in his day, studying in Paris, Vienna, Padua, London and Edinburgh and finally practising with much success in Manchester;

- Edward, who went to sea as mate in one of the Watts ships, and who was drowned in 1836, aged only 26;

- George, who migrated to London and died without children;

- Andrew Hodgson Watts, who married Mary Ann Smith of Whitby and had a numerous family;

- Richard Hannay Watts, whose daughter Mary Hannay Watts (1806-1867) married a Mr. Adshead of Stalybridge, Cheshire, a cotton spinner. Benjamin Disraeli in one of his novels used Mary as the pattern for his Mrs. G. O. A. Head;

- Ann, who married James Wright of South Blyth of a firm of timber merchants and importers who had supplied most of the timber to the Hannay and Watts shipyards, and who are still in business in Blyth today;

- Alice Hodgson Watts, who married a Newcastle attorney, William Chater and died in 1846 without children.

## 4.2. Edmund Hannay Watts of Cowpen (b. 1805)

Edmund was succeeded by his son Edmund Hannay Watts of Cowpen. He nearly met his death when only a few weeks old by a chimney being blown down which fell and broke over his cot which was standing in the garden of the house. Edmund was mercifully unhurt.

In 1823 he married Sarah, the youngest daughter of Edward Adshead of Stalybridge, Cheshire. He continued with the shipyards and particularly with the ownership of vessels trading in coal. Towards, the end of his life his activities shifted to South Wales, although he continued to live at Malvin's Close and operate his business interests there.

In 1822 he attempted to claim the Baronetcy of Mochrum. On what title it is not clear, and he certainly had little or no right to it.[237] In 1877, Malvin's Close was sold and the family moved to South Wales whither their shipping interests had shifted.

He had four sons and five daughters:

- Edmund Hannay Watts who succeeded his father;

- Edward Adshead Watts born in 1833, a Master Mariner, who was drowned at Montreal, unmarried, on 16th July 1872;

- Thomas, also a Master Mariner and a bachelor, who was drowned the previous year, 1871;

- William Hannay Watts, born in 1846. was resident in Galatz and died in Cairo in 1890. He married Isabella the daughter of Gilbert Ward, a surgeon in Blyth, and had a daughter who died unmarried.

- Mary Hannay Watts, who married the Reverend Thomas Clifton;

- Sarah Adshead Watts, who married James Gibson, a nail and chain manufacturer in Bedlington;

- Eliza, who was married to Thomas Drummond a Master Mariner, part owner of a ship trading with Spain and Portugal, and a descendant of the Duke of Perth who served with the Prince at Culloden; he was a master mariner. They had one son Edmund Hannay Drummond who married Blanche

---

[237] In the 1ˢᵗ through 3ʳᵈ editions, Stewart Francis stated "A large number of letters to his solicitors are in existence, and have been published in my other volume of notes, where they can be consulted." Unfortunately, this volume has not been found. It may never have been published.

Brittain, the daughter of Captain Brittain. His only son died in 1900 from appendicitis. There are still a few Drummonds in Houghton le Spring.

- Catherine, who married Archibald Cowie of Airdrie, Lanarkshire.

- Alice, who, at her sister Catherine's wedding, set eyes on Alexander Cowie, her brother-in-law Archibald's younger brother and an extremely handsome man. In October 1860, she married him. Both brothers were ironmasters in Airdrie and Coatbridge. They lived at Hall Craig, Airdrie. The author Stewart Francis is Alice and Alexander's descendant.

### 4.3. Edmund Hannay Watts, Jr (1830-1902)

E. H. Watts, Junior, as he was called, lived both in South Wales and later at Devonhirst, Chiswick, and became the director of a very large shipping concern with many other ramifications. He was director and owner of the Old Black Vane Colliery in Monmouthshire, and the Watts Ward Shipping Company, whose main business was the shipping of coal from South Wales to London and abroad. He was also a director of the National Steam Coal Company, The London South West Coal Company and the Abercairn Coal Company. The Watts Ward Shipping Company had offices in Barry, Newcastle, Blyth, Paris, Newport, Nantes, Genoa, Savona, Milan, Barcelona, Cardiff and London.

E. H. Watts, Junior was a Justice of the Peace for Monmouthshire, and a member of the Committee of Lloyds. He married twice, firstly Fanny Ward, the daughter of Fenwick John Shadforth of Overdinsdale in May 1856; she died in 1878 leaving him nine sons and two daughters. Secondly he married Martha Roberts of Paris, a daughter of Joseph Roberts of Falmouth, Jamaica, in 1882.

His and Fanny's children were as follows:

- Edmund Hannay Watts married, in 1889, Francis Lillian, the daughter of Thomas Jones Price of Greenway, Neath. They had two daughters, Irene Hannay Watts and Edna Hannay Watts. He lived in Newport Friars in Monmouth and was a partner in his father's shipping concerns. He died in 1894, six years before his father. Irene Hannay Watts married W. T. L. Becker; they had two daughters and resided at Eccleston Square in London.

- Fanny Shadforth Watts who married Colonel James Williams of Bryn Glas, Newport, and whom the author Stewart Francis' father visited frequently as a child. The old house is now a children's home.

- Emily married William Munro, M.A., sometime incumbent of All Saints, Newport.

- Sir Fenwick Shadforth Watts, who was born in 1858, and the only robust member of a very large family. Sir Fenwick entered the Watts Ward Shipping Company and during the 1914 War became Controller of Shipping for the Board of Trade, for which service he was made a Knight Bachelor in 1919. He also at various times served as Chairman of the Shipping Federation, as President of the Chamber of Shipping for the United Kingdom and Principal Representative of the ship owners on the National Maritime Board. In 1901 he bought the old Norfolk County School at Elmham, renovated it, and handed it over to the Dr. Barnado's Homes charity, which ran it as the Watts Naval School, a home for up to 300 orphans and destitute boys until 1953. Sir Fenwick married Julia, the daughter of A. T. McGovern of the 52$^{nd}$ Foot[238], and died without children on April 25, 1926.

- Augustus Norris, Edgar, Frank, Hensliegh Harold, Hugh, Arthur Wellesly, Alfred Ernest, and Henry Watts. Of these only Henry Watts of Newport lived to any reasonable age, and he only to 34, and none of them married.

## 4.4. Alice Watts

Alice Watts, the sister of E.H. Watts Jr, married Alexander Cowie in 1860 and had three children. Unfortunately, she found her husband Alexander's drinking habits not to her liking. It must have been six of one and half a dozen of the other, as he was a jolly type, perhaps a little too addicted to the bottle, and she, at this time perhaps, a bit of a prig. However, one night she decided to return to her family at Malvin's Close in Northumberland. Leaving in her coach, with her three children, she crossed the border at Carter Bar.

Alexander on his return finding she had gone, gave chase and came in sight of them when they were just on the English side of the border. This was too much for him; he refused to cross the border and rode reluctantly home. Finally he went to Canada, and Alice moved to London, after Malvin's Close had been sold. She behaved extremely

---

[238] A light infantry regiment of the British Army from 1755-1881. Saw action in the American War of Independence, India and the Napoleonic Wars.

badly with her coachman, the result being Eddie, who at one time was employed as tutor to the author Stewart Francis' father.

Alexander and Alice's children were George Edmund, William and Alice.

George Edmund was born in November 1861. He was a Bachelor of Arts and a Doctor of Medicine, in fact a man who took degrees for the fun of it, and never put them to useful purpose. After a short stay in Watts Ward and Co., he became theatrical agent for his brother William. George Edmund never married.

William, known on the stage as Leonard Rayne, went to South Africa, where just before the South African War he owned most of the theatres and became an impresario of note. He married and had a son William, regrettably known to the family as "Little Willie," who died without any claim to fame but a capacity for hard liquor difficult to surpass.

## 4.5. Alice Watts Cowie

Eliza Watts Drummond and E. H. Watts, Jr, took charge of their niece, Alice and Alexander's daughter Alice Watts Cowie, who subsequently married Frederick Francis, the son of Nathaniel Draper Francis, a family of Huguenot extraction. On her wedding day Alice received a letter from her father, written six years previously and withheld by her mother, asking Alice to come and join him in the United States and speaking of her portion of the inheritance. Her father's address at the time of writing was Providence, Pennsylvania.. This story reads like a Victorian melodrama, which is precisely what it was.

Alice and Frederick had four sons and two daughters: Aubrey Nathaniel, Frederick, Harold, George, Marie and Winifred. Aubrey Nathaniel was the eldest. Frederick married Eva Stapleton and was an experimental chemist for Caribonum Ltd; they in turn had a son Derek. Harold married Mary of St. John, New Brunswick and settled in Canada before World War I, serving during it in the Canadian Forces; they had three children, Ernest, Clifford and Winifred, and resided in Fredericton, New Brunswick. George, the fourth son, died as a child. Marie married Arthur Hill, an official of the Civil Service; they had a daughter Christine in Canada. The other daughter, Winifred, married Andrew P. Currie, lately of Glasgow, and had one daughter Anne, who married Eric Gittins of London, an estate agent for the Duke of Westminster; they resided in Eccleston Square and had a son Christopher, born in 1957.

Alice Cowie died in 1936 on her way back from visiting Harold in Canada. Her husband Frederick died in 1928.

197

## 4.6. Aubrey Francis (1890-1976)

Aubrey Nathaniel, their eldest son, was born in 1890 and educated at Merchant Taylors School. He entered the family business of N. D. Francis and Sons of which he remained a director until its demise in 1948, when it was sold out to Hudson's Ltd. In 1914 he enlisted in the Public Schools Battalion of the Middlesex Regiment. and, in September 1914 was commissioned as a second lieutenant in the South Lancashire Regiment. He served with the 9th Battalion in France and Macedonia, ending the war after the second Battle of Doiran commanding his battalion. Of his military exploits in the First World War, there are two worthy of note. The first concerns a spy catching and is fully reported in Lesley Ingram Crawford's 1929 book on the Salonika Campaign, *On the Anvil*. Secondly he commanded a composite mounted regiment made up from transport drivers of the 22nd Division, which advanced from Salonica to the Tatalja Forts on the Bosporus. whilst the rest of the Black Sea Army went to Constantinople by sea. Strangely, his son, the author Stewart Francis, commanded a similarly constituted squadron at the end of the 1945 War, when he marched from the River Po in Italy to Austria. After leaving the regular army in 1922, Aubrey Nathaniel joined the 10th London Regiment, subsequently a Territorial Battalion of the Royal Berkshire Regiment (5th Hackney Battalion), a liaison for which he was entirely responsible. He commanded both the 10th London and the 5th Royal Berkshires, retiring in 1938, only to be recalled in April 1939 to raise the 7th (Stoke Newington) Battalion, The Royal Berkshire Regiment until 1940. He was then transferred, on account of his age, to the command of 33 Group, Royal Pioneer Corps[239] and in 1941 was sent to raise the first Group No. 53 of the East African Pioneer Corps in Kenya. This he took to Egypt, taking part in the Battle of Alam el Halfa, (September 30 – August 5, 1942), part of the Western Desert Campaign between Montgomery and Rommel. Aubrey Nathaniel was in command of a composite force, when he was wounded, aged 53. Later that year he returned to England and after a short period in command of a Group at Shrewsbury, was appointed Deputy Director of Pioneer and Labour at Western Command, as a full Colonel, retiring in 1946 on account of ill health.

He was a founder member of the Boy Scout Movement and raised the 2nd North London Group (1st London Caledonians) in 1908. He became a District Commissioner for Scouts in London. Of his other interests, he was President of the Suffolk Congregational Union of 1955 and was Convener for Men's Work for the Congregational Union of England

---

[239] British Army light engineering corps that became part of the Royal Logistics Corps in the 1990s.

and Wales and was elected International President of Men's Work whilst at the Congregational Conference in Hartford, U.S.A., in 1958.

He was appointed an O.B.E. in 1938, received the Territorial Decoration and became a Deputy Lieutenant for the County of London and a Justice of the Peace.

He married, on April 6, 1918, Hilda Martha, the daughter of Charles Frederick Knight of London, and had two sons, Stewart Frederick Benedict and Roy Wallace, born in 1920 and 1922 respectively.

## 4.7. Stewart Francis (1920-1996)

Stewart Frederick Benedict Francis, the primary author of this book, was born in 1920. He was educated at Forest School and entered the 5th Battalion, the Royal Berkshire Regiment in 1938, later serving in the 7th Battalion, and during World War II at Headquarters, 78th Division, on the General Staff and in the 1st Battalion of the East Surrey Regiment in North Africa and Italy, and for a short time as an A.D.C. at General Alexander's Headquarters, and finally in the Greek Army 1947-8. During the war he became a regular officer in the Royal Berkshire Regiment and was mentioned in despatches.

Subsequently he served in the Arab Army of South Arabia and took part in the Radfan and South Arabia campaigns between 1964 and 1967. These campaigns were part of the Aden Emergency, an insurgency which eventually led to the independence of Yemen, in 1967, which had been under British rule since 1839. He finally served as a Lieutenant Colonel in the Zambia Regiments. In 1960 whilst serving in Nigeria he rode two Nigerian polo ponies from Nigeria to England, a journey of 7000 miles. He was a well-known polo player in Nigeria and played for the British Army touring Team in 1966 in Aden. He was a Fellow of the Royal Society of Arts.

In 1941 he married Joyce Stafford Anderson, the only daughter of John Allan Anderson, late of Gubeon, Morpeth in County Northumberland, the early seat of this branch of the family. They had two sons, Stewart Charles John Aubrey and Lloyd Wayne, born in 1943 and 1947 respectively. Stewart Charles was educated at Oundle School and became a solicitor. Lloyd was at the University of Ulster and became a Territorial officer in the Royal Artillery.

Until his death in June, 1996, Stewart Francis resided at Armathwaite Castle in Cumberland.

# XII: The Hannays of Grennan

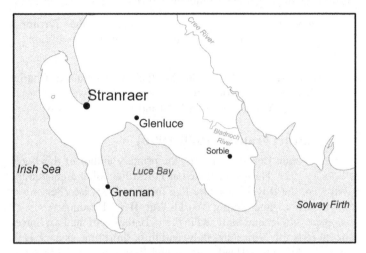

**Figure 50: Grennan**

The property of Grennan in the parish of Glenluce was little more than a good sized farm, with a fair amount of land attached to it, lying on the high ground just above Luce Bay. But by all standards it was a pleasant and satisfactory little estate.

## 1. Gilbert Hannay of Grennan

Gilbert Hannay was the second son of John Hannay of Sorbie and Elizabeth Stewart, the daughter of Sir Alexander Stewart of Garlies.

The first mention of Grennan in the family is in 1530, when Gilbert was escheated for £133.6.8d. for the murder of Alan Story, his surety being John Hannay, baillie of Wigtown. Gilbert is described as a fugitive from the law and his lands were granted to John, probably his father, for the duration of his escheat. The entry in the register reads:

> "10th July 1530. Letter to John Hannay Burgess of Wigtown his heirs and assigns the gift of all goods moveable and immovable that pertain to Gilbert Hannay in Grennan and now pertaining to our Sovereign Lord by reason of escheat through the said Gilbert in Grennan fugitive from the law and at the Horn for airt and part of the slaughter of Alan Story granted to John Hannay baillie of Wigtown subject to

amercement [240]of £40 if John does not bring Gilbert to underlay the Law at Dumfries for the said murder."

In 1535 Findlay, one of Gilbert's sons, was granted a remission for his part in the murder.

Gilbert_was a man of great influence in Wigtownshire. He became sheriff of Wigtown in 1546. Gilbert accompanied Gilbert Kennedy, Earl of Cassilis, against Queen Mary of Guise, and with him laid siege to the Castle of St. Andrews (1546-1547). For this action he was again escheated. He however seems to have survived without much apparent loss, as he again appears in a case in 1547 regarding the curacy of Glenluce parish, and the induction of Sir Andrew Sanderson to that appointment.

In 1551 on April 30, Gilbert appears again, with William his son, when they took an action against Findlay Hannay before the Lords, in Council. Findlay was ordered to make certain payments to them.

Gilbert had four sons, William who succeeded to Grennan, Gilbert of Drygollis, Findlay and Andrew in Gass.

---

[240] **amercement**: fine assessed as an alternative to imprisonment.

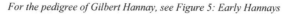

*For the pedigree of Gilbert Hannay, see Figure 5: Early Hannays*

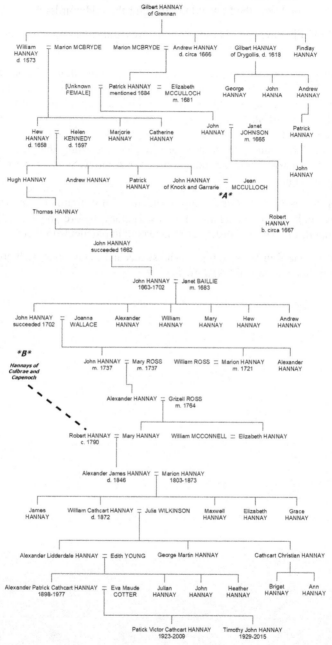

*A*: See Figure 54    *B*: See Figure 8

**Figure 51: The Hannays of Grennan**

202

## 1.1.  Gilbert Hannay of Drygollis (d. 1618)

Gilbert of Drygollis is mentioned in his brother William's will. Of the Drygollis family there is not much to tell. Gilbert was succeeded by his son Andrew who was still infeft of Drygollis[241] in 1618. Andrew seems to have been rather a wild character and was charged before the Presbytery of Wigtown in 1608 with adultery with Marion Clugiston. He did not bother to turn up at the Kirk Session and was excommunicated. George and John in Drygollis, his brothers, appear in William of Grennan's will but we know nothing further of them.

## 1.2.  The Family of Andrew Hannay in Gass

After his brother William's death, Andrew Hannay in Gass married William's widow Marion McBryde. In 1582, John Kennedy (Andrew's nephew Hew Hannay's father-in-law) sued Marion. One suspects without the agreement of "the overman," regarding the lands of Grennan, probably to secure them for their rightful owner, Hew.

Andrew in Gass was granted lifetak of Gass in 1591, the property consisting of three merkland. In 1622 he was arraigned for housebreaking with another Andrew Hannay, the son of a John Hannay of Barlay. They broke into the house of Ucthred McDowell in Edinburgh with twelve other men. This was not an ordinary case of theft, but part of the feuding which was so popular among the Gallovidians of the period and which was frequently carried as far as Edinburgh.

Andrew was succeeded by his son, Patrick in Gass who is mentioned in the Register of Deeds for 1666. Also mentioned in 1681 is she who is obviously Patrick's second wife: "Elizabeth McCulloch, the relict of a ..... McKie." This contract binds Patrick to infeft Elizabeth in "350 merks furth of the lands of Gass" and Elizabeth to bring £100 Scots. In 1665 John Hannay, the son of Patrick Hannay in Gass, married Janet Johnson.

There were several children of this marriage of which the names of David and Andrew only have come down to us. There was a third son whose descendants now hold land still in the immediate area of Old Gass farm.

## 1.3.  Robert (of Gass) and Janet (of Spital)

From this union of two branches of the Hannays, the family now holding the lands and farms of Dirnow and West Culvennan descend. Their family tree is shown in Figure 52: Descendants of Robert Hannay

---

[241] The exact location of Drygollis is unknown.

and Janet Hannay. Robert Hannay of Gass was born in 1742. His connection to the earlier Hannays of Gass is unclear, but Robert married his distant cousin Janet Hannay, daughter of Robert Hannay and Janet McKie. Their son James Hannay had these farms in about 1830. James married Elizabeth Patterson, and their son James married Grace Stewart Morgan. Their son, yet another James, was born in 1836. He married Mary McAvery, and it is thought that he was born at Clugston.

James and Mary had four children:

- James, born 1861, emigrated to Canada and married a French Canadian. They had five son and three daughters. James is buried at Keefers, British Columbia.

- John, born 1863 also emigrated to Canada and later lived in Boise, Idaho. He was unmarried.

- Robert, born 1865, stayed in Scotland and married Mary Hughes. His son, Robert Hannay, farmed Dirnow farm, Kirkcowan. Robert the younger's sons subsequently farmed there: yet another Robert (along with his sister Mary, who lived with him) at High Drumskeog adjoining the Boghouse farm Mochrum; James at Dirnow; and John owned and farmed West Culvennan, the latter two both in Kirkcowan Parish.

- Isabella, born 1868, and who married Robert Stewart.

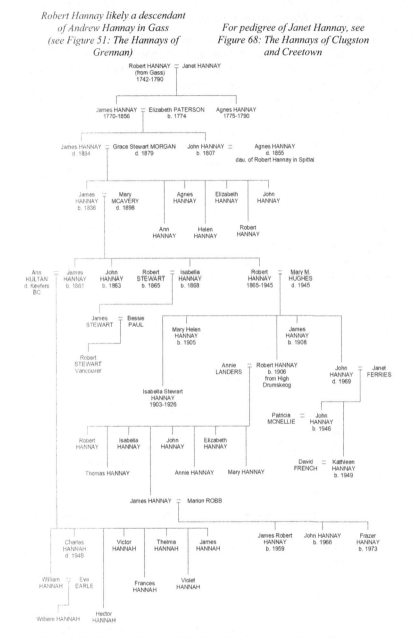

**Figure 52: Descendants of Robert Hannay and Janet Hannay**

## 2. William Hannay of Grennan (died 1573)

William Hannay succeeded to the property of Grennan about 1560. He also possessed the lands of Stancher, Strabrechan, Gass and other property stretching towards Ayrshire. The early Grennan titles are either lost or illegible but there exist enough (they eventually passed into the possession of the family of Sir John McTaggart, to whom the property now belongs) to provide some information as to the family. On October 15, 1590, there is mention of a John Kennedy of Grennan. It may be that William's son Hew got the final possession of the property through his wife Helen Kennedy, John's daughter, particularly as William is shown as being "in Grennan" in 1569, and therefore might have just been renting it.

William married Marion McBryde of Balmurrie, Wigtown. She, after William's death, married his brother Andrew in Gass. He had three children, Hew who followed him at Grennan, and two daughters Marjorie and Katherine. He was buried at his request at St. Michael's Church, Glenluce, on July 2, 1573. His will was proved at Edinburgh on November 3, 1580.

There are two boys mentioned in his will who were probably his bastards, John and James Hannay. He directs most kindly that they will be "held as brother with my ane bairns till they come of perfyt age..." His will shows William to be a most thoughtful and kind man with a real concern for his children's welfare for he:

> "ordainis Alexander Hannay of Sorbye overman and defender of my wyf and bairnes to remain togidder in all my roomes induring her widowhood and if she marries with advys of the said Laird of Sorbie scho to remain in lykemanner in roumes with my bairns to their perfyt age, failing thereof the roumes to be left to my bairnes and they to use the councill of the overman."

The consideration William had for his children is touching particularly in such violent times as Scotland was then experiencing. He was still a Catholic at the time of his death, and strangely this family became one of the strongest Covenanting families in Wigtownshire.[242]

## 3. Hew Hannay of Grennan (d. 1658)

Hew, William's son, succeeded to Grennan and later married Helen Kennedy, the niece of Lady Katherine Kennedy (wife of Sir Patrick

---

[242] William's will, included in earlier editions, can be now found at
https://clanhannay.org/will-of-william-hannay-of-grennan/

Vaus of Barnbarroch). Helen was the daughter of John Kennedy of Grenare, a natural son of Gilbert Kennedy, 3rd Earl of Cassilis.

In 1582, Archibald A'hannay and Margaret McKie, his wife, sued Helen's father John Kennedy concerning the production of the titles to the six merkland of Grennan, of which Archibald was tenant. He was probably acting as tutor to the Grennan property.

Hew's wife Helen died on November 18, 1597, and her will was confirmed on September 15, 1599. She seems to have owned a proportion of the farm stock worth a considerable amount of money. It would appear that she was part owner of the estate, or at least had liferent, as in her will amongst the debts owing to her is the remark "to Johne[243] Earle of Cassilis master of the ground for duty of the lands of Grennan in ann Lxxxxviij yearis ijc xxi j merks."

Hew was quite a young man when his father died, and lived till 1658. Helen must have died shortly after their marriage, but lived long enough to bear him four sons, Hugh (the eldest), Andrew, Patrick and John, afterwards of Knock and Gararrie. Hew was about ninety when he died in 1658 and was probably about five years old at his father's death in 1573, and so he would therefore have been married in about 1588.

In 1631 Hew's uncle, Andrew Hannay of Gass, , renounced some property in his favour, that is "six merkland of Grennan with houses etc lying in the regalty of Glenluce on repayment of £1000 in bond." Whether Uncle Andrew was in trouble due to the feud with the Murrays of Broughton, or just in debt, we do not know.

Hew's son Andrew served in the Scottish Army against Cromwell's forces at Dunbar where he was an ensign. He was captured after their defeat and imprisoned by Cromwell for a period. Hew's son Patrick became an early signatory of the Solemn League and Covenant in 1637, and was subsequently M.P. for Wigtown in the Scottish Parliament, and a Colonel of Horse in General Leslie's army of which mention is made in Chapter VII: The Family of John Hannay, M.P.. Hew's son Hugh predeceased his father, and little is known of him, except that he had a son, Thomas, who succeeded his grandfather.

## 3.1. Hannays in the Turbulent 17th Century

The religious troubles in Scotland, in which the Hannays were very much involved on both sides, sprang from a fervent natural desire for independence and a strong dislike for any control from London.

---

[243] i.e., John Kennedy (1575-1615), 5th Earl of Cassilis, who would have been her first cousin.

Charles I considered it to be his religious duty to bring to Scotland the order of service and ritual contained in the English prayer book. To carry this through he employed Archbishop Laud and the Earl of Traquair. The former was ill-informed as to the feelings of most Protestant Scotsmen and the latter was not strong enough to advise the King against such a measure. Robert Baillie, a Presbyterian minister of the time, wrote:

> "Those which are adverse from all cirimonies wherof ther is a great
> number yea almost all our Nobilitie and Gentrie of both sexes
> counts the booke little better than a Masse and are farr on a way to
> seperate from all who embrace it."

The actual signal for the breach came with the reading in St. Giles Kirk in Edinburgh of the service from the Prayer Book on July 23, 1637 by Dean James Hannay, as described in Chapter VII: The Family of John Hannay, M.P.. But the ultra-Protestant faction had been working for some time to build up a solid opposition to it, led by Archibald Johnston, Lord Warriston, and Colin Campbell, Lord Lorne, who soon afterwards became the 1st Earl of Argyll. These two pillars of the Covenant had constructed it with great care throughout the winter of 1636-7. The National Covenant was written as a bond, so dear to Scots hearts of the period, through which the King's disquieted Protestant subjects should manifest their union. In a speech before the Council on December 21, 1637, Mr. Thomas Ramsay showed the mood of this opposition:

> "That ther had been many weightie affairs befoir ther Lordships but
> never any of such importance; that he himself had been in tymes
> befoir them about papists and never parted but with great
> contentment, which he expected much more being before them
> about poperie itself, the seids of whose superstition and idolitrie
> were which sown in the service book, and to hierarchicall tirrany in
> the Canons and High Commission, that Augustine on the (110)
> Psalm made mention of three sorts of Anti-Christ, whereof the first
> was cruel, the next craftie; and the third and main anti-Christ was
> cruel and craftie; that in the service book was craft and in the Book
> of Canons crueltie."

A number of Commissions were sent out to get signatures to the National Covenant. Among the Scottish magnates who sided with the Covenanting party was John Kennedy, 6th Earl of Cassilis, to whom the Hannays of Grennan owed some allegiance, both by marriage and as their heritable superiors. When the Bishops' Wars[244] (1639-1640) started, Hew's son Patrick was sitting in Parliament in Edinburgh. The

---

[244] The initial conflict of the Wars of the Three Kingdoms (1639-1651), which entwined England, Scotland and Ireland, and involved religious disputes as well as the abolition – and re-establishment – of the monarchy.

situation in England drifted from bad to worse and certain Scots saw their opportunity, backed by Covenanting religious fervour, to throw off the unpopular control of London. The Covenanting Army was formed under Alexander Leslie, 1st Earl of Leven largely as a bargaining factor between both sides in England, although nominally on the side of the Parliament. In the end in 1646 it sold King Charles I, whom, at this time, it was pledged to support, to Parliament. Hew's son Patrick raised a regiment of Horse and held a colonel's commission. It is interesting to note that in 1662 another of Hew's sons, John of Knock and Gararrie, is mentioned by Woodrow as being fined for Nonconformity.

In 1647 in the Kirk Session records of Dumfries there is an interesting reference excommunicating a number of notable people including Lord Herries, the Countess of Nithsdale and Sir John Maxwell and Margaret A'Hannay in Kirkgunzeon saying that:

"It is to be intimated out of all the Pulpits therein (presumably
Dumfries) that the persons aftermentioned are excommunicated and
that none reset them nor resort to them, without licence of
Presbyteries or other Kirk Judicatories upon evidence of the
necessary and just cause, asked and given under peril of
ecclesiastical censures."

## 4.  Thomas Hannay of Grennan (succeeded 1659)

On Hew's death in 1658, his grandson Thomas succeeded and was served heir in a sasine January 4, 1659.

The sasine reads, "Sasine in favour of Thomas Hannay as nearest and lawfull heir to Hew Hannay his guidsir of Six merkland of Grennan for a yearly payment of £16 Scots money at two times in the year."

On January 16, John Kennedy, 6th Earl of Cassilis is shown as feudal superior of Grennan in a charter in favour of Thomas. Thomas married, but unfortunately we do not know his wife's name, and only the name of one child, John, his heir. He no doubt had others but they probably died in infancy.

## 5.  John Hannay of Grennan (succeeded 1662)

John Hannay of Grennan survived his father and has sasine of the property in 1662. At this service (of heirs) John Kennedy, 6th Earl of Cassilis, was the sponsor.

## 6.  John Hannay (junior) of Grennan (1663-1702)

The succession here is somewhat difficult to follow, but from the sasines it would appear that John the elder, who had sasine in 1662 and on July 2, 1663, had a son, John, who succeeded in 1684. This second John is shown on June 23, 1684 as

> "sasine in favour of John Hannay of Grennan as son and heir of the deceased John Hannay of Grennan in the lands of Grennan."

This second John married Janet Baillie, and in the marriage contract dated April 23, 1683, proved in a further document of June 23rd 1684 there is the following provision:

> "Compaired John Hannay of Grennan and in the terms of his marriage contract dated April 23rd 1683 gave and granted to his wife Janet Baillie liferent and sasine of the lands of Grennan."

The family are shown in the Parish list of 1684, as consisting of John Hannay, his wife, Alexander, William, Mary, Hew and Andrew. John died in 1702, and on July 16 his son, another John, had sasine of Grennan.

## 7.  John Hannay III of Grennan (succeeded 1702)

In 1707 John married Joanna Wallace, the daughter of John Wallace of Herochilen. They had two sons, John and Alexander. The boys later had sasine of half the lands of Grennan in 1737.

## 8.  John Hannay IV of Grennan (m. 1737)

This last John succeeded his father and married Mary, the daughter of Alexander Ross of Cairnbrook, in the parish of Kirkholm in 1737. The marriage settlement is dated October 26 and 29, 1737. They had a son, Alexander.

## 9.  Alexander Hannay of Grennan (m. 1764)

Alexander also married a Ross of Cairnbrook, Grizzel, the daughter of John Ross in 1764.

In passing it may be mentioned that from this John Ross were descended the well-known Antarctic navigators, Sir John Ross and his nephew Sir James Clark Ross, both of Balsharroch, Wigtownshire. The former was born in 1777 and died in 1856, the latter in 1800 and died in 1862. They took their ships the *Erebus* and *Terror* to the Antarctic regions, a wonderful feat in those days of sailing ships.

By his marriage with Grizzel Ross, Alexander had two daughters, Mary and Elizabeth. Mary, the elder, married Doctor Robert Hannay of Capenoch and Culbrae in Wigtownshire. This branch of the family had been independent as early as 1457 when Dougal Hannay of Culbrae and Capenoch appears in the early registers. Dr. Robert was latterly Collector in Portpatrick. Elizabeth married William

McConnell, later to become Sheriff of Wigtown. The property went to Mary Hannay, who by her marriage to Dr. Robert had four daughters and two sons.

## 10. Alexander James Hannay of Grennan (d. 1846)

The eldest child of Mary and Robert, Alexander James Hannay, had a distinguished medical career. He graduated at Edinburgh University in 1812, his treatise being on the subject of Apoplexy. He was Professor of the Practice of Medicine at Andersons College of Medicine in Glasgow from 1828 to 1846, and President of the Royal Scottish Medical Society of Edinburgh in its 87th Session 1823-24. His wife Marion McDowell Hannay was born in 1803, and married Alexander James on November 13, 1826. She was the daughter of James Hannay of Barlinnie and Lockbank. They had five children: James; William Cathcart; Maxwell; Elizabeth, who married a Mr. Hunter; and Grace who married a Mr. Ross. Alexander Hannay died in 1846. Marion outlived him and died in 1873.

James the eldest son died without issue. He was killed as a result of an accident at sea on his way home from India. His mother Marion sold the lands of Grennan to Sir John McTaggart of Ardwell about 1852 shortly after the death of her husband Alexander James. There was a severe financial crisis in the country at this time and she was advised by her trustees to sell on account of a small bond which was out on the place.

## 11. William Cathcart Hannay (d. 1872)

William and his brother Maxwell both went into business in Singapore. William married in 1869 Julia Christian the daughter of the Reverend D. S. Wilkinson, the minister at Tongland in Kirkcudbrightshire. They had three sons, Alexander Lidderdale, George Martin and Cathcart Christian. William was very interested in family history and did a considerable amount of work on the subject. Before he died he produced a short memorandum from which much of this chapter has been adapted. William died in 1872 at Singapore.

His son George entered the King's Own Scottish Borderers and served with distinction in World War I, becoming a colonel and being awarded the D.S.O. Colonel George died without any children.

George's brother Cathcart also entered the Army, serving in the Dorset Regiment where he also became a colonel and gained a D.S.O. Colonel Cathcart had two daughters, Briget and Ann.

211

## 12. Alexander Lidderdale Hannay (m. 1898)

William's eldest son Alexander Lidderdale went into the Indian Civil Service in the Madras Presidency and in later life became a J.P. for Kirkcudbrightshire. He married, in 1898, Edith, the daughter of Jasper Young of Garroch in Kirkcudbright and had four children, three sons and a daughter.

## 13. Alexander Patrick Cathcart Hannay (1898-1977)

Alexander Lidderdale Hannay's eldest son Alexander Patrick Cathcart Hannay was born in Madras, India, in 1898. He entered the Cameron Highlanders and served in France in World War I. He won a Military Cross as a Lieutenant in Russia at the close of the war. He was seconded for part of his service to the Royal Air Force for flying duties. He commanded the 1st Battalion, Cameron Highlanders, and was also the O.C. (Officer Commanding) of No. 53 Army Co-operation Squadron RAF from 1937 to 1939. He also served in No. 100, No. 20 and No. 16 Squadrons for periods from 1920 to 1926 and 1934 to 1936. He was awarded the O.B.E. in 1946 and invalided out of the army in the same year. For some time, he lived at Bowden Knowe near St. Boswells and lived in Chester Street in Edinburgh where he moved in November 1954. He married Eva Maude Cotter the daughter of the Reverend W. H. Cotter, LL.D., of Bullevant. County Cork, on December 28, 1921. They had two sons, Patrick Victor Cathcart (1923-2009) and Timothy John (1929-2015).

### 13.1. Patrick Victor Cathcart Hannay (1923-2009)

Patrick Victor served in World War II in the Rifle Brigade in Italy and North Africa. He was mentioned in despatches for gallantry in Italy. Whilst he was serving with the 10th Battalion in B Company. On May 25, 1944, the battalion moved through the Hitler line by a gap made by the 1st Canadian Infantry Division and the 5th Canadian Armoured Division. At first light on May 26 an attempt was made to cross the river Melfa under heavy fire, Victor Hannay, as his regiment called him, an hour later waded over the river on a reconnaissance patrol to find the only remaining enemy were a few deserters. The battalion, due to his action, crossed the river immediately, and, having established a bridgehead, allowed the 1st Guards Brigade to pass through. After the war he gained an Honours degree at St. Andrew's University in 1950 and entered the Colonial Service in Malaya in 1952. He married Elvira Pachetti of Milan on February 8, 1948. He subsequently served in Tanganyika.

## 13.2. Timothy John Hannay (1929-2015)

Patrick's brother Timothy was christened in St. Margaret's Chapel in the Castle of Edinburgh. Timothy went to Edinburgh University where he served in the Air Training Squadron and as a Flying Officer in the RAF and Adjutant of 257 Fighter Squadron. He married Judith Butler in 1956; they divorced in 1974 after raising two sons. Subsequently, he married Linda Callan, with whom he had two more sons.

# XIII: The Hannays of Knock and Gararrie

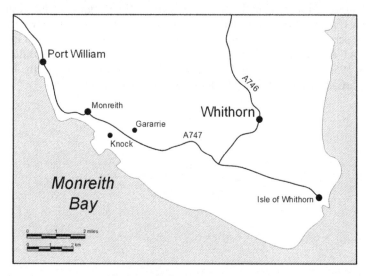

**Figure 53: Knock and Gararrie**

This branch of the family begins with John Hannay, the third son of Hew Hannay of Grennan. He is first mentioned in the will of his mother Helen Kennedy, when she appoints her husband Hew "hir spous as father and laufull administrator to Andro, Johnne and Patrick Hannay," 2 January 1597. See Figure 54: The Hannays of Knock and Garrarie

John and his descendants held the farms of Knock and Gararrie from the Maxwells of Monreith on friendly terms "Or as long as wood grew and water ran." They were connected with the Maxwells by marriage, both families having married into the family of the McCullochs of Myretoun near Monreith. John married Jean, the daughter of John McCulloch of Myretoun and his wife, Mary Couper.

## 1. *John Hannay the Younger of Knock*

John, the son of John and Jean, succeeded to the property. Little is known of him except that he is shown as being fined £400 for Nonconformity in 1662, having no doubt been one of the early Covenanters. He had two sons and a daughter, John, James and Isabella.

There is another John who may have been related to the Knock and Gararrie family: John Hannay, Writer to the Signet in Kirkcudbright, was flourishing in 1684 and became Sheriff Clerk for the Stewartry. There are many entries in the Sheriff Court records concerning him and he is still a very active lawyer up until 1699.

214

*For the pedigree of Hew Hannay (d. 1658), see Figure 51: The Hannays of Grennan*

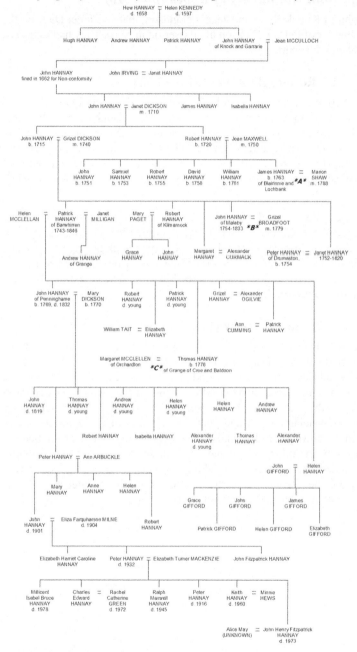

*A*: See Figure 55    *B*: See Figure 63    *C*: See Figure 64 and Figure 65

**Figure 54: The Hannays of Knock and Garrarie**

215

## 2. John Hannay III of Knock (m. 1710)

John of Knock, John and Jean's grandson, married Janet Dickson the daughter of Patrick Dickson of Glasserton in 1710. They had two sons, John and Robert.

### 2.1. Robert Hannay (1720-1793)

Robert, the second son of John Hannay III of Knock and Janet Dickson, was born in 1720 and married Jean, the daughter of Alexander Maxwell of Newland and Balmagon in Kirkcudbrightshire in 1750. Alexander was a direct descendant of John Maxwell, Lord Berries (1512-1583), the loyal friend of Queen Mary, who after the battle of Langside conveyed her to sanctuary at Dundredden Abbey, which is close to Balmagon.

Robert and Jean had six sons: John born in 1751, Samuel born in 1753, Robert in 1755, David in 1758, William in 1761, and James in 1763. Samuel matriculated at Glasgow University at the age of 14 and subsequently became a Doctor of Medicine. Robert, who had made a fortune in Glasgow in business, died in 1793. The eldest five brothers all died unmarried.

### 2.2. James Hannay (1763-1820)

James, Robert's youngest son, succeeded him. He acquired the property of Lochbank, near Castle Douglas, and also Barlinnie in Kirkcudbrightshire. He married, on August 21, 1788, Marion the daughter of James Shaw of Mid Kelton and his wife Jean Brown of Carsluith, who was the cousin of Professor Thomas Brown, a metaphysician, author and poet. The Browns of Carsluith are a very old Galloway family, whose members included the last Abbot of Sweetheart Abbey. James and Sir William Douglas of Castle Douglas founded the Galloway Banking Company. in 1806. He was a magistrate for the Stewartry and clerk to the Lieutenancy of the County, as well as the Earl of Galloway's agent.

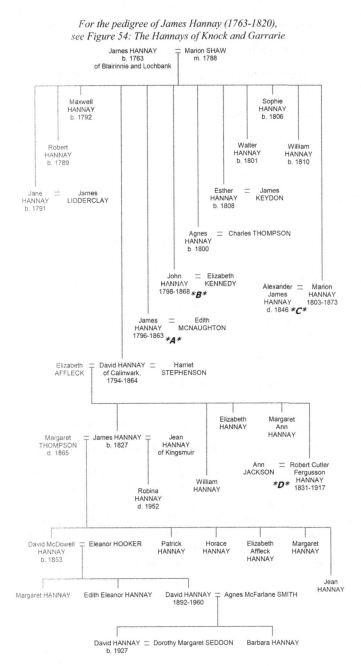

*For the pedigree of James Hannay (1763-1820),
see Figure 54: The Hannays of Knock and Garrarie*

*A\*: See Figure 57    \*B\*: See Figure 56    \*C\*: See Figure 51    \*D\*: See Figure 60

**Figure 55: The Hannays of Blairinnie**

217

James and Marion had a large family of six sons and six daughters:

- Robert was born in 1789.

- Jane, born in 1791, married James Lidderdale, who bought Lochbank from her brother David.

- Maxwell was born in 1792 and died unmarried.

- David was born in 1794.

- James, born in 1796, founded a large family from whom the Hannays of Spring Hill descend.

- John, born in 1798, also had a large family.

- Agnes, born in 1800, married Doctor Charles Dunbar Thompson of Torhousemuir near Newton Stewart.

- Walter, born in 1801, was an artist in London and died there unmarried in 1880.

- Marion McDowell, born in 1803, was later the wife of Doctor Alexander Hannay of Grennan from whom the present Grennan family derives.

- Sophie, born in 1806, died unmarried.

- Esther, born 1808, married a Mr. James Keydon of Glasgow.

- William was born 1810. He went to India in the East India Company's Cavalry and died in Calcutta in 1836.

## 2.2.1.    John Hannay (1798-1868), son of James

John (1798-1868), son of James and Marion, was born on April 30, 1798, and died exactly seventy years later in 1868 on his birthday. He married Elizabeth, the daughter of Captain James Kennedy of Lincluden in Dumfries by Margaret, daughter of James Lennox. She was born in 1796 and died two years before her husband in 1866. He was a Writer to the Signet in Edinburgh. As a result of this marriage he became possessed of the Estate of Lincluden.

*For the pedigree of John Hannay (1798-1869), see Figure 55: The Hannays of Blairinnie*

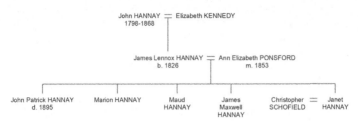

**Figure 56: The Hannays of Lincluden**

His son, James Lennox Hannay of Lincluden, was born on September 20, 1826, and entered the legal profession. He became Recorder of Pontefract and Metropolitan Police Magistrate of the Marlborough Street Police Court in London. He was a J.P. for Kirkcudbrightshire and for Middlesex and also a Deputy Lieutenant of Kirkcudbright.

On June 16, 1853, James Lennox married Anne Elizabeth, the daughter of James Ponsford and had two sons and two daughters, of whom one son, James, and one daughter, Jane, widow of the late Christopher Schofield, survived him. The property of Lincluden has now passed out of the family. This family tree can be seen in Figure 56: The Hannays of Lincluden.

## 2.2.2.  James Hannay (1796-1863), son of James

James and Marion's son James, who was born in 1796, entered the army and became a Captain in the 8<sup>th</sup> Foot. His portrait can be seen in Figure 58. James lived nearly all his life in Ireland at Ballylough, Co. Antrim. He was a very tall man, being 6ft. 4 in. Many of his descendants were remarkable for the same trait, more especially three of his granddaughters who were all over six feet tall and strikingly handsome to boot. They were the daughters of his eldest son, Colonel Edmund Alexander Hannay.

*For the pedigree of James Hannay (1796-1863), see Figure 55: The Hannays of Blairinnie*

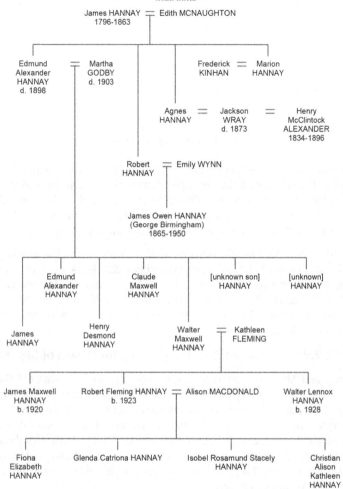

**Figure 57: The Hannays of Spring Hill**

James married Edith, the daughter of Edmund McNaughton of Beardsville, Co. Antrim, by Hannah, the daughter of John Johnson of Belfast. James died in 1863 and left four children: Edmund Alexander; Robert; Agnes, who married first Captain Wray of Roan Kelly, Co. Antrim, late of the 6th Foot, and secondly Rear Admiral McClintock Alexander of Dunduan, Co. Antrim; and finally Marion, who married

220

Frederick Kinhan[245] of Belfast. Their tree is shown in Figure 57: The Hannays of Spring Hill.

**Figure 58: James Hannay (1796-1863)**

## 2.2.3.      Robert Hannay (1835-1894)

James and Edith's second son, Robert (1835-1894), went to Trinity College, Dublin, and became a Doctor of Divinity and in 1857 the Vicar of Belfast. He married Emily, the daughter of the Reverend

---

[245] possibly spelled Kinahan or Kinaghan

William Wynne by Elizabeth the daughter of the Rt. Reverend James Saurin, D.O., Bishop of Dromore.

### 2.2.3.1. James Owen Hannay (1865-1950)

The son of the Reverend Robert also entered the Church: James Owen Hannay (1865-1950) became Canon of Saint Patrick's (Protestant) Cathedral in Dublin. He is better known as a writer, novelist, and playwright under the pseudonym of George A. Birmingham. His best known play is entitled *General John Regan*, and among his other works are included *The Wisdom of the Desert* (1904), *The Seething Pot* (1905), *The Bad Times* (1908), *The Search Party* (1909), *The Northern Iron* (1909), *Lalage's Lovers* (1911), *The Major's Niece* (1911), *The Simkins Plot* (1912), *The Lighter Side of Irish Life* (1912), *Priscilla's Spies* (1912), *The Red Hand of Ulster* (1912), *Spanish Gold* (1912) and *The Inviolable Sanctuary* (1912). James Owen Hannay died in 1950.

**Figure 59: James Owen Hannay (George A. Birmingham)**

### 2.2.4.    Edmund Alexander Hannay (d.1898)

Edmund Alexander, James and Edith's eldest, married Martha Godby. He entered the army and served in the Royal Horse Artillery in the Crimea; after the war he transferred to the Militia and commanded the Antrim Militia Artillery. He died in 1898 and his wife in 1903. They had fourteen children, of which the sixth, Walter Maxwell Hannay, purchased the estate of Spring Hill in Co. Worcester.

Walter served in World War I as a Captain in the Coldstream Guards and married Kathleen, the daughter of Robert Fleming of Nettlebed, Oxfordshire, by his wife Sarah Kate Hindmarsh. They were married in the Guards Chapel, Wellington Barracks, on May 15, 1918. They had three children: James Maxwell born August 11, 1920; Robert Fleming born September 30, 1923; and Walter Lennox, born on July 13, 1928, who joined the Army through the Royal Military Academy Sandhurst and was commissioned into the Royal Scots Greys on October 21, 1948.

Robert Fleming married Alison MacDonald and had four children: Fiona Elizabeth, born April 26, 1949; Glenda Catriona, born April 29, 1951; Isabel Rosamund Stacely, born February 18, 1956; and Christian Alison Kathleen, born November 17, 1957. Robert Fleming was a barrister at law and served in the Coldstream Guards until invalided out. He retired from the Bar in 1963 and was ordained Priest in 1966, becoming Rector of Garsingham near Oxford.

## 2.3.  David Hannay of Calinwark (1794-1864)

David, son of James and Marion, was born in 1794 at Lochbank. He was educated first at Annan, where Thomas Carlyle was one of his school fellows, and later in Edinburgh. Robert, his elder brother, was not interested in the family estate and much of its administration was left to David. Finally, David wound up the Bank of Galloway which was likely in considerable financial difficulty. He took over the estate from Robert, incidentally becoming responsible for its debts as well as Robert's personal ones and granting to Robert an annuity of £500 a year. He contracted these responsibilities and fulfilled them, which says much for his business acumen and tenacity.

There are a few notes extant written by David, presumably from information given to him by his father concerning the family finances which are of interest.

> "Various lawsuits existed, notably one with Napier concerning the Galloway Bank. The Rental from the landed estate was £1,100 a year after the Peace (i.e. 1815). Legacies to the children amounted to £15,000-£1,500 each. Debts owed by James of Blairinnie

(deducting £2.000 in Lord Galloway's hands) £3,000. Galloway bank £5,000. Robert's debts £1,000. Robert's Annuity £500 a year."

It would seem that the young man had bitten off more than he could chew with any profit. It is fair to say something here about Robert, who appears to have been something of a waster. He was not. He was merely a man who was not interested in—or good at making—money. He was an advocate of the Scottish bar, but he may not ever have practiced law. Robert was also a Master of Arts of Balliol College, Oxford. After his resignation of the family property, he left Scotland and settled in Kew, where he died unmarried at the age of 78. He was an author of several books on Judicial History and Jurisprudence generally. He visited the libraries of the Vatican and Stockholm, and in 1836 published a "Report on the British Museum." In the same year gave evidence before a Committee of the House of Commons concerning that Institution.

David married in 1822 Elizabeth Affleck, the daughter of Capt. William Affleck R.N., of Whitehaven, Cumberland. The Afflecks were an ancient Scottish family related to the Auchinlecks and had a long naval tradition. The house at Lochbank was sold shortly afterwards to James Lidderdale who had married David's elder sister Jane. In 1824 David bought Carlinwark House. He seems, however, to have divided his time between a house in Bank Street, Dumfries, and Carlinwark. They had five children: James, William, Elizabeth, Margaret Ann and Robert Cutler Fergusson. Tragedy overtook this happy and prosperous family. In August, 1833, Elizabeth Affleck set out with her three elder children in a phaeton[246] driven by her husband. Something had been forgotten, and when not far from the house they drew up. Elizabeth alighted with the intention of going back, and at that moment, the horse took fright, the vehicle was upset and she was thrown under the wheels, was trampled on and died within an hour. "Thus perished," says the Dumfries Courier, "in the prime of life, a beloved wife, the mother of five fine children, and one who was universally admired and esteemed, not more for personal loveliness, in which she was almost peerless in the South of Scotland, than for her amiable disposition, unostentatious charity, sound sense and polished manners." She was only twenty-eight years of age. Two years later her husband married again, a Miss Harriet Stephenson, daughter of the vicar of Dacre in Cumberland. Maybe she was a friend of his first wife, for Victorian widowers often chose a friend of their first wife to be the stepmother of their children. Harriet outlived him and is the Mrs. Hannay referred to in James's correspondence and diaries, though the family called her Mama. She seems to have been a good stepmother, for one of the children who died

---

[246] light, horse-drawn carriage with four wheels.

young chose to leave her his share of the inheritance to come to him from his maternal grandfather. There is also a letter in existence to James when Consul in Barcelona. It is a very affectionate, warmhearted letter with bits of family gossip and she addresses him as Hamish, the Scottish form of James and obviously a pet name.

David was in partnership in the Galloway Bank (which his father had helped found), with his second cousin Alexander Hannay, the son of John Hannay (1754-1833) and Grizel Broadfoot, who was living in the house in Bank Street many years later. In remodeling Carlinwark, David had once more taken on rather more than he was able to afford. The house was originally an inn and having it enlarged was an extremely costly undertaking. He unfortunately involved his bank with one of the London Joint Stock Banks which crashed, and within three years of Elizabeth's death he went bankrupt. He, however, paid the creditors of the Galloway Bank twenty shillings in the pound. At the bankruptcy proceedings it was remarked that if he had kept the bank's books as well as Mrs. Hannay (Harriet) kept her household ones, there would have been no bankruptcy. The Hannays seldom seem to be good at arithmetic; they never seem to be able to keep money, although they appear to have from time to time made a number of fairly sizeable fortunes.

As soon as his affairs were wound up he left Scotland and settled at Barnet in Hertfordshire. Here his elder daughter died and later his son William, and his younger daughter. Finally, he left Ridge, the house near Barnet and moved into lodgings in North London, until his death in 1864.

Two pleasing stories throwing some light on his attitudes are to be found in letters from his daughter-in-law Margaret, wife of his oldest son, James. Writing to her father in Australia soon after the birth of her first-born child she says:

> "Baby is getting on nicely, James is more and more fond of him every day. He has been short coated and we expect he will grow very much this summer as we intend spending it with Grandpapa Hannay, very much to the delight of that old gentleman I am happy to say."

Some years later, writing to her brother-in-law Robert, who had just got married, she says:

> "James had a letter from Papa this morning in which he threatens evil consequences to someone from the want of commonsense of someone else about your marriage. I cannot clearly understand from his letter whether it is Mama or myself that is wanting in the valuable sense, you or he who are to suffer from the lamentable defect in us womankind. In case it should be me that is meant I write just a few lines that we may not misunderstand one another."

225

She goes on to express warm feelings of affection and to welcome the new sister-in-law and ends up by saying:

> "Do you remember I always said you would make a good husband and you used to say you would be a very jealous one? Now you may be better informed, but the only one to cause you to suffer from that painful weakness will be Papa. He, I am sure, has always been nearly as much in love with your wife as yourself."

Robert's wife, who was good and gentle and much loved, was not a great social catch, so that David's insistence on her receiving the right attention from the start shows a generous spirit.

### 2.3.1.    Robert Cutler Hannay (1831-1917)

Robert Cutler Fergusson, David and Elizabeth's second son, lived in Eastbourne where he was in business.

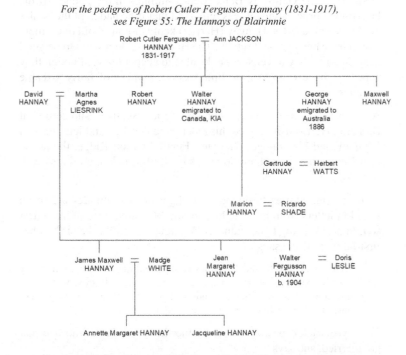

*For the pedigree of Robert Cutler Fergusson Hannay (1831-1917), see Figure 55: The Hannays of Blairinnie*

**Figure 60: The Family of Robert Cutler Fergusson Hannay**

Robert wrote poetry for a hobby and had an astonishing memory. He was at one time literary editor of the Morning Post. His wife was a noted beauty of her day, Ann Jackson by name. They had five children:

- David, his oldest son.

- Robert died unmarried.

- George went to Australia in 1886.

- Walter went to Canada. He did not marry and was killed in the Canadian Army in World War I.

- Marion married Ricardo Shade.

- Gertrude married Herbert Watts.

- Maxwell, of whom nothing is known.

### 2.3.2.    David Hannay (b. 1861)

David, the eldest son of Robert Cutler Fergusson Hannay and his wife Ann, married Martha Agnes Liesrink. She was the daughter of an eminent surgeon in Hamburg. She was quite wealthy, but David succeeded in getting through most of her money in a remarkably short time. The inevitable happened, and she left him and set up house at Kingsclere in Berkshire. She was a very strict person and somewhat sombre and entirely Germanic in her outlook on life, but none the less full of great energy and decision, for at 83 she went to Australia to see her second son, James, who had retired to Perth.

There were three children:

- Jean Margaret went to Malta to stay with Captain Henry Harwood (who later sank the Graf Spee) and was killed there whilst riding.

- James Maxwell, the eldest, went to Thames Nautical Training College aboard HMS Worcester for his education, and became a captain in the British India Line and eventually their harbour representative at Calcutta. In World War II he was appointed to command the Lascars in Calcutta and made a colonel in the Indian Army. He finally retired in Perth, Australia, where he farmed. He married Madge White and had two daughters, Annette Margaret and Jacqueline.

- Walter Fergusson was born in 1904 and expressed a desire to be a surgeon at a very early age, announcing to the family doctor at the age of six , "I want to cut up Grandpa's tummy." He entered the medical profession and served for some time in the R.A.M.C., retiring in 1928. He was an eminent physician in Harley Street and a prolific writer to the national newspapers both on medical and other subjects. He was knighted in 1951 and was for some time personal physician to

Earl Attlee[247]. In 1936 he married Doris Leslie (1891-1982), a well-known historical biographer, fiction writer, and novelist. Walter died in 1961.

## 2.4. James Hannay (1827-1873)

James, the eldest son of David Hannay and Elizabeth Affleck, was born in 1827 and had perhaps one of the most varied and interesting careers of any member of the family. His remarks on the family motto were characteristic: "In my case," he would say to his children, "it probably means through great pecuniary difficulties to the gallows." In spite of this characteristic quip he took his family traditions and history very seriously. Genealogy and heraldry were among his chief interests. He held strong, and, to our generation, odd theories concerning aristocratic lineage; yet he was never a snob in the vulgar sense. Primarily he was a believer in an aristocracy of character and intellect, and that in the main this would be found to consist of those whom he would call of "good blood." He inclined to despise mediocrity and detested above all the worship of financial prosperity and success for their own sakes. Democracy, the growth of which he saw to be inevitable, he regarded most dubiously.

An extract from "A Book of Recollections" by John Cordy Jeaffreson, published in 1894, shows James' and his father David's views on ancestry and that both of them were gifted with a neat sense of humour:

> Delighting to expatiate on the grandeur and romantic vicissitudes of patrician houses with which he had no ancestral connection, Hannay did not omit to speak much and handsomely of the Hannays of Sorbie, and all other groups of Hannays who were genealogically related to his particular family. There were times when he would have been in better company if he had said less of the virtues and alliances of his progenitors. I recall with amusement how his father (a charming old gentleman) on a certain occasion checked his brilliant son for being rather too eloquent about his ancestors. I was sitting one Sunday afternoon with the father and the son in the dining room of the Pleasant Row house, when Mr. Hannay the elder, putting down his whiskey toddy, checked my friend's loquacity on his favourite topic by remarking gently, "There, there, Jamie you have said more than enough about your pedigree, Don't you see you are just wearying your friend with o'er-much speech about people in whom he of course is not greatly interested? The Hannays were no such great people as you like to think them. One of your grandfathers, Jamie, was a highly respeckit Scotch shopkeeper, and I wish I could say as much of my ain son."

---

[247] Clement Attlee, former prime minister of the United Kingdom.

> For a moment my heart bled for my friend as these words came to
> him at one end of the table from the lips of his father, sitting
> directly opposite him. But Jamie was neither abashed nor rendered
> in any way uncomfortable by the parental rebuke, accompanied as
> it was by what I of course regarded as a domestic revelation that
> could fail to shock my friend and pain him acutely. On the contrary
> the staggering speech brought a smile of amusement to Jamie's
> handsome face and caused his magnificent eyes to overflow with
> silent laughter. "Very good, wasn't it?" Hannay the younger
> observed in a low voice as he covered me with his merry eyes.
> "The Dad has a happy vein of humour and I never knew him in
> better trim."

His greatest, most enduring love was for learning; knowledge for its
own sake. He was, above all, a natural scholar. He venerated the
classics and adored the beauty of his own language. Literature, history,
philosophy and poetry were his religion. He taught himself to read
Greek and acquired with almost no help from anyone a deep and wide
scholarship which was recognised and respected by his
contemporaries.

There was, however, another totally different side to his nature, which
reveled in good company, good wine, good talk, laughter, wit and
loved the stir and movement of life, politics, discussion, argument and
a good fight, too. In politics he was a Conservative, but not by any
means an orthodox one, for some of his ideas were far ahead of his
time. He had a great power of invective and enjoyed using it but,
strangely, one finds among his very good friends some of those same
"advanced Liberals" he roundly abused with his pen, and it is rather
surprising to read his witty impertinences and then learn from his diary
that within a very short time he and his victim are welcoming each
other to their respective homes. I think perhaps they "gave as good as
they got and no bones broken" in Bohemian London, where his
happiest years were spent. Perhaps, too, though a good hater, he would
have said with Charles Lamb, "If I knew him, I couldn't hate him."

The novelist William Makepeace Thackeray speaks from his great
height and surely in affection of "little" Hannay; but James was not
what that word suggested. James was, to be precise, 5 ft. 8 ins. in his
shoes, squarely and rather heavily built. He was, as a young man,
handsome, with bright dark eyes that could flash with anger or beam
with benevolent humour, vital, enthusiastic, volatile, witty and his
friends loved him, admired him and sought his company.

And this is his story. In August, 1833, when James was six and a half,
his mother Elizabeth was killed in a carriage accident before the eyes
of her husband and elder children. She was only twenty-eight, said to
have been a great beauty and much loved. So, here was the first

entrance of tragedy into the little boy's life. *The Courier* also reports that "the eldest boy, James, made a miraculous escape, as the seat he had sat on a moment before was literally dashed to pieces."

David Hannay sold Carlinwark three years after this disaster and moved to London. He married a second time two years after his first wife's death.

James, when he was ten, went to school in Westmorland until, in March, 1840, he entered the Navy as a midshipman. He joined HMS *Cambridge* at Sheerness, and in the autumn of the same year served in this ship in the Mediterranean fleet, taking part in the blockade of Alexandria during the [Second] Syrian War (i.e., the Egyptian-Ottoman War, 1839-1841). Later he served in the sloop HMS *Snake*, the corvette HMS *Orestes* and the 84-gun HMS *Formidable*.

He served for five years in the Navy until he was court-martialed for insubordination and discharged the Service. He was accused of striking a superior officer, when under the influence of drink. He told his daughter that the officer in question had spoken insultingly of a lady, "and," she commented, "I have no doubt both were telling the truth." He insisted on defending himself before the Court Martial, and when the papers were sent to the Admiralty the conviction was quashed as "vindictive," and no slur rested on his character. However, he wanted to leave the Navy and therefore resigned his commission and came to London, living at first with his father. Immediately, he began his regular attendance at the British Museum.

In 1846, his first job, immediately after leaving the Navy, was as a reporter on the *Morning Chronicle*. By the time he was twenty-three, he had written *Biscuits and Grog, King Dobbs* (both of these later published in his collection *Sketches in Ultra-Marine),* and a novel, *Singleton Fontenoy,* which had considerable success.

He began to keep a diary in April 1852 when he was living in lodgings at 15 Huntley Street near the British Museum. He was now twenty-five and well launched. Among his friends were Thomas Carlyle, William Makepeace Thackeray , Douglas William Jerrold, Charles Dickens (he never knew Dickens well but wrote for him) and (nearer his age and very intimate) Dante Gabriel and William Rossetti, Coventry Patmore, William Allingham and many more. Dante Gabriel Rossetti sketched a gathering at James' house in 1851 (See Figure 61: Reunion at Hannay's by Dante Gabriel Rossetti).

**Figure 61: Reunion at Hannay's by Dante Gabriel Rossetti**

He wrote for *The Westminster Review, Daily News, Punch, The Press, Household Words, All The Year Round, Illustrated Times, Temple Bar, Cornhill, Athenaeum,* and *Blackwood's* (introduced by John Chapman, Editor of *The Westminster Review*). There is an amusing glimpse of him, as he appeared in these early days to his "rivals," in Edmund Tates' *Reminiscences.*

In 1853 he gave his first course of lectures in London, on "Satires and Satirists," and drew a good and quite distinguished audience. All the time he was reading, teaching himself Greek, studying history, acquiring knowledge. One of his books is *A Course of English Literature.* Published as a volume in 1866, it was written as a series for a popular periodical *The Welcome Guest,* in 1858-1859. Remembering that he was then thirty-two and that everything needed to write that book he had taught himself in the fourteen years since he had left the Navy and while he was earning his living at the same time, it is understandable that Thackeray once spoke of him as "the cleverest man I ever knew." This book is interesting as it shows a wide tolerance and balanced judgement, and inherent reasonableness in contrast with the militant, dogmatic side of his nature.

When the diary begins, James is in love with his future wife, Margaret Thompson. They used to walk from Islington where her home was, across the fields to Highgate, Homsey or Hampstead. They were married on February 24, 1853. Margaret Thompson—the "M" of the diary—was both beautiful and good. "Beautiful as the personal attractions of M. are," James notes after an evening spent with his love during their betrothal, "her character and sentiment always leave the final, the predominant impression after you have been talking to her. She reminds of the Daphne story. You chase her as the nymph and end by worshipping her as the laurel." The year before his wedding, he took Dante Gabriel Rossetti to visit her, and the artist drew a sketch of her and gave it to them (see Figure 62).

**Figure 62: Margaret Hannay, by Dante Gabriel Rossetti**

It is a charming portrait - an early Rossetti, not at all stylistic. Later, she sat to Rossetti as "Beatrice" for the preliminary water colour he made for his "Dante's Dream".

His description in a letter of April 6, 1853 to Kingsmuir about his marriage is characteristic:

232

It was my intention, as you know, to proceed to Wigtonshire from Edinburgh, and there to examine the ruins of Sorbie, and to proceed to my Uncle John's. The plan was frustrated by a piece of unexpected news; for Mr. Thompson of the Oriental Bank, whose daughter and I had been on terms of courtship for some time (though as nothing was definitely arranged, I did not speak of the matter to you) - Mr. Thompson, I say suddenly agreed with the Bank to proceed to Melbourne and found a "branch" for them for the purchase of bullion. - He saw his way to good business from this notion, and at once consented to proceed with his family to that distant region: - As suddenly he wrote off to me, and gave me the option to conclude my marriage, or to let his daughter go with them to Australia.

Here you observe my dear Sir, was what the newspapers call a "Crisis". I had to resolve and to resolve and to resolve , at once - the case required that promptness of action which in old times was doubtless displayed by the family in War, and which is as necessary as ever in matters of importance ........ to go wandering about Sorbie, while a girl whom I loved was sailing to the Antipodes was a proceeding to which not even my reverence for Sorbie could permit; my affection and my amour both pulled one way. My circumstances were not such as to make me afraid of entering on a modest gentlemanly household. So, I left for London a few days before the end of January.

I had not been many days in town before the above-mentioned rheumatism laid me up. It came on with severe pain in the wrists and knees, accompanied by fever etc. I had good advice and as you may suppose "pulled foot" to get well - and managed to conquer the first foot of it just in time for my marriage, which was on the 24th Feb at the Scotch Church in this parish. I began to walk abroad a little too soon, - so got a second dose of the nuisance - and had to be fed with beef-tea by my wife, half the honey-moon: You will admit that this was rather hard on one, but there was nothing for it, but to submit with grace, and swallow your honey out of a gallipot[248], and be thankful. Thank God, April has begun mild and balmy; I am once more well and very happy. My kindred were astonished at my sudden wedding, but when the matter was explained, of course, they (as my Uncle John wrote the other day) saw that I had done right and sent me their congratulations. Mr. Thompson sailed in the *Madagascar* on the 2nd March.

You ought now, by rights, to have some account of the kind of wife I have got, though I could not write half a description of her, and could not expect you to believe half, of that half, if I did. But I feel pretty certain that you will take my word for this much, that she is a very ladylike sensible, modest girl of 19, and extremely handsome. I have succeeded to the quarters of my father-in-law and have

---

[248] a small ceramic jar used for holding medicine

hoisted my flag in a comfortable house in a quiet terrace, with a garden leading down to the New River. I now feel that I shall better employ my time than ever I did, and hope to realize what Mr. [John] Marshall, Patrick [the Poet] Hannay's friend says of him:

> ...thou art shown
> By Pen, times changing, Hannays are active
> in acts of worth - be 't peace or war.

Five days after the wedding, Margaret's father with all her family sailed to Australia where they settled permanently. Her brother Joseph was one of the original thirteen students to be enrolled in the University of Melbourne. Her maternal grandfather was John Henning, the sculptor (1771-1851), a character of considerable interest. John Henning, junior, also a sculptor, was her uncle. He did, amongst other works, the frieze on the Athenaeum and the frieze round the triple Arch at Hyde Park Corner. Another of her uncles, Archibald Henning, was an artist, and early contributor to *Punch*; he drew the very first *Punch* cover cartoon. Her uncle by marriage was also an artist, Kenny Meadows. She seems to have been a thoughtful, intelligent young woman with independent ideas, common sense and a vein of quiet humour. Little is known of her short life and she was only a memory to her elder children.

The diary continues till 1860. During those years James, in addition to reading, writing and lecturing, kept up his genealogical studies and also indulged in his other hobby: debate. He belonged to several debating societies and, of course, to more than one convivial club. Besides his literary associates he had a circle of good friends among young men studying for or practising at the Bar (probably met through his cousin, James Lennox Hannay, barrister and later London Police Court Magistrate), and would carouse and celebrate with these in their Chambers or in taverns in and around Fleet Street: "The Cheshire Cheese", "The Cock", and "Dick's". Sometimes he visited "The Cider Cellars", "Evans", or further afield, "Fish Ordinary" at Billingsgate. He visited, walked and talked regularly with his father, and his young brother was constantly at his house.

Nevertheless, it seems that the trouble that later beset him was already faintly showing like a dark cloud in a fair sky. He knew his own weakness but not its terrible power. He wrote happily on January 1, 1856, "The year begins tolerably well, with no great debts, work reasonably abundant, health of the household good. I begin (as usual) with a whole string of good resolutions—hard reading, attention to work, increased knowledge, and moderate use of banquets." But moderation was never one of his characteristics.

234

"Reading less than I should had I not been so full of our own present politics," he wrote in the Spring of 1857. And off he went, to Dumfries to contest the Dumfries Burghs, which constituency his father had twice contested unsuccessfully. Though records seem to show that he stood as a Tory, he made very clear in his election addresses that he would not pledge himself to vote for either Party but certain principles that his conscience approved. He went with no money in his pockets and backed by none except his local supporters, and he had a grand time. He spent one riotous week electioneering, which must have been just after his own heart. His opponent was William Ewart, a much older man than himself, a politician of distinction and experience, an advanced Liberal with several really good reforms to his credit. However, wherever James spoke, "the mob," as he called his audience, loved him, roared with laughter at his wit and cheered him heartily. On the Nomination Day, both candidates spoke to big crowds in Queensbury Square. They spoke at considerable length and a show of hands was called for. The victory was to James. "I think there can be no doubt", announced the Sheriff Mark Napier, "that the greatest show of hands is in favour of Mr. Hannay." It was "roses, roses all the way," but at the polling booths it was another matter. William Ewart had represented the Dumfries Burghs for sixteen years and was to continue to do so for the rest of his life. It was a Liberal constituency and laugh and cheer though "the mob" might, the hard-headed Scottish voters knew when they were well served. "So was beat thoroughly, but time and all things considered didn't come off so badly after all," says James. After the declaration of the Poll, he spoke again from the hustings and "populace again enthusiastic" he notes.

The whole affair seems to have delighted and amused him. He put in a further three weeks enjoying himself. He was dined and wined, and entertained at the theatre where a special performance was given "under his patronage" ("Lord preserve us," he remarks); and after visiting his kith and kin around Kirkcudbright he returned to London, where he found it a little hard to settle down again.

But politics, much as he enjoyed them, were far more to him than a pastime. He had a good grasp of affairs, and although he had no particular social or political standing, his writing attracted the attention of Lord Stanley[249], Colonial Secretary in the Conservative administration of 1858-1859. In December 1859, Lord Stanley wrote him a letter of several pages which, beginning "My dear Sir, I have read with much interest your sketch of French trends," and goes on to discuss very fully the existing Anglo-French situation and Napoleon III. The letter is marked "Private" and concludes: "I don't know if you

---

[249] Edward Henry Stanley (1826-1893), 15th Earl of Derby

can make any use of these remarks but they are quite at your service. Of course, I wish this letter private. Pray always communicate with me if I can in any way assist you."

All his life James was pressed for money. He was not a good businessman and one of his two weaknesses was extravagance. When he had any money, he spent it; that is what is for he would have argued. The Dumfries jaunt may possibly have been the beginning of more serious difficulties. At any rate, after his return he insured his life, borrowed on the policy and sent off a cheque to Dumfries to cover his election expenses.

In 1860 he had a small legacy—a few hundred pounds only. He went around paying his bills as soon as the cheque came, and the following day took his family to Worthing, where he rented a furnished house on the seafront for the summer. He was at this time doing two leaders–an "Inside" and "Front"—for the *Illustrated Times* every week, as well as much reviewing and was writing a book of his own. He had a happy time at Worthing, riding, bathing and sailing with his family, and of course his friends followed him there, as they always did wherever he went.

The holiday was cut short by the offer of the editorial post from the *Edinburgh Evening Courant*. He went at once to Edinburgh and took a house at 28 Buccleuch Place, and there the family remained for four years.

He assumed the editorship on August 31. He kept up his diary only till December, sometimes making up two weeks at a time. Then it stopped. The *Courant* was a daily evening paper, so there could have been little leisure.

I think he must have found this change in his life very irksome; he must have missed his beloved British Museum, his friends and his Bohemian existence, and the amount of mere routine work he had to do must have been very uncongenial. Within four months Margaret wrote to her brother-in-law: "James is looking very well but complains bitterly of the restraint." Perhaps, all things considered, it is surprising he stood it as long as he did. His views on the Crimean War and the extension of the franchise make interesting reading. In a letter from 16 Pleasant Row, Cannonbury, on Nov 3, 1854, he says:

"In London, nothing is talked about but Sebastopol—shells,
gunboats and what not. The people are full of war, and one
excellent result is that the Manchester party are kicked out of all
importance in consequence. So ahead are all notions of the great
changes & mighty progress of the 19th Century—as if human nature
would ever be content with cheap cotton, Polytechnic schools and
Ragman eloquence—which is what those fellows call Enlightened

Tranquility. Not a drummer but is rather more popular than Cobden at present. And those battles by bringing men of family, such as that grand old fellow Sir Colin Campbell, before the whole world, covered with honour, have an excellent effect on public opinion. War is a great conservatiser. And if this War be well concluded, it will help to show the Masses that there is still ability left to carry on the Country without calling for their enlightened assistance through the medium of increased suffrage and otherwise proposals."

And again in a letter of Jan 6, 1855 to George Francis Hannay of Kingsmuir:

"I suppose that you are shocked as everybody here is, at the way in which the Crimean Expedition has been bungled. I remember scarce anything so disgraceful, and the handle it gives to the enemies of the existing system of Government to assert that it is "useless" is only too obvious and dangerous. In fact, it has done much to neutralise the excellent effect of the battles in a contrary direction. It seems not improbable that this war will lead to a great many important consequences, and the radicals openly propose their faith in it as an agent in the general cause of revolution all over Smoke. For this reason, it is said, that peace is the real object of the Kings just now but no peace in the present state of affairs can be brought about without dishonour to England. Meanwhile, we must await the news, and see whether Sebastopol has been assaulted which if successfully done will somewhat redeem the past.

Just as affairs are so bad in the Crimea my cousin is going out from Templemore in Ireland; he is well up in the Lieutenants' list and will either be shot or get his company I fancy soon. But he is such a long fellow that he could scarcely have escaped at Alma or Inkerman. His elder brother Edmond is going into the Kerry Militia I believe, for want of something to do, but I have not seen him gazetted yet. It seems that Wray whom their sister married is not a Naval, but a Military Captain, a man of good family and some hereditary property in the County."

He returned to London in 1864 and took a house in Bloomsbury, 31 Tavistock Place. He continued to send contributions to the *Courant*.

In 1864 his father, with whom he had kept in very close touch all his life, died, and on December 29, 1865, he lost his Margaret. She died painfully and tragically after months of illness (though she still carried on her normal life and duties to within a short time from the end), as the result of a neglected discharge from the ear. Medical science at that time had not the knowledge or skill to deal with this and a general blood poisoning developed and spread. She was only thirty-two and she left six children, the eldest of whom just twelve, the youngest, two.

It is now necessary to speak of the weakness which destroyed James Hannay, as it has many other men of brilliant promise. He was never a "tippler" or a "soaker", he drank in bouts—periodic fierce bouts of indulgence which may have been beyond his power to resist. It is not clear when this trouble first gained ascendancy over him; no doubt it began gradually, insidiously, as such habits do. It is certain that a terrible fear followed his wife's death.

Margaret had been attended at her end by a faithful friend of long standing who had also been governess to the little girls. Charlotte Cole was a daughter of Dr. Cole, a friend of Charles Lamb. She must have had a stout as well as a loving heart. She took charge of the six children, cared for them, worked for them and stayed with them (even accompanying them to Spain), till they were grown up; and when she was very old they took care of her.

Her task must sometimes have been a grim one; for the first time there was real poverty. There is a story that one night James, coming home late and seeing the old crossing-sweeper on the corner shivering with cold, emptied his pockets of all the silver he carried. In the morning the old man called on Miss Cole and returned the money. "The gentleman wasn't himself," he said. "I couldn't rob the little children." James was not by the best standards a good father, that much is obvious, but he was a very loving one, understanding and kind. He wanted his children's love intensely and longed for their company.

At the end of that year he pulled himself together. He went to Southend (then a charming fishing village), took lodgings, cut himself off from his friends and worked hard. Just before Christmas he wrote to Miss Cole: "When I find how much work I get through in this place, I curse my folly in not having come long ago, and in having wasted money and time in such miserable ways this twelvemonth." "There are excellent houses in the best situation here at two guineas a week furnished," he writes. "How should you like to Xmas it here? I confess if I could avoid passing the anniversary—you understand—at 31 it would be a great blessing. Of course, I am always thinking of her here but here she was never anything but well and happy." There is a postscript: "Private—If you hear any suggestion of visits to me here except from my own household, please discourage them. I want to be alone for every reason."

So, he was trying his best. He was never a secret drinker. His friends were part of the fatal temptation: the talk, the laughter, perhaps the assuagement of some deep melancholy within—who can understand this thing? "Don't let the Bard forget me," he writes, referring to his youngest child, Horace, named for the Poet. "I long to see his stout little legs on the Pier and we must have you here soon."

They went down at Christmastime but not to a furnished house. He bought a turkey and they had Christmas dinner at his lodgings.

He stayed in Tavistock Place nearly three years after his wife's death. Sometimes things went well, sometimes ill. Some of his writings were collected and published in volume form in this period.

And then Fate gave him another chance.

In 1868 the Tory Party was again in power and James' old admirer, Lord Stanley, was Foreign Secretary. In those days the Consular Service was a branch of the Diplomatic, and Stanley offered James the Consulate at Brest; he asked instead for Barcelona and got the appointment.

He went to Scotland in the summer and proposed to his distant kinswoman Jean Scott Hannay of Kingsmuir, a very old friend of his and also of his late wife. She accepted him and he wrote to his little daughters in London (the eldest of them now thirteen) to give them the news direct:

> "Miss Jeannie Hannay has consented to become my wife, and I
> hope she will accompany me to Barcelona on my first going there.
> She is an old friend of mine and was a dear friend of your Mother's.
> She is, moreover, of the chief or main branch of our family, a
> thorough gentlewoman, as well as one of the kindest, most amiable
> and most sensible ladies I ever knew. I trust you will be prepared to
> receive her with the highest respect and affection and will help me
> to regain the happiness which I once knew during your dear
> Mamma's lifetime."

And they did. She proved to be an affectionate and kind stepmother. The marriage took place at once and they departed for Barcelona. Miss Cole and the children followed later.

James was four and a half years at the Consulate. It is a very great pity there is no diary of these years. The first thing of note to his credit after his arrival was the release of a British subject, a sailor who had been seventeen months in prison without trial, from a Spanish jail. James set to work and never rested till he got him out.

In 1870 there was an outbreak of yellow fever in Barcelona. The Hannays were then living at Putchet, a suburb above the town. All the consulates closed except the British. James stayed in his office at the Consulate, right down in the docks where the fever raged. "Looking after his nationals," he said, but the town of Barcelona presented him with a medal in commemoration of his services during the outbreak. It is recorded that when told of the medal James remarked: "What for? For not running away?" This medal belonged in later years to his second son Patrick, who had engraved round the edge of it the words

Thackeray had spoken of his friend: "You may search little Hannay through and through and you won't find a white feather."

In July 1872, six months before his death, he began to keep his diary again. He was once more trying to pull himself together. It makes sad reading. Things had been getting very bad in the last years. The drinking bouts were terrible and no doubt increasingly frequent. His money affairs got into a shocking tangle: he was in debt and living on promissory notes. One of the last things he did was to send his agent in London a cheque to pay the insurance on his life, but he had to borrow the money he sent. He was still working at the Consulate, of course, and still writing for the English press. He sent an essay on St. Simon to Smith, Elder and Co., and for this received £30 which went at once on arrears of interest on loans and rent.

There are still happy moments recorded. "Took my boys bathing." "Went shopping with my girls." And his reading is still carefully noted down: rereading Carlyle, Thackeray, Scott, Macaulay, a good deal of history and French literature, Thomas à Kempis, Burton, and "my old friend Boswell." The classics as ever, of course, His much-loved Horace did not fail him, and in the last weeks of his life he read the New Testament in Greek.

For no known reason, the diary stops just four weeks before the end. His death was sudden and totally unexpected. On the morning of January 9, 1873, he was found dead in his study by his second son, Patrick, only thirteen years old at the time, who loved him dearly and never forgot him. His eldest daughter, too, loved, admired and understood him.

He left his young family, the eldest of whom was only nineteen, penniless. The subsequent history of this young family is material for a novel of the period. Everything is there: setting, plot, characters, and, in the person of his eldest daughter, a heroine worthy of any pen.

In 1852, when James was twenty-five, he had edited and written a preface and notes to *The Poetical Works of Edgar Allan Poe: With a Notice of His Life and Genius*, the first English edition of the Poe's poem. Poe had died prematurely and sadly, as everyone knew. On page 25 of the preface James writes:

> "Of his character what is there to say? Let us be charitable.
> Southey's doctor when he heard of a toper[250] was wont to say
> compassionately, "Bibulous clay, Sir, bibulous clay." I would not
> put forward this compendious excuse for Poe; but we must allow
> for infirmity in the man. He was indulged early; he was seduced by

---

[250] a heavy drinker

example. Because he left traces of something high and beautiful in him in spite of this, don't let us make that a reason for being harsher on him than on the frail mortals of his race. One pious scribbler told us very soon after his death that his faults were many, his virtues few. But I learn from those who knew him, men like my friend Buchanan Reid, himself a fine, graceful. tender poet, that his friends loved him and that those who understood him pardoned his infirmities."

I have thought that when James, in the springtime of life, wrote these words, he was, with prophetic foresight, writing his own epitaph.

Between 1872 and 1873 there are a number of his reports to the Ambassador in Madrid, the Hon. A. A. Layard, in the British Museum concerning the Carlist[251] Rising in Spain which are most interesting and give some indication of the respect that Britain and James Hannay in particular was accorded in 19th century Spain.

One last note before leaving James: at an Anglo-Scottish dinner, the Scots challenged the English to drink them under the table. At last when all the English were prostrate, James staggered to his feet and said, "Gentlemen, Flodden is avenged."

James' children by his first wife Elizabeth were three sons and three daughters:

- David McDowell, his eldest son, discussed below.

- Patrick who married a Miss Katy Watson and lived as a banker at Hove, whose son James was a planter in Assam.

- Horace, who died unmarried in 1897.

- Elizabeth Affleck, who married Robert Clement Wyatt (Robert's daughter, Mrs. Eleanor Witty, married Margaret's son Frank Witty and supplied much of the information for this chapter, particularly concerning James her grandfather),

- Margaret, who married Herbert Witty and had a son Frank of whom we have already spoken, and

- Jean, who married Phillip Ray.

By his second wife Jean Scott, James had a daughter Robina who married Fred Salveson. She died in 1952 leaving no children.

---

[251] Carlists were part of a political movement seeking to place a member of the Bourbon dynasty on the throne of Spain.

## 2.5.  David Hannay (1853-1933), son of James

David McDowell Hannay, James and Margaret's eldest, was born in 1853. He became a naval historian of note. He married Eleanor Hooker and had two daughters, Margaret and Edith Eleanor, and a son David. He died in 1933 and the following "Times" obituary notice was published at his death:

> "Mr. David Hannay, who died suddenly in London on Thursday at the age of 80, was an able writer and lecturer on Naval History. As one of the group of journalists who helped before the war to form public opinion on sea power and the need of an adequate fleet he rendered national service, no less than by his influence on young officers at the Royal Naval College. Mr. David McDowell Hannay was born in London on December 25th. 1853. David was educated at Westminster School and was for some months Vice Consul at Barcelona where his father had been Consul. Over a period of many years he contributed to *Henley's Scots Observer* and the *Nautical Observer, The Times Literary Supplement, The Pall Mall Gazette, The Saturday Review,*. and the *St. James Gazette.* He did much work for the magazines, and a selection of his essays in Blackwood's and elsewhere was reproduced under the title "Ships and Men" in 1910. He first book was a monograph on Admiral Blake, in the series *English Worthies* edited by Andrew Lang, which appeared in 1886. To another series on Great Writers he contributed lives of Smollet (1887) and Captain Marryat (1889) both of which were well received. On the works of Marryat, he was a recognised authority and in the nineties he contributed an introduction to an illustrated edition. To "English Men of Action" he contributed a biography of Admiral Rodney in 1891. His hereditary interest in Spain led him to study Spanish Literature and he wrote an excellent biography of Don Emilio Castelar."

His daughters married as follows: Margaret to James McCaig of Stranraer, Edith Eleanor to Stephen Lang. His son David married Agnes McFarlane Smith of Mull and had two children, David and Barbara.

## 3.  *John Hannay (b. 1715) of Knock*

John Hannay of Knock, the son of John Hannay and Janet Dickson, was born in 1715, and married his cousin Grizel Dickson in 1740.

There were three sons, Patrick, Robert and John, and two daughters, Janet and Margaret. Janet was born in 1752 and married Peter Hannay of Drumaston. a descendant of William Hannay of Kirkdale, the branch of the family the Hannay Thompsons now represent. Margaret married Alexander Cormack.

## 3.1. Robert Hannay of Kilmarnock

John and Grizel's second son, Robert of Kilmarnock, went to Glasgow, as did so many younger sons, to earn a living in business. Little else is known of him other than he married Mary Paget and had two children, Grace and John.

## 3.2. John Hannay (1754-1833) of Malaby

The third son of John Hannay and Grizel Dickson, John of Malaby (1754-1833), is an interesting person who was called "The Galloway Saint", though the reasons why have defied investigations[252].

*For the pedigree of John Hannay (1754-1833), see Figure 54: The Hannays of Knock and Garrarie*

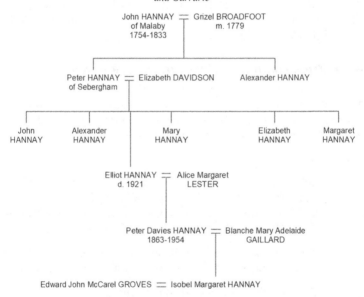

**Figure 63: The Hannays of Sebergham**

John married Grizel Broadfoot who bore him two sons, Peter and Alexander. Alexander became a banker in Dumfries, and Peter a noted agriculturalist. For a family tree, see Figure 63: The Hannays of Sebergham. Peter bought the property of Baldoon and married Elizabeth, the daughter of the Rev. Elliot William Davidson, then minister at Sorbie. Finally, he purchased the property of Sebergham

---

[252] No mention can be found regarding this moniker for John Hannay of Malaby other than ones that obviously refer to earlier editions of *The Hannays of Sorbie*. Indeed, the only "Galloway Saint" which can be found is Saint Ninian, i.e. a literal saint from Galloway. It is unclear where Stewart Francis originally discovered this reference.

Castle, near Carlisle, which incidentally is noted for its primroses. His wife Elizabeth had three sons and three daughters. His sons were John, Alexander and Elliot, and his daughters, all unmarried, Mary, Elizabeth and Margaret lived at Sedbergham Castle until they died in the early 1920's when the place was sold to a man of the name of Knote of Newcastle.

Elliot married Alice Margaret, the daughter of John Lester, and served for many years as a civil servant in the War Office. He died in 1921, leaving a son Peter Davies Hannay, born in 1863, who claimed the title of Hannay of Sorbie and is shown in Burke as such, although Hannay of Knock would have been more suitable: Hannay of Sorbie he certainly was not. He married Blanche Mary Adelaide, the daughter of Alois Gaillard of Italy. He died in 1954 and left a daughter Isabel Margaret, who married Colonel Edward John McCarel Groves, D.S.O., M.C., of Lymn, Cheshire.

## 4. Patrick Hannay of Barwhirren (1745-1836)

John and Grizel's eldest son, Patrick, born in 1745, married Helen McClellan of Carleton and purchased the estate of Barwhirren. He married secondly Janet Milligen, who bore him one son, Andrew. It was Andrew who bought the property of Grange.

Patrick's children by his first wife Helen were:

- John, who succeeded to the estate at Penninghame, married Mary Dickson (born 1770) and had a large family. He died in 1832. His first son, also named John, predeceased him in 1819. His second son Peter, thus succeeded.

- Elizabeth, who married William Tait of Wigtown and had a family, some representatives of it are still living there today

- Robert and Patrick, who died in infancy

- Grizel, who married the Rev. Alexander Ogilvie

- Helen, who married John Gifford of Grange of Bladnoch,

- another Patrick, who married a certain Ann Cumming and went to America, where they settled and raised a large family of four daughters and three sons.

- Thomas, who purchased the Grange of Cree.

## 4.1. The Family of Thomas Hannay (born 1776)

Thomas Hannay, the son of Patrick of Barwhirren and Helen McClellen, purchased Grange of Cree and Baldoon, and married Margaret McClellen of Orchardton.

*For the pedigree of Thomas Hannay (b. 1776), see Figure 54: The Hannays of Knock and Garrarie*

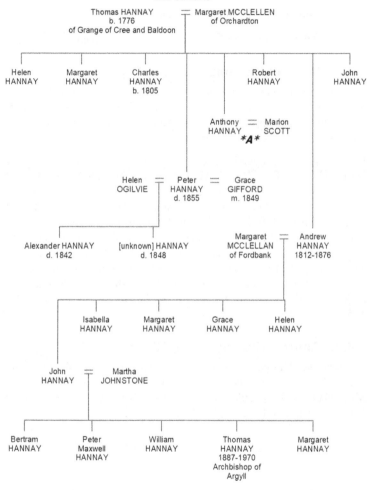

*A*: See Figure 65

**Figure 64: The Hannays of Grange of Cree**

Thomas and Margaret had six sons and two daughters:

- Helen married Mr. Thomas Miekle, the founder of Crieff Hydro[253].

- Margaret died young.

- Charles was born in 1805, married Elizabeth Beath of Cowper and Garthland and died in 1875.

- Robert and John both died young.

- Peter, Andrew, and Anthony are discussed below.

## 4.2. Rev. Peter Hannay (died 1855)

Thomas and Margaret' son Peter entered the Church and was for many years minister at Wigtown. He published a book of sermons, and a biographical note appears in one of the editions which is rather long but worthy of study. Some of the salient points follow:

Peter went to the University of Edinburgh, and then was at Theological Hall under Dr. Dick[254]. He was licensed to preach by the United Presbytery of Wigtown on March 14, 1826. Ordained at Glasgow on May 6,1835, he went to Oban to a missionary station. He was Inducted to Creetown on July 26, 1837. On April 30, he married Helen the daughter of the Reverend Alexander Ogilvie of Wigtown. He had a son and daughter. His son Alexander died in 1842 aged three; his daughter followed, aged 11, in 1848, and his wife between the two. He became minister at Wigtown and in 1849 married secondly Grace, the daughter of Mr. George Giffard of Grange of Bladnoch. He died on May 26, 1855.

## 4.3. Andrew Hannay (1812-1876)

Thomas and Margaret' son Andrew, went to Liverpool, where he engaged in business concerned with shipping. He married Margaret McClellan[255]of Fordbank and had one son John and four daughters, Isabella, Margaret, Grace and Helen.

---

[253] Crieff Hydro – the Crieff Hydropathic Establishment – is a resort hotel in Perthshire.

[254] Professor John Dick, DD, 1764-1833

[255] It is curious that Andrew would have married someone with the exact same name as his mother, though from a different village. It is possible that this is an error. There is a record of an Andrew Hannay or Hannah in Wigtown marrying a Margaret *Thomson* around this time.

246

John continued in business in Liverpool and married Martha Johnstone. John and Martha had four sons – Bertram, Peter Maxwell, William, and Thomas, and a daughter, Margaret.

*For the pedigree of Anthony Hannay, see Figure 64*

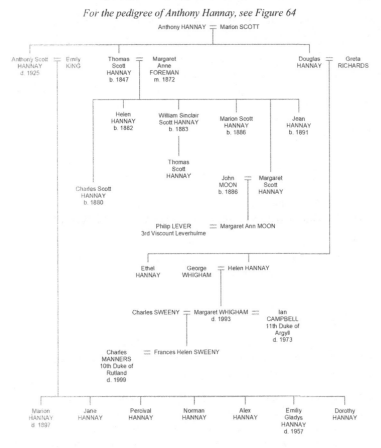

**Figure 65: Hannay of Baldoon and Garthland**

John and Martha's son Thomas was born in 1887, took a B.A. at the University of Liverpool in 1907 and went to Queen's College, Cambridge, securing a B.A. there also in 1910, and proceeded to M.A. in 1914. He entered the Church of England and was ordained in Wakefield Diocese in 1911. From 1933-40 he was Principal of the College of the Resurrection at Mirfield. In 1942 he was asked to accept the Bishopric of Argyll in the Episcopal Church of Scotland, which he did, being appointed Primus in 1952 and Archbishop of Argyll and the Isles. He was awarded a Lambeth Doctorate of Divinity in 1954 and made a Fellow of Queen's College, Cambridge, in 1952. He died on January 31, 1970.

247

### 4.4. Anthony Hannay

Thomas and Margaret' son Anthony married Marion Scott and had three sons: Anthony Scott, Thomas Scott and Douglas.

The family tree of this branch can be found in Figure 65: Hannay of Baldoon and Garthland.

Douglas married Greta Richards and had two daughters, Ethel, who married Fred Todd, and Helen, who married Col. George Whigham. Helen and George's daughter Margaret became Duchess of Argyll. Margaret was involved in a series of scandals throughout her life, the most notorious of which was a very messy divorce from Ian Campbell, the Duke of Argyll.

Thomas Scott, the second son of Anthony, married Margaret Anne ("Annie") Foreman and had two sons, Charles Scott and William Sinclair Scott, and four daughters, Helen, Marion Scott, Margaret Scott, and Jean. Margaret Scott married John Moon, and their daughter Margaret Ann married Philip Lever, the 3rd Viscount Leverhulme.

Anthony Scott was educated at Merchiston and entered the cotton business. He was the founder of the Cotton Clearing House in Liverpool and a prominent businessman then till his death in 1925. He married Emily King, and they had eight children.

## 5.   Peter Hannay (m. 1818)

Patrick Hannay's son John was succeeded by John's second son, Peter. Peter married Ann Arbuckle and had two sons, John and Robert, and three daughters, Mary, Anne and Helen.

John was the factor at the Gavenwood and Fife estates and subsequently on the Caithness and Sutherland estates. John owned the Cairnhill estate in Aberdeenshire and had a top Aberdeen Angus stud. He was deputy lieutenant for the county. His wife was Elizabeth Farquarson Milne, the only daughter of Dr. and Mrs. Milne of Moncopper House, Banff.

John and Elizabeth's son Peter emigrated to Australia, where he married and started a family. Peter's son, John Henry Fitzpatrick was born in 1884 at Lentesfield. At 7 years of age he travelled, on the death of his parents, back to Scotland and lived with his grandfather, John Hannay, at Stirling. He attended Dollar Academy. John Henry Fitzpatrick returned to Australia in 1901 and became a resident of Bassletown, New South Wales. He married and had three sons and two daughters. His brother, Charles Edward Hannay, had three sons and a daughter.

# XIV: The Hannays of Clugston and Creetown

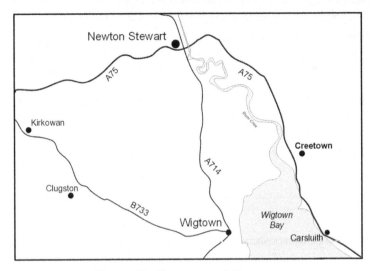

**Figure 66: Clugston and Creetown**

As an introduction to the Clugston and Creetown branch of the family, it is a suitable place here to discuss the various Scottish contingents that fought in continental armies almost up to modern times. Many of the family served in these corps. The presence of Scottish contingents in the French armies dates from the period of the Hundred Years' War (1337-1453), when both France and Scotland had England as the common enemy. Perhaps the most famous commanders were John Stewart, Earl of Buchan, the victor over the English at Beauge in 1424, and his father-in-law, Archibald, Earl of Douglas, both of whom were killed at the battle of Verneuil, 1425. Scottish participation in the French army culminated in the establishment of the *Garde Écossaise* bodyguards to the French King—under the French King Charles VII (1403-1461). This guard lasted, in name, until the French Revolution, although the number of Scotsmen in it dwindled rapidly after 1603, when the English and Scottish crowns were united.

The heyday of the Scottish regiments in Germany was the period of the Thirty Years' War (1618-1648), when Scottish contingents fought in both the Imperial and Protestant armies, primarily those of the Swedish king Gustavus Adolphus. The name of Leslie was particularly renowned: Alexander and David (who later won with Cromwell the victory of Marston Moor) in the Swedish king's forces, and Walter, later a Count of the Empire, with the Swedish king's opponent Albrecht von Wallenstein.

249

In the Netherlands the Scots played a large part in the wars of Independence and were eventually formed by the States into the Scottish Brigade (known in Scotland as the Dutch regiments).

In the 18th century, although many individual Scots, Jacobite refugees, served in European armies – for example the famous James Keith(1696-1758), son of the Earl Marischal of Scotland, who served as a field marshal in the service of Frederick II of Prussia – in the service of Prussia and Russia, they took service as individuals rather than as commanders of Scottish companies. Many members of the family served in these various corps.

*For the pedigree of John Hannay (d. 1614), see Figure 20: The Hannays of Kirkdale*

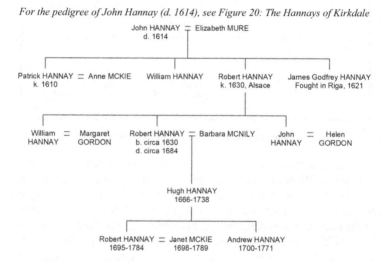

**Figure 67: Early Hannays of Clugston and Creetown**

## 1. Robert Hannay (d. 1630)

It is in the context of one of these Scottish expeditions to the continent that we first hear of the Clugston and Creetown branch, which split off from the Kirkdale line (see Figure 67: Early Hannays of Clugston and Creetown). The first of the name was Robert, the brother of Patrick Hannay of Kirkdale. He served as a Major in Lord Reay's Regiment in the Thirty Years' War, and after campaigning in Alsace he was killed in 1630. Robert's descendants can be found in Figure 68.

*For the pedigree of Robert Hannay (k. 1630), see Figure 20: The Hannays of Kirkdale*

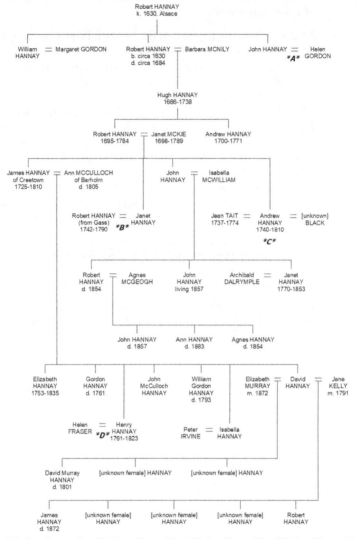

*A*: See Figure 69    *B*: See Figure 52    *C*: See Figure 73    *D*: See Figure 71

**Figure 68: The Hannays of Clugston and Creetown**

Robert had three children, so the Parish list of 1684 informs us:

- William who married Margaret Gordon, and who is mentioned in an assignation of James McColm, a burgess of Wigtown in 1668.

251

- Robert, born about 1630 and who lived at the Mill of Clugston of whom more anon.

- John, of whom the Register of the Scottish Privy Council for 1679 reads, "John Hannay at the Myle of Clugston gives a bond not rise in arms against his Majesty dated at Wigton on September 4th 1679." This was presumably after the Battle of Bothwell Brig[256], in which he must have been concerned when the Covenanters were so severely defeated by Dundee. John was out with the rebels at Bothwell Brig. Shortly after the battle the Dragoons came into Galloway, burned houses and removed the cattle. By the Sheriff's order, John had the roof of his house removed and the house demolished. However, September 4, 1679, a John Hannay of the Mill of Clugston, probably John of Penninghame (his brother was William of Clugston), made a bond at Wigton as follows:

  > "That whereas his Majesty's proclamation of 27th July last has indemnified him for being in the late rebellion on his signing this bond, he will hereafter abstain from taking arms against his Majesty."

In 1684 it appears he had been declared rebel again as William McCalmont was summoned for communicating with him. John's family can be seen in Figure 69.

---

[256] Also called Bothwell Bridge

*For the pedigree of John Hannay, see Figure 68.*

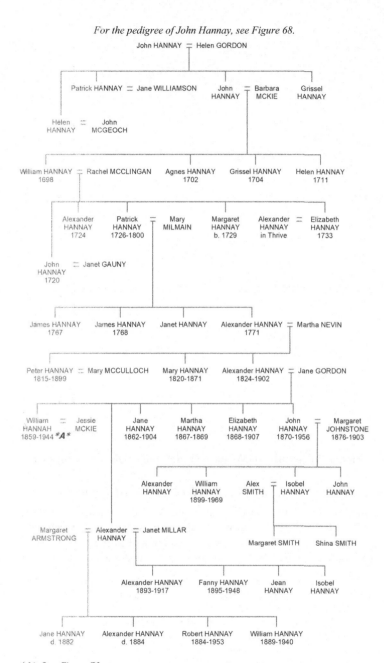

*A*: See Figure 70

**Figure 69: The Hannays of Altercannoch**

*For the pedigree of William Hannah, see Figure 69*

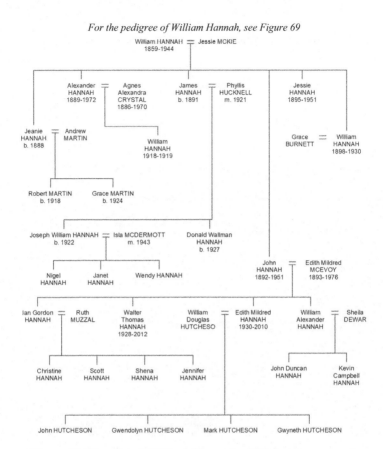

**Figure 70: Family of William Hannah of High Altercannoch**

## 2. Robert Hannay (1630-c.1684), son of Robert

Robert was the miller at Clugston. The date of his death is given as 1682 on the family tombstone. As the stone was erected much later, this year may be incorrect, for he is mentioned in the Parish List of 1684 with Barbara McNily his spouse. The tombstone reads as follows:

"Here lies the corps of Robert Hannay millar of Clugston who died in 1682 aet 52 also Hugh Hannay his son who died in 1738 aet 72. As also lies the corps of Andrea Hannay son of Hugh who died 24 Dec 1771 aet 71 as also the Corps of Robert Hannay and Janet McKie late of Spittal who died Jan 8 1784 and she aged 80 years and also the corps of James Hannay[257] and Agnes Forsyth his spouse late in Gass who died aet 72 and she uel 71. Also Agnes Hannay daughter of Robert Hannay in Clugston who died 1790 aet

---

[257] Pedigree unknown

15 years and also the corps of Robert Hannay who died Aug 18
1790 aet 48."

## 3. Hugh Hannay (1666-1738), son of Robert

Robert's son Hugh, born at Clugston in 1666, also mentioned in the
Parish list in 1684, continued as the miller of Clugston, dying in 1738.
He had two sons, Robert (more below) and Andrew. Andrew was born
in 1700 and died in 1771 unmarried.

## 4. Robert Hannay of Spital (1695-1784), son of Hugh

Robert, born in 1695, married Janet McKie and is referred to as of
Spital near Wigtown. This is, in fact, probably only another name for
the Mill of Clugston, as it might be said to be in Spital. They had
several children:

- James of Creetown is discussed in more detail below.

- Janet married her cousin Robert Hannay in Gass Robert and
  Janet had a son James and a daughter Agnes. See Figure 52:
  Descendants of Robert Hannay and Janet Hannay.

- John married Isabella McWilliam, and had three children:

    o Robert, who became the miller of Clugston and
      married Agnes McGeogh, having a son John, and
      two daughters Ann and Agnes.

    o John, who was still living in 1857.

    o Janet, who married Archibald Dalrymple and died in
      1853.

- Andrew, married Jean Tait and was the founder of the
  Stranraer and Powton [Pouton] families. He is covered fully
  in the next chapter.

## 5. James Hannay of Creetown (1725-1810)

Robert Hannay of Spital's eldest son James of Creetown, was born in
1725 and died in 1810. He married Ann McCulloch of Barholm in 1752
and had a large family:

- Elizabeth, born in 1753, died unmarried in 1835.

- Gordon and John McCulloch both died in 1761, aged three
  years and two months respectively.

- William Gordon died aged 18 in 1793.

- Isabella married Peter Irvine and had issue.

255

- David married twice: first Elizabeth Murray who bore him a son, David Murray who died in 1801, aged 17, and two daughters; secondly, Jane Kelly whom he married in 1791. Jane and David had a son James who died unmarried in 1872, and another son Robert, also unmarried, as well as three daughters.

- Henry, who was born in 1761 and is listed below.

## 6. Henry Hannay (1761-1823), son of James

Henry was the only son of James and Ann to produce a surviving male heir. He married Helen, the daughter of Simon Fraser of Pollhillick, a cadet branch of the Lovat family, by his wife Rachel, the daughter of Lewis Cuthbert of Castlehill, Inverness. Henry's family tree can be found in Figure 71.

Henry and Helen had four sons and six daughters:

- James, born in 1799, was a lieutenant in the Royal Navy and died unmarried at an early age in 1823.

- Alexander Fraser died in infancy

- Huntly Gordon died unmarried in 1866.

- Simon Fraser is discussed in detail below.

- Rachel died unmarried in 1876.

- Ann McCulloch, who died in infancy.

- Frances Grey who also died unmarried.

- Catherine Fraser married William Thomas.

- Mary Pemberton married Colonel Comber Augustus Kirkland of the Bengal Staff Corps.

- Mary Madgdelene married Captain Charles Carew Pigott in 1839 and died in 1843.

*For the pedigree of Henry (1761-1823), see Figure 68: The Hannays of Clugston and Creetown*

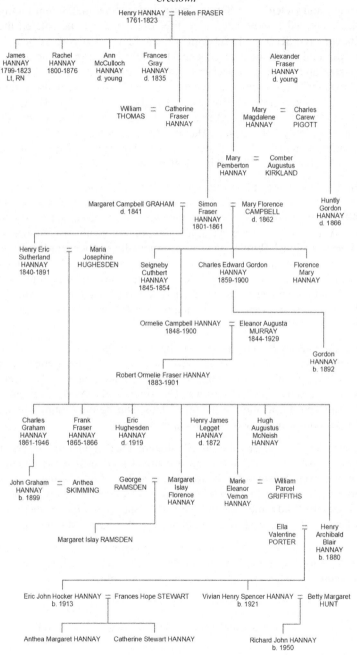

**Figure 71: Family of Henry Hannay (1761-1823)**

257

## 7. *Lt. Col. Simon Fraser Hannay (1801-1861)*

Henry and Helen's son Simon Fraser, from whom the present family descends, led a most interesting life. Born in 1801, he entered the Indian Civil Service and subsequently the Indian Army where he rose to the rank of Lieutenant Colonel. In 1822 the Burmese subjugated Assam and the British declared war on February 24, 1824. Colonel Hannay took a very prominent part. He joined his regiment, the Assam Light Infantry (now the Royal Gurkha Rifles) on May 14, 1838, and when the Commanding Officer was killed in action at Sadiya on January 28, 1839, Captain Hannay took over command. He was confirmed in the rank of Lieutenant Colonel on March 25 that year and remained in command until his death in January 1861.

In 1837 he wrote an article for the *Journal of the Asiatic Society* describing his journey into Upper Burma. He was at this time in the 40th Regiment of Native Infantry and went from the capital of Ava to the Amber mines of the Hakong Valley on the south east frontier of Assam. Colonel Burney, then his commanding officer, ordered this mission to the mines. His party consisted of the newly appointed British Governor of Moyaung and several Burmese officers of inferior rank with a number of troops. He left Ava on November 22, with 34 boats of various sizes, and returned on April 9, 1836 arriving back in base on May 2.

On the journey he must have seen the wild tea bushes which led him eventually to start the Hannay Tea Gardens in Assam, a concern in which the family is still actively interested—for example, Eric John Hooker Hannay (1913-1976) was Chairman of the Assam Branch of Indian Tea Association in the mid-1950s. During the Mutiny, Simon Fraser commanded the troops in upper Assam.

His first wife, Margaret Campbell Graham, the daughter of Alexander Graham of Glasgow wrote a most detailed journal of the regiment's march from Mysopoorie to Mhow in 1829, and also wrote another journal beginning in 1839 when they were posted in Sadiya, Upper Assam. In 1840 Simon and Margaret had a son, Henry Eric Sutherland. Margaret died in 1841, likely of cholera, and is buried at Gauhati.

On Margaret's death, Simon married again with the family governess, Mary Florence Campbell, the daughter of Alexander Campbell of Calcutta, by whom he had three sons and a daughter:

- Seigneby Cuthbert, born in 1845 and died in 1854.

- Ormelie Campbell, born in 1848 of whom more anon.

- Charles Edward Gordon went to New Zealand, married, and had a son Gordon, who served in the Royal Navy settling in Australia.

- Florence Mary, who died in Assam.

Here are some extracts from Margaret's journal which show some of the difficulties of life in India and some of the customs good and bad of the period:

"A JOURNAL
Commencing from Mysopoorie
19th January 1829.
Written by Mrs. Simon Hannay

Camp Bickry-

We left Mysopoorie early this morning where I have spent nine happy months. Every tree and shrub—I felt some attachment to—they were all planted and arranged by myself—but it has not been my fate to see them come to perfection—and my beautiful flowers will now in all probability go to ruin—I have been in low spirits all day—after Breakfast I was very industrious and mended some of my stockings—a rare thing for an Indian lady to do—it is dreadfully cold and the encampment is on a large dreary plain—I dined at the Mess where I am to be a guest of the Officers during the march. There is nothing at all interesting about this place—it is merely a small village. A poor man died in Camp today of a few minutes' illness—such is the uncertainty of human life. God no doubt sends these awful warnings to us to check us in the career of folly we are all too prone to run on in and how thankful we ought to be to our Almighty God Who spares us to repent—may I and all who are dear to me improve the time granted us on earth, and may God preserve us from sudden death.

This Journal I intend to keep regularly (If God spares me) during the whole march to Mhow. It will perhaps afford my much loved Mama more amusement than a common letter and I will write down whatever comes uppermost knowing that my darling mother will consider the motive for which it is written, so making up for its deficiency in good language and interesting material.

Camp Arowan—Jan 20th, 1829.

I did not arrive at the ground this morning till nine o'clock—Last march I used to go between the advance guard and the Corps, but now I find it a better plan to keep between the rear guard and the Regt. I read my Bible for an hour after Breakfast and then sat down to work. I had visits from several of the Officers—they are all so attentive and so anxious to please me that I find it very pleasant dining at the Mess. This is a very pretty place—the village is on a rising ground. Hannay and I walked there after dinner. The houses are generally built with mud and have flat roofs. There is also the

259

ruins of a mud fort here. The country is rather thickly wooded and the view from the little hill on which the town is built is really very pretty at least it appears so to us, after seeing flat sandy plains for so many months. I regret poor old Mysopoorie more the farther I get from it and my beautiful garden that I took so much trouble with. I feel as if I were going to a large town and leaving the country where I enjoyed perfect freedom. At Mysopoorie I did just as I pleased. I could look after the garden and the farmyard and never was intruded on, but at a large station such as Mhow if you associate with the people you must in some measure conform to them—to their habits and customs—and a young woman requires some strength of mind to withstand mixing with the gay and thoughtless crowd. If my kind friends the Monktons had been gay worldly people I should have profited little by their society, but it was the contrary and their good example has I trust brought me to think more seriously of Death and Eternity.

Camp Shackohabad [Shikohabad]—Jan. 21st, 1829.

I have been very unwell and very lazy this morning. I lay down to read after breakfast and did not get up till it was time to dress for dinner. It has been very cold all day. If I am spared to go back home once more to dear dear Scotland, I know my beloved Mama will never get me from the fireside. I really cannot bear the cold and strange to say I always feel in better health when others are suffering from extreme heat of weather.

Mr. Davidson—a nice young man and a great friend of ours—came to spend the day in Camp with the Officers of the Regt. He spent some hours with us. It was very late ere I could get up from the dinner table, but I persuaded Hannay late as it was to take me to the city of Shackohabad. We walked through it but I saw nothing worthy of note but a beautiful little Mosque. It has three domes with a slight elegant front. It is enclosed with a high brick wall. Hannay and I were allowed to go inside but there were no figures in the niches and no carving of any kind. Consequently, external appearance was all the Mosque could boast, but that being of the purest white and an elegant form relieved by a clump of dark green trees made it look extremely pretty. Shackohabad is an old Musselman City, and the immense number of ruins of old, and very large, brick buildings tell that it has once been a place of some renown. The word Shackohabad means the Glorious City, though it now looks a poor crowded, and I should think an unhealthy place.

Maggy has forgot to mention the crowd of old women, men and children that followed us thro' the town staring at us as if we were beings of a different world. It is not proper for a lady to go into these large towns where the greater proportion of the inhabitants are Musselmen, as you are almost always liable to insult by being crowded with faquers or Holy beggars who scruple not at abusing the Europeans whenever they can. Maggy chatters and makes such a noise, calling out O Hannay look at this, and O Hannay look at that. I am obliged to call her to order. She is as much pleased to look at an Olde Tomb or Temple as if it was a Palace. The fact is if you see one of either Hindu or Musselman, you see the whole, the only difference is the size, they being all of the same shape and built of the same materials with the exception of those you may meet with when stone is procurable. I allude to those met with in the Company's provinces. The temples of the Hindus in Assam and the ruins of those of former days are more splendid in the part of India we are going to, and I expect Maggy will be agreeably surprised.

Camp Agra—Jan. 25th, 1829.

This is Sunday and I might have gone to church but I thought it would be more profitable for me to have a service at home so I had my 8 scholars—the band boys— to join me. I do not read the service of the Church of England but I have got Beans Prayer Book and I try to keep as near to the Church of Scotland as I can. I have been teaching these eight boys for some months—they are very attentive to what I tell them and I trust God will yet bless my poor endeavours to teach these little orphan Boys. I read all day and then went in the evening to take another peep at the splendid Taj—the fountains were playing—but I was disappointed in them, they are quite unworthy of the place—the echo there is the finest thing you can imagine in the large dome, the voices below in common conversation sound above like sacred music. The building cost upwards of £700,000[258]. The Emperor Shajehan who built this splendid place to the memory of his wife the beautiful Nourjehan is buried by her side—he intended to have thrown a marble bridge across the Jumna and to have built a Tomb for himself exactly like that of his wife, but he died before it could be put in execution.

Camp Kutghur—4th Feb. 1829.

It is just a year today since we left Dinapore on our march to Mysopoorie and we little thought to be so soon again on the move—it is certainly a hardship on the Regt. but none to me—I enjoy a March so much that I must have been cut out for an Officer's wife—today we are encamped on the Bed of the River Gumber—part of which is quite dry in this season–the banks are steep and rugged with a good deal of Jungle – the Country round here is barren broken ground with very deep ravines—so much so it is dangerous travelling in the dark. Hannay would not let me leave Hindown till daybreak. I was up however in time for Breakfast—I worked and read in the forenoon and walked in the evening with Hannay and Mr. Shuckburgh to try to get some pretty pebbles—but we found no nice ones—I am still rather an invalid and get very tired towards evening—Mr. Long spent this evening with us.

---

[258] £60,500,000 in 2018.

Camp Burrana—Feb 17th, 1829.

We have had a halt today from a most unlooked for circumstance.
Brigadier Duncan who is to command the Station at Mhow is
travelling three marches in rear of our corps and has been taken
dangerously ill on the road. Our doctor has been applied to and we
are obliged to stop till he returns. I have been alone in Camp all
day. Hannay has been out and brought home some fine fish and a
few splendid stones. I went to the riverside in the evening and took
the Band Boys with me and they picked up some very nice pebbles.

Camp Burrana—Feb. 18th, 1829.

Here we are still at a stand—we could not move without the Dr.
Hannay has been out all day and I have been trying to grind down
some of the pebbles to see what they are like. I went to look for
more pebbles in the evening with Hannay and Mr. Shuckburgh and
they took me such a road that I shudder at the very thought of it—
we walked at least six miles on the very edge of a very steep Bank
of the river and the water so deep right behind me that if my foot
had slipped I must have been drowned but this was not all for we
staid out so late that we lost our road and we got home by climbing
and scrambling through some of the most frightful ravines I ever
saw—the Jungle here is almost all the babool tree which is covered
with a strong thorn at least an inch long. I jumped on some
withered branches of this and got my poor feet full of these horrid
thorns—the pain I endured was dreadful. I scolded Hannay—I
scolded Mr. Shuckburgh—declared I never would walk with them
again if they did not promise to take me home by daylight—but
they laughed at me—we got home safe at last but I am very tired
and my feet swelled as large as two pairs of common feet—the
Natives make a very strong liquor from the Babool—I believe it is
from the flower Hannay says—when well distilled it is a very good
and not unwholesome spirit—our servants have all been tipsy
today.

The weather is now getting very hot—I am obliged to have
recourse to my light muslin gowns already—poor Hannay is so
tired—he has gone fast asleep already. I too dearest Mama must
say goodnight my eyes are winking very fast.

Camp Sousneer—March 2nd, 1829.

Our march was only six miles this morning so that I was not
obliged to leave the ground till daybreak; however I was up and
dressed by 4 o'clock in order to let the servants strike the tent, and
as I found it very cold in the open air, I had a fire of rushes made
where I sat till it was time for me to start. I began to think of home
and fancied what would my dearest Mama think could she only see
me at this moment, sitting in the middle of a camp in the centre of
India warming myself at a fire of rushes, wrapped up in a large
Tartan silk cloak and surrounded by natives, camels, and elephants.

I came through Sousneer in the morning. It is a large fortified town—the natives came out in crowds to stare at me I never shut the doors of my palanquin in passing through a town or village—most ladies would—but I like to see everything that is to be seen and as it does me no harm—the natives staring at me—the curiosity of both parties is satisfied.

The soil here is not good and there is very little cultivation. We walked out in the evening and got some pretty pieces of Agate. We are encamped in a horrible place. The tents are close together and we are quite surrounded by ravines—our tent is on the very edge of one—and as it is blowing very hard I don't quite like it.

The Officers are all quite disconcerted at hearing that the Mess wines are out. People in this country cannot bear to want any comfort and I do think unless a man marries young, he is apt to get very selfish. You would be quite astonished dearest Mama could you see or know how selfish ladies are in India. They would not give up one comfort which they have been used to for anyone. I hope I am not selfish for I do despise it in others. Laziness too is what grows on one most imperceptibly. I try to guard against it as much as I can. I always dress myself, brush and dress my own hair and take care of my own clothes. I am not praising myself dear Mama but only wish to show that it is quite possible for a lady to exert herself in this Country. I keep no Ayah (Lady's maid) which diminishes the expenses of our establishment not a little. Hannay often insists on my having one but I will not indulge in such laziness unless obliged to by bad health.

Sudiya—August 21st, 1839.

Got up at 6 o'clock-dressed, took coffee and read with Mr. Dalton till 10 o'clock, by which I mean that he read to me while I worked. Hannay was engaged in writing. He reprimanded me sharply for what he calls lounging away the morning. I think it unkind his doing so, as I considered my morning as both pleasantly and profitably employed.

Little does Hannay know how many a sore heart he has given me by the harshness of his language when he is angry. True it is that he makes up for it by generosity and indulgence, and as he immediately forgets his anger, and the cause of it, he wonders that I remember it, but in the same proportion, as kindness and attention, attaches me, so does harshness estrange me. It is a very weak point in my character, that I cannot bear an unkind look even from those I love and often has my poor Grandmother told me that this quick perception and extreme sensibility would render me miserable in passing through this world. And I have found her words but too true. Things that would pass totally unobserved by others strike home to me and wound my feelings, so that this fault of mine may be viewed as a misfortune, although I do not possess the slightest feeling of an unforgiving disposition. But of all the forgiving tempers I have ever met with, Hannay's is the most so, and I believe him to be too generous to take revenge on his greatest enemy.

Breakfasted at 10, Hannay called it 11. Commenced my school at 11 and got over it at 2. Read till 4, Dressed, Dined at 5. Wet evening. Could not walk out. Hannay sleepy. Myself stupid. Mr. Dalton bearing all, most philosophically. Went to bed at 10."

More details about Margaret's life and journal can be found in the book *Army Wives: From Crimea to Afghanistan: The Real Lives of the Women Behind the Men in Uniform* by Midge Gillies (Aurum Press, 2017).

## 8. Henry Hannay (1840-1891), son of Simon

Simon and Margaret's son, Henry Eric Sutherland, was born in 1840, and died on October 24, 1891. He joined the East India Company's Navy and served in the Persian Gulf campaign[259] and in The Indian Mutiny[260]; first in the HMS *Calcutta* and then with Captain Reall's Naval Brigade on shore. He is listed as a Midshipman in 1857[261]. He retired in 1859 while in Dibruggarh, where he was serving with the Naval detachment attached to the First Abor expedition.

Henry married Maria Josephine the daughter of Charles Hughesden, a merchant trading with China in Calcutta. They had a large family, six sons and two daughters:

- Frank Fraser died aged one in 1866.

- Eric Hughesden did not marry and died in 1919.

- Henry James Legget died in 1872 as a child.

- Margaret Islay Florence married George Ramsden of Maltham, Huddersfield, and had a family.

- Marie Eleanor Vernon married William Parcel Griffiths of Merion, Pembrokeshire.

- Hugh Augustus McNeish was a Knight Bachelor and married Raine Roe. His son, Richard Neish, was killed in a polo accident in Nowsherain 1938.

- Henry Archibald Blair was born in 1880 and brought up by Sir Joseph Hocker the eminent botanist. He was educated at Bedford School. He was a noted polo player in his early days in India and also an East India merchant,

---

[259] Anglo-Persian War, 1856-1857

[260] also known as the Sepoy Mutiny, 1857-1859

[261] Clark, F., *East-India Register and Army List for 1858*, Allen and Co., London, 1858

owning the Hannay tea gardens in Assam. He married Ella Valentine Porter and had two sons:

- o Eric John Hocker, was born in 1913 and became a tea planter in Assam. Eric married Frances Hope Stewart and had two daughters, Anthea Margaret and Catherine Stewart

- o Vivian Henry Spencer, born in 1921, was a Major in the Royal Engineers. He was awarded a Military Cross in World War II, and married Betty Margaret Hunt. They had a son, Richard John, born in 1950.

- Charles Graham, born in 1861, married and had a son John Graham Hannay. John married Anthea Skimming and became a councilor for Chelsea. Charles tried to claim the baronetcy of Mochrum, which is discussed below.

## 8.1. Charles Hannay and the Baronetcy

Charles Graham Hannay put forward a claim to the baronetcy of Mochrum through Ramsden, Sykes and Rawsden, solicitors of Huddersfield in 1901. The claim was based on Sir Samuel Hannay's claim in 1783 as the 3$^{rd}$ Baronet of Mochrum. In 1853 the family had applied for a general service of heirship to the Sheriff Clerk of Wigtown. The Sheriff substitute of Wigtown, Mr. Rhind, endorsed the petition as follows:

"Wigtown 2nd June 1853. Having considered the foregoing petition and seen the abstract Petition with a certificate attached thereto of the Publication Edictally in Edinburgh allow the petitioner a proof of his propinquity as specified in the aforesaid petition, in terms of the statute 10 and 11 Vict, cap 47."

No doubt further action was taken due to the caveat placed on the Baronetcy by George Francis Hannay of Kingsmuir, who had a prior claim, of which there is no doubt. But by the death of the last of the Kingsmuir male descendants the succession would rightfully fall to Kirkdale and his descendants. And these failing and becoming Rainsford Hannays, the succession would quite rightly be transferred to the nearest male heir who would be in the family of Robert Hannay of the Mill at Clugston, and of whom Charles Graham Hannay was the senior male representative.

In 1901 he issued the following declaration of intention to assume the baronetcy:

" ...Now be it known to whom all these presents may concern that I, the said Charles Graham Hannay have assumed the said baronetcy and will hereafter be known only as Sir Charles Graham Hannay

265

Baronet at present of Romai in the District of Debrughar [Dibrughar, Assam] aforesaid. In witness whereof I have set my hand at Great Portland Street in the county of London this 26th day of September 1901."

For want of a nearer heir, and at present it does not seem that there is one, in Stewart Francis' opinion, the baronetcy should be assumed by this branch of the family.

## 9. *Ormelie Campbell Hannay (1848-1900)*

Ormelie Campbell, Simon Fraser's son by his second wife, Mary Florence, was born in 1848. He joined the 93$^{rd}$ Highlanders, now the Argyll and Sutherland Highlanders, as an ensign on October 5, 1867, and was a gazetted lieutenant in 1871. He was promoted captain in 1878 and went to South Africa for the Zulu War, where he was employed on special service. He was transferred to the 91$^{st}$ Highlanders in 1889 and present at the Presentation of New Colours when HRH Princess Louise took the Queen's Colour from Major Hannay and handed it to Lieutenant Thorburn. The next year, 1893, he was given command of the 91$^{st}$. He gave up command in 1899 and was promoted colonel.

At the outbreak of the South African War he was sent to the seat of war and placed in command of a brigade of mounted infantry. He had a great reputation as a horseman and was known as one of the hardest riders to hounds with the Bicester Hunt.

He was a magnificent salmon fisher and a good shot. At cricket even in his fiftieth year he would hold his own with any subaltern.

His tragic death at the Battle of Paardeburg on February 18, 1900, caused wide felt grief. The way of it is described in *The Times History of the War in South Africa*. Field Marshal Lord Roberts was sick on February 27 and had handed over to his Chief of Staff Herbert Kitchener, 1$^{st}$ Earl Kitchener, the conduct of the battle for the day. This was Kitchener's first experience of fighting the Boers. As usual, this officer, whose great fault was impetuosity, galloped forward with virtually no staff, dashing from point to point as at the Battle of Omdurman in Sudan issuing a string of verbal orders. He hurled battalion after battalion at the Boer Laager in the river bed and, suffering heavy casualties at one point, he ordered Colonel Ormelie Hannay, to charge the Boer Laager with the mounted Infantry. Ormelie, who had been pressing forward in the orthodox role of mounted infantry—they are not cavalry and not equipped to charge—and who had reported he could make no further progress, took this order as a reflection on his personal courage. He charged forward with a handful of men, galloped forward himself in advance of them, and

266

fell riddled with bullets. The day became known as Bloody Sunday due to the number of casualties (almost 300 within the Highland Brigade), and Kitchener was severely criticized for this action. When *The Times History of the War in South Africa* was being written, the proofs concerning Paadeburg were sent to Kitchener, who wrote to General Sir Ian Hamilton at the War Office, trying to get the account changed, as it reflected on his ability as a General, and to lay the blame for the loss of fifty lives at the door of Colonel Hannay. Fortunately *The Times*, as is its wont, printed the truth, and whilst Ormelie's charge was perhaps not war, it was the only action a soldier and a man of honour could have taken in the circumstances.

Ormelie had a son, Robert Ormelie Fraser, who was commissioned as a 2nd lieutenant in October 1902, in the 91st Highlanders. He went out to South Africa to his regiment and died of enteric at Pretoria on March 5, 1903.

# XV: The Hannays of Powton and Stranraer

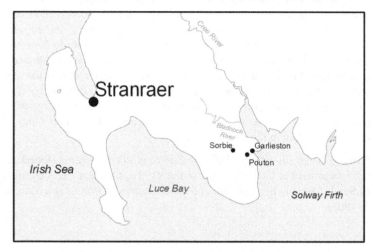

**Figure 72: Pouton (Powton) and Stranraer**

These families, comparatively modern branches from the main tree, break off from the Creetown and Clugston family in about 1750 with Andrew Hannay, the son of Robert Hannay of Spittal and Janet McKie (see XIV: The Hannays of Clugston and Creetown).

## 1. Andrew Hannay (1740-1810), son of Robert

Andrew was born in 1740 and lived at Barhoise, where he was a miller. He married Jean Tait of Stranraer and had three children who survived:

- William, his heir.

- John, who founded the Powton [Pouton] family.

- Margaret, who married John Dalrymple of Barlennan.

An old tombstone in Kirkcowan churchyard says the following:

> "Here lies the corps of Jean Tait spouse of Andrew Hannay who died August 20th 1774 aet 37. Also Robert Hannay his son who died May 1770 aet 8. Also the above Andrew Hannay who died 15 December 1810 aet 70."

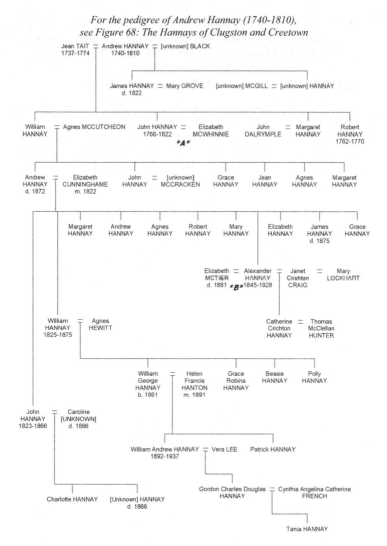

For the pedigree of Andrew Hannay (1740-1810),
see Figure 68: The Hannays of Clugston and Creetown

*A*: See Figure 74    *B*: See Figure 75

**Figure 73: The Hannays of Stranraer**

Andrew married a second time a Miss Black, who bore him two
children:

- James, who was a miller at Barhoise and married Mary Grove.
  He died in 1822.

269

- A daughter whose name is unknown, who married a Mr. McGill and became the grandmother of James McGill, sometime Mayor of Sunderland in County Durham.

## 1.1. John Hannay (d. 1822), son of Andrew

John, the son of Andrew and his first wife Jean, was a miller in Monreath. He married Elizabeth McWhinnie and died aged 56 in 1822 at Kirkcowan. John and Elizabeth had three sons: John of Corshulloch; Robert of Sleuhebert (an old Hannay property of many years standing), who died in 1865; and James who died aged 23, in 1862.

*For the pedigree of John Hannay (1766-1822), see Figure 73: The Hannays of Stranraer*

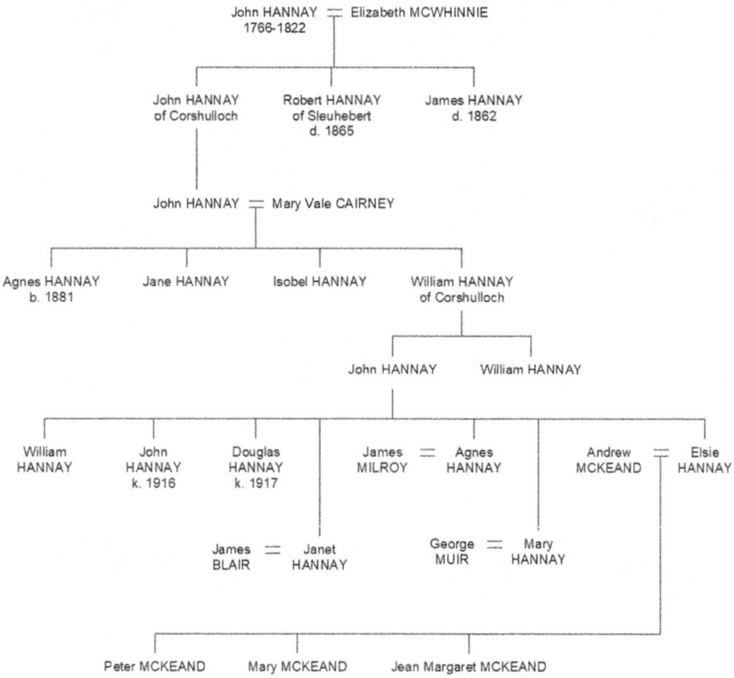

**Figure 74: The Hannays of Powton**

John, the son of John of Corshulloch, succeeded to Sleuhebert and Powton and married Mary Vale Cairney. There were three daughters, Agnes (b. 1881), Jane and Isobel, and a son William who succeeded to Corshulloch.

William had two sons, John and William. William's son John had three sons and six daughters:

- William his eldest served in the Boer War and settled in South Africa. In World War I he served again with the South African Forces in the East African Campaign and in German East and West Africa in 1914. He died later in South Africa as a result of war wounds.

- John and Douglas, the other two sons, were both killed in France in World War I, one at Paschendale, and the other at Courcellete.

- Janet married James Blair.

- Agnes married James Milroy.

- Mary married the Reverend George Muir.

- Elsie married Andrew McKeand of Airlies, who served in Rangoon from 1901 to 1925. They had three children: Mary, Jean Margaret, and Peter McKeand. Peter was a Wing Commander in the RAF and married Frances Wylie. He had three daughters: Patricia, Jane and Alison. He was educated at Fettes and for his war service in India and Burma, he was awarded the D.S.O .. D.F.C. and Bar, the A.F.C. and the American Air Medal.

## 2. William Hannay, son of Andrew

William, Andrew's eldest son, succeeded to the Kirkcowan Mills. but decided that Portpatrick would be a more profitable site for his operations, so he drove the millstone towed by horses from Kirkcowan to Portpatrick some forty miles and started operations there. He married Agnes McCutcheon who was descended from the Hannay family, and whose people had farms at Kynloch, Craigally and Brabreck. William's business prospered and he had a large family, two sons and four daughters:

- Andrew, the eldest, succeeded to the Mills, but first spent some time at sea.

- John, the second son, married a Miss McCracken and also went to sea. He was killed as the first mate of the ship *Hastings* at Calcutta in 1834.

- Grace married a Mr. McDowell of Pinminnoch.

- Jean married a Mr. Urquhart, who was an exciseman.

- Agnes married a Mr. Anderson.

- Margaret married a Mr. Witter.

271

## 3. *Andrew Hannay (d. 1872), son of William*

In 1816, William's heir Andrew was bound apprentice to Michael Wallace and John Baird and Company, Shipowners in the ship *Mary and Jane*, a brig. He was embarked at Stranraer and completed his indenture in 1818. Subsequently he left the sea and followed his father's business, establishing the firm of Hannay and Sons, Millers at Corswell Mill in Stranraer. A letter of 1861 shows that business was not always a bed of roses and that prices were keenly competitive:

> "I am in receipt of your letter of the 1st instant quoting your price
> for oatmeal, and in reply I have to inform you that the price you
> have quoted will not answer me at present as I am selling it out
> here just now about your quotation, it is country meal that we are
> receiving just now at the County fair price which is 19/8d. a boll
> this year delivered in the store."

Andrew married Elizabeth Cunninghame in 1822 and died in 1872. They had a very large family, six sons and five daughters:

- John (the eldest), William (who served in the Indian Police) and Alexander (who succeeded to the Corswell Mill) are each described in detail below.

- Margaret married James Brown, a great friend of her brother William in his younger days.

- Andrew married a Jean Rankin.

- Agnes married an Alexander McCullam.

- Elizabeth married firstly a John Anderson and secondly a James Euston.

- Mary and Grace died unmarried.

- Robert married Janet Crichton

- James died unmarried in San Francisco.

### 3.1. John Hannay (1823-1866), son of Andrew

John, the eldest son of Andrew and Elizabeth, was born in 1823, joined the Royal Artillery and went to India where he became a Sergeant in C Battery of the 16th Battalion at Allahabad. An omnibus letter from him to his brother Robert and his mother shows something of his life in India, written from Barrackpore in 1863:

> " ... I soon found William [his brother] after I received my father's
> letter and I have correspondence with him about once in a fortnight.
> I had a letter from him two days ago, they are all well and I hope
> doing well. He has changed his employ he is now a first class

Inspector of Police in Cuttack it is about 150 miles from here, I would have paid him a visit ere this but there is no conveyance except by bullock cart and that would be twelve days march so I do not like to try twelve days there and twelve days back that would spoil a months leave, but I will see him if God spares us before I leave India.

This is the most unpleasant month in India, just the close of the monsoon that is the rainy season, we will have four months pleasant weather after this month, and then fearful hot. We have plenty of drills here, it is all the morning and evening. Our first parade is at five oclock and again about eight, and then one parade at six oclock in the evening. We are not allowed out during the day but I often go a fishing under the shade of a tree, the best prescription for health is plenty of exercise in this country. We have fine horses to ride all entire arab horses and I have a good gallop every morning at drill."

To his mother he says:

"my wife poor body is not very strong and the weather close, she expects to be confined in about a month, this is a miserable country for a european in a perfect state of health. I am now nearly smelting and it is about 10 oclock at night."

John had served in the Crimea and was awarded two medals. He presumably went to India with the troops sent to quell the mutiny in 1857[262] and then stayed on there with his regiment.

His brother William made several attempts to get him out of the Army into Government employ in India, but John never actually got round to it. He had married a Miss Caroline in India and had two daughters, one called Charlotte Elizabeth; the other's name is not known. He, his wife, and the daughter whose name is not known all died in 1866 from some epidemic. A letter from William gives the details:

"16th June 1867. .. Dear Father, I am sorry to inform you that I have been unable to claim little Charlotte yet, on account of my brother and I not knowing the same officer which is required to be done according to the Military regulations before I can claim the child, and what I now request of you, is to send on receipt of this, a copy from the Parish register book regarding our birth and baptizmal certificates together with a copy of your marriage lines .. . I am sorry I cannot inform you who died first but I think it must have been her mother [Caroline] as John died on the 9th August afterwards his effects were immediately sold and his child placed in school."

---

[262] The Indian Rebellion of 1857 started with a mutiny of Indian soldiers in the employ of the British East India Company, and grew to widespread revolt instigated by harsh British laws and taxation.

## 3.2. Alexander Hannay (1845-1928), son of Andrew

Alexander, the son of Andrew Hannay and Elizabeth Cunninghame, was born in 1845 and married Elizabeth McTier, who died in 1881, leaving him four children. He married again twice subsequently, secondly Janet Crichton Craig who gave him a daughter Catherine Crichton, who married Thomas McClellan Hunter, and thirdly Mary Lockhart. In 1878 he was admitted a burgess of Stranraer.

*For the pedigree of Alexander Hannay (1845-1928), see Figure 73: The Hannays of Stranraer*

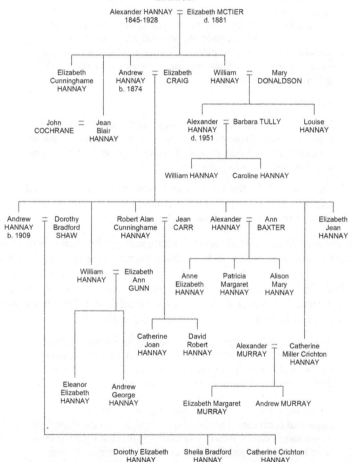

**Figure 75: The Family of Alexander Hannay of Stranraer**

By his first wife he had two daughters and two sons:

- Elizabeth Cunninghame did not marry.

274

- Jean Blair married John Cochrane.

- Andrew was the director of the family business at Corswell Mills and is described in more detail below.

- William built the present mill in 1947 and was also a director of the firm.

### 3.2.1. Andrew Hannay (b. 1874), son of Alexander

Alexander's son Andrew, born in 1874, married Elizabeth Craig and had four sons and two daughters, including:

- Andrew, his eldest son, was born in 1909 and married Dorothy Bradford Shaw and had three daughters.

- His second son, William, married Elizabeth Ann Gunn in Singapore had a daughter Eleanor and one son, Andrew George, born in 1957.

- The third son, Robert Alan Cunninghame, married Jean Carr and had a daughter Catherine Joan and a son David Robert.

### 3.2.2. William Hannay, son of Alexander

William, Alexander's second son, married Mary Donaldson and had a son Alexander, who married Barbara Tully, and was killed in the RAF in 1951, leaving a son William and a daughter Caroline.

William and Mary also had a daughter Louise who married a Mr. Douglas and had a daughter.

## 4. William Hannay (1825-1875), son of Andrew

John's brother William had also served in the army, probably also in the Crimea and the Mutiny but had very soon retired and entered the Indian Police where he became a First class Inspector. He writes from Cuttack soon after entering the Police, and in a rather newsy letter gives much information of his life there:

"9th October 1863…I am trying to get him [John] a situation somewhere near me in the same employ so as his former service counts for pension, at the same time I have lost mine, on account of being employed by a private company for twelve months between leaving the army and joining my present employ, however it will affect me very little or nothing where it would be a very serious loss for John who cannot speak the language, I am learning another language called Orissa, the name of the part of the country we are in, and I hope to live in for some time. Dear Parents we are living at present in Cuttack a very large military station situated on an island

275

a beautiful place, a large river called the Mahanadi or in English the mother of rivers and on the other side the river Kathajodi each of the rivers is upwards of 1½ miles broad and at this time of the year from 30 to 40 feet with a current of 5 to 7 miles an hour and so you can form an idea of the millions of cubic feet of water that passes daily in fact it is more like the sea...I am going to a much more beautiful place called Puri 50 miles on the sea beach it will remind me of happy days I spent at home only that from here the surf is terrible that small boats could not live one minute and it is so all along the Coromandal coast except at the change of monsoons...My salary is at present £20 a month with free quarters, medical attendance which enables us to live very happily and if I can pass my language test next month my salary will be doubled..."

In 1864 his wife Agnes (nee Hewitt) writes:

"... Since William wrote we have been constantly on the move until very lately. It will take some time to settle ourselves again in India-it is foolishness having more than one carriage and a couple of small carts drawn by bullocks which is the general mode of travelling. William was transferred from Puri on the 28th September and had to leave us behind him and proceed to Hooghly from whence he was again transferred to Serampore, myself and the little ones left Puri on the 20th November and arrived in Calcutta on the 11th of December after a very tiresome journey. I was confined of a daughter on the 10th of November and we have named her Grace Robina. ... William was again transferred to this district (Murshidabad) which is certainly a much better place than Serampore but in the middle of the country where it would take but very little for them again to mutiny, for they are a forward race of people ... "

There is a passage that most Service families will fully appreciate which follows now in this same letter:

"We left Puri for the purpose of getting to a station where there is a good school. I am sorry to say I have met with the same misfortune here, there is neither a boys or girls school here, so I shall have to take my eldest daughter to Calcutta and leave her there as soon as the weather becomes a little cooler."

In 1867 William and his family attempted to make the journey to Madras to place his daughter in a school there. The journey can hardly be described as a success. He had to ship from Puri to another place down the coast to pick up the Calcutta-Madras packet. On arrival they were told to wait as the ship was unloading rice, the ship from Calcutta never came and William was faced with waiting several days at £2 12s. a day or footing it home, he says:

"We went ashore at the mouth of the river, without a bite to eat (the ship he had left had run short) or a drop of fresh water to drink or a stitch on which to lay down in and that with a sick wife and four little children. Luckily when about six miles up the river, we met a european gentleman on his way to the steamer who gave us all the help he could ... there is nothing but a lid of low dense jungle full of tigers and other animals, the greatest part in- India is the like. However, we arrived on terrafirma next morning. And thus, we had to eat what the natives gave us which was very sweet indeed ... "

They finally got home having enlisted some coolies, a distance of 100 miles. Travelling off the beaten track in those days was hardly the thing for a family but is demonstrative of the hardiness of these early settlers in India.

John had got into some trouble at this time and was silent, William wrote to his brother Robert, saying:

"I know he (John) is poor and I have offered any assistance I can give if will but only let me know but no answer. My wife wrote many letters to his wife but she too is silent. I would freely give all I am worth, which is not much, to know the cause, but of no use. I am afraid the poor fellow is ashamed at being reduced and so full of hopes of going home when here on his two bob a day, but that is foolish of him as it cannot be . . . "

Not long after this John died, and eventually his daughter came into William's custody. William died in India in 1875 leaving one son William George, and three daughters Grace Robina (b. 1864), Bessie and Polly.

## 5.  *William George Hannay (b. 1861), son of William*

William George, the son of Inspector William Hannay and his wife Agnes, entered the Merchant Service as an apprentice on the ship *Mowlam* under Captain F. R. Patsy. Between 1893 and 1896 visited Portland Oregon, Australia, Belfast, San Francisco, and Puget Sound. He rounded the Horn on at least three occasions in one of the last sailing ships in regular service there. Finally, he became Assistant Shipping Master to his Company. He married Helen Francis Hanton in 1891 and had two sons, William Andrew and Patrick.

## 6.  *William Hannay (1892-1937), son of William*

William Andrew was born at Kiddipore in India in 1892 and entered the R.M.C. at Sandhurst, afterwards serving in the King's Liverpool Regiment and the 19th Hyderabad Regiment. He retired as a result of war wounds in the mid-1920's.

He served from 1916 in the Royal Flying Corps, and was at some time during World War I the chief flying instructor to the United States Air Force. He compiled a document which may be said to be one of the

277

earliest directives on Fighter tactics. William Andrew returned to the army in 1920 having won the Air Force Cross. Whilst in America, Major Hannay had met with a serious flying accident, and as a result he died in 1937 aged only 45.

He married Vera Lee, the daughter of Charles Lee, and had a son Gordon Charles Douglas Hannay (1930-1994) who served in the Royal Army Service Corps and retired from the army in 1954 to become the director of a shipping concern.

Gordon Charles married Cynthia Angelia Catherine French in 1956 and had a daughter Tania, born in October 1957. They lived in Cavendish Court in London.

# XVI: The Hannays of Drumaston

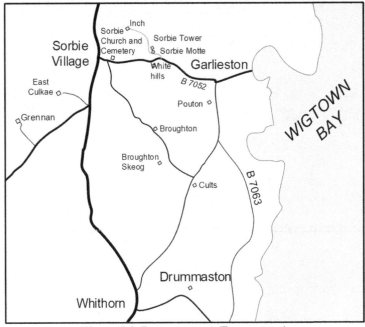

**Figure 76: Drummaston (Drumaston)**

This family is a scion of the Kirkdale line, and beginning with John Hannay of Bargallie, the brother of Samuel Hannay of Kirkdale, and son of William Hannay of Kirkdale.

John married Marion Murdoch, and on his death the Bargallie property must have reverted to Kirkdale for the latter still had it in 1790. John had two sons, James and John.

A family tree is shown in Figure 77.

James, born in 1717, married Helen McCredie and died in 1792. Both are buried in Cruggleton old churchyard, and as far as we know they had no surviving children.

*For the pedigree of John Hannay of Bargallie, see Figure 20: The Hannays of Kirkdale.*

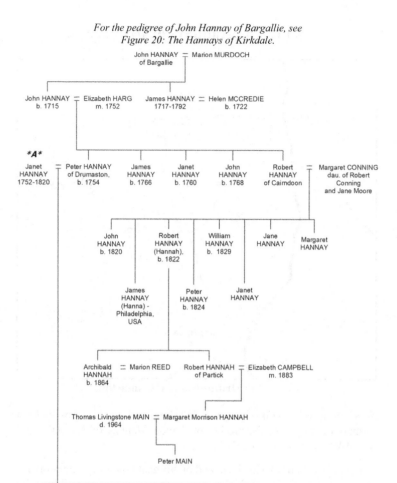

*A*: From Figure 54    *B*: See Figure 78

**Figure 77: The Hannays of Drumaston**

## 1. John Hannay (b. 1715), son of John

John, the other son of John and Marion, was born at Cults on June 19,1715, and married, in March 1752, Elizabeth Harg. Their children included the following:

- Peter, born 1754, and discussed below.

- James, born in 1766 who died unmarried.

280

- John, born in 1768.

- Janet born in 1760.

- Robert, who married Margaret Conning of Liverpool, the niece of Capt. Conning[263], and had a large family, of which we shall mention James and Robert.

  o James went to Philadelphia, U.S.A. and changed the spelling of the family name to Hanna. James became an attorney at Law in Philadelphia and New York. He visited England just before World War I and worked on the family history with the object of claiming the Baronetcy for his cousin[264], Robert Hannah of Partick. However, due to lack of funds the project was shelved.

  o Robert the younger, born in 1822 at Whitehouse, moved to Partick near Glasgow changing his name to Hannah and worked for Barclay Curle and Co., Ltd., shipbuilders on Clydeside as a foreman shipwright; during his early years he had been to sea in some of their sailing ships. Robert the younger had seven daughters and two sons. The sons were Archibald and (yet another) Robert.

  Archibald, born in 1864, was a marine engineer and on one of his voyages just disappeared for ever. His wife Marion Reed, son and small daughter never heard of him again.

  Robert (the grandson of Robert and Margaret) was also indentured as an apprentice marine engineer and eventually sailed as chief engineer in many ships of the Donaldson and Clan Lines. He was shipwrecked off Newfoundland early in his career, and also acted as chief engineer in an American yacht in the Spanish American War. He retired from the sea and became foreman engineer to John Brown and Co., working on such vessels as the *Aquitania*. He married Elizabeth Campbell in 1883 and had five

---

[263] Unclear who this is, but it may refer to a John Conning from Liverpool who is mentioned in several shipping records from 1791-1793 as the captain of the *Clarence*.

[264] Although Francis says "cousin", from the text it appears that Robert was James' brother or nephew, depending on which generation of Robert of Partick he was referencing.

281

sons and four daughters. One of his daughters Margaret married Commodore Thomas Livingstone Main, OBE[265], of Glasgow, and their son Peter Main very kindly supplied this information.

## 2. *Peter Hannay of Drumaston (b. 1754), son of John*

John and Elizabeth's son Peter was born at Clugston in 1754. He married Janet Hannay of Knock. She was born in 1752 and died in 1820. Peter purchased the house at Drumaston, a rather charming spot on the Wigtown coast. They had three sons, George, John who died in 1804 aged 22, and Peter who died the same year aged 17, both no doubt carried off by some epidemic. They are buried in Mochrum Kirkyard. There was a daughter Elizabeth who died unmarried, and another, Jenny, who married John Martin of Kintreoch. Their son, John, married Jessie Stewart of Prestry but unfortunately had no children.

## 3. *George Hannay (1790-1867), son of Peter*

George Hannay of Drumaston, the youngest and only surviving son of Peter and Janet, was born in 1790 and married Isabella McConnell circa 1824. She was the daughter of John McConnell of Chapel Heron and Margaret Stewart of Cults near Sorbie. Isabella was a direct descendant of Robert the Steward and a very charming lady. In her latter days she regrettably went blind. To amuse herself and to train her memory, she used to teach her grandchildren hymns and Scottish poetry in the summer house at Drumaston on summer evenings. Amongst her favourites was Bishop Ken's lovely hymn "Glory to thee my God this night."

---

[265] More information on Commodore Main can be found in the British and Commonwealth Shipping Company staff register archive http://www.bandcstaffregister.com/page2597.html

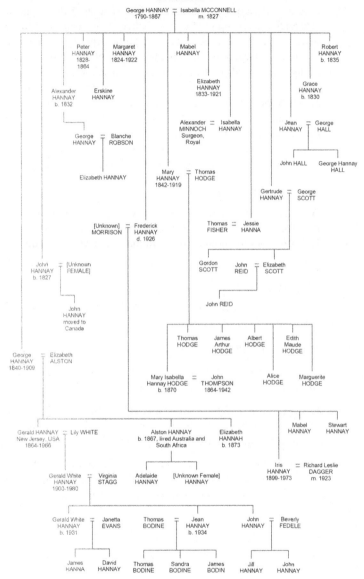

**Figure 78: The Family of George Hannay**

George and Isabella had a prodigious family:

- John, born in 1827, married and had a son John, who went to Canada, and of whom no more is known.

283

- Peter was born in 1825 and died in 1864.

- Jessie Anne, born in 1829, married a rich cigar merchant of Rochdale, a certain Thomas Fisher, who was sometime Mayor of that town. He was so large that the mayoral coach had to be enlarged in order that he might get into it. Rochdale, being truly proud of this magnificent son, preserved one of his waistcoats in the local museum—it would accommodate three ordinary people in a sufficient degree of comfort. Tragedy unfortunately overtook this family, there were twelve daughters and a baby son, all save one daughter, Isabella, and his son, George, were drowned in Black loch whilst out on a skating party. George had a daughter Jessie.

- Grace was born in 1830.

- Alexander, born 1832, moved to Newcastle upon Tyne. and married leaving a son, George, who married a Blanche Robson. Their daughter Elizabeth married a Mr. Mawson.

- Elizabeth was born in 1833. She lived with her sister Margaret and died at the age of 87.

- Margaret (born 1824) married Mr. Millar and died in 1922 at Midtoun in Galloway aged 98.

- Robert was born in 1835.

- Isabella was born in 1836 and was the wife of Dr. Alexander Minnoch, R.N.[266] She also died at the age of 98.

- George, born in 1840, became a banker in South Shields, Co. Durham and married Elizabeth Alston. George apparently changed the spelling of his family name to "Hannah."

  o Their son Gerald, born 1864, went to the U.S.A. and became the manager of the Oscar Barnett Foundry of New Jersey in 1910. He married Lily White of New

---

[266] Stewart Francis mentions additionally in the 3rd and earlier editions that Isabella married a Reverend Campbell and had a son Hugh. It is of course possible that Isabella was married twice, but her marriage to Dr. Minnoch is confirmed in *Scotland Marriages, 1561-1910* database, FamilySearch (https://familysearch.org/ark:/61903/1:1:XYWQ-ZY6 : 8 December 2014), Alex. Minnoch and Isabella Hannay, 27 Dec 1866; citing Whithorn, Wigtown, Scotland, reference ; FHL microfilm 6,035,516. It is of course possible that the almost identically-named but not directly related couple George and Isabella (mentioned in an earlier footnote) may have had an Isabella of their own who married Reverend Campbell.

York and died in 1966. He had a son, Gerald White, born in 1900, who married Virginia Stagg.

o   Their son Alston, born 1867, went to Australia where he married and became a successful business man in Adelaide. Later he removed to South Africa and started a large business in Johannesburg. He had two daughters, Adelaide who died unmarried, and another who married a Mr. Anderson.

o   Their daughter Elizabeth, born 1873, married Joseph Collins in 1898. Elizabeth spoke for the Queen Mary's Army Auxiliary Corps before the queen herself at the Albert Hall Convention after World War I.

- Mary (1842-1919) is discussed in detail later.

- Erskine lived in South Shields and was also a banker.

- Frederick married a Miss Morrison who had two daughters and a son: Iris married Dr. Richard Leslie Dagger of Morpeth. Mabel married a Mr. Carrick of Newcastle. There was a son Stewart, also Walton and another John died young, and Robert died, aged 22 in 1860.

- Gertrude became the wife of George Scott of South Shields and had at least one son and a daughter.

- Mabel died young.

- Jean married George Hall and they had two sons: John and George Hannay, who was killed in the London Scottish (a volunteer infantry regiment) in World War I.

## 4.  Mary Hannay (1842-1919), daughter of George

George and Isabella's daughter Mary Hannay of Drumaston was born in 1842 and married Thomas Hodge of Burnfoot, Stirlingshire, in 1863. They moved to Newcastle upon Tyne, but still retained the house at Drumaston. She died there in 1919 leaving seven children:

- Mary Isabella born in 1870, of whom more below.

- Thomas, who married Annie Wentworth and died without children.

- James Arthur, who married Emily Simpson.

- Albert, who became a doctor.

285

- Alice, who died unmarried.

- Edith Maude, who married H. J. Criddle of Newcastle. Her son John married Nancy, the daughter of Sir Alexander Kennedy, K.B.E. of Fairford Shipyards. They had three children, John, David and Peter. Edith Maude's daughter Elaine married General John Oakshott.

- Marguerite married George Wilson and had a daughter Eleanor Mary and a son Richard Hannay Hodge.

## 5. *Mary Isabella Hodge (b. 1870)*

Mary Hannay and Thomas Hodge's daughter Mary Isabella Hodge was born in 1870, and married John Thompson who took the name Hannay Thompson. He was born in 1869 and died in 1942. John Thompson was a civil engineer and General Manager and Engineer of the Admiralty Harbour at Dover. He was awarded the O.B.E. for his services. He was a Justice of the Peace, a Master of Science of Durham University, a Member of the Institute of Civil Engineers, a Fellow of the Royal Society, Edinburgh. He had two French distinctions, first an Officer of the *Académie Française*, and second an Officer "*de l'Instruction Publique de France*." He was sometime a Captain in the 2nd Volunteer Battalion of the Black Watch. Mary Isabella and John Thompson had two children, Marjorie Hannay Thompson and John Horace Hannay Thompson.

### 5.1. John Thompson (1904-1949)

John Horace Hannay Thompson was born at Broughty Ferry in 1904 and married Winifred Brayshay of Leeds. He was a Doctor of Philosophy of Edinburgh University and a civil engineer. John was regrettably killed whilst supervising the construction of a new bridge in 1949. He had two daughters, Catherine and Winifred Mary. The latter married Jan Kenworthy of Kilmarnock and had a daughter Catherine Margaret.

### 5.2. Marjorie Hannay Thompson (b. 1896)

Marjorie, the daughter of John Hannay Thompson was born at Dover in 1896. She married Cecil William Meredith of Craigyard, Broughty Ferry in 1922. He was a civil engineer on the Dundee Harbour Board and a fellow of the Royal Philatelic Society of London. He also built and operated one of the largest model railways in the country at the time, the Craigyard Railway.

Marjorie had a formidable record of public service. She served as the British Red Cross Service Assistant County Director and Commandant for Dundee during the latter stages of the Second World War[267]. She received a Distinguished Conduct Certificate from Her Majesty Queen Elizabeth at Holyroodhouse after the war. She entered local politics in 1945, becoming a councilor of the City of Dundee. She was made a Baillie in 1947 and was Hospital Master for the City from 1949 to 1952.

They had three children:

- Mary Edith Hannay Meredith who married John Hugett Wood of Croydon

- Isabella Marjorie Hannay Meredith who married Hugh Hunting of Slaley, Sevenoaks, Kent, a director of Hunting Clan Airlines. They had a daughter Linda Mary Hannay Hunting, born in 1957.

- David Cecil John Hannay Meredith, who was born in 1933 at Broughty Ferry. He was a Territorial officer in the Fife and Forfar Yeomanry, a civil engineer, and a Bachelor of Arts of Cambridge University.

---

[267] Stewart Francis stated First World War in earlier editions, but surely he is referring to WWII, as Marjorie would have been only 22 years old at the end of the Great War, and Elizabeth (George VI's consort, not Queen Elizabeth II), from whom she received a distinction following the war, would not have been on the throne yet.

# XVII: The Hannays of Rusko

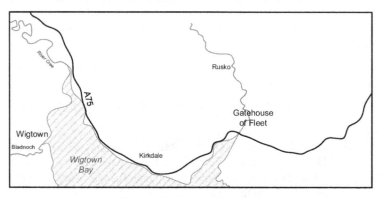

**Figure 79: Rusko (Ruscoe)**

The origins of this family are obscure, but they appear to be descended from John Hannay in Skeog, near Whithorn, who is shown as an elder of the kirk of Whithorn in 1712 and was probably a descendant of the Hannays settled in Broughton as early as 1520. He had a son, John, in Skeog, of whom we know nothing.

## 1. The Family of George Hannay

However this second John's son, George (at least it is supposed that is the relationship although definite proof is not available), was a Baillie and Burgess of Whithorn. He married Grizzel Martin and had several children (see Figure 80: The Hannays of Ruscoe). George Hannay was a wright and lived till early in the 19th century. His wife died in 1786, aged 73. The children who grew up were: Alexander; Robert; Andrew; Agnes, who married Alexander Conning; Jean; and John, a seafaring man.

Alexander was apprenticed in 1765 to Anthony McGuffock in Whithorn who bore witness to his faithfulness, capability, honesty and good character. Alexander emigrated to New York in 1774 in a ship with 300 people which took eighty days to do the voyage. He thought they were overcrowded; but during the crossing they spoke to a vessel from Londonderry to Philadelphia with 590. He could find no work in New York and went on to Norfolk, Virginia, where he obtained employment in building. Neither the crossing nor the arrival in America was all these emigrants had wished for. Many failed to get satisfactory employment and drifted here, there and everywhere. Only the hardier spirits made a go of it.

288

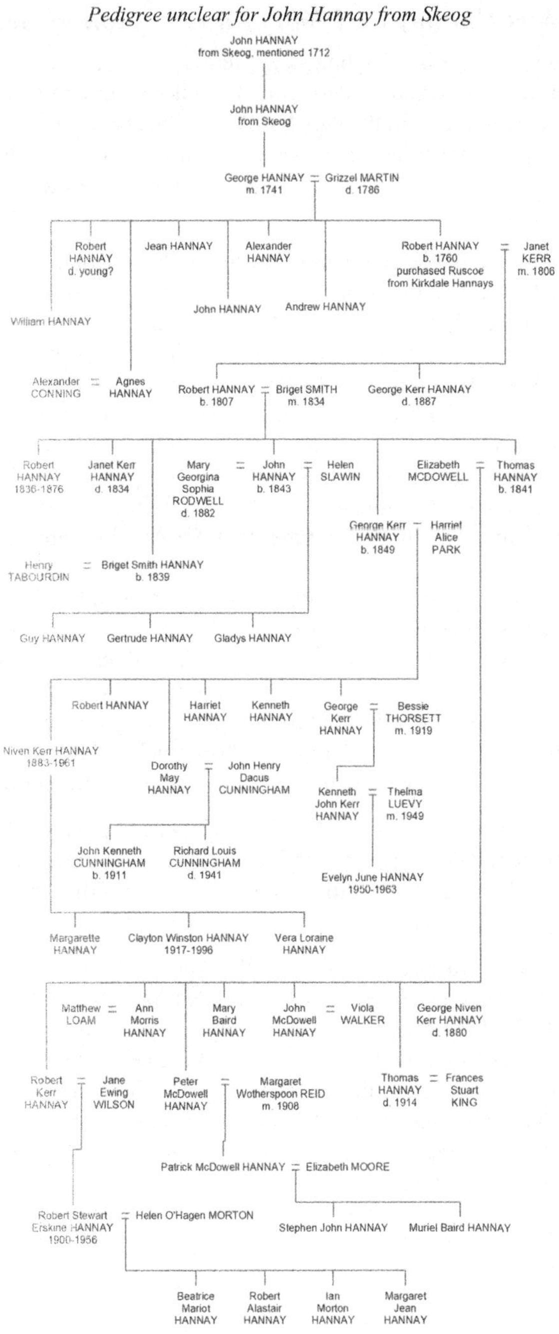

John HANNAY
from Skeog, mentioned 1712

John HANNAY
from Skeog

George HANNAY = Grizzel MARTIN
m. 1741          d. 1786

Robert HANNAY d. young? — Jean HANNAY — Alexander HANNAY — Robert HANNAY b. 1760 purchased Ruscoe from Kirkdale Hannays = Janet KERR m. 1806

William HANNAY

John HANNAY     Andrew HANNAY

Alexander CONNING = Agnes HANNAY     Robert HANNAY b. 1807 = Briget SMITH m. 1834     George Kerr HANNAY d. 1887

Robert HANNAY 1836-1876     Janet Kerr HANNAY d. 1834     Mary Georgina Sophia RODWELL d. 1882 = John HANNAY b. 1843 — Helen SLAWIN     Elizabeth MCDOWELL = Thomas HANNAY b. 1841

George Kerr HANNAY b. 1849 — Harriet Alice PARK

Henry TABOURDIN = Briget Smith HANNAY b. 1839

Guy HANNAY     Gertrude HANNAY     Gladys HANNAY

Robert HANNAY     Harriet HANNAY     Kenneth HANNAY     George Kerr HANNAY = Bessie THORSETT m. 1919

Niven Kerr HANNAY 1883-1961

Dorothy May HANNAY = John Henry Dacus CUNNINGHAM

Kenneth John Kerr HANNAY = Thelma LUEVY m. 1949

John Kenneth CUNNINGHAM b. 1911     Richard Louis CUNNINGHAM d. 1941

Evelyn June HANNAY 1950-1963

Margarette HANNAY     Clayton Winston HANNAY 1917-1996     Vera Loraine HANNAY

Matthew LOAM = Ann Morris HANNAY     Mary Baird HANNAY     John McDowell HANNAY = Viola WALKER     George Niven Kerr HANNAY d. 1880

Robert Kerr HANNAY = Jane Ewing WILSON     Peter McDowell HANNAY = Margaret Wotherspoon REID m. 1908     Thomas HANNAY d. 1914 = Frances Stuart KING

Patrick McDowell HANNAY = Elizabeth MOORE

Robert Stewart Erskine HANNAY 1900-1956 = Helen O'Hagen MORTON     Stephen John HANNAY     Muriel Baird HANNAY

Beatrice Mariot HANNAY     Robert Alastair HANNAY     Ian Morton HANNAY     Margaret Jean HANNAY

**Figure 80: The Hannays of Ruscoe**

289

## 2. Robert Hannay (b. 1760) of Ruscoe, son of George

Robert, born in 1760, was bound apprentice to Alexander Lillie in Whithorn in 1777. At some date after 1780 he emigrated to Jamaica, where he is found later in the parish of Vere, County of Middlesex. He appears to have been joined by his elder brother Andrew in about 1789. Alexander also, considerably senior, seems to have left the States and come to Jamaica.

Alexander's will, made in the parish of St. Andrew, County of Surrey, in 1794, left bequests to his father, to his sisters Agnes and Jean, to his brothers John and Andrew and the residue to "my dearly beloved brother Robert" his sole executor. On May 10, 1795, Robert wrote to his sister, Agnes Conning, about Alexander's marriage to "that damned jaid." He did not think there would be much left, "the way they had been going on." Alexander was worth £3,000 to £4,000 before his marriage. He asks to whom had Alexander left his property in Scotland, and says he thinks of coming home as Jamaica is in a bad way. Andrew was still living with him at this time. In 1796 Andrew returned home by the *Active* from Milk River to Lancaster. Robert, who was in the habit of sending money to his father, wrote in November 1796 about Alexander's will saying there would probably be about £1,100 to £1,200, of which £300 or £400 was tied up. He said that he himself had sold all his property and was hoping to return home in 1797. There was a general fear on the island at that time of invasion by the 'bragans from St. Domingo". He also says Jamaica is "very sickly". Robert paid off Alexander's profligate wife with £165 and sent her home to England.

Robert must have returned in 1797, for in 1799 he bought Ruscoe from Hannay of Kirkdale[268]. He married Janet Kerr of Stranraer on April 28, 1806. Robert had made quite a fortune in his building business in Jamaica and was now able to settle down to a quiet life.

His father left him Bruce Hall near Whithorn, which in a letter of September 1812, he states he has no intention of selling. Robert certainly looked after the rest of his family, for in 1818 his wife Janet writes to Agnes Conning, Robert's sister, asking her if she is in need of money. There is a charming postscript to this letter by one of the children thanking Aunt Agnes for some tops and informing her that they now have a donkey to ride. In 1836 he sold Bruce Hall to provide an annuity for the daughters of his sister Agnes. Robert had two sons: Robert; and George Kerr, who died unmarried in 1887.

---

[268] John Hannay of Kirkdale bought Ruscoe in 1786, then died in 1797. Robert likely purchased from John's heirs.

### 3. Robert Hannay of Ruscoe (b. 1807), son of Robert

Robert and Janet's son Robert married Briget, the daughter of Thomas Smith of London, 1834. A letter from his mother to Aunt Agnes says "Feb 10th 1834, Our son Robert was married about a fortnight ago to a young lady in London of the name of Smith. They have gone as far as the Isle of Wight."

Their children were six in number:

- Robert (b. 1836) died unmarried in 1876.

- Janet Kerr died in 1834.

- Briget Smith (b. 1839) married Henry Tabourdin and had a family.

- John (b. 1843) married Mary Georgina Sophia Rodwell, who died at the birth of their son in 1882. The child did not survive, and John married again, a Helen Slawin, and had a son Guy, and two daughters Gertrude and Gladys.

- George Kerr (b. 1849) is discussed below.

- Thomas (b. 1841) is also discussed below.

### 3.1. George Kerr Hannay (b. 1849)

George Kerr married Harriet Alice Park, who brought to the family the place of Ruscoe which was connected with the Park Mines at Barrow and Dalton in Furness. He was a Captain in the Ulverstone Detachment of the 10th Lancashire Rifle Volunteers (1879).

George Kerr and Harriet had six children: Niven Kerr, born 1883, who died in Canada in 1961; Dorothy May, married John Henry Dacus Cunningham(1885-1962), who joined the Royal Navy in 1895 and became an Admiral of the Fleet and Second Sea Lord, as Admiral Sir John Cunningham of Mediterranean fame; Robert; Harriet; Kenneth; and George Kerr, who married Bessie Thorsett in 1919, and had a son, Kenneth John Kerr, who married Thelma Luevy in 1949. Kenneth's daughter, Evelyn June, born in 1950, died in 1963.

### 4. Thomas Hannay (b. 1841), 2ⁿᵈ son of Robert

Robert and Briget's son Thomas became an iron master at Ulverston in Lancashire. He started his first blast furnaces at Barrow-in-Furness. There was some considerable trouble and legal wrangling over this firm and Thomas was forced to sell Ruscoe to settle various debts. Thomas married Elizabeth McDowell, and his family was a large one:

- His eldest son Robert Kerr Hannay is discussed below.

- Ann Morris married Matthew Loam.

- Peter McDowell (born c.1870) emigrated to California and married Margaret Wotherspoon Reid in 1908. Only one son survived, Patrick McDowell Hannay who married Elizabeth Moore. He was a designer for the North American Aircraft Corporation and worked on the design of the Sabre Jet fighter. He had a son Stephen born in 1940 and a daughter Muriel Baird.

- Mary Baird became an eminent doctor.

- John McDowell also emigrated to the United States and married Viola Walker.

- Thomas married Frances Stuart King; he died in 1914 in East Africa and they had no children. She moved to the United States.

- Lastly, George Niven Kerr died as a child.

## 5. *Robert Kerr Hannay (died 1940), son of Thomas*

Robert Kerr Hannay was a great Scottish historian, and for the later part of his life Historiographer Royal for Scotland in succession to Professor Sir Robert Sangster Rait. He was a Master of Arts, Doctor of Laws, Fellow of the Royal Society of Edinburgh, Professor of Ancient History and Palaeography at the University of Edinburgh, and an Honorary member of the Royal Scottish Academy. He also held the Fraser Chair of Scottish history at Edinburgh University in 1920. He became an Elder of the Kirk of St. Giles in 1938.

Robert Kerr was educated at Glasgow University, from whence he went to University College at Oxford. He entered the University with the intention of reading history but turned to a study of the classics—a fortunate choice, as it happened, since his deep knowledge of Medieval Latin was an immense advantage to him in his future work.

It was as a classical scholar that he began his teaching career, being appointed in 1894 as assistant lecturer in Classics at University College, Dundee. On the affiliation of that College with St. Andrew's University three years later he became Lecturer in Latin Language and Literature, but in 1901 the University Court recognised his special abilities and appointed him to the lectureship of Ancient History.

Students both at St. Andrew's and Edinburgh remembered Professor Hannay not merely for his erudition but for his broad humanity and what has been described as the "democratic camaraderie" which marked his relations with his students.

When he was at Oxford he founded a literary and essay society; as a lecturer at St. Andrews he was also the Chapel Choir Master and conductor of the Musical Society. As Fraser Professor at Edinburgh he took a very active interest in the Workers' Educational Association, himself lecturing on outstanding features of Scottish History. He was President of the Scottish Historical Society and a great devotee of music. He had a fine singing voice and was no mean organist.

The Professor was a great campaigner for the better teaching of Scottish History and for the preservation of Scottish Records. He had been at one time in the Scottish Record Office. *The Scotsman* described his address at a meeting of the Edinburgh City Business Club as follows:

> What he described as "an alarming lack of expert history teachers" in Scotland was explained by Professor R. K. Hannay, LL.D.. Historiographer Royal for Scotland, in the course of an address on "Scottish Interest in Scottish History," which he gave yesterday at the weekly luncheon of the Edinburgh City Business Club in the North British Station Hotel. The president, Mr. J. E. Dalgleish, C.A., was in the chair.

> Speaking of the neglect of the Scottish historical records, Professor Hannay said that the damage was mainly done between the 1840's and 1860's, when no particular attention was given to records of a historical character. The fact of the matter was that in Scotland no pressure had been put upon the Government to see that special provision was made for studying, classifying, and indexing the records.

> After referring to the foundation of special Chairs for history in the Scottish Universities, Professor Hannay said that the result had been a tendency to turn away from the romantic side of Scottish history, initiated by Sir Walter Scott, to the institutional history of Scotland. One could not believe that a people so endowed with character as the Scots had nothing to give to humanity in respect of institutions. The history of Scottish law, for example, to which the Stair Society was turning its attention, had a significance outside Scotland.

> On the subject of history generally in education, Professor Hannay pointed out that in Scotland it had come into the field much later than in England. History in Scotland had had to be grafted on to our old-fashioned history.

> "When I was at school, I was taught history," he said, "and I simply loathed it. I believe it must not be so much my own incompetence as the incompetence of the teacher.

> "It is quite true that history has not been satisfactorily taught in Scotland, and it is not satisfactorily taught yet."

293

The problem in Scotland was that there was a traditional training in the schools in English language and literature, and now that history was coming to be a special subject, what place was it to have in the curriculum?

There was an economic question, proceeded Professor Hannay. In the Universities a student would spend four years in an honours course in English language and literature, and another in history, and the two went out together. A vacancy occurred in a provincial secondary school, and the Education Committee believed that the man who had studied English language and literature was qualified to teach history but the man who had studied history was not qualified to teach English language and literature. Could we afford the luxury of two specialists?

"We have as a consequence," he declared, "an alarming lack of expert history teachers, and that creates a vicious circle between the Universities and the schools."

People who had been taught history at school, but not decently, went up to the University, where they had to be taught history. A great many of them were very well qualified to teach it when they went out, but there were not enough appointments for them.

"What is the place of Scottish history in our education?" asked Professor Hannay. "It is a very difficult question to answer. Obviously Scotland is in a very special position. It is a part of Great Britain, and it is also an intensely patriotic country interested in its own past. You have the inevitable tendency for young Scots who are passing through higher education, and who are necessarily on the make, to take up the subjects which will pay them.

"One thing that has troubled us very much is the English attitude towards Scottish history. It is very much the result of the altitude which followed upon the romantic work of Sir Walter Scott. The English attitude is 'Oh, it's Mary Queen of Scots and Robert the Bruce. We know all about them.' It is not institutional history."

Along with Sir Robert Rait of Glasgow, they had obtained some kind of recognition for Scottish history in the Civil Service examination – not quite satisfactory, but still it was a step. It never used to pay a Scotsman to know anything about his own country.

Both in school and University, said Professor Hannay, Scottish history was absolutely necessary as a means of instruction. He would like more Scottish history, but especially better Scottish history.

"Our aim," he said in conclusion, "is to make Scottish history, whatever place you give it, not merely an intellectual study, not merely patriotic pabulum, but a moral discipline for both teacher and pupils. I think in Scotland we are justified in believing that our history is worth studying."

In the Times was a short biography of him on his appointment as Historiographer Royal:

"It is announced that Professor Robert Kerr Hannay, the Fraser Professor of Scottish History and Palaeography in the University of Edinburgh, has been offered, and has accepted, the office of His Majesty's Historiographer in Scotland. This office, it will be recalled, was rendered vacant by the resignation of Professor R. S. Rait upon his appointment as Principal of Glasgow University. As Mr. Forbes Gray points out in an article on another page, the office of Historiographer was continuously associated with Edinburgh lawyers and Edinburgh professors for two hundred years from the days of Robertson down to 1919, when Professor Rait succeeded the late Professor Hume Brown. The choice of Professor Hannay once more associates the office with Edinburgh University.

Professor Hannay came to Edinburgh University in 1919 from the Record Office in the Register House. His experience as Curator of the Historical Department has undoubtedly helped to determine his objective as Professor, and an important feature of his work at Edinburgh has been his determination to bridge the gulf between the Record Office and the academic study of history. In a sense Scottish history may be said to be in special need of this correlation, and it is fitting that the choice of an Historiographer should have fallen on one who by reason of his own special interest and because of his position at the centre where research into Scottish documents is most easily conducted is able to some extent to guide that research and direct it to channels likely to prove most fruitful. Professor Hannay wrote in collaboration with the late Sir John Herkless the five volumes of the 'Archbishops of St. Andrews.' His more recent work has been in the field of legal and constitutional history— especially in connection with the Scottish Parliament and the origins of the Court of Session. Professor Hannay was educated at Glasgow University and University College, Oxford. He was Lecturer in Latin Language and Literature, and later Lecturer in Ancient History, at St. Andrews, before his appointment in 1911 as Curator of the Historical Department in the Register House. In 1923 he received the degree of LL.D. from St. Andrews."

On the preservation of family records, he has this to say, writing in 1921:

"My attention has been drawn to a letter by Sir Frederic Kenyon which appeared the other day in Scottish newspapers. The purpose of the letter—to avert the destruction of family records which may be of historical value—will have the sympathy of all historical students; and they will be grateful to the Director of the British Museum for his timely action.

From internal evidence, however, it is not quite clear that the letter was drafted to include Scotland; and its publication here may

295

involve misunderstanding. As Secretary of the Scottish History Society, and formerly Curator of the Historical Department in the Scottish Record Office, I feel bound to advert to the matter.

Not long ago Mr. James Curle, W.S., took occasion at a meeting of the Scottish History Society to invite the cooperation of those— particularly the law agents—who might be able to contribute charters and documents for national and historical purposes; and he indicated the Register House as the proper repository for distinctively Scottish records. That invitation might be extended to any who at the present time intend to dispose of family collections. No doubt some papers have a high marketable value and will inevitably be sold. Charters, however, and similar documents have, as a rule, slight monetary worth. On the other hand, their historical importance is never negligible; and at the Register House there are already upwards of 10,000 charters, 4,000 of which, prior to 1603, have been admirably calendared and fully indexed by the industry of my predecessors and colleagues. This collection, too little known and used, is a valuable national possession; and it should be developed as a pure matter of historical business.

Again, the Advocates' Library contains much material which must be taken in conjunction with what is in the Register House; and, in addition, it is the most suitable repository for Scottish documents which have a predominantly literary interest.

The Unions of 1603 and 1707, apart from other causes, have led to an accumulation of Scottish documents in London; and it is unfortunately necessary for the student of Scottish affairs, especially in the later periods, to go South. The London repositories are suitable enough for documents of mainly British or Imperial significance. At the same time, it would, from the point of view of the historical student, be most un-businesslike to ignore the obvious fact that documents relating specially to Scotland should be deposited in Edinburgh. The proper line of action is clearly determined by the progress of historical events; and the principle indicated should not be very difficult to apply in practice.

It is unfortunate that in Scotland there is as yet a very faint appreciation of the central importance of our own record repositories. In England the energy of Professor Pollard has resulted in the foundation of an Institute for Historical Research, connected with the University of London. A similar development on a modest scale is necessary in Scotland, if we are to keep pace with the advance of historical education. Donors of Scottish charters and documents, acting upon the principle indicated above, will do a national service, without prejudice to what may be considered the legitimate functions of the British Museum."

He died in 1940, and Professor E. W. M. Balfour-Melville wrote of him:

"Will you allow one who was proud to be for twenty years a junior colleague of Professor Hannay to say something of what he means to students of his subject, who one and all looked up to him as the doyen of Scottish historians. Trained in the classical schools of Glasgow and Oxford, he brought to the study of History a mastery of Latin which turned to good account of an archivist. While Curator of the Historical department of H.M. Register House he edited for the Scottish history Society "Rentale Sancti Andrea, 1538-1546," and "Rentale Dunkeldense 1506-1507." His inaugural lecture on becoming Professor of Scottish History in 1919 foreshadowed that the fuller use of the records in the academic teaching of his subject which marked his tenure of the chair. It was perhaps as a pioneer in the constitutional history of Scotland that his best work was done. Among the more important of his articles and pamphlets were "Parliament and the General Council," "Conventions of Estates" and "the Scottish Crown and the Papacy." His larger works included "The Foundation of the College of Justice" and the "Early History of the Scottish Signet." His introductions as editor of "The Acts of the Lords in Council 1501-1554" and "The Register of the Scottish Privy Council 1684-9" were also valuable. At the time of his death he was editing a calendar of the "Letters of James III and James IV" for the Scottish History Society (of which he had been chairman of the Council since 1938) and the "Latin Letters of James V" as a Record publication. Unrivalled as was the place he had won in the esteem of historians in Scotland his friends will remember him not less for his sympathetic interest; his kindly disposition, his fund of anecdote, his love of music and unfailing bonhomie."

His wife, Jane Ewing Wilson, was also a truly remarkable woman in her own right. She was the daughter of the Reverend John Stewart Wilson, D.D., of New Abbey, Galloway, and was born in 1868. She was awarded the C.B.E. and was a Justice of the Peace. She had many connections with St. Leonard's School at St. Andrews both as a student, Mistress, Housemistress and Governor. She attended Girton College, Cambridge, and London University. An extract from the Scotsman of April 15, 1938 will be of interest:

" ... After her marriage she became prominently known in Edinburgh and the East of Scotland for her social welfare work ... In the Scottish capital Mrs. Hannay found wide scope for her activities. She became a member of the Scottish Savings Committee shortly after its inception and it was for her support of the movement—a support that embraced a considerable amount of public speaking, for which she had a distinct gift—that her name was included in the 1933 New Year's Honours List as a Commander of the Order of the British Empire.

During... [World War I] ...Mrs. Hannay played a leading part in setting up in Scotland of Women's Patrols... [an early step in the progress of integrating women into police forces in the UK] ... A

297

member of the Church of Scotland and a daughter of the manse, Mrs. Hannay served on various Church committees and upon two Assembly Committees, having had the honour of addressing the General Assembly of the Church from the floor of the house."

The Dean of the Thistle, The Very Reverend Charles Warr, preached an address at her funeral in St. Giles and pays this rather splendid tribute to her:

"Today all that is mortal of Jane Ewing Hannay is being laid to rest amid the sequestered peace of her childhood's home. It is indeed fitting that her dust should sleep in the soil of Galloway for she loved that soil with all the passion of her heart. Life led her far from its immemorial quiet, but it was to the last the land of her dreams. The memory of the Manse of New Abbey ever glowed like an altar lamp in the sanctuary of her soul. Now she has gone back to her own country and her own people 'her work accomplished and the long day done.' And we her friends have gathered here, in sorrow of heart, yet in calm and trustful confidence, for these last tender offices of faith and love.

We are each poignantly aware of the depth of our own personal loss. Jane Hannay had a genius for friendship, and when she gave her affection she gave it without measure. Friendship and affection constituted for her the only atmosphere in which she could freely breathe. 'It is good to be loved' she said in a lucid period during her last illness, when told of sympathetic enquiries of her friends. And we who knew her understood just how much of herself was revealed in these few simple words.

In her passing there has gone from us a remarkable personality. Her intellectual gifts were of an unusually high order, and she made herself a unique place among the women of her generation. It is no exaggeration to say she was one of the most accomplished Scotswomen of her time. And those capacities of mind and qualities of character which God had bestowed on her, she put unreservedly to the public service. I need not recapitulate the many and varied activities of her busy and devoted life. They are known to you all. Nor need I remind you that, amid her divers and engrossing duties and interests, her fairest piece of creative work was the gracious home she made for her husband and son. With a multitude throughout the land we give grateful thanks to God today for all she was enabled to do and achieve.

We remember her smile that was like sunshine; the swiftly stirred deeps of emotion and sympathy; the quick and clever speech; the nimble wit; the capacity for fun and the quaint reaction of her humour; the spirit that was so brave and free ; the alert and cultured mind that scorned the second rate, that was always on guard to defend conviction and principle, but which never left estrangement in the wake of controversy. We remember her love of God, her wise and lofty patriotism, her profound concern for humanity. We

298

remember, in short, a gifted, gracious, and gallant lady and remembering we realise how much the poorer is our individual and corporate life because she is no longer here.

With her marked aptitude for practical affairs, Jane Hannay combined a deep mystical perception. She lived very close to the unseen world. Those who sensed the secrets of her life knew that she worked in fellowship with the Risen Lord, and in communion with the saints in light. She has fought a good fight, she has finished her course, she has kept the faith. Elsewhere, we believe she has entered upon greater and more abounding service. We remember in sympathy and affection those near and dear to her; we commend her soul to God."

## 6. *Robert Hannay (1900-1956), son of Robert*

Robert Kerr and Jane had one son, Robert Stewart Erskine Hannay, born in 1900 and educated at Edinburgh Academy. He entered the Royal Navy and was a midshipman in HMS *Iron Duke* in 1921, being transferred to HMS *Victory* in 1922, and to HMS *Vivid* in 1926 and thence to *Furious* later that year. He was Lieutenant Commander (E) of HMS *Renown* in 1930 and retired in 1932. During World War II Robert was recalled to the Navy and was employed at the Boom Defence Department of the Admiralty. He received the OBE in 1942 and was promoted Commander.

He married Helen, the daughter of Sir James Morton, LL.D., F.R.S.E., J.P., of Dalston Hall, near Carlisle in 1930, and entered his father-in-law's firm, Morton Sundour Fabrics where he was a director till his death in 1956.

In the obituary notice in his firm's journal is a very striking description of him:

"The dominant feature of his private life was his supremely happy marriage blessed with four children, in whom he delighted without in any way doting over them, and supported by an overriding belief in spiritual values which he was not afraid to proclaim ... An underlying seriousness and deeply religious outlook did not in any way diminish, and in many ways served to throw into relief, his humorous and almost boyish outlook on life which was so exhilarating to all who he met ... "

There were four children: Beatrice Mariot, named after a 15th century ancestor Mariot Hannay, the daughter of Odo of Sorbie; Robert Alastair; Ian Morton; and Margaret Jean.

# XVIII: The Hannays of North America

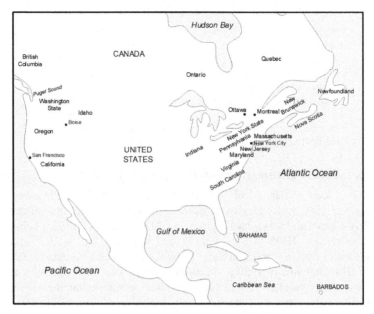

**Figure 81: North American locales mentioned in this book**

The Hannays, Hannas, Hannahs and Hanneys of North America deserve a volume of their own; when Stewart Francis first wrote *The Hannays of Sorbie*, he concentrated primarily on the roots of the family in Scotland. This chapter should be considered a starting point for further research. Great challenges, of course, arise when attempting to connect the Canadian, American and Caribbean branches of the family back to Scotland. Often trails can only be traced back to a particular ship which sailed from Scotland or Ireland. Beyond the passenger rolls, identification may or may not even include the town from which the emigrating family originated. Nonetheless, relatively complete trails are sometimes discovered, and family members continue to research the connections.

In 1653 a John Hannay of West Quarters, Carrickfergus, one of the Scots planted in Ulster during Charles I reign probably by Sir Robert (see Chapter VI: The Sons of Alexander of Sorbie) or David Hannay (see Chapter VIII: The Hannays of Kirkdale), who were in the Irish Civil Service, and in some way was responsible for arranging for suitable Scots to come over to people Ireland. John was ordered to be removed on account of "his monarchical and Presbyterian leanings" by Cromwell's Government. He is supposed to have gone to the Americas. There were between Maryland and Pennsylvania many "Scotch-Irish" emigrants placed to make a barrier between Penn's Quarter and the Catholic Marylanders. It is probably with these that John went. After the battle of Bothwell Brig in 1679, when the Covenanters opposed Dundee and were decisively beaten, 250 Scots who had been taken prisoner were banished to America, including a Samuel Hannay of Kirkmabreck, probably a relation of Kirkdale. As a result of the Test Act troubles, several members of the family were banished to the plantations. A William Hannay was sent to East New Jersey Plantation, and another William was banished to the Barbados. No doubt there were others whose names have not been vouchsafed to us.

In 1700, we hear of a Robert Hannay in the Council of Massachusetts being given permission to erect a "timber building covered with rough caste and slates in Kingslane, Boston." In 1730 John Hannay is licensed by the Presbytery of New Brunswick, New Jersey, as a minister, first in Bethlehem in 1730, and then at Kingwood in 1742 and finally at Alexandria, New Jersey about 1752. In 1760 the Presbytery of Dutchess County, New York received a William Hannay into its communion.

From the diary of the Reverend David McClure are these entries about a certain Robert Hanna living in the Scottish-Irish enclosure between Maryland and Pennsylvania, who appears by this time to be a man of some substance:

"1772, 11th Oct, Last Sabbath preached at Proctors tent and today Wednesday at the house of Esq Robert Hanna about 30 miles from Pittsburg ... some rigid Presbyterians in this settlement objected to me because I did not belong to a Presbytery but was a New England Congregational minister.

1772 12th Oct, Esq Hanna accompanied me to Ligonier.

1772 19th March, Preached at Robert Hanna Esq and next day Ligonier."

This may be the Robert Hanna (1744-1821) who is mentioned by the Reverend Hanna (see later in this chapter) in his book as being born in Prince Edward County, Virginia, a descendant of Robert Hannay (probably the son of Alexander of Sorbie), and through whom the Reverend Hanna and his family are descended. He moved to Pennsylvania, where we find him in this extract, and thence to South Carolina and finally to Brookville, Indiana. He served in the American War of Independence, and married Nancy the daughter of James Park. He is mentioned in White County History, Indiana, published in 1915.

Robert's uncle Joseph, who was probably born in Ulster, travelled over with Robert's father, John. He settled in South Carolina; the

301

Revolutionary War was fought on his farm, known then as Hanna's Pens or Hanna's Cowpens.

During the whole of the eighteenth and nineteenth centuries there were many members of the family settling in the States, and Canada: George Hannay of Kingsmuir was there for 20 years from 1764 until driven out by the War of Independence, and many others from the main branches of the family have settled there from time to time.

Captain Patrick Hanna (1699-1758) who went over to join his brother Robert and settled in York County, Pennsylvania, had a son Robert who founded Hannastown there. This family is still represented there today.

## 1. The Family of Thomas Hannay of Stonykirk

There is one family which is particularly worthy of note, that of Thomas Hannay of Stonykirk (on the Rhinns of Galloway in Scotland).

James Hannay his eldest son, born in 1798, attended Glasgow University and went as a missionary to Richibucto in New Brunswick, Canada, in 1833.

He returned to Scotland to the cure of Cairn Ryan in 1845 and died at Port William in 1858. He married and had five sons, Thomas, John, Andrew, David and James. On his death his wife returned to Canada, and James her eldest son, who was born there in 1842 entered the legal profession and was called to the Bar in 1867. He was later the official reporter to the Supreme Court. Between 1867 and 1873 James published two thousand volumes of reports. In 1873 he resigned and became assistant editor of the St. John *Daily Telegraph* and in 1883 he went over to the staff of the Montreal *Herald* and then on to the staff of the Brooklyn *Daily Eagle*. In 1888 he returned to St. John, to be editor of the *Gazette*. He published several historical works about Canada and the United States. James married Margaret Ross in 1844 and died in 1910. John his brother was born in Scotland but removed to U.S.A. and became the Cashier of the Farmers and Merchants Bank of Edison, Washington State. Of his sons, Arthur B. Hannay went into the press gallery of the Canadian Parliament, and N. B. Hannay became the President of the first National Bank of Mount Vernon, State of Washington.

## 2. Andrew Hannay (1733-1808)

William Vanderpool Hannay carried out a great deal of very useful work concerning the members of the family resident near Albany, New York State. He published in 1913 a "Genealogy of the Hannay Family", which gives an outline of the family in Scotland as he knew it, and a

302

very detailed genealogy of the branch of the family from which he is descended.

Andrew Hannay came to America in the 18ᵗʰ Century. The following is taken From *Biographical Sketches of Andrew and David Hannay* by A. M. Hannay:

Andrew Hannay was born in the town of Galloway, County of Galloway, Scotland, in the year 1733. Concerning his boyhood life scarcely anything is known, but it is presumed, however, to have been quiet and industrious. He at some time learned the cooper's trade and worked at that business in his native town. His education was limited, but he was possessed of a strong constitution and vigorous mind, plodding at his unremunerative business, but this it seems did not satisfy his ambition. He was resolved upon a change, whether for the better or not, time only would decide. No branch of business being open where he could secure profit and advancement, he, at the age of twenty-four, enlisted in the King's service, in Col. T. Brudenell's company, 51ˢᵗ Regiment of Infantry, Major Montgomerie's command. He served in the army six years and was discharged on account of a stiff finger produced by a felon [abscess caused by a bacterial infection]. The original document was in the hands of his late son David, filled out and signed by Col. T. Brudenell.

At some period of his service in the army he was married, his wife being a German lady. After getting his discharge, he returned with his family to his native town, where he was engaged, in company with another man, in building houses for some ten or twelve years, gaining but small profit. Indeed, it was barely possible in his native country for a poor man to secure a scanty living. The land was all owned by the aristocrats and all business controlled by them, while the poor were servants and little cared for.

He now formed the resolution of coming to America, and sometime in the year 1774 carried it into effect. He landed at New York with but four shillings left.

During the forepart of the first day he secured a place for his family to live, and in the afternoon found work for himself, and earned two shillings tending a mason. Thus, situated he continued for some length of time. His great desire was to obtain land on which to raise substantial food for his family, and if possible to leave as an inheritance for his children.

He soon fell in with a Mr. Kortright who owned a large tract of land in Delaware County, New York State, and was by him induced to go there and settle. So, after making a contract he took the following directions, and proceeded thence to make a home. He was to go from New York to Albany, from there to Schoharie, to Breakabeen, to the township of Kortright, which was thirty miles from Schoharie.

There were four families with him, and leaving their wives and children in Schoharie, they pushed on to Kortright and there immediately commenced and finished in four days, four houses, one for each family. Then they returned to Schoharie for their families. When they returned they found their houses filled with snow, it being the wintertime. Now he had a house and land but surrounded by almost unending woods, inhabited more or less by the savage Indians and wild beasts, in a country subject to heavy snows, with very few inhabitants, and with scarcely anything but his strong arms with which to clear off the woods and prepare the crops in the spring.

How well he succeeded is not known, as he did not live here very long. Want of means and the difficulty of procuring provisions compelled him to seek a home somewhere else.

One day after he had been thirty miles to the mill, and returning with the meal upon his back, he told his wife before it was used up she must prepare to move. He sold his possessions for three pounds and returned to Schoharie, where he settled and remained less than a year, after which for some length of time he was not permanently settled. He used to say, "I moved nine times in nine years and was never without bread for my family." At last he settled in the town of Rensselaerville, Albany County, where he took land to work upon shares. He succeeded pretty well in raising grain, and lived here three or four years, but was finally driven away by the Indians who were very troublesome.

One day when he had gone from home, some Indians came to the house where his wife was alone and demanded pork. Upon being told that she had none, one of the foremost of them drew his scalping knife and struck her a severe blow in the breast, with the intention, no doubt, of killing her, but the blade striking the breast bone, thus prevented the wound from being a fatal one. To be more secure against the troublesome Indians he moved his family to Bethlehem, in the same county, he and his son returning to take care of the crops.

One time as they were on their way home from labour, they stopped at the house of a Tory to stay overnight and took rest upon the floor near the fireplace. Late in the night they were all awakened by a noise at the door. Upon the door being opened it became known that a band of Indians were outside, whose object seemed to be to make their friend a visit. Two or three of their number entered and after some conversation roughly asked who was lying in the bed on the floor. Being positively assured that only a part of his own family were there, they were induced not to disturb them but they threatened that if they had any Yankees about the house they would take their hearts' blood in a minute. He and his son had lain almost breathless through the interview, and after the departure of the Indians, they carefully made their way into the adjoining wood to obtain rest for the remainder of the night. At one

304

time the Indians were so troublesome that some of the inhabitants built a fort in which to place their families in case of attack.

He used to tell an amusing incident in relation to this fort. The people were constantly on the watch lest the Indians should steal upon them. One morning a sharp firing of musketry was heard at no great distance from the settlement. The inhabitants immediately becoming alarmed, ceased their employment and proceeded to the fort for safety. Upon gathering it was ascertained that one man had been left ploughing in his field ignorant of danger. A call was made for someone to volunteer to go and notify him and bring him to the fort. Andrew Hannay was the first to offer. The horses were quickly stripped of their harness, and himself taking one and the ploughman the other, they hastily returned to the fort. Some time was now spent in preparing for the expected attack. Finally, a council was held, and it was determined that some scouts should be sent out in the direction of the firing to ascertain if possible its cause and object.

Andrew Hannay again offered his services and with two or three others sallied forth. The locality was reached and his discovery soon made known the fact that the firing proceeded from a few Indian boys shooting squirrels.

Andrew's sympathies were entirely against the English in the Revolutionary War, but the need of his presence at home always prevented him from joining the army. In the year 1777 when Burgoyne's campaign was brought to a crisis, he raised a company of volunteers and started with them to join General Gates. Upon reaching Albany, the news came of Burgoyne's surrender and they disbanded and returned to their homes.

Soon after his removal to Bethlehem his wife died, leaving him with four children, three boys and one girl. He continued to live on here a year or two when he became acquainted with and married a widow named Towsick. Her maiden name was Elizabeth Ricord and she lived about twenty miles southwest of Albany, in what was then the Town of Coeymans. Her husband and only son had been carried to Canada by the Indians and died there, leaving her with nine daughters to provide for as best she could. They managed to cultivate the land with their own hands and procure a comfortable living.

They were always more or less harassed by fear of the Indians, who were often lurking about committing horrible crimes in the vicinity. Once they were taken to Albany for safety and remained there for some time until the country became more quiet and less dangerous. Andrew Hannay now obtained possession of a large tract of land principally covered with timber lying on both sides of what was called the Passic Creek (now called Basic Creek) in what is now the Town of Westerlo, Albany County.

305

The country was becoming more quiet and settled, and markets to some extent were being established, especially at Albany. It seems that the days had really come for realizing the fond hope he had entertained when leaving his native land. Peace and prosperity were not his lot for a long term of years. He remained here successfully engaged in farming and clearing off the land for the remainder of his life.

The offspring of his second marriage was one son David. In the year 1800 Andrew's second wife died, and he was some time afterward married to a widow, Hannah Wendell, who had formerly lived in Dutchess County. He lived with her until his death which occurred in the year 1808, he being the age of 75 years. At his request his remains were buried near the road in a beautiful field on his own farm. Such in brief is the history of his life. He was one of many who would not submit to live under the form of society, where the most sacred rights of man are held only by a few privileged characters. He chose rather to endure privation and hardships in a distant, wild and unsettled country, but where industry and perseverance were necessary for anyone to secure all the blessings of this life.

The names of his children by his first wife were James, John who married Adrian Whitmarch, Andrew who married Mary Ann Swop, and Elizabeth who married George Swop. The boys settled on lands given them by their father. Elizabeth and her husband moved to Pennsylvania, from thence to Canada, and afterwards back to Genesee County, N.Y., where she died. The names of his step-daughters were: Mary who married Chris John Price, and moved to Canada, and Hannah who married a Fineout, and moved to Schenectady, N.Y., and Catherine who married a Fineout, and moved to Canajoharie, N.Y., Elizabeth who married Peter Grant, and moved to Delaware Co., N.Y., and Eve who married a Ramsay, and lived in Bethlehem, Albany Co., N.Y., and Christine who married a Helega, and lived in Berne, Albany Co., N.Y., and Sarah who married a Swop and moved to Holland Purchase, Genesee Co., N.Y., and Laney who married John Sager, and moved to Canada, and Margaret who married a Helega, and moved to Berne, Albany Co., N.Y.

Andrew Hannay sailed from Scotland on the *Tate of Whitehaven* on May 7, 1774. There were six other Hannays on the passenger list, presumably his family. He was aged 40 at the time and his residence given as Gatehouse of Fleet. Of the 67 passengers on board 37 were from Gatehouse, which shows the state of the West of Scotland at the time. He had four children, James, John, Andrew and Elizabeth whose names appear on the passenger list. Another son, David, was born in America.

Andrew had previously served from 1757-1763 in Col. Thomas Brudenall 's 51st Foot (now the King's Own Yorkshire Light Infantry).

It is thought that Andrew's father was another Andrew married to Margaret McCaw and that his father was, in turn, yet another Andrew from Minnigaff. A family tree can be found in Figure 82: Pedigree of Col. William V. Hannay. William, who collected much of this material, was a banker and retired Colonel of the U.S. Army, living in Albany, New York State.

*Pedigree unclear for Andrew Hannay of Minnigaff*

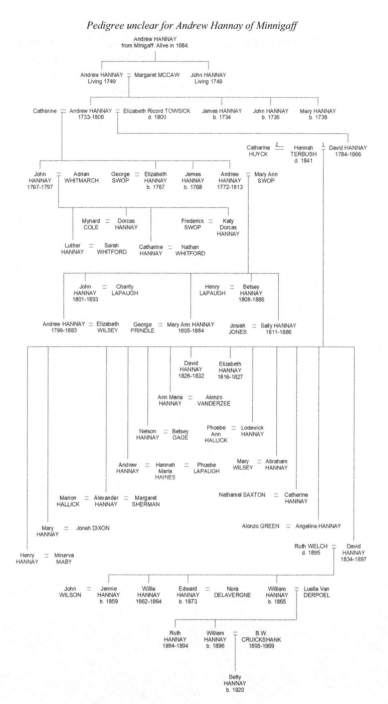

**Figure 82: Pedigree of Col. William V. Hannay**

308

## 3. *David Hannay (1784-1866)*

Andrew Hannay's son David by his second wife is also listed in *Biographical Sketches of Andrew and David Hannay* by A. M. Hannay:

David Hannay was born October 5th, 1784. He was the only child resulting from the marriage of Andrew Hannay and Mrs. Elizabeth Towsick. The description given of the house in which he was born is, that the floor was made of basswood trees split, and the split surface smoothed with an axe; the roof was composed of basswood bark. Patience and industry, however, had rendered his humble abode pleasant and comfortable. His boyhood days, from the time he was possessed of sufficient strength, were almost entirely spent in hard labour, assisting his father upon the farm. The conveniences for farming used at the present time were then almost unknown. Even the most simple tools were of home manufacture, so that it then required to perform the same amount of work much more hard labour than in later times.

The simple tool, the plough, which is now constructed in a thousand varieties, was then hewn out of wood and plated with strips of iron, the wheels of a wagon were frequently sawed from the huge body of a white oak tree. Pitchforks were cut from small crotched saplings, and similar expedients were resorted to in all instruments of farm labour. These were looked upon as being the best that could be procured and were used with patience and were considered sufficient and effective.

Progress was necessarily slow in clearing the land of heavy timber and fitting it for producing crops. Here in peace and contentment they were satisfied to labour and to live.

Neighbours commenced gathering about them so that a society began to be established, but in many respects a very different society from that of the present day. The difficulty of raising extensive crops and a limited market caused everyone to live with the utmost economy. Neither men, women or children desired anything better than good stout home-made clothes for wearing apparel and it was not often that children obtained boots and shoes to wear until they became grown up men and women. On all occasions a rude sleigh or wagon drawn by an ox team formed the conveyance, and some farm vegetables with bread made of corn meal or rye flour composed the usual satisfactory repast. Form and fashion and all the frivolities of society were the great lessons of life.

The people lived principally in log houses with huge fire places for cooking purposes and to protect them from the cold, and a feeling of brotherhood pervaded all who lived in the vicinity and each seemed to possess a full share of earthly enjoyment, as much if not more so, than the people of the present time. Trouble from the Indians, especially in the earlier times, was occasionally feared.

A novel custom was ordained by which the whole neighbourhood could be quickly aroused in case of danger. Each family possessed a tin horn, and at the approach of danger, the family in trouble would sound the horn a number of times in quick succession, his neighbour would repeat the sound and so on until the remotest family was notified. In case they wished to communicate with each other to understand if all things were well, one long sound was given. The advantage of schools was then almost unknown.

David Hannay had the privilege of attending a common school some two or three months before he became a man. He, however, acquired principally by his own efforts a sufficient knowledge of the common branches to be able to read, and write, and to understand common business transactions. At the age of twenty-one years, October 10th, 1805, he was married to Miss Hannah Terbush. Three years later his father died.

He now came into possession of fifty acres of land which included the house where he was born. The old house, however, was in due time replaced by a larger dwelling. He soon after purchased more land, sufficient to make a large farm. This farm, on which he lived until he died, is situated in one of the most pleasant localities in that part of the State. A beautiful stream of water called Passic Creek (now called Basic Creek) runs through nearly the centre of it. The eastern half is slightly uneven forming a gradual slope down to the creek, while west of the creek is a broad, beautiful, flat even land which in cases of a severe freshet[269] overflows with water, making permanent and very productive mellow land, while the upland is adapted to grain and pasture. Portions of the uplands are stony and it is interesting to see how by patient hard labour the whole farm except the flat has been divided into fields and each surrounded by a high stone wall. It is difficult to imagine how a man in one life-time could provide for the wants of a large family and change the wild forest into such cultivated fields.

In the course of a few years he began to be surrounded by children among whom were boys who soon became able to assist him. He usually enjoyed excellent health, and so with some exceptions did his children, but his wife for a long term of years was more or less affected with sickness, which many times caused him sorrow and which tried his energies and sometimes darkened his prospects. In the War of 1812, he was harassed by the difficulties and uncertainties incident to the war and by the fear of being compelled to leave his dependant family of little ones and join the army. Twice he had the good luck to escape the draft but the third time he was forced to prepare for duty in the army. On his way to the rendezvous he had the good fortune to secure a substitute who agreed to take his place for the amount of forty dollars and he immediately returned home to the utmost delight of his family. His

---

[269] Flood of water from heavy rain

good judgment and unexceptional habits of life won for him the confidence and esteem of all who knew him.

During his whole life he was never personally engaged in a lawsuit. He was often honoured by town offices but had the self-denial to refuse them when he feared he was not competent.

Much of the land in this part of the country was a portion of the famous rent land and at many times there was much trouble and contention on account of paying the rent to the land holders. One odious feature in the conditions of the rent was the "Sixth Sale" by which the occupants in the case of selling were obliged to pay their land holders one-sixth part of the money received. Through the efforts of David Hannay and other prominent men a suit to recover the "Sixth Sale" was resisted.

After being ably prosecuted and defended in the various courts of the State, it reached the Court of Appeals, and was finally decided in the favour of the occupants of the land, and the unjust condition was forever removed. His whole life was marked by peace and quiet, and in all his transactions of private and public affairs, he was distinguished for good judgment, candour and honesty.

A trait of his unambitious character is shown in the fact that he never rode in a public conveyance—railroad, steamboat, or even a stagecoach. Though sometimes required to travel a long distance, he always preferred to provide a good conveyance of his own.

Concerning the public topics of the day, he was always well informed and able to discuss them with interest and intelligence. In politics he was an earnest Democrat.

The energies of his life were by no means altogether devoted to worldly affairs. During his entire life he was a member of the Baptist Church and held various positions of responsibility and trust in the Church. Many delicate questions pertaining to church matters were entrusted to his deliberations, judgment and decision. His leisure hours were usually spent in studying the Bible or in perusing religious books or newspapers. His Christian course of life was ever marked by strict devotion to duty, calm but firm pursuit of right and by always setting an example of Christian conduct. What a pleasure after a life of over four score years to be able to reflect that so many of those years have been spent in the true and earnest service of his Master.

His wife died November 2nd, 1841, aged 53 years. By her he had fourteen children; eight sons and six daughters. Two of the daughters died, one when an infant, the twelfth child, and the other named Elizabeth, the fifth child, after a protracted illness, when nearly approaching to womanhood. One son, the eleventh child, named David died in infancy.

July 16th, 1842, he was again married to Miss Catherine Huyck, who was during his old age and feeble health, an agreeable and pleasant companion.

At the age of eighty-two years when he died, his mental and physical powers were remarkably well preserved. He was buried on a beautiful mound in a field near the brook that was the scene of his boyhood sports.

## 4. The Reverend James A. M. Hanna (1925-2007)

In Jackson County, Ohio, the late Reverend James Arthur MacClannahan Hanna did some outstanding genealogical work for the Hannay diaspora. He collected a great deal of most valuable information which formed the basis of his book *Hanna of Castle Sorbie, Scotland and Descendants*, which was published by Edwards Brothers of Ann Arbor, Michigan, in 1959.

He was descended from Robert Hannay, likely the son of Alexander of Sorbie. The Rev. Mr. Hanna's family emigrated to Northern Ireland and thence to Pennsylvania and Delaware about 1680. In time they moved on into Virginia and, lastly, Ohio. They are a large family who produced many eminent Presbyterian divines, and of whom the Reverend James Hanna has written very fully.

He was born in Marietta Ohio in 1925. A decorated infantryman in the U.S. Army during the Second World War, he later studied at Marietta College and Louisville Presbyterian Theological Seminary. James Hanna died on April 17, 2007.

## 5. John Francis Hanna (1843-1885)

John Francis Hanna was born in Philadelphia on Aug. 20, 1843, the son of Francis Hanna and Eliza F. Keefe and grandson of James and Elizabeth Hanna. He attended Gonzaga College High School conducted by the Jesuits and subsequently entered Georgetown University, becoming a BA. From Georgetown he entered the Virginia Military Institute in 1862. At the Battle of New Market in May 1864 the 257 cadets of VMI fought with the Confederate Army against the Union Army as part of the American Civil War. Their charge in the battle was described by Capt. Franklin Town, a Union officer, as follows: "Their line was as perfectly presented as if on a dress parade or in the evolution of a review." John Francis Hanna was cadet first lieutenant in D Company. The jacket worn by John is now preserved in the VMI Museum, along with a diary kept by John from April 17-May 9, 1864. He continued to serve in the Confederate Army until the end of the war.

312

Returning home after the war, he studied languages and read philosophy with a German professor. He spent one year abroad in company with Mr. James M. Johnston, who was later his law partner. They both entered the office of Judge Walter Cox of Washington, D.C.

He attended George Washington University Law School in 1867-68. He received his degree in 1869, and practised in the Court of Claims and the U.S. Supreme Court. His portrait hangs in the Jackson Memorial Hall at VMI. He was injured by the falling of his horse, October 25, 1885, and died at his home at Mt. Vernon, VA. October 31, 1885. His Cross of Honour was sent to his sister, Miss Cecelia Hanna, who then lived at 1435 Fairmount Street, Washington, D.C. His classmate, Captain B.A. Colonna, wrote a tribute to his memory from which the following brief abstract is quoted:

"... Mr. Francis Hanna and his son, John Francis Hanna, were my companions for the first time early in January, 1862, on a night stage ride from Goshen to Lexington, Va., and on that stage coach were laid the foundation of friendships that lasted during our lives ... we were second classmen and cadet sergeants when Stonewall Jackson's remains were brought to VMI and laid in State in his old class room. Hanna was sergeant of the guard and without precedent or advice he conceived his duty readily and clearly and saw that the cadets on duty at the bier, one at the hand, another at the foot, stood at parade-rest continually day and night so long as 'Old Jack' was with us for this purpose. They were relieved hourly .... After graduating in June following the Battle of New Market, Va., he was along with others of the class of 1864 appointed second lieutenant in the provisional Army of the Confederate States and served with distinction on the staff; first with General Imboden and next with General Echols. He also during a critical period of some weeks served as captain of infantry in the trenches in front of Fort Harrison and for his proficiency and bravery received the thanks of his commanding officer ... "

"The Washington Law reporter", Vol. XIII, p. 596, Nov 7, 1885, in an editorial too long to be reproduced here in full, says:

"Perhaps the most positive and conspicuous trait of Mr. Hanna's character was his absolute fidelity in the discharge of the duties of life. His unusual physical and moral courage never allowed him to temporize for an instant. His duty once determined he reckoned not the risk in performing it. Neither times nor places nor the fear of bodily harm nor the taunts of men could swerve him from the line he had laid down..."

He had two sisters, Sheila Hanna and Mrs. Anna Hanna Ferrney of Washington.

313

## 6. John Spragins Hannah (1845-1901)

Also present at the Battle of New Market was John Spragins Hannah, born on March 21, 1845 in Cedar Hill, VA, the son of George Cunningham Hannah and Ann Eliza Spragins. His grandfather George was a captain in the War of 1812. His people on both sides were descended from prerevolutionary settlers in Virginia. One of his ancestors being a sea captain who carried non-combatants, women, and children from Yorktown, during its siege in 1781 by General George Washington during the American Revolutionary War. Another commanded a company of students from the Hampden Sydney College at the 1781 Battle of Guilford Court House.

On January 1, 1863, he matriculated at VMI, and in the following session served as a cadet private in Company D in the Battle of New Market. After the battle he entered the Confederate Army, and was made $2^{nd}$ lieutenant in Captain Summers' company, then in east Tennessee, under the command of General Hood. Soon afterwards his regiment was sent to Salisbury, North Carolina, to guard the Federal prisoners there. When General George Stoneman's raid released these prisoners, he was captured and carried off to Tennessee to prison. While a Federal prisoner he was mistaken by the notorious guerilla commander Kirk for Capt. Isaac Avery, to whom he bore a close resemblance, and at whose hands Kirk had suffered serious discomfiture. Hannah narrowly escaped being shot.

After his release from prison he went into business with Daniel and Marshall, of Smithville, VA, then to Hull, Atkinson & Co., a dry goods house of Baltimore, for which firm he was a travelling salesman. After two years he entered the firm of W.P. Harvey & Co., wholesale grocers. He soon gained control of the southern trade of this firm which he built up and placed upon such a solid basis that he was entrusted with the management of their branch house in Chicago and was finally made a partner. He was a member of the Board of Trade, Chicago.

He married Annie Carrington in 1884 and had two children, Elizabeth and Miles Carrington Hannah. He died on July 5, 1901. He had three brothers who were also cadets at VMI: Samuel Baldwin in 1863, George Baxter in 1865 and Joel Morton in 1868.

## 7. David Blythe Hanna (1858-1938)

David Blythe Hanna was born at Thornliebank on December 20, 1858, the son of William Hanna, the foreman of Crum Cotton Mills and Janet Blair. He was educated at Thornliebank and in Glasgow.

He emigrated to Canada after working on the Caledonian Railway in Scotland in 1882 and joined the Grand Trunk Railway in Montreal. In

1902 he was third Vice President of the Canadian Northern Railway, and during his term of office the line was taken from Saskatoon to Calgary. In 1918 when the Railway was taken over by the Canadian Government, he was appointed First President until 1922 when he was appointed to the Liquor Control Board of Ontario.

His life is perhaps best dealt with in his book *Trains of Recollection,* being the story of his early railway career written with Arthur Hawkes.

The town of Hanna in Alberta is named after him. In their 50th Anniversary publication they said this of him:

> "D.B. Hanna takes his place in a long line of the founders of the West. He played an important and proud role in making his contribution to Western Canada, we who were to follow and those generations yet to come are proud indeed to be residents of a county which as the history of Canada reveals is the bearer of a distinguished name."

## 8. *Mary Ann Hannah (1783-1852)*

Mary Ann Hannah, born January 3, 1783 in Augusta County, Virginia, married Daniel Stover Jr. (1780-1860) at Trinity Episcopal Church in Staunton, Virginia, on March 30, 1803. She died on March 23, 1852, at Mount Sidney, Virginia, where she was buried next to her husband in Mount Pisgah Cemetery.

The Daniel Stover Sr. Family and a Joseph Hanna/h family were both in the Naked Creek region of Augusta County in the Shenandoah Valley from the 1740s/1750s onwards, making this Joseph Hannah family the most likely line leading to Mary Ann Hannah. Both she and her husband, Daniel Stover Jr., seem to have not moved from the Naked Creek/Mount Sidney area throughout their lives. She was likely a Presbyterian Protestant by birth and he from a restrictive German Protestant sect. They got married in an Anglican/Episcopalian Church in Staunton, which suggests this cross-Protestant denominational marriage was not approved by both families. The Joseph Hanna/h family migrated down the Shenandoah Valley from Pennsylvania in the mid-18th century with the great Scotch-Irish migration from Ulster at the time.

Mary Ann and Daniel's fourth son Simon P. Stover (1822-1872) married an Elizabeth Ida Link (1822-1867) in Augusta County; they had a daughter, Ida Elizabeth Stover (1863-1946) who married David J. Eisenhower (1863-1942) in Kansas.

Ida and David were the parents of General Dwight D. Eisenhower (1890-1969), 34th President of the United States of America.

## 9. John Hanna (b. circa 1777)

John Hanna of Castlebar, County Mayo, was born roughly 1777. He appears to have fought in the Peninsular War as a Corporal of the Coldstream Guards in Colonel (later Field Marshal) William Gomm's company. John emigrated to Canada sometime after 1817, bringing with him his family, which included his brother Robert (c. 1781-1856) and his son James. The family settled in what was then the Huron District of Canada West, now Huron County, Ontario. See Figure 83 for a family tree.

### 9.1. James Hanna (1817-1896), son of John

John's son James married Elizabeth Givens, who was born in Ballymena, County Antrim. After Elizabeth's death in 1881, James was married a second time to a Miss Hanna (probably a distant cousin). James had two sons, James Edward and Givens.

### 9.2. James Hanna (1861-1935), son of James

James and Elizabeth's son James Edward was born in Plum Hollow, Ontario in 1861. James Edward married Eva Jane Eliza Henderson; they had two sons, Frederic James and Herbert Edward, and one daughter, Eileen.

### 9.3. Frederic Hanna (1899-1969), son of James

James Edward and Eva's son Frederic James—known to the family as "Eric"—was born in Ottawa, Ontario, in 1899. He was educated at the Royal Military College of Canada and the University of Toronto. He fought in World War I as an officer in the Royal Canadian Army and eventually rose to the rank of Major. After the war he became an attorney. He married Victoria Muriel Boyce (1898-1991), the daughter of Arthur Cyril Boyce, KC, MP, DCL, a Conservative member of the Canadian House of Commons from 1904 to 1917. Frederic and Victoria had three children, James Eric, Elizabeth Muriel and Barbara Jane. Frederic James died in Ottawa in 1969.

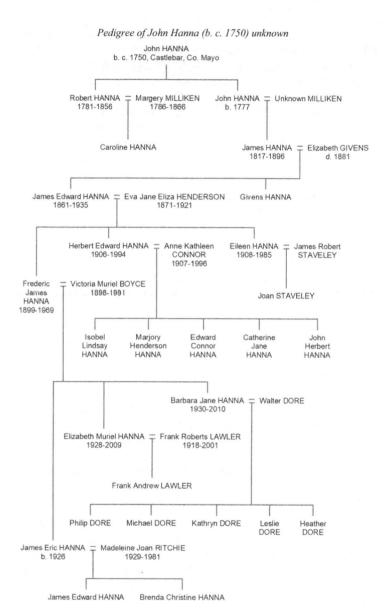

*Pedigree of John Hanna (b. c. 1750) unknown*

**Figure 83: Family of John Hanna of Castlebar, County Mayo**

## 9.4. James Hanna (born 1926), son of Frederic

Frederic and Victoria Muriel's son James Eric was born in 1926 and earned a bachelor's degree in engineering at the University of Toronto before joining the Royal Canadian Air Force. James was a test pilot for the RCAF in the 1950s and served as a liaison officer between the

317

Canadian government and Avro Aircraft during the development of the CF-105 Arrow supersonic interceptor. In the 1960s, he served with the United Nations Emergency Force (UNEF) in Gaza. In 1975-76 he was defence attaché to the Canadian Embassy in Paris. He returned to Canada to command the 22nd NORAD region based in North Bay, Ontario for three years before his final career assignment as Commander of Canadian Forces Europe (CFE) in Lahr, Germany. He retired from the Canadian Armed Forces in 1982 with the rank of major-general.

James subsequently became head of government and military sales for De Havilland Aircraft in Downsview (Toronto), Ontario. A Clan Hannay Society member since the 1960s, MGen Hanna served on the Clan Hannay Council in the 1990s and early 2000s.

### 9.5. Elizabeth Hanna (1928-2009)
Frederic and Victoria Muriel's daughter Elizabeth Muriel was born in 1928. She married the Rev. Frank Roberts Lawler, Canon of St. Andrews at Christ Church Cathedral in Ottawa. Their only child, Frank Andrew Lawler, has been a member of the Clan Hannay Society since the 1990s and is the co-author of the fourth edition of this book.

### 9.6. Barbara Hanna (1930-2010)
Frederic and Victoria's youngest child Barbara Jane was born in Ottawa in June 1930. She married Walter Dore of Montreal. During the course of their 60-year marriage, they lived in Nova Scotia, Ontario and British Columbia, experiencing Canada from coast to coast. They had five children: Philip, Michael, Kathryn, Leslie and Heather. Barbara died in White Rock, British Columbia, in November 2010.

## 10. Certainly Not the End of the Chapter
Right up to the present day, the family is still sending its emigrants to both Canada and the United States where no doubt they will carry the traditions of their native Scotland to the general benefit of their adopted country. It is impossible to name them all here, but it is hoped that future editions of the *Hannays of Sorbie* will add many more of their stories.

For those interested in further research into the family diaspora in Canada and the United States, the following works are some starting points:

- **Hanna, Rev. James A. M., *Hanna of Castle Sorbie, Scotland and Descendants*, Edwards Brothers, Ann Arbor, 1959**. This book attempts a fairly broad approach to

318

Hannas in the United States, although tends to emphasize Ohio and Pennsylvania.

- **Hannay, William Vanderpoel (b. 1896),** *Genealogy of the Hannay Family,* **Albany, New York, U.S.A., 1913.** A short, eclectic work comprising a genealogy descending from the author's ancestor Andrew Hannay (1733-1808; he or his son emigrated from Scotland to New York State) and a dozen or so anecdotal references to various other Hannay branches.
- **Rice, Charles Elmer,** *A History of the Hanna Family,* **Pim and Son, Damascus, Ohio, 1905.** This book covers branches of the family in Virginia, Kentucky, Indiana, Tennessee, Pennsylvania and Ohio.

# XIX: The Hannay Poets

The Hannays have been distinguished in art as well as war. In Edinburgh there is a delightful entry in the accounts of the Lord High Treasurer for 1536 "sent to the kingis grace with Sir Constantine Hannay a dousane lute strings price 6 /-." It seems that historically, however, Hannays may have had a particular bent towards the literary arts. James Hannay of Barcelona, author, scholar and diplomat, has already been mentioned in earlier chapters, as has the Reverend James Owen Hannay, who wrote under the pen name George Birmingham.

## 1. Patrick Hannay the Poet (d. 1665)

The most famous of all Hannay literary men is Patrick Hannay the Poet, a royal courtier. His origin is uncertain, but it has been said that he was born in 1594 a grandson of Donald Hannay, who was the son of Robert, Laird of Sorbie (d. by 1593). However, Patrick the Poet may have been Sir Patrick, the son of Alexander of Sorbie (d. 1612). This Patrick (see Chapter VI: The Sons of Alexander of Sorbie) served James I's government in Ireland with his brother Robert, the 1st Baronet of Mochrum Park; in this case the aforementioned Donald Hannay would have been his Great Uncle. Then again, Patrick the Poet may have been yet another Patrick Hannay whom we have not been able to tie to the family tree, for example the Patrick Hannay who served as a member of parliament in Edinburgh in 1637.

There were then so many Patrick Hannays that it is quite conceivable there were two contemporary Patricks in royal service, one in Ireland and one in London. Both appear to have had some form of military service, and some references online have conflated elements of each of the biographies so that it is difficult to distinguish between the two.

The 1662 collection of Patrick the Poet's works contains contradictory clues as to his pedigree: The complimentary lines written in the preface refer to his "father's father **Donald**", implying a descent from the *Kirkdale* line (See Chapter VIII: The Hannays of Kirkdale) while the coat of arms shown in the frontispiece would indicate that he was a third son of the Laird of *Sorbie* (See Chapter II: The Rise of Sorbie), in which case his "father's father" would have been named **Patrick**.

Perhaps it is best to let readers decide for themselves the Poet's pedigree based on their interpretation of the conflicting evidence.

### 1.1. Two Patricks or One?

The arguments **for** Sir Patrick and Patrick the Poet being one and the same include the following:

- In 1619, **Patrick the Poet** wrote a series of elegies upon the death of Queen Anne, consort to James I. He dedicated these to her son Prince Charles (later King Charles I). In 1625, **Sir Patrick** was commended by King Charles I for his closeness with his late mother, Queen Anne.

- In 1621, King James sent **Sir Patrick** on a diplomatic mission to Sweden. In 1622, a preface to **Patrick the Poet's** collection of poems, Patrick is praised for his service in the field in Bohemia. Both Sweden and Bohemia were participants in the 30 Years' War.

- The 1622 collection of poems includes a preface written by Sir Robert Hannay, 1st Bt. Mochrum, who was **Sir Patrick's** brother.

- It appears that much of **Sir Patrick's** official role in Ireland was on paper only, which would accommodate a majority of time spent in London and on the continent.

- The coat of arms in the 1622 collection implies that the poet was a younger son of the laird of Sorbie, which fits **Sir Patrick**.

Arguments **against** include:

- **Sir Patrick** supposedly died at sea in 1629. **Patrick the Poet** apparently died in 1665.

- **Sir Patrick's** grandfather was named Patrick; **Patrick the Poet's** grandfather was supposedly named Donald.

- **Sir Patrick's** will was apparently proved in Edinburgh in 1641. **Patrick the Poet's** will was proved in Surrey in 1665.

## 1.2. The Life and Works of Patrick the Poet

It is likely that 1594, the date of his birth given by historian George Chalmers, is wrong, as by 1619 (he would only be 25) Patrick had published a considerable number of works, and had been to the wars, but it is not impossible.

Patrick came to Court in London likely at the insistence of his kinsman Sir Robert Hannay of Mochrum.

He was a poet of some distinction, and Queen Anne took a considerable interest in him. His work was well known in his own time, and the original editions published in 1619 and 1622 are now very rare and of great value. The following is a list of his known works:

- *Two Elegies on the Death of Queen Anne with Epitaph,* London.

- *A Happy Husband, or, Directions to a Maid to Choose her Mate,* London, 1619 (See Figure 85).

- *A Wives Behavior Towards her Husband After Marriage,* 1619.

- *Philomela the Nightingale, Shertine and Mariana, Songs and Sonnets,* published by Nathanial Butler, London 1622. (See Figure 84)

Of the last, Thomas William Lowndes in his 1859 *Bibliographer's Manual of English Literature,* vol. IV, says "a rare volume in five parts... engraved title by C [Crispin] de Passe in eleven compartments, the bottom centre occupied by a portrait of the author." An original copy is in the possession of the family of Dr. David Rainsford Hannay, 2nd Chief of Clan Hannay.

An edition was privately re-printed in 1875 so that copies could be presented to members of the Hunterian Club by Thomas Russell. It is seldom now that a copy comes on the market. This edition has a memoir of the author by David Laing, 1793-1878, a Scottish antiquary and bookseller. It also includes complimentary lines by a certain John Marshall, written in 1622, that imply that the tomb of Galdus (a Caledonian Chief who resisted the Romans in the 1st Century) is buried at Cairnholy, on the Kirkdale estate. The lines also imply a particular genealogy of Patrick's descent which may not be accurate. See Chapter II: The Rise of Sorbie for a discussion on this topic.

In the 1619 edition of the Elegies he calls himself "Patrick Hannah, Master of Arts." It is not known when he became an M.A., but in later editions he dropped this designation and substituted "Gent."

In 1622 he published his collected poems in one volume divided into five portions each with a separate title and dedication.

The first portion of the volume, entitled "Philomela the Nightingale", is dedicated to "the most illustrious Princess Frances, Duchess of Lennox, Countess of Hertford and Richmond."[270] It consists of over a hundred stanzas and of 1,700 lines all of which he set to music.

---

[270] Frances Howard (1578-1639), who was briefly married to a cousin of King James I. She incidentally bankrolled the production of Captain John Smith's book *The Generall Historie of Virginia* in 1624.

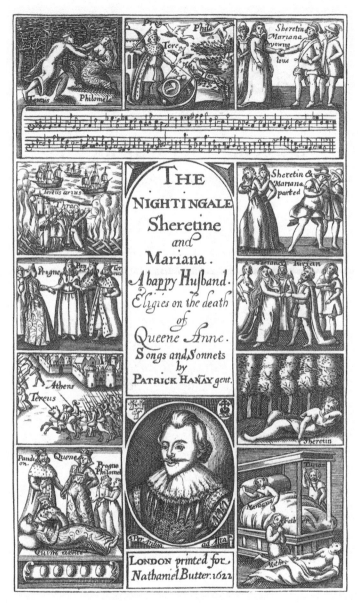

**Figure 84: The frontispiece of The Poetical Works of Patrick Hannay, London, 1622**

# A
# Happy Husband

*OR,*

Directions for a Maide to
*choofe her Mate.*

As alfo,

A WIVES BEHAVIOVR

towards her Husband after
*Marriage.*

By *Patricke Hannay*, Gent.

To which is adioyned the *Good Wife*;
*together with an Exquifite difcourfe of* E P I-
T A P H S, including the choyfeft thereof,
*Ancient or Moderne.*

By *R. B.* Gent.

*Exemplo iunɛlæ tibi fint in amore Columbæ,*
*Mafculus & totum fœmina coniugium.* } Propert

Printed at *London* for *Richard Redmer*, and are to
be fold at his fhop at the Weft end of Saint
*Pauls Church,* 1619.

**Figure 85: Title Page to 'A Happy Husband', 1619**

It is a peculiar measure probably suggested by the "Cherrie and the Slae" by Captain Alexander Montgomerie[271], with which Patrick would be familiar. "The Cherrie and the Slae" is supposed to have been written at Cumpston Castle in the Stewartry. The poem is founded on a legend given in the sixth book of Ovid's *Metamorphoses*. Here is the fifth stanza of "Philomela," followed by the opening verse of the "Cherrie and the Slae."

### *Philomela, The Nightingale*, **Patrick Hannay, 1622 or earlier:**

"With pleasure which that place did bring,
Which seemed to me perpetuall spring;
I was enforc'd to stay;
Leaning me lowly on the ground,
To hear the sweet celestiall sound
These Sylvanes did bewray,
Ravish'd with liking of their songs,
I thought I understood
The severall language to each longs,
That lodges in the wood.
Most Philomel
Did me compell
To listen to her song,
In suger'd strains
While she complaines
Of tyrant Tereus wrong."

### *The Cherrie and the Slae*, **Alexander Montgomerie, 1597 or earlier:**

"'About a bank with balmy bews,
Where nightingales their notes renews
With galland goldspiks gay;
The mavis, merie, and Progne proud,
The lintwhite lark, and laverock loud,
Saluted mirthful May;
When Philomel had sweetly sung,
To Progne she deplor'd,
How Tereus cut out her tongue,
and falsely her deftower'd;
Which story, sae sorry,
To shew herself she seemed
To hear her, sae near her,
I doubted if I dream 'd."

The second portion of the volume, "Sheritine and Mariana", is dedicated "To the Truly Honourable and Noble Lady Lucie, Countess

---

[271] Alexander Montgomerie (c.1550-1598) was a poet in James VI's court in Scotland.

of Bedford[272]," and is of quite different character from the preceding poem. It is prefaced by "A brief Collection out of Hungarian History for the better understanding of the ensuing poem." It has reference to the reign of Solyman the Magnificent, fourth Emperor of the Turks and to the wars in Hungary following the death of the tributary King John. With the absence of Sheratine on service in Hungary at the battle of Mohacz (1526), Nicholas Turian, who accompanied the Emperor Maximilian, fell deeply in love with Mariana of Vienna, and she was forced to marry him against her will. When Sheratine returned and learned of the inconstancy, as he thought of Mariana, he sickened and died. Mariana's love for him, however, had never changed and when she learned of his end and sought death too. The story is recounted by the heroine's ghost.

"A Happy Husband or Directions for a Maid to Choose her Mate," as also "A Wife's behaviour towards her Husband after Marriage" fills the third portion of the volume, and is dedicated to "The Virtuous and Noble Lady, the Lady Margaret Home, eldest daughter to the Right Honourable Alexander, Earl Home, Baron of Dunglas, &c."[273] Hannay refers to the "not to be requited favours which have wholely obliged me to you." Unfortunately, we know nothing of the nature of these favours.

"The Elegies on the Death of Queen Anne" follow, dedicated "To the Most Noble Prince Charles." After the elegies come two epitaphs, the first of which reads thus:

> "Power to do ill, and practice only good,
> Humblest in heart, highest in place and blood,
> Fairest, and Fre'st from loose desires in thought,
> Pleasures to tempt; yet not distained in ought;
> With anxious care, in courage ne're dejected,
> Though cause of joy, with no vain-joy affected,
> Know, reader, whensoe're these lines you scan,
> Such (and none such but she) was our Queen Anne."

The last portion of the book contains some ten songs and twenty sonnets and is dedicated "To the right Honorable Sir Andrew Gray, Knight, Colonel of Foot Regiment and General of the Artillery to the

---

[272] Lucy Russell, Countess of Bedford, 1580-1627, was a lady of the bedchamber to Queen Anne. She was also a noted patron of the arts as well as a strong advocate of King James's daughter, Elizabeth, the Electress of the Palatinate. Since Patrick was both a poet as well as a soldier who had fought for Elizabeth's husband Frederick's cause on the continent, it is not surprising that he dedicated one of his works to her.

[273] Margaret Home (c. 1607-1683) later married James Stuart, 4th Earl of Moray, and became Countess of Moray.

High and Mighty Prince Frederick, King of Bohemia." In the dedication he says:

> If of these labours I did none direct,
> Brave sir to you for offering or for shield,
> Since you so fatherly did me affect,
> When first you did conduct me to the field;
> I justly might be taxed as ingrate,
> Deservedly your love might turn to hate.
> Let shriller musket, cannon culvering.
> Give place a space while I do entertain.
> Your ears with musick of a milder strain
> …I have been by
> When thy hot courage well-nigh crack'd the raines
> of strict command…

This shows that Patrick had seen service abroad under Gray, but of that service we know very little.

Edward Vernon Otterson edited a series of reprints of rare poetical works, which were privately printed from 1840 to 1843, the number of copies not exceeding twelve to sixteen of each. Number 10 of the reprints was this last portion of Hannay's 1622 volume and there were fifteen copies, with an additional leaf, on which the editor refers to the author's military career:

> Hannay appears to have been one of the heroic spirits who, in the latest age of our expiring chivalry drew their swords in the cause of the unfortunate but high spirited daughter of James I, the wife of the Elector Palatine and titular King of Bohemia. The influence of her beauty, spirit, and manners (in the low Countries she was called the Queen of Hearts), allured a gallant body of the young nobility and gentry of England to the Standard of her unfortunate husband, attracted as much by a romantic admiration of the virtues of the woman as a generous feeling· for the misfortunes of her husband. Of the disastrous issue of the war, in which all their hopes blasted, no one is ignorant."[274]

Andrew Agnew in his "Hereditary Sheriffs of Galloway" (published 1893) says that Patrick served with distinction.

One of the sonnets in this final section is entitled "Alluding to Hope":

> Hope makes the sea bee plow'd in furrows white,
> That in the end sweet gain may thence arise;
> Hope makes the toyling tradesman take delight
> To labour ear' and late with watchful eyes.

---

[274] Elizabeth Stuart, James I's daughter, was married to Frederick IV, Elector Palatine and King of Bohemia.

Hope makes the Shepherd in the winter care
to tend his flock, and lodge them from the cold;
Hope makes the soldier fight, senseless to feare
Mongst hot alarmes; both watch and ward and hold.
The seaman's hope rich merchandise repaies;
The Tradesman's hope is answered with his hyre,
Young lambs and wool the shepheards charge defrayes;
The soldiers wage is that he doth require
I doe for hope more then all these sustaine,
Yet hope with no regard repaies by paine."

The book closes with the following prayer:

"O Father-God who by the word didst make
The azur'd-vault and all the host of heaven,
The hills, vales, plaines, fresh streames and brinie lake,
And unto each inhabitants hast given;

O Word which (for our sakes) did'st flesh become,
With sinners to purge sinne had'st habitation;
Crimeless accus'd, condemn'd, the crosse thy doome,
Suffredst Death, Buriall, rose for our Salvation.
Oh Holy Ghost which does from both proceed,
Sweet soule-inspiring spirit with peace and love;
comfort to all, cast downe from sinful deed,
Lessening their woes with hopes of heaven above
O Triune one, one God and persons three.
Reforme my waies and draw me unto thee."

The title page of the original edition bears the Hannay motto "Per ardua ad Alta." In the commendatory poems before the Nightingale is one from Sir Robert Hannay of Mochrum which reads:

Thy Philomena's sad (yet well sung) note;
Wrong'd Sheretine and Mariana's love;
Home's husband Anna's Elegies so wrote,
Thy songs and sonnets passion deep did move;
Do well approve that thy ingenious wit,
For every measure, every subject's fit.

Two of his dedications are worth repeating: First, the dedication to "Sheretine and Mariana."

"To the truly Honorable and Noble Lady Lucy, Countess of Bedford.

It is a continued custom (Right honourable) that what passeth the Press, is Dedicated to some one of eminent quality; Worth of the personage to whom, or a private respect of the party by whom it is offered, being chief causes thereof, the one for protection and honour, the other for thankful remembrance. Moved by both these, I present this small Poem (now exposed to public censure) to your Honour: first knowing the fore-placing of your Name (for true worth so deservedly well known to the world) will not only be a defence against malignant carpers, but also an addition of grace. Secondly, the obligation of gratitude (whereby I am bound to your ladyship's service) which cannot be cancelled, shall be hereby humbly acknowledged. If it please (that being the end of these endeavours) I have my desire. Deign to accept thereof (Madam) with a favorable aspect, whereby I shall be encouraged, and more strictly tied to remain

Ever your Honour's, in

all humble duty,

PATRICK HANNAY.

And secondly the Author's note before "A Happy Husband."

"To Women in General.

In things of weight and moment, care and circumspection are to be used, with a truly grounded judgement before resolution. Now in human actions none is of more consequence than marriage, where error can be but once, and that never after remedied. Therefore, in it is great caution required before conclusion, the sequel of staid deliberation, or unadvised rashness, being a happy, or a wretched like. And therein is another's counsel most necessary (though through the whole course of man's life it be safer than the self-conceived): for affection which in other affairs doth oft overrule reason (even in the wise) doth in this ever hide the faults of the affected under the blinding veil of love. This hath caused me for the weal of your Sex to produce this Husband to the light, not gain, or glory: knowing well the vulgar and critic censurers in this age do rather detract than attribute: but I care not much for their opinion: who dislike, may freely abstain: if any give better, I shall willingly assent; take it as it is meant, for your good, to displease none, and to content all.

P. Hannay."

In 1623, William Lithgow, a Scot who had journeyed far afield over a 20-year period, documenting his voyages, published a collection of his *Travels*. Patrick Hannay wrote the following preface to this work:

To his Singular Friend
Mr. William Lithgow

The double travell (*Lithgow*) thou hast tane,
One of thy Feete, the other of thy Brane,
Thee, with thy selfe, doe make for to contend,
Whether the earth, thou'st better pac'd or pend.
Would *Malagaes* sweet liquor had thee crownd,
And not its treechery, made thy joynts unsound,
For Christ, King, Countrey, what thou there indur'd
Not them alone, but therein all iniur'd :

329

Their tort'ring Rack, arresting of thy pace
Hath barr'd our hope, of the world's other face :
Who is it sees this side so well exprest,
That with desire, doth not long for the rest.
Thy travell'd Countreyes so described be,
As Readers thinke, they doe each Region see,
Thy well compacted matter, ornat stile,
Doth them oft, in quicke sliding Time beguile,
Like as a Mayde, wandering in *Floraes* Boures
Confind to small time, of few flitting houres,
Rapt with delight, of her eye pleasing treasure,
Now culling this, now that Flower, takes such pleasure
That the strict time, whereto she was confin'd
Is all expir'd ; whiles she thought halfe behind,
Or more remayn'd : So each attracting line
Makes them forget the time, they doe not tyne :
But since sweet future trauell, is cut short,
Yet loose no time, now with the *Muses* sport ;
That reading of thee, after times may tell,
In Travell, Prose, and verse, thou didst excell.

Patrick Hannay.

The above dedication was reprinted with some modification – perhaps
by the poet, perhaps by the editor – in Lithgow's 1632 edition. More of
Patrick's life is not known, but it is thought that he died in Lambeth,
County Surrey, according to a will dated 18 Oct, 1665 in the Register
of Confirmed Testaments.

## 2.  *John Hannay (1802-1854), son of John*

John was the son of John Hannay of Creetown, a builder. There were
three brothers, all of whom learned the building business. One moved
to a neighbouring town and one to Glasgow and thence to the West
Indies. John, the eldest, remained in Creetown and married Janet the
third daughter of John Bralt, a farmer in Chapelton. He called himself
Hannah, as he was always getting mail addressed to the other Hannays
of Creetown. John and Janet had nine children; the eldest, another
John, wrote poems.

He was born in Creetown on November 10, 1802, his early youth being
spent at Chapelton on his grandmother's farm. He accompanied
Captain Dennision on shooting and fishing expeditions. Dennision had
a literary bent and translated and edited several old Scottish poems, etc.
John went to work for Dennision, who encouraged the boy's literary
efforts. Later he moved while still young to Diss in Norfolk and in 1829
entered business in Ipswich. He died in 1854.

After his death his poems were published by Richard Crisp of Beccles
in a work entitled *Posthumous Rhymes by John Hannah*.

The book's dedication reads:

> This volume is dedicated to the memory of a man of equal
> intelligence and modesty, of generous heart and sterling
> uprightness; and to those by whom his character was appreciated,
> his friendship valued, and his death lamented.

Here is a sample of his work, entitled "Ellen and the Banks of Cree"
(1827):

Young Edwin's gone to Ellen's bower,
His lip has felt the parting kiss;
Soft sorrow on his brow did lower,
And tear-drops mingled with the bliss:
'Farewell! I go, perchance, to see
No more my Ellen, nor the Cree.'

Young Edwin felt the sacred glow
Of honour all his soul inflame,
And burned to meet the ruthless foe
And earn a wreath of martial fame;
To fight for home and liberty,
His Ellen and the banks of Cree.

For these he left his Ellen's arms
And crossed the foaming billows o'er,
And rushed amid war's rude alarms,
The sabre's flash and cannon's roar; —
For honour, love, and liberty,
His Ellen and the banks of Cree.

And still, when loudest pealed the gun,
And fiercest rose the battle's yell,
Where densest rolled the war-cloud dun,
And the most heroes fought and' fell,
He stood and shouted ' Liberty! — '
For Ellen, and the banks of Cree! '

Alas, upon thy fatal shore,
Corunna, Edwin died at last;

He fell beside the gallant Moore;
And as to heaven a look he cast,
He faintly breathed a prayer for thee,
His Ellen, and the banks of Cree.

## 3. *Thomas Hannay*

Thomas was also a native of Galloway. His book *Mort Aratsch and
Other Poems* was published in 1911 by Fraser, Asher and Company,
Glasgow and Dalbeattie.

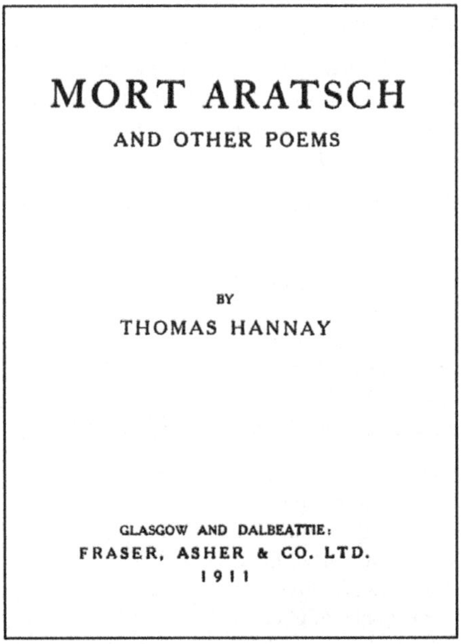

**Figure 86: Collected works of Thomas Hannay**

The title work refers to the Morteratsch Glacier in the Swiss Alps. The dedication reads:

TO MY WIFE.

> If there was one who could dispel
> The cloud upon my brow,
> If there was one who loved me well,
> 'Twas thou.

Thomas lived for some time in London and studied chemistry and botany. He later went to the continent and in 1912 was living in Switzerland. He spoke German as fluently as his native tongue, was well versed in Italian and spoke French with a strong Scots accent, which he himself averred that of all things in the world he was least likely to lose. He was a noted skier and mountaineer.

## 4. *Advice to the Prime Minister by Robert Hannay*

Of Hannay writers there are many; putting pen to paper seems to be an occupational disease of the family. A certain Robert Hannay, who had pretty strong views on the system of usury and rates of interest about 1823, wrote considerably on the subject to Sir Robert Peel, the Prime Minister. Two of his letters are quoted here:

"It is more than twelve months ago I used the freedom of submitting to your consideration a proposal to lower the legal rate of interest.

Subsequent thought and observations have strengthened my opinion which I now present to you in a different form. Having observed with regret the repeated efforts made in Parliament to repeal the Usury laws, and the prevelant notions of their impolity, I thought I should be rendering a service to the public by an endeavour to open up the true motives of those laws and to prove from the experience of ages that they are grounded upon justice and indispensible to security.

The proposal to lower the legal rate of interest is chiefly designed to lessen the distress of the landowners. This measure as you know has often been resorted to, and never without the happiest effects.

It is therefore no project of mine, but a great instrument of State policy recommended by the practice of our ancestors and confirmed by experience.

I trust you will, therefore, pardon me when I again interest your consideration of the subject.

Your obedient servant

Robert Hannay:

18th April 1823"

Again in 1828 he addressed himself to the Prime Minister, this time on the subject of thefts of money from the mails:

"10th March 1828,

The frequent robberies and thefts of money, banknotes and valuables from Public coaches, cannot have escaped your notice. Never a month, seldom a week, passes over without such a loss. My present object is, to propose a plan, that shall secure the public from such losses for the future, while it provides an addition to the revenue.

The plan is simply this, that there be established in the Post Office a department similar to that in France, when bullion, banknotes, jewels and other things precious may be entered, as letters are, and the government becomes responsible for delivery in conditions of moderate insurance.

Such an office has long been established in France to the security and advantage of commerce and to the profit of the revenue.

My only object here is to suggest the subject to your notice without entering upon debates, nor proofs to shew, that such an institution, if useful in France, would be much more so in England."

# XX: Irish Hannas

There are many members of this family who it is not, without very considerable research, possible to tack on to one of the main well-known branches. From early times, many of the family went far and wide in search of fortune; the less adventurous but no less industrious stayed at home. Some became great and wealthy, others honest poor folk, as is the pattern of all clans. Some served the greater ones of the family, some emigrated from Scotland, first to Ireland, where Sir Robert and his son held great power in the early seventeenth century, and from there, both great and small, sprang the large numbers of Hannas now scattered in Ulster. Some of their descendants have migrated to England, many more to America.

The topic of Hannas in Ireland is vast. Stewart Francis barely touched on it when writing the first edition of *The Hannays of Sorbie* in 1958, and the subject deserves an entirely separate book. Fortunately, such a book, *Hanna of the Close*, by R. Keith Hanna, Genealogist for the Clan Hannay Society, was published in 2008. It is highly recommended for a far more detailed account of the family's history on the Emerald Isle.

Also of interest for its information on the Irish branch (though it also covers Hannas in Scotland and the United States) is *Hanna of Castle Sorbie, Scotland, and Descendants*, by the late Reverend James Arthur MacClannahan Hanna (published 1959).

A map of Ireland, with some of the place names mentioned in this chapter (and others), can be found in the Maps section at the back of this book.

As a guide in determining dates and locations of settlement in Ireland, the family name in itself may present some difficulty. The use of "ay" "a" or "ah" as an ending seemed to have been quite indiscriminate. In fact, so indiscriminate is the use of these names that the same man is often referred to as A'Hannay, Hanna or Hannah in the same document. During the seventeenth century the form begins to crystallize, for Lady Ann Hannay of Kingsmuir writes to Captain William Hannay that she "knows many who spell it with an 'A' but few with an 'Ay'".

The Irish branch of the family settled in the vale of Wicklow and around Belfast seems to have favoured the "a" whilst much of the Scottish branch have preferred the "ay", although in the Lowlands "ah" is the most common form.

334

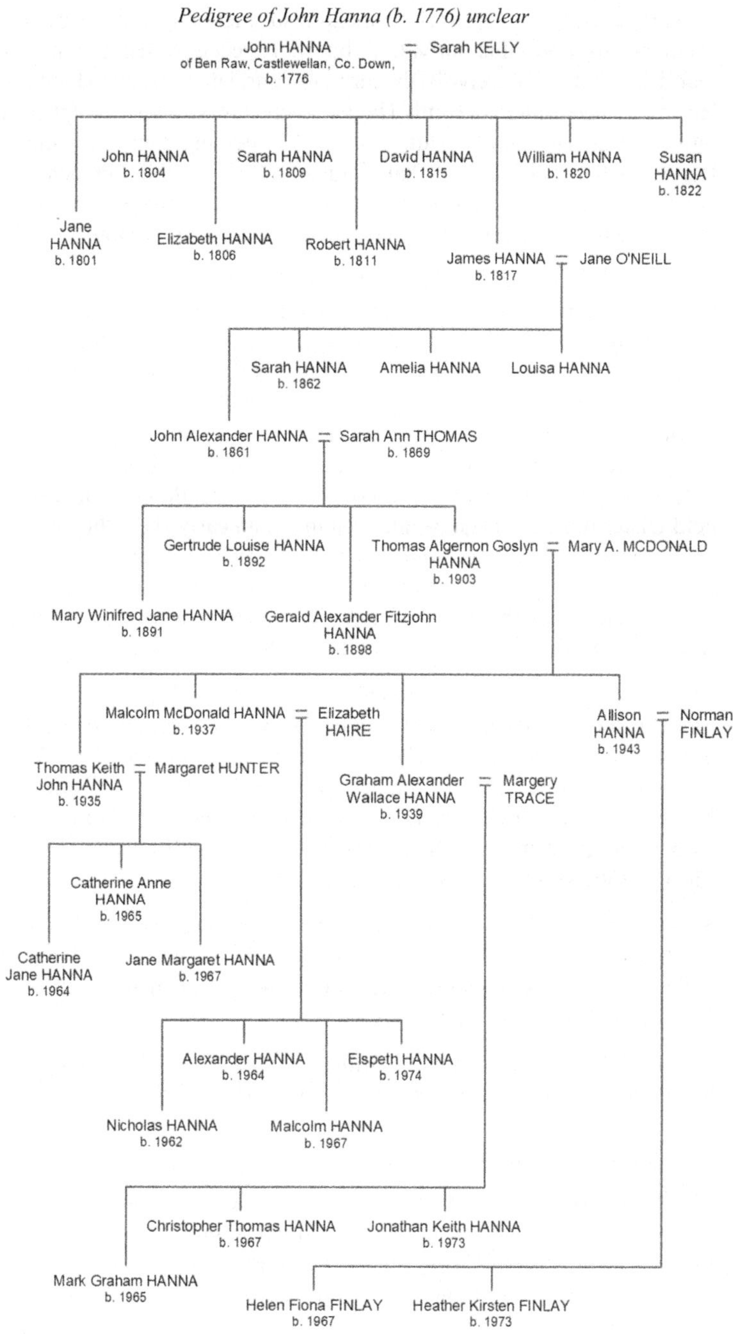
Pedigree of John Hanna (b. 1776) unclear
John HANNA
of Ben Raw, Castlewellan, Co. Down,
b. 1776
Sarah KELLY
Jane HANNA b. 1801
John HANNA b. 1804
Elizabeth HANNA b. 1806
Sarah HANNA b. 1809
Robert HANNA b. 1811
David HANNA b. 1815
James HANNA b. 1817
Jane O'NEILL
William HANNA b. 1820
Susan HANNA b. 1822
Sarah HANNA b. 1862
Amelia HANNA
Louisa HANNA
John Alexander HANNA b. 1861
Sarah Ann THOMAS b. 1869
Mary Winifred Jane HANNA b. 1891
Gertrude Louise HANNA b. 1892
Gerald Alexander Fitzjohn HANNA b. 1898
Thomas Algernon Goslyn HANNA b. 1903
Mary A. MCDONALD
Thomas Keith John HANNA b. 1935
Margaret HUNTER
Malcolm McDonald HANNA b. 1937
Elizabeth HAIRE
Graham Alexander Wallace HANNA b. 1939
Margery TRACE
Allison HANNA b. 1943
Norman FINLAY
Catherine Jane HANNA b. 1964
Catherine Anne HANNA b. 1965
Jane Margaret HANNA b. 1967
Nicholas HANNA b. 1962
Alexander HANNA b. 1964
Malcolm HANNA b. 1967
Elspeth HANNA b. 1974
Mark Graham HANNA b. 1965
Christopher Thomas HANNA b. 1967
Jonathan Keith HANNA b. 1973
Helen Fiona FINLAY b. 1967
Heather Kirsten FINLAY b. 1973

**Figure 87: The Hannas of Castlewellan, Co. Down**

In earlier editions, Stewart Francis also mentioned the surname "Hannan" as a possible derivation, but more recent research indicates that it's likely a purely Irish surname unrelated to the Hannays. However, according to Keith Hanna, there are known examples of those bearing the family name Hannan 'anglicizing' their surname to Hanna in the wake of the Plantation of Ulster in the 17th century, although maintaining their Roman Catholic religion. Such seems to be the case with the Hanna family near Ardglass in County Down.

In Ulster during the Plantations of James I, Charles I, the Commonwealth and Charles II, many families from Galloway crossed over the narrow strait. Keith Hanna suggests the crossing took place from Portpatrick to Donaghadee, which was the shortest route in the 17th century. All over Ulster they were given land and took over control of the county from the Irish natives, becoming the forerunners of today's "Scotch Irish", the Ulstermen. Of similar Celtic background but industrious and fiercely Protestant they drove the Catholic Irish out and held Ulster for the Protestant succession. At an early stage they had to decide whether they would fight for James II or for William of Orange. In most cases they chose William, and at the Battle of the Boyne in 1690 several Hannahs took part, notably the Hannahs of Castlewellan (For some of their descendants, see Figure 87).

Present-day Hannas can be found across the Northern counties. In Strabane there is the family of Hugh Hanna, who was an active member of the Clan Society in its early years. Hugh was from the Scots Irish settlement of the late 17th century, and his family have farmed in Northern Ireland in County Down for many generations. He married Isobel Pettigrew and became a wholesale grocer in Strabane. His son Mervyn followed his father into the business.

Stewart Francis also mentions that a family "connected with Ireland" are Alexander Hanna, his wife Elizabeth and their son John living in Aldermanbury and Westminster, who were buried in the Abbey in 1778, 1786 and 1814 respectively.

All over Ulster there are many families who have lived there and given it and the Crown great service, including the Hannas of Newry.

## 1. The Hannas of Newry

The Hannas of Newry (see Figure 88) are an old family, who branched off from the Kirkdale line at the same time as the Hannays of Kelso. Indeed, the Hannas of Newry should perhaps, in fairness, come under Kirkdale: They are used here as an illustration of the variants of the same.

*For the pedigree of John Hannay (d. 1614), see Figure 20: The Hannays of Kirkdale*

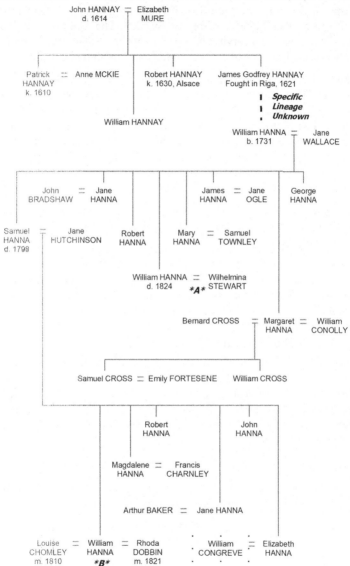

*A*: See Figure 90   *B*: See Figure 89

**Figure 88: The Hannays of Newry**

Patrick Hannay (d. 1610), the Laird of Kirkdale, David Hannay, his son from whom the Hannays of Kelso descend, and James Godfrey, Patrick's brother, were all engaged in either recruiting, dispatching or commanding soldiers for Gustavus Adolphus's army in Sweden.

337

David, who was a civil servant at Dublin Castle, recruited them and despatched them to the Laird of Kirkdale, who shipped them from Leith to brother James Godfrey in Sweden. The Laird's other son, Alexander, was also serving in Sweden and James Godfrey's brother Robert was killed in Alsace in 1630 in Gustavus Adolphus's army.

The Gold Medal given to James Godfrey by Gustavus Adolphus for his services in the Bohemian War of 1620 and struck in commemoration of the taking of Riga[275] in 1621 has been handed down through the generations of the Newry branch[276]. It bears the name James Godfrey Hanna, and the town of Lubeck, a Hanseatic town on the Baltic. The specific lineage linking James Godfrey Hannay and William Hanna (born 1731), the earliest Newry Hanna in the written records, is unknown.

The family acquired property in Co. Down by intermarriage with the Wallaces of Crobane, at whose house hangs a portrait said to be of the great Sir William Wallace.

It may be of interest that Canon James Owen Hannay (who wrote novels under the pen name George Birmingham), the Irish author, was referred to by the Hannas of Newry as a cousin. He is discussed in more detail in Chapter XIII: The Hannays of Knock and Gararrie

## 1.1. William Hanna (1731-1803)

The first to settle at Greenwood Park, Newry was William Hanna, who was born in 1731 and died in 1803. He married Jane Wallace, the daughter of Robert Wallace of Newry by his wife Jane Stuart. Jane's mother was Mary Scott of Harden, a descendent of the Mary Scott of Harden celebrated in song as "the Flower of Yarrow"[277]. William and Jane had eight children:

- Samuel the eldest with whom we shall deal later.

- Jane who married John Bradshaw, now represented by the family of Canon Bradshaw of Inisheen, Dundalk.

- Robert, who died unmarried in China.

---

[275] Although now the capital of Latvia, at that time the city of Riga was in the Polish-Lithuanian Commonwealth.

[276] Stewart Francis noted that the medal was (at the time of the 3rd edition, i.e., 1977) in the keeping of Alexander Hannah, but it is unclear to whom exactly he was referring. The whereabouts of the medal are, as of 2018, unknown.

[277] A traditional Scottish air. The Mary Scott of the song was also an ancestor of Sir Walter Scott.

- William, who became the progenitor of the Stewart Hannas, whom we shall see later.

- Mary, who married Samuel Townley of Newry

- James, who married Jane, the daughter of William Ogle of Newry. They had two children: Samuel, a doctor in Dublin, who married Emily Fortescue and had no children, and William, who died unmarried.

- Margaret, who married first Bernard Cross and secondly William Conolly.

- George, who was living in 1820 and died unmarried.

## 1.2. Samuel Hanna (1759-1798), son of William

Samuel, the eldest child of William and Jane, held land in Newry and also Acton Manor, County Armagh. He was born in 1759 and died October 12, 1798, at Aldermanbury in London. He married Jane the daughter of John Hutchinson of Grange, Co. Louth on December 2, 1785. They had six children:

- William the eldest, mentioned in more detail below.

- Magdalene who married Rev. Francis Chomley, and is now represented by the family of Francis Chomley of Clermont Rathew, Co. Wicklow.

- Robert, who died unmarried.

- Jane, who married Arthur Baker of Dublin.

- John, who died young.

- Elizabeth, who married William Congreve.

## 1.3. William Hanna (m. 1810, 1821), son of Samuel

William, Samuel and Jane's eldest son, was a barrister at law and best known as Councilor Hanna. He lived at 5 Gardiners Place in Dublin and at Corduff House, Lusk, Co. Dublin. His family tree can be found in Figure 89.

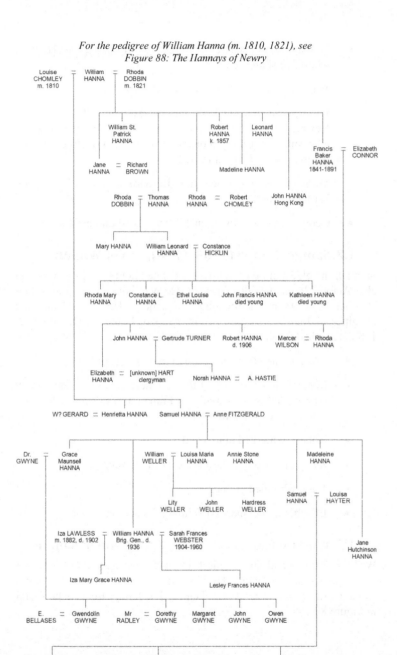

*For the pedigree of William Hanna (m. 1810, 1821), see*
*Figure 88: The Hannays of Newry*

**Figure 89: Family of William Hanna (m. 1810, 1821) of Newry**

340

In 1810 he married Louisa Marion Chomley, the daughter of John Chomley and Henrietta Baker. There were two children:

- Henrietta Rebecca, who married W. Gerard of Belfast.

- Samuel, of whom more anon.

After the death of his first wife, William married again on 27 December 1821, Rhoda Dobbin, the daughter of Thomas Dobbin of Armagh, and had nine children. They were:

- Jane, who married Richard Brown of Newry.

- William St. Patrick, who died unmarried.

- Thomas who lived at 5 Gardiners Place and married Rhoda, the daughter of Leonard Dobbin of Armagh. They had two children: Mary; and William Leonard, who went to the U.S.A. and settled in Morgan, Texas. William Leonard married Constance Ellen, the daughter of John W. Hicklin of London.

- Rhoda, who married Robert Chomley.

- Robert, who was a Civil Engineer and lived in Cawnpore, who was killed in the massacre arranged by Nana Sahib in 1857. Hanna Pass in present-day Pakistan is named after him.

- Madeline, who died unmarried.

- Leonard, who died young.

- John who went to the Far East as a Hong Kong Merchant[278] and owned the famous racehorses *Hackney* and *Garter*. He died unmarried.

- Francis Baker (1841-1891), who was a Civil Engineer on the Madras Railway and Colonel of the Madras Engineer Volunteers. He designed and oversaw the building of three impressive bridges over the Beypore (Chaliyar) river.[279] Francis Baker married Elizabeth, the daughter of John Connor of Innismore, Delgany, Co. Wicklow and had four children:

---

[278] In Morris & Co's list of foreign residents of 1870, John is listed as a merchant living in Tientain.

[279] Francis referred to him as "building the 'Hanna Bridge' over the river Toongubundra at Ferak", but no reference could be found to any of these terms. According to the Institution of Civil Engineers obituary for Francis Baker Hanna in their 1892 proceedings, he was, however, quite well respected and deeply missed, being eulogized with a tribute from the Governor.

341

Elizabeth, who became Mrs. Hart; John, a Colonel of the Royal Artillery, who became a censor of plays and films and had one daughter, Norah; Robert, a civil engineer in India was killed in a train crash at Avignon returning to India with his wife. Lastly, Rhoda, who became Mrs. Mercer Wilson.

## 1.4. Samuel Hanna, son of William

Samuel, the eldest son of William, by his first marriage, owned Corduff House at Lusk. He served in Ceylon as a District Judge and later as the Resident Magistrate at Carrick on Suir in Co. Tipperary, and later at Bray in Co. Wicklow. He married Annie, the daughter of the Rev. James Fitzgerald of Shepperton, Co. Clare. There were seven children:

- William, the eldest, mentioned in more detail below.

- Grace Maunsell, who married Dr. Gwynne of Sheffield and had issue.

- Louisa Maria who married William Waller of Castletown Manor, Limerick, and had three children, Lily, John and Hardress. Hardress had issue.

- Annie Stone, who died unmarried.

- Samuel, who followed the family calling of civil engineering, spending much time in Argentina and Chile, married Louisa Hayter[280], and had three children: Walter, a colonel in the Royal Engineers, who married Kathleen Grey and had two daughters; Godfrey, who died unmarried; and Constance who married Christopher Pryor. They had two children.

- Madeleine, who [may have] died unmarried[281].

- Jane Hutchinson, who died unmarried.

## 1.5. William Hanna, Son of Samuel (d. 1936)

William, the eldest son of Samuel, succeeded to Corduff. He joined the Royal Artillery and served in India, the Boer War and World War I, rising to the rank of Brigadier General. In 1882 he married Iza, the daughter of William Lawless of Ardmeen, Blackrock, Co. Dublin, and granddaughter of Field Marshal Baron Lawless, one of the Irish

---

[280] In Table VIIA of the 3rd (1991) edition of *The Hannays of Sorbie*, Samuel's wife is listed as Eliza Jane. It is unknown if this is a typo for "Louisa Jane" or if Samuel married a second time.

[281] Francis notes Madeleine as being married to Hayters Chomley in Table VIIA of the 3rd (1991) edition of the Hannays of Sorbie.

Generals who served under Napoleon in France. She died in 1902. There was one daughter of this marriage, Iza Mary Grace.

In 1904 General Hanna married again, Sarah Frances T. Webster, the daughter of the Rev. Robert Webster. There was one daughter, Lesley Frances.

When General Hanna was commanding in Rouen in 1918, his wife, Sarah Frances, drove an ambulance for the French. At the time, two American cousins, Constance and Ethel, daughters of William Leonard Hanna of Texas, came to France with a nursing contingent and landed up at Rouen. Iza Mary Grace Hanna, General Hanna's daughter was also there in an ambulance at *Le Treport* and they all managed to meet. All three were great granddaughters of William Hanna of Newry.

Sarah Frances was awarded the *Croix de Guerre*. In World War II she worked for Soldiers, Sailors, Airmen and Families Association (SSAFA, the UK's oldest military charity) in Palestine, Greece and Syria and was awarded the MBE. She died in 1960.

General Hanna was deeply interested in genealogy and did a very considerable amount of work. Unfortunately, this was all destroyed by incendiary bombs in the Second World War. In World War I he raised the 61st Divisional Artillery which he commanded until 1916 when he went to America on behalf of the Ministry of Munitions to buy brass for making shells. Miss Iza Mary Grace Hanna, his daughter, recounted that at one time he considered he could prove his title to the Hannay Baronetcy, and that Colonel Henry Bathurst Hanna, his cousin, urged him to do so and was prepared to pay the cost. However, they never proceeded further. It is significant, however, and would point to the family coming from Kirkdale. He died at Braiswick Hall, Colchester, in 1936.

Thus, this line, descended from James Godfrey Hanna came to an end.

One interesting fact of this branch of the family is that they have, in common with the Hannays of Kelso, the tradition of wearing the Stewart Tartan. The reasons for this are obscure, but it may possibly be in connection with the Earls of Galloway. The Coat of Arms is Argent, Three Roebucks heads azure collared or with a pendant thereat Gules. Their motto: 'Ad Alta Virtute' (To the Heights of Valor).

## 2. The Stewart Hannas

The Stewart Hannas start in 1801, when William Hanna, younger son of William Hanna of Greenwood Park, Newry, married Wilhelmina Stewart, a daughter of William Stewart of Wilmount, Antrim. In 1803, when William Hanna the elder of Greenwood Park died, he left most of his property to William the younger, as Samuel, his eldest son, was already dead. A family tree of the Stewart Hannas can be found in Figure 90.

*For the pedigree of William Hanna (d.1824), see Figure 88: The Hannays of Newry.*

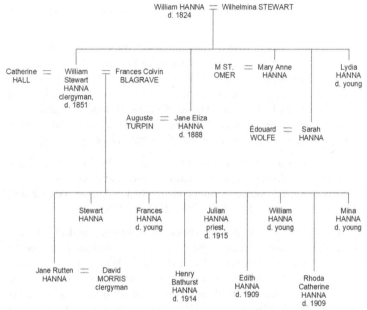

**Figure 90: The Stewart Hannas of Newry**

In 1824 William Hanna died intestate. His widow Wilhelmina made a will leaving her Newry and Doran's Hill property to her four daughters, subject to the sum of 5/- per annum to her remaining son, Stewart William Hanna. She appointed guardians to her children: the Rev. W. Mathias; George Hanna, a brother-in-law; and John Bradshaw, the husband of her sister-in-law. She then took herself, with her children, to Paris where she settled. Wilhelmina died in 1833. The three eldest daughters all married Frenchmen, as follows:

- Jane Eliza, married Auguste Turpin of Paris and died in 1888. She bequeathed her share of the Newry property to two unmarried daughters of her brother Rev. Stewart William Hanna, Edith and Rhoda Catherine.

- Mary Anne to M. St. Omer.

- Sarah to Édouard Wolfe.

The fourth daughter, Lydia, died in her mother's lifetime. In 1834 James Hanna of Newry, one of the trustees, died and his son, Dr. Samuel Hanna, took on the trusteeship.

344

## 2.1. Stewart Hanna (d. 1851), son of William

The Reverend Stewart William Hanna, William and Wilhelmina's son, was sometime curate of St. George's, Jamaica, and wrote *Notes of A Visit To Some Parts of Haiti* in 1835. He returned to England and took up the Ministry of Woolwich and later of St. James in Marylebone. He married first Catherine Hall, who died without children.

He was married a second time, to Frances Colvin Blagrave, and together they had nine children:

- Jane, who married the Rev. David Rutten Morris of the Isle of Wight.

- Stewart, a civil engineer at Naini Tal in India.

- Frances who died young.

- Henry Bathurst, who was a colonel in the Bengal Staff Corps and Quartermaster General of that province. He was well known as a writer on military matters in India. He was wounded in the mutiny and in Afghanistan. He died at Petersfield in 1914.

- Julian, a British priest in France who died in 1915.

- Edith and Rhoda Catherine, who both died in 1909 unmarried. They had inherited the Newry property from their late aunt Jane Eliza. In their wills, Rhoda and Edith left the property in equal shares to their cousins, Catherine Bradshaw, who died in 1929, and Iza Mary Grace Hanna, who died in 1980.

- William, who died young.

- Mina, who died young.

The Rev. Stewart William Hanna died in 1851.

## 3. *Hugh Hanna (1821-1892) of Dromara, son of Peter*

One of Ulster's most explosive characters and one of the family's many ecclesiastics, Hugh Hanna (1821-1892) of Dromara must surely be one of the most forceful products of our family. He was the son of a farmer, Peter Hanna, and Ellen Finiston. His grandfather John, also a farmer, was a great influence on his early years. John had a strong covenanting streak, and a strict religious atmosphere was the order of the day. His family gave up farming and moved to Belfast where Hugh was apprenticed to John Holden a woolen draper. He entered the Belfast College in 1843 and the Old Assembly College in 1847 and was licensed to preach by the Presbytery of Belfast in May 1851. He was installed in Berry Street in 1852.

345

A series of open-air Services at the Customs House steps was planned in 1857. These were to be conducted by Thomas Drew, William McIlwaine and Thomas Roe, all of whom, as well as being ministers in the Anglican Church in Ireland were prominent in Orange circles and well-known anti-Catholic controversialists. During Lent, McIlwaine had preached a series of anti-papal sermons and issued them in pamphlet form. Of these, the Commissioners who investigated the riots said:

> "These lectures and leaflets were in language not unnaturally considered offensive by some of the Roman Catholic people, for whose sake they were stated to be delivered."

Owing to the tension, the magistrates requested the Belfast Parochial Mission to postpone its meetings during July. Then on August 9, McIlwaine preached and on August 23 a riot was only narrowly averted. As a result, the Parochial Mission decided to cancel the remainder of the meetings.

This action was not approved by everyone, and Hugh Hanna declared that he would preach on September 6. It had been reported that Drew would preach at the Customs House steps on that date, and a Roman Catholic crowd occupied the area, but he did not appear. Hanna held his meeting. When the Roman Catholics realised that the meeting was not to be held at Customs House steps and were about to disperse someone told them where Hanna was preaching. Immediately they headed for Corporation Square. The meeting up to this apparently was quite orderly, but now a riot developed. *The Irish Presbyterian* gives a lengthy account.

So serious was the situation that the Presbytery of Belfast held a special meeting to be "an apostolic practice", and to have been "customary during the entire history of the Presbyterian Church in Ireland". Also, that it was determined "by all legitimate means" to maintain this right. On the specific events which necessitated the holding of the meeting it was resolved:

> "That under the existing circumstances of this, we do affectionately entreat our brother, Mr. Hanna, as a matter of Christian expediency, to desist from open-air preaching till, in the mercy of God, a reasonable time be afforded for excited passions to cool and subside..."

They also appointed a committee "to confer with Mr. Hanna in reference to these resolutions" and "to take such measures as to them shall appear desirable for maintaining... the constitutional and Christian privileges of this Church".

346

The open-air meetings ended, and the Commission of Inquiry published its report on the riots on November 20, placing most of the responsibility on the Orange Society and the clergy and ministers who despite warnings from the magistrates, persisted in provocative open-air preaching.

On December 15, at a public meeting in the Music Hall, Mr. Hanna was presented with a watch, bearing the inscription:

> "Presented Hugh Hanna, with a purse of 100 sovereigns by the Protestants of Belfast and vicinity, in approval of his character as a Christian minister, and in testimony of his able and successful maintenance of the right of open-air preaching, especially on Sabbath, 6th September, 1857".

In these early days Hanna perhaps did not realise the disservice to peace in Ireland he was doing by his desire to preach the gospel freely. His associates had other motives. Hanna had not distinguished between freedom to preach and an anti-Catholic campaign. He had played into the hands of those who believed in violence and thus contributed to the increasing bitterness.

As time went on Hugh modified his position and became a High Tory, opposing Gladstone's first Home Rule Bill in 1886 with all the force Presbyterianism could muster.

Hanna not only opposed Home Rule but was an ardent advocate of the Tory cause, addressing many meetings in its interest in England and Scotland as well as Ireland. For this he was highly praised by those of Tory sympathies and condemned by the Liberals. Hanna was entitled to his political convictions and to be a Tory if he wished; at the same time, his presentation of his cause and his condemnation of the "apostacy" of Gladstone left him open to accusations of prejudice and bigotry.

In 1871 the liberals repealed the Party Processions Act, passed in 1850 by the parliament of the United Kingdom to prohibit organized marching in Ireland; thus, both Orangemen and Nationalists were able to hold parades. On August 15, the Nationalists decided to hold a parade. Hugh, now at St. Enoch's, which was at the time the largest Presbyterian church in the UK, petitioned the Town Hall to have his church property protected. The result was disastrous. When the Nationalists came to assemble at Carlisle Circus, they found it occupied with some 8,000 people prepared to defend St. Enoch's. The inevitable rioting followed. That evening Hanna drove along the Shankill road and addressed the crowd, thanking them for saving St. Enoch's from destruction. There were riots again on August 15, 1876, and July 12, 1878. In the 1886 riots, the worst ever, the mayor asked him to try and restrain the crowds on the Shankill Road. He failed and

347

had to seek shelter in the house of a Mr. and Mrs. Shanks, who were parishioners of his. A letter from the town hall received that evening is significant:

> Town Hall, Belfast,
>
> 11th June 1886.
>
> Dear Mr. Hanna,
>
> Your services on the Shankill Road last night were of great use in assisting to keep the peace, and the Mayor hopes that you will be able to continue them again this and tomorrow evening, until quietness in the neighbourhood is restored.
>
> Yours very truly,
>
> Samuel Black, Town Clerk.

At the same time, it has to be remembered that Hanna was a militant Tory and absolutely opposed to Gladstone. Neither did he hesitate to issue a call to arms:

> "Ireland at this moment is within arm's length of civil war. The possibility, the probability of an appeal to arms as the inevitable settlement of the Irish question is discussed in calm and heroic resolution at ten thousand homes in Ulster...
>
> Every capable loyalist should be enrolled in a loyal defensive union to meet any emergency that may arise. Let captains of hundreds, captains of fifties and captains of tens be elected and their corps constructed to meet the day of danger."

There, however, is another side to all this. Hanna, as we have seen, tried to prevent disturbances on the Shankill during June. We also find him standing alone between "both mobs" on August 9 and succeeding in getting them to return home. We find him personally cutting down "the chain across Townsend Street to trip the horses of the military", and, again, sending the mob home on the Shankill while Father Greene, a Catholic clergyman, was doing the same on the Falls. The last, however, does not appear to have been a joint action.

With regard to Father Greene, Hanna, in his evidence to the Commissioners, said:

> "Father Greene is a personal friend of my own ... the most genial Roman Catholic cleric in Belfast, a great favourite with many Protestants against whom, however, he organises his fighting minority."

He told how he worked with Greene on the Board of Management of the Royal Hospital, declaring: "I like him very much."

When asked, "Do the Catholic and Protestant clergy associate as they do in other towns where I have seen them walking through the streets together, met them dining together, and that sort of thing—does that take place in Belfast?" Hanna replied, "Not that I am aware of, but I would not object to dine with Father Greene, particularly if the dinner was a good one." When asked if it would be good if this happened in Belfast also, Hanna answered, "I have no doubt it would have a great influence."

In addition, there is an oral tradition, which the author Stewart Francis was not able to confirm, that a Roman Catholic priest from St. Mary's, Chapel Lane, was one of the special guests at the opening of St. Enoch's, and that he occupied a seat in the front pew.

It seems that Hanna's political anti-Catholicism may not have been carried over into his social relationships.

The fact that there were riots before his day suggests that Hanna was not principally to blame for the disturbances. At the same time, there can be no denying that many of his actions, sermons, speeches and pamphlets were extremely provocative and contributed to them.

He was appointed a Doctor of Divinity by the Presbyterian Theological Faculty for Ireland and a Doctor of Laws by Galesville University, Wisconsin.[282]

His church flourished; he had a great interest in revival movements. He was a great and forceful preacher—he was not called "Roaring Hanna" for nothing.

He died in 1892, and the City of Belfast raised a statue to him in Carlisle Circus. Blown up in 1970, it did not survive the Troubles.

---

[282] The institution no longer exists. The entity went through several operators and name changes between its founding in 1854 and the present day. Between 1877 and 1901 (during Hugh Hanna's time) it was run by Chippewa Presbytery. Ironically (given the Reverend Hanna's anti-Catholic leanings), the school was subsequently run by the Society of Mary between 1941 and 1985, functioning as a Catholic novitiate and retreat center. It is now a museum and performing arts venue called Old Main.

**Figure 91: Hugh Hanna (1821-1892)**

# XXI: More Family Branches

## 1. The Hannays of Leeds

There is a branch of the family originating in Gatehouse of Fleet, near Kirkdale, whose members were employed as estate workers on the Kirkdale estate. They eventually moved to Glasgow before settling, three generations later, in Leeds[283].

The names of the sons of this family are interesting as they follow nearly exactly those of the Kirkdale Hannays during this period. It was the fashion to call one's children after one's employers or benefactors. There were Ramsay, John, Johnstone and Alexander amongst them. Perhaps Sir Samuel set up one of his worthy tenant farmers in Glasgow as a baker and certainly his influence could have secured him an entry in the guild. The family lived in Glasgow for many years and prospered.

Alexander Hannay (b. 1749) was a master joiner in Kirkcudbright. He married Margaret McMillan. They had two sons, Ramsay and Alexander.

Ramsay married Mary Glen, and from them descend the family in Leeds (see Figure 92)

Alexander Hannay, born in 1781, was a miller in Dundee. He married Jane Rae and had a son, yet another Alexander, who became a distinguished Congregational minister.

---

[283] Stewart Francis also stated in earlier editions, "There was, in Glasgow in 1784, a John Hannay burgess and guild brother, who on September 13th that year married Margret, the daughter of Matthew Wylie, also a baker and burgess of Glasgow." He added, however, no evidence connecting this particular John Hannay with the Hannays of Leeds.

351

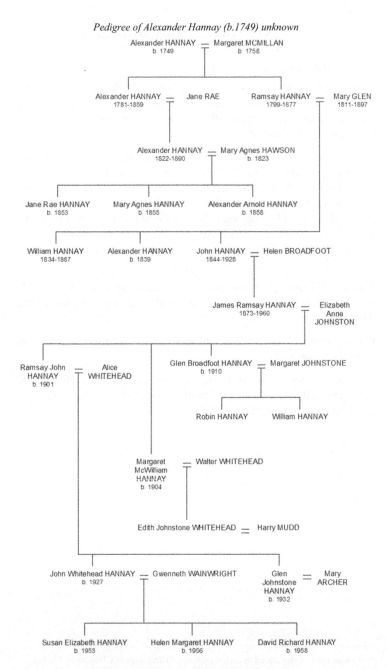

*Pedigree of Alexander Hannay (b.1749) unknown*

Alexander HANNAY b. 1749 — Margaret MCMILLAN b. 1758

Alexander HANNAY 1781-1859 — Jane RAE

Ramsay HANNAY 1799-1877 — Mary GLEN 1811-1897

Alexander HANNAY 1822-1890 — Mary Agnes HAWSON b. 1823

Jane Rae HANNAY b. 1853

Mary Agnes HANNAY b. 1855

Alexander Arnold HANNAY b. 1858

William HANNAY 1834-1867

Alexander HANNAY b. 1839

John HANNAY 1844-1928 — Helen BROADFOOT

James Ramsay HANNAY 1873-1960 — Elizabeth Anne JOHNSTON

Ramsay John HANNAY b. 1901 — Alice WHITEHEAD

Glen Broadfoot HANNAY b. 1910 — Margaret JOHNSTONE

Robin HANNAY

William HANNAY

Margaret McWilliam HANNAY b. 1904 — Walter WHITEHEAD

Edith Johnstone WHITEHEAD = Harry MUDD

John Whitehead HANNAY b. 1927 — Gwenneth WAINWRIGHT

Glen Johnstone HANNAY b. 1932 = Mary ARCHER

Susan Elizabeth HANNAY b. 1953

Helen Margaret HANNAY b. 1956

David Richard HANNAY b. 1958

**Figure 92: The Hannays of Leeds**

352

## 1.1. Alexander Hannay (1822-1890)

Alexander and Jane's son Alexander Hannay was born in Kirkmabreck on February 27, 1822. He, early in his life, showed his ability as an orator and a leader. Always interested in politics he used to tell with glee that one of his earliest recollections was standing on a box and haranguing his playmates on the Reform Act of 1832.[284] He was in due time apprenticed to a printer and publisher in Dumfries. However, he decided to become a minister and entered the University of Glasgow and the Theological Hall of the Scottish Congregationalists where he remained from 1841 to 1846, matriculating in 1843.

In 1846 he accepted the charge of the church at Princess Street, Dundee, where his fervour, energy and eloquence made a notable mark on the City.

He moved to London in 1862 and took the pastorate of the City Road Church. During this time, the strain on his voice proved too great for him. When looking at his portrait – see Figure 93 – one can imagine this huge man booming forth his carefully thought-out and eloquent sermons. As a result of this trouble he moved in 1866 to West Croydon. In 1867 he was appointed the Secretary of the Colonial Missionary Society, and he acquitted himself so well that on the death of Dr. George Smith in 1870 he succeeded as Secretary of the Congregational Church of England and Wales. He had of necessity to give up his pastorate in Croydon. His work for this body was magnificent and he guided his denomination through many troubled seas.

---

[284] The Reform Act of 1832 expanded voting rights in the United Kingdom. Its most well-known effect is possibly the demise of "rotten boroughs", electoral districts in which a handful of voters controlled a seat in parliament.

**Figure 93: Alexander Hannay (1822-1890)**

His greatest work was probably the foundation of Mansfield College at Oxford. The course of his work took him to America, Canada and Australia and in 1880 he was made a Doctor of Divinity at Yale University. During his tenure as secretary, the church built Memorial Hall, the building housing the headquarters of the Congregational Union in Farringdon Street, London, until it was demolished in 1968. Alexander's portrait, which used to hang in the hall, is now in the possession of the Congregational Memorial Hall Trust.

He married Mary Agnes Hawson and had two daughters and a son. Alexander died on November 12, 1890. He was a powerful, eloquent man who had great organising ability.

## 2. The Hannays of Townhead, Sorbie

The farm at Corwar has been held by the Hannays for centuries: On July 31, 1583, the Testament of Nevene McGilter in Borance references William Hannay in Corwar. Again, on June 28, 1594, in the Testament of John Mure, a notary burgess of Whithorn, John Hannay in Corwar gets a mention.

In 1665 and 1684 they are still in occupation. In 1665 an Alexander, and in 1684, in the parish list, John, Margaret, another John, Janet and a Robert are listed. In 1696, both Robert and John appear as witnesses to bonds.

The origin of this family is not known, nor is the connection of these earlier Hannays in the area to John Hannay (d. circa 1815) of Townhead of Sorbie who is the earliest member of the line for which we have an unbroken line to the present day. In addition to his son Alexander who resided at the farm in Corwar) and a daughter Barbara, he probably had other children. A sketch pedigree can be found in Figure 94.

## 2.1. Alexander Hannay (b. 1782), son of John

Alexander married Mary Broadfoot in 1807 and lived at Corwar. They had a large family, with four sons: John, born in 1811; Andrew, born in 1815; William Cooper, born in 1817; and David, born in 1819 and died unmarried.

They also had four daughters: a second Marion in 1813 to replace the first Marion who died young in 1808; Elizabeth Cooper; and Barbara.

## 2.2. William Hannah (b. 1817), son of Alexander

William Cooper Hannah, the son of Alexander and Mary, seems to have changed the spelling of the family name to "Hannah". He was apparently employed in India, one imagines with the East India Company, for his third son Herbert Bruce Hannah was born there in 1862. He married Agnes Bruce Stephen Johnson and had a daughter, Louisa, and four sons, William Lennox, Garlies Stuart, Herbert Bruce and Andrew Stuart.

Shortly after Herbert Bruce's birth, his mother Agnes sailed home from Calcutta with him on the *St. Lawrence,* and crammed into these few weeks a whole gamut of unpleasant experiences. They amounted to a storm in the Atlantic and being driven over to the South American Coast, the ship losing first her masts and then her jury masts, finally arriving in Bahia for repairs, as they could not go to Rio de Janeiro, for that city had decided to have a revolution. At São Salvador she saw the cells of the Inquisition, and a woman of the place offered her child for sale. One piece of luck on an otherwise luckless voyage was that the *St. Lawrence* arrived in the Bay of Bengal just in time to escape the great cyclone of 1864.

Their next journey home was overland to Alexandria on the cross-country route used before the Suez Canal opened. The family then moved to Jamesfield in Manor Place, Edinburgh. In 1869 they moved down to Amherst Road, Stoke Newington, where they had some Lennox cousins. The boys were educated at Vermont College in Lower Clapton, and then went on to various endeavors:

- William Lennox wrote a short book about the family, and was responsible for the material from which this chapter has been culled. The first 44 pages of his book have been regrettably lost. These might have given a clue to the family's origins. He died unmarried in 1909.

- Garlies Stuart (born 1860) died in 1923 and was father of the family holding the farm at Townhead as of 1960. More about him below.

- Herbert Bruce (born 1862) was sent, on leaving school, to the office of Messrs. Robert Monteith and Co., ship brokers and agents of Lime Street, London. In 1879 he and his mother returned to India, where he was articled to William Casey Morgan of Messrs. Roberts, Morgan and Co., Solicitors of Calcutta. He was admitted a Solicitor at the Calcutta High Court on September 11, 1886 and remained with Morgan's firms till 1890. He returned to England in 1894 and was admitted to the Inner Temple through the good offices of Lovell Keays without any preliminary examination. He was called to the Bar in 1897. During this time, he was a member of the Hardwicke Debating Society. He returned to India and was admitted Advocate of the High Court at Calcutta.

In 1913 he edited the first part, on the subject of Trusts, of Collets Specific Relief Act. He wrote a manual of the Tibetan language, and several other works on diverse subjects. He was a lecturer for some years in History at Calcutta University, in addition to his duties as High Court Judge. He died unmarried in 1930.

- Andrew Stuart, the fourth son, was born in Chorlton Cum Medlock near Manchester in 1865. He was also educated at Vermont College and went into the merchant navy, being appointed aboard the *City of Athens* from 1882-87. In 1888 he entered the service of the South India Steam Navigation Company. and became a Master Mariner being in command severally of the *SS Kerbela*, *Nudden*, *Putaa*, *Byculla*, *Amra*, *Aska*, *Chilka* and *Chapra*. In 1902 he transferred to Messrs. Haxton and Co. He was finally marine superintendent for the Eastern Bengal Railway. He returned to England in 1920 and died shortly afterwards at Boscombe. He was unmarried.

356

## 2.3. Garlies Hannah (1860-1923), son of William

Garlies Stuart Hannah, the second son of William Cooper and Agnes, married Lillian Esther Pittar in 1887 and had a large family: Agnes Maria born in 1888, Garlies born and died in 1890, Mary Kathleen born 1891, John Stuart born in 1893, Charles William Cooper born in 1894 and Esther Mabel born in 1901.

Charles William Cooper Hannah was educated at Exeter School and entered the National Bank of India in London. On the outbreak of war he was commissioned in the Devonshire Regiment and was killed as a second lieutenant on September 28, 1916 in France by a stray bullet through his head on a misty day about a fortnight after his arrival there. He was unmarried.

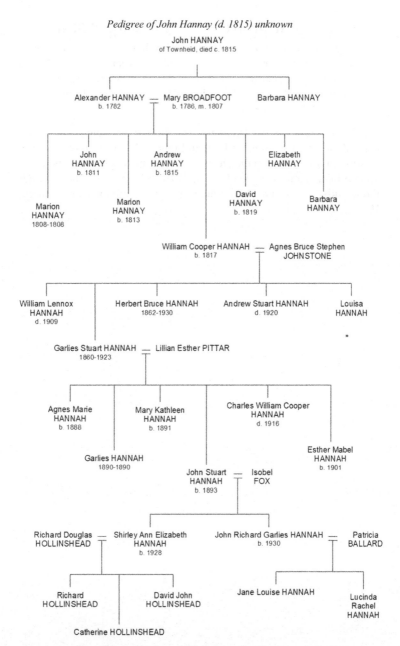

**Figure 94: The Hannahs of Townhead, Sorbie**

## 2.4. John Hannah (b. 1893), son of Garlies

John Stuart, the only married son of Garlies Stuart, was born in 1893, and also went to Exeter School. He joined the India Police for the Province of Bengal in 1913. In 1916 he was appointed to the India Army Reserve of officers and joined the 127th Baluchis. Shortly after he was transferred to the 89th Punjabis with whom he served on the Frontier and in the Mohmand and Chitral Campaigns. In 1917 he went to Mesopotamia and during this campaign he was awarded a Military Cross.

He rejoined the India Police in 1917, and was appointed Deputy Midnapue and Khulna districts, retiring in 1929. He then joined the B.N. Railway as superintendent of the Watch and Ward Department, serving in Chakradhapur in Bihar, Orissa.

In 1930 he was a member of the International Kanchenjunga expedition, a failed attempt to ascend Mount Kanchenjunga, the third highest mountain the world. He married Isobel Fox and had two children: Shirley Ann Elizabeth, born in 1928; and John Richard Garlies, born 1930.

## 3. The Hanneys

In England there are a number of Hanneys who spell their name with an "ey" instead of an "ay". Some live in Lincolnshire where a Hanney produced the stone and timber, provided for the stands, at the Coronation of Richard II in 1372. Others come from Berkshire, Durham and Somerset from the villages of Publow and Windford. Harold Huntingdon Hanney represented this branch and had a son John Huntingdon Hanney who worked with the World Bank Organisation in Washington. His uncle William Weston Hanney was a successful businessman in London.

From Berkshire, serving in the Royal Berkshire Regiment was Brigadier Walter Hanney. Len and Hilda Hanney, from Nottingham, have been longtime members of the Clan Hannay Society, and their son Ian Hanney, from Nottingham, is a member of the Clan Council.

No doubt there are many others, all of whom it would appear sprang from the same Norse strain as the Hannays of Sorbie.

## 3.1. Hanney's Band

The Hanneys of Marksbury, Somersetshire, were presumed to have come from Ireland and settled in Marksbury, Somerset. James Hanney was a talented musician who inspired the whole of his family to such an extent that without exception all became musicians in a practical way. He moved to a suburb of Swansea, where later his children, who by now had married, also moved and joined him.

A small band was formed by him consisting of his sons, and his grandsons also, which was called Hanney's Band. After his death the band was taken over by his eldest son, George, as conductor and managed by George's fourth son, William. It became very successful and won innumerable prizes at the different band contests and was considered one of the finest bands in South Wales. After George's death, the conductorship was taken over by Samuel, George's fifth son, the band now being called Hanney's Military Band as it now consisted of both woodwind and brass. In 1911, the band took part in an international band contest in Paris, competing against some of the best bands in Europe—French, German, Italian, Austrian and Dutch. The band won first prize and was met at Swansea Station on their return by a mass of people, since it was the only British Band ever to have won an international contest. The score of one of the best pieces—the "William Tell" overture by Rossini—was lodged, together with a record of its success, at the Town Hall, Swansea. After World War I it became very difficult to keep the band going successfully, owing to a number of members leaving the district and aftereffects of the war. Therefore, a concert was arranged in January, 1920, before the disbandment for the benefit of Major Samuel Hanney, the conductor. It was conducted by Major Reginald Hanney, Licentiate of the Royal Academy of Music, Associate of the Royal Conservatory of Music, Bandmaster 1st Battalion Dorsetshire Regiment, by kind permission of Lt. Colonel C.C. Hanney, D.S.O.[285], who commanded the battalion. Of the items in the programme, one was a march composed by Major Reginald Hanney, the conductor of the award-winning 1911 performance of the "William Tell" overture. So ended over a half century of success in music to this branch of the Hanneys. Major Reginald Hanney, after his retirement from the Army, became a lecturer in music at various public schools, some of which were Hurstpierpoint College, Lancing College and Sevenoaks School, specializing in wind instruments and also doing concert work on the oboe and clarinet. The pedigree of this family can be seen in Figure 95: The Hanneys of Marksbury, Somersetshire.

---

[285] C.C. Hanney was understood to be from one of the Irish branches of the Hannays.

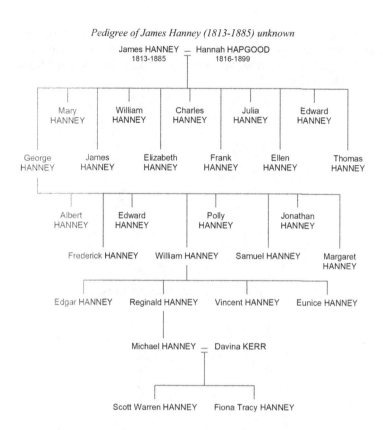

Pedigree of James Hanney (1813-1885) unknown

James HANNEY — Hannah HAPGOOD
1813-1885 — 1816-1899

| Mary HANNEY | William HANNEY | Charles HANNEY | Julia HANNEY | Edward HANNEY |

| George HANNEY | James HANNEY | Elizabeth HANNEY | Frank HANNEY | Ellen HANNEY | Thomas HANNEY |

| Albert HANNEY | Edward HANNEY | Polly HANNEY | Jonathan HANNEY |

| Frederick HANNEY | William HANNEY | Samuel HANNEY | Margaret HANNEY |

| Edgar HANNEY | Reginald HANNEY | Vincent HANNEY | Eunice HANNEY |

Michael HANNEY — Davina KERR

| Scott Warren HANNEY | Fiona Tracy HANNEY |

**Figure 95: The Hanneys of Marksbury, Somersetshire**

## 4. Hannas in Australia and New Zealand

In Australia on the River Yarra at Melbourne, Pat Hanna operated the ferry now replaced by the Queen Street Bridge. He was originally apprenticed to George Stephenson, the engineer, and constructed the Chain Ferry over the Yarra powered by a steam engine of his own design and construction. He was also a noted builder of bridges. He came from Ulster and became a member of Parliament and a minister. He bought the old Government House in Melbourne, where he died in 1888. Hanna Street, which leads to the site of the Chain Ferry, is named after him.

The grandparents of another "Pat", George Patrick Hanna (1888-1973), who so greatly assisted in fostering the Clan Society, came to Australia in 1840, then moved to Whitianga, New Zealand. Typical of many pioneers of the Empire, they raised a house of kauri trees. Pat himself had a distinguished career, first as an entertainer in the ANZAC forces

361

in World War I and later as the producer of the first two Australian talkie films, *Diggers* and *Diggers in Blighty*. He subsequently became the producer of many stage presentations and films. He died in 1973 in Bedfordshire, England.

**Figure 96: Pat Hanna's film "Diggers in Blighty"**

## 5. James Ballantyne Hannay (died 1931)

James Ballantyne Hannay, who was born in Glasgow, made a considerable contribution to science. His father Alexander owned the Prince of Wales (later the Grand) Theatre in Cowcaddens. James was educated at Larchfield Academy but did not like school and left to help his father in the theatre. Like most boys, chemistry attracted him first as a means of making fireworks. An additional incentive was the colour fires which were used in the theatre for producing scenic effects. With a young friend, Ralph McIvor (who eventually became an agricultural chemist of note in Australia), he set up a laboratory. There was nothing superficial about his study; he was a single-minded young man. The tradition in his family was that he was self-taught as a dentist. He joined the firm of J. & J. White, chromate manufacturers in Glasgow, in 1873. In 1874 he joined the Chemical Society and the next year published five papers in the Chemical News, the journal of the Society. In 1876

362

he was elected a member of the Royal Society of Edinburgh. He then entered Anderson's College and by 1877 was on the staff. In 1878 he was also appointed assistant lecturer on the staff of Owen College, Manchester.

In 1883, he bought an impressive house called Cove Castle in Cove, Argyll, designed by Scottish architect James Sellars in 1867.

His chief claim to fame, however, was his production of a synthesized diamond in 1880. There has been considerable controversy over this. Its genuineness was proved by X-ray examinations as late as 1943. In 1962, however, Professor Kathleen Lonsdale (by then head of the department of crystallography at University College London), who had conducted the 1943 study, revisited the samples and changed her mind about their authenticity.

James married—and was later estranged from—Caroline Johnston. Together they had three daughters, Eva, Ethel and Edith.

James wrote numerous scientific papers, but late in life he turned to historical and philosophical studies, writing several controversial works about the origin of religion. He died at Cove Castle in 1931.

## 6. Sergeant John Hannah, VC

Not to be forgotten in this history of the family is Sgt. John Hannah of the Royal Air Force. On the night of September 15, 1940, the RAF raided a concentration of German barges at Antwerp. Flying Officer C.A. Connor piloted a Hampden bomber of No. 83 Squadron. In the nose of the bomber sat the navigator; behind and above him was Connor, penned into his seat for the duration of the flight, for the aircraft had only one set of flying controls. At the rear of the deep-section part of the fuselage were the rear gunner and the wireless operator, Sergeant John Hannah, occupying the upper and lower gun position from which both could crawl from one end of the aircraft to the other.

The Hampden made a first bombing run, but Connor was dissatisfied with it and circled to make another, this time meeting heavy flak. The Hampden was hit in the wing several times as it dived and shook so much that Connor found it difficult to keep control. The aircraft dropped its bombs, and about now Connor noticed flames reflected in his Perspex windshield, but was so busy taking evasive action that at first he gave them no serious thought. As he avoided shells, Sergeant Hannah called him on the intercommunication system and said, very quietly, in his broad Scots accent, "The aircraft is on fire."

363

**Figure 97: John Hannah, VC**

"Is it very bad?" Connor asked.

"Bad," the young Sergeant said, "but not too bad." However, Connor gathered that the situation was serious but that John did not want to alarm him. Connor warned the crew to prepare to abandon the aircraft. At the same time, he was still "throwing the machine all over the place to dodge shells, some of which were ripping through the fuselage while others seemed to be bouncing off. Besides this, the ground defenders were spraying the air with tracer bullets and Connor knew his men would have little chance of landing unharmed.

In the meantime, the fire was getting a firmer hold, but gradually the plane drew out of range of the gunners. About this time the navigator and rear gunner jumped for it; the rear gunner had no option, for he was burned out of his bottom cockpit.

Sergeant Hannah could have followed the rear gunner through the bottom escape hatch or come forward, closed the bulkhead door and escaped through the navigator's hatch. He did neither but remained in the rear cockpit. A large explosive or incendiary shell, which burst inside the bomb compartment of the aircraft, set parts of the interior alight and turned the whole of the compartment into a sort of blowlamp, the wind coming through the large hole caused by the direct hit. The alloy sheeting on the floor of John's cockpit was burned away, leaving only a grid formed by cross-bearers. The melted metal was blown backwards and plated in great smears on the rear bulkhead. The electrical leads and all other inflammable equipment were alight, drums of ammunition blew open and thousands of rounds exploded in all directions. The outer layer of sheet metal on the door and bulkhead of the rear compartment melted and blistered.

Sergeant Hannah could remain in his position only by using his oxygen mask, as he fought the flames with fire extinguishers and even by hitting them with his logbook. Connor could feel heat on the back of his neck, and when he turned his head he could see the flames about four or five feet away. Even with his mask on, John found the fumes too strong and was beginning to suffocate. He ripped off the mask and dashed through the fire, getting badly burned in the process. After about ten minutes Connor, feeling a cool breeze on his neck, asked John how things were going; the communication system had somehow escaped damage.

"The fire's out, sir," he said cheerfully. On the captain's instructions, he investigated and found that the other two members of the crew had gone. He then scrambled into Connor's cockpit, bringing the navigator's maps so that Connor could steer a course for home. When the plane finally landed, the sergeant jumped out "as though what he had done had been an everyday occurrence," Connor reported.

John's conduct was an act of very deliberate bravery for he knew that by delaying his escape he deprived himself of getting away from the aircraft; his parachute was burned with the rest of the equipment in the cockpit. His action almost certainly saved Connor's life, and he saved the aircraft. The many officers who inspected the plane were astonished that such a wreck could have been brought home, amazed that such a fire could be fought, for somehow John had managed to keep it away from some of the fuel tanks, which had many holes in them. He was awarded the Victoria Cross.

## 7.  *Robert Hill Hanna, VC (1887-1967)*

Another Victoria Cross was won in World War I by Sgt. Major Robert Hanna of the Canadian Infantry on August 2, 1917. The citation reads:

> "This Warrant Officer, when the enemy machine gun posts had beaten back three attacks with heavy casualties putting all officers out of action, coolly collected the survivors, rushed through the wire, personally bayonetting three and braining a fourth enemy soldier. By his action he displayed courage at this most critical moment of the attack and handled a desperate situation and is deserving of the highest possible award."

Robert Hill Hanna was born on his father's farm in Aughnahoory Townland, near Hanna's Close, Kilkeel, County Down in the north of Ireland on August 6, 1887, the second of 11 children born to Robert Hill Hanna, Senior, and his wife Sarah. Educated at Ballinran School in the Kingdom of Mourne, he left school at 14 and worked on the family farm until age 18 when he decided to emigrate to British Columbia in Canada. There he became a lumberjack, and after an apprenticeship, he started his own prosperous lumber business prior to World War 1.

At the start of the War, this diminutive lumberman (a mere 5' 5 ¾" tall and 140 lbs.) enlisted as a private on November 7, 1914, just after Canada declared war into the 29th (Vancouver) Battalion, 2nd Division of the Canadian Expeditionary Force. After extensive training for 6 months, the battalion was shipped to England on May 20, 1915. They arrived for service in northern France on the September 17, 1915.

By the middle of 1916 he had been promoted to corporal having seen action on the Somme, and he had also served at Ypres, Arras, and Paschendale, having gone "over the top" 22 times in total prior to Vimy Ridge in 1917.  By December 20, 1916, he had become a Sergeant and by August 1917 this veteran volunteer soldier had become Company Sergeant Major just before his thirtieth birthday.

**Figure 98: Robert Hill Hanna, VC**

As the War was coming to its denouement, and during a bitter 10-day struggle around Vimy Ridge — from August 15-25, 1917— the Canadian Corps overran a much-contested treeless hillock on the north side of the French mining centre of Lens called "Hill 70" (so called because it was 70m above sea level). On August 21, during the start of the second phase of the fighting for the hill, both the Canadians and Prussian Guards had decided to attack each other on the same day at almost the same pre-dawn time such that desperate bayonet fighting ensued in no-man's land. The Canadian 29th Battalion's right-hand Company B pushed forward to meet its objective, suffering crippling losses as it crossed the open fields.

All the officers were killed or wounded, whereupon the company-sergeant-major Robert Hanna, assumed command of the remnants of the force and determined to take the German strongpoint that three assaults had failed to seize. It was a stub German trench with parapet machine gun and it was flanking the Canadian battalion's attack with the potential to destroy the whole of the 29th Battalion. Hanna coolly collected a party of men and then led them against the position amid a hail of rifle and machine-gun fire. He personally forced his way through barbed wire, used a grenade to silence the gun and then killed the four remaining German gun crew with his bayonet and rifle. He then advanced down the trench and destroyed two dugouts with German stick grenades he found in the trench after his own ammunition had run out.

He was joined by the rest of his company at this stage and they consolidated their position by hastily building a fortification block, because Germans from the town below had regrouped after dawn to counter attack in force. However, Hanna and his party bravely held on against repeated assaults by the Prussians until they were relieved later in the day. For his initiative, act of leadership, and personal courage Hanna was recognised with the award of the Victoria Cross at Buckingham Palace later that year. He was also promoted to lieutenant and served for the remainder of the war as an officer before being demobilised on the May 24, 1919.

After the war Hanna continued to run his logging camp before taking up his original vocation of farming near Mount Lehman outside Vancouver, returning to Ireland several times to visit family and friends over the years. He married and had two sons, one of whom, John, died in infancy. Robert Hill Hanna died on June 15, 1967 and is buried in the Masonic Cemetery in Burnaby, British Columbia. His Victoria Cross is still in the possession of his son Robert who was born in 1940 and served in the RCAF and as a civil pilot with Canadian Airlines before his retirement.

## 8. South African Hannays

David and George Hannay emigrated from Stoneykirk in Wigtownshire to the Western Cape in 1834. They named their farm Begelly.

David married Louisa Fetherstone. His son, Captain Angus Hannay, distinguished himself in the Langenburg Campaign serving in the Vryburg Volunteers and subsequently in Dennison's Scouts in the South African War. The Hannays moved to Vryburg after the Warren Expedition in 1884-85. Their descendants still reside in the Western Cape, represented by the Hannay Sampson family of Grahamstown.

# XXII: Stirlingshire Hannas

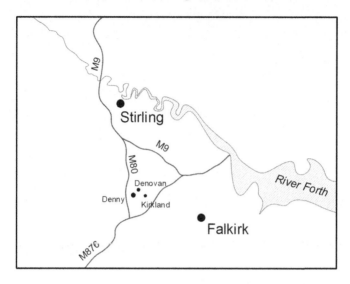

**Figure 99: Stirlingshire**

This branch of the Hannay Family (see Figure 100) claim descent from
Dr. James Hannay (c. 1595-1661), who was Dean of Edinburgh from
1633 to 1638 (For more information, see Chapter VII: The Family of
John Hannay, M.P.).

## 1. *John Hannay (born 1626), son of James*

John, the eldest son of Dean James, was born in Edinburgh on
December 17, 1626. The witnesses were his grandfather William
Braune, John Maxwell, and Patrick Braune.

John Maxwell, A.M., was Minister of Trinity College at the time of
John Hannay's birth, and two years later became Minister of St . Giles.
When Dean James became Dean of Edinburgh, John Maxwell was
appointed Bishop of Ross. Maxwell was a staunch supporter of Charles
I's project of liturgical revision. Along with Dean James he was in July
1633 made a Freeman of Stirling.

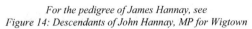

For the pedigree of James Hannay, see
*Figure 14: Descendants of John Hannay, MP for Wigtown*

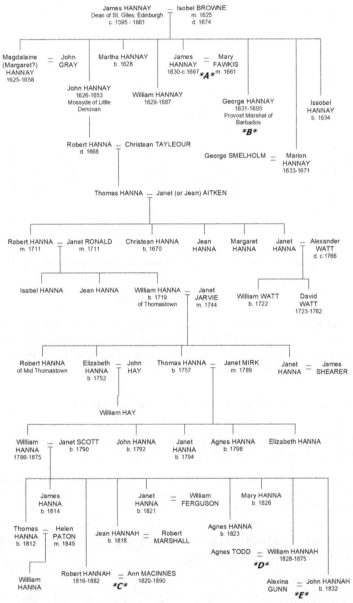

*A*: See Figure 44    *B*: See Figure 14    *C*: See Figure 104    *D*: See Figure 102
*E*: See Figure 103

**Figure 100: The Family of James Hannay, Dean of St. Giles**

370

John Hannay's third witness was his uncle, Patrick Braune, who succeeded his father as Clerk to the Exchequer.

Not a great deal is known of John. He became a doctor in Edinburgh, no doubt accompanied his father to Dunipace, and likely is the John Hanna in Mossyde of Little Denovan who died in February 1653. His descendants appear to have dropped the "Hannay" spelling entirely and changed it, depending on the branch, to "Hanna" or "Hannah."

In the Stirling Testaments is given his testament dative. At the time of John's death he had "no guds nor geir", but there was a total of £80 owed to him by James Cuthell in Little Denovan (£66:13:4) and Alexander Rennie in Kirkland (£13:6:8). There were no debts owed by the deceased apart from £20 disbursed at the time of his funeral. The testament is dated December 30, 1664. That he had "no geir" is not surprising as at the time he and his father were impoverished. His executor dative and heir was his son, Robert Hanna.

From John Hannay are descended the Hannas of Thomastoun and the Hannahs of Leith whose arms are differenced from Sorbie by a tower between two lymphads[286] on a red chief. Their crest is a cross-crosslet issuant an open boat both sable with the motto *Per Laborem ad Alta*. Evelyn Hannah who was for many years the Membership Secretary of the Clan Hannay Society, also directly descended from this line.

### 1.1. John Hanna of Drumheid of Little Denovan

Two years after John Hanna(y)'s death, we find a further death recorded, that of John Hanna in Drumheid of Little Denovan. He died in June 1655 and his heir was his son, James Hanna.[287] He was slightly more affluent, and his "guds and geir" included "two kye [cows], three guyes of one year old, ane year old foil [foal] ", farm produce, utensils, furniture etc., in all, £132:6:8. His debt included rental of £12 and a loan of £80 from David Foster of Denovan. The exact relationship between John Hanna in Mossyde of Little Denavan, John Hanna in Drumheid of Little Denovan and Margaret Hannay, spouse of John Gray, indweller of Stirling, is not established, but it seems very likely that they were closely related.

John's son James of Drumheid married Grizell Cuthell, no doubt daughter of James Cuthell who owed his kinsman, John of Mossyde,

---

[286] **lymphad**: heraldic charge consisting of the image of a single-masted ship

[287] Stewart Francis states in earlier editions that the John Hanna who died in 1655 "is probably a son of John in Mossyde of Little Denavan." This, however, makes little sense, as John in Mossyde was only 27 years old when he died in 1653. It is barely biologically possible for his purported son John Jr to himself have had a son James by 1655.

£80. Their children were Marion (born January 22, 1693), Margaret (born February 10, 1695), James (born July 22, 1696), John (born 1699), James (born November 23, 1701) and Mary (born March 16, 1704).

## 1.2. Delayed Stipends

Although the deaths of John of Mossyde, John of Drumheid and Margaret, in Stirling, were 1653, 1655 and 1658 respectively, it was not until 1661 and 1664 that confirmation was obtained. It was at this time, June 21, 1661, that Parliament ordered that £100 be paid to Dean James Hannay's children out of vacant stipends on account of their father's sufferings. No doubt James of Drumheid and Robert of Mossyde had to be served heirs before they were entitled to the pension provided by the Government.

## 2. *Robert Hanna (d. 1668), son of John*

John Hannay's son, Robert, described as being in Little Denovan, died in October 1668. His executor dative was his wife Christean Tayleour. His assets consisted of:

| | |
|---|---|
| "ane kow and ane stirk" | £ 8 |
| "four hoggs" | £ 0:12: |
| "in the barne and barne yard 6 bolls corne" | £ 20 |
| "fodder" | £ 4:13:4 |
| "utenceilles and domicetlls for the house estimat" | £ 6 |
| Suma of the Inventor | £ 40:08: |

The debt due by Alexander Rennie in Kirkland of £13:6:8 with interest of 16/- due to Robert's father was still outstanding. In addition, George Robertsone in Torrwoodhead was also due £13:6:8. The total of the inventory and loans was £67:17: .

Against this amount Robert's debts were:

| | |
|---|---|
| Rent | £25 |
| Wages to his servant, Margaret Baird | £8 |
| Funeral Expenses | £30 |

## 3. *Thomas Hanna, son of Robert and Christean*

In the testament mention is made of Robert's son Thomas Hanna, merchant in Falkirk, who married Joane Airbon (probably Janet or Jean Aitken). Their children were:

372

- Robert, born in Thomastoun, described below.

- Christean, born on September 16, 1670, who married Charles Hough on December 13, 1689, and had three children, Christean, Jean and Thomas.

- Jean

- Margaret

- Janet, described in more detail below.

Thomas Hanna appears frequently in the Falkirk Parish Records as a witness of births from April 27, 1672 to November 9, 1718.

### 3.1. Janet Hanna, daughter of Thomas and Jean

The family of Janet Hanna are mentioned in detail in James Love's 1908 book *Antiquarian Notes and Queries of Falkirk*. She married Alexander Watt (died about 1766), merchant and baron bailie, who at the time was one of Falkirk's most prominent citizens. She was his second wife. Children by their marriage were William Watt, born 1722 , and David Watt, born on July 27, 1723, and who died in December 1762 .

David Watt was a vintner and carried on his father's business at the Red Lion Inn, Falkirk. One of the stories gathered by Robert Kier (1807-1827), who in 1827 wrote a *History of Falkirk* and passed on by him to Robert Chambers, the historian, concerns David, who was said to have been a "flaming Jacobite". Prior to the Battle of Falkirk, David was

> brought out to the street by a party of Highlanders who set him down on the causeway and deliberately eased from his feet a pair of new shoes adorned by silver buckles. To save his fine shoes, David protested his Jacobitism, but the spoilators, perhaps accustomed to such shallow excuses, disregarded his declaration, observing: "Sae muckle ta better, she'll no grumble to change a progue for the Prince's guid."[288] It is added that David's principles were a good deal shaken by this unhappy incident.

David married Lilias Morrison of Falkirk Parish in 1747 and had three daughters.

---

[288] Roughly, "So much the better, one shouldn't object to us hocking this for a dagger if it benefits the prince"

## 4. Robert Hanna, son of Thomas and Jean

Robert Hanna is recorded as being in Thomastoun near the Haggs, Stirlingshire, on August 28, 1711, where he married Janet Ronald at Denny Parish Church.

Robert Hanna may have been married twice, as a Robert in Thomastoun is recorded in the Parish Records as marrying Agnes Liddell at Denny Parish Church on March 26, 1706. By this marriage there was a son, Thomas, born on March 23, 1707.

By the marriage with Janet Ronald of Thomastoun the following children are recorded:

- Isabel Hanna, born February 8, 1713.

- Jean Hanna, born March 3, 1717.

- William Hanna, described below.

## 5. William Hanna (b. 1719), son of Robert

William Hanna was born March 15, 1719, and married Janet Jarvie on the December 1, 1744. They had at least two children: Elizabeth Hanna (born August 23, 1752) and Thomas Hanna (born March 9, 1757), and possibly two more, Robert and Janet.

It is possible that Janet Jarvie may be descended from the Huguenot family of Gervaises who, before the Edict of Nantes[289], left France and fled, whence they sailed to Grangemouth and settled at Torwood. In Vol. XII pp. 719-720 of the Privy Council Register of 1622 appears a complaint by William Wallace, Messenger, against Sir James Forrester of Torwood and some of his tenants who included John Jarvie in Forresteris Maynis. They afterwards went to Boghall, near Bathgate; part of the wood is called Jarvie's Neuk to this day. Mary Jervais, daughter of the farmer of Balbardie Mains, near Bathgate, married in 1792 David Simpson, and their son, born June 7, 1811, was the famous physician Sir James Young Simpson, 1st Baronet, known for his pioneering use of chloroform as an anaesthetic.

### 5.1. Robert Hanna, son of William

William Hanna and Janet Jarvie may have had a son, Robert Hanna of Mid Thomastoun, who was served heir to Alexander Shaw, tenant in

---

[289] A proclamation by Henry IV of France in 1598, establishing freedoms and protections for Protestants, who had up to then been persecuted, sometimes brutally (e.g., the St. Bartholomew Day Massacre of 1572, when Catholic mobs killed thousands of Huguenots throughout France).

Bonnybridge and Helen Ronald, co-heir of provision general[290], May 28, 1783. Recorded July 5, 1783. In 1784, John and William Shaw, Bookbinders, Glasgow, and Robert Hannah of Mid Thomastoun are recorded as heirs of provision to Alexander Shaw:

> "Seised April 2nd, 1784, in half of Wester Thomastoun and part of Muir adjoining in the Parish of Denny and half of 40/land of Torbrex Wester Lenzie; on Post Nupt Mar, Con. between Alexander Shaw and Helen Ronald, his spouse, July 27th, 1775 and Rec. General Seis May 28th, 1785.

> On March 7th, 1796 William Kirkwood in St. Ninians was seised in 2/6 land of Wester Thomastoun with part of the Common Muir thereto adjacent. On disposition by John and William Shaw, book binders, Glasgow, and Robert Hannah of Mid Thomastoun 17th-19th November 1787."

## 5.2. Elizabeth Hanna (b. 1752), daughter of William

William and Janet's daughter Elizabeth Hanna, born August 23, 1752, seems to have made a romantic marriage with John Hay, as the following entry appears in the Falkirk Marriage Records:

> "John Hay and Elizabeth Hanna, both of Denny Parish, clandistinaly married at Falkirk on January 9th, 1775".

A son, William Hay, was born on October 10, 1775. They later emigrated to the United States of America as is shown by the following entry which appears in the Stirlingshire Register of Sasines of 1828.

> "William and Alexander Fraser, Masons, Dunmore, seized April 7th, 1828 in 1 Rood and 17 falls of ground with the houses thereon, being part of the lands of Longcroft to Elizabeth Hanna, spouse of John Hay, Mason, sometime at Longcroft Burn now at Pittsburgh, North America, April 17th 1828 and disposed and assigned by her with consent of the said John Hay April 7th 1828."

## 5.3. Janet Hannah, daughter of William

Janet Hannah, who married James Shearer, may have been another daughter of William and Janet. The Sasine Register of Stirlingshire records as follows:

> "Janet Hannah spouse of James Shearer, Merchant, at Haggs of Bankier. James Mirk, Hollandbush seized October 9th, 1804 in 30 falls of ground being the South West corner of the park called Hags

---

[290] A **heir general** is a one who inherits both heritable (i.e. lands and associated buildings) and moveable (everything else) property. A **heir of provision** is someone who receives an inheritance by means other than a line of succession (e.g. a contract, settlement or other provision). Thus, a **heir of provision general** combines these two definitions.

on the North side of Highway, East from Hollandbush, parish of
Denny on Feu Contract between him and James Shearer, December
14th, 1802 and Janet Hannah his spouse, seized cod die in liferent
of said piece of ground and houses thereon propries manibus of the
said James Mirk."

If Janet was indeed William's daughter, it is likely that James Mirk was
related to Janet's brother Thomas' wife, Janet Mirk.

## 6. Thomas Hanna (b. 1757), son of William

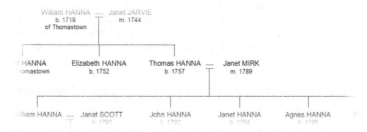

**Figure 101: Thomas Hanna and Janet Mirk**

Thomas Hanna, son of William Hanna and Janet Jarvie, was born on
March 9, 1757, and married Janet Mirk in May 1789. For a while he
worked on the family farm of Thomastoun but about 1807 he moved
to the Haggs of Bankier where he became an innkeeper. The following
entries appear in the Register of Sasines for Stirlingshire:

> "Thomas Hannah, Thomastoun and Janet Mirk his spouse and
> William Hanna their son seized in liferent and fee respectively
> January 23rd, 1809, in a piece of ground at Haggs of Bankier on the
> North side of the High Road leading from Denny loanhead to
> Kilsyth, parish Denny- on Disp by James Henry at Haggs of Bankier,
> April 11th, 1807.

> "Thomas Hannah, Innkeeper, Haggs, seized August 9th, 1814 in the
> Wester half of a piece of ground and West half of the dwelling house
> thereon and in Haggs of Bankier, Parish of Denny- on disposition by
> John Buchanan, Haggs, August 9th, 1814."

Thomas and Janet had the following children:

- William Hanna, who is described in more detail below.

- John Hanna, born February 29, 1792.

- Janet Hanna, born July 29, 1794, and married William
  Anderson, Haggs, on February 14, 1817. They had two
  daughters, Mary and Hanna.

- Agnes Hanna, born April 26, 1798.

- Elizabeth Hanna, who married Alexander Stirling.

## 7. *William Hanna (1786-1875), son of Thomas*

Thomas and Janet's son William Hanna was born in 1786 and married Janet Scott (born July 5, 1790) on March 23, 1811. Janet Scott was the youngest daughter of James Scott of Seabegs and Jean Shearer.

The Scotts of Seabegs had held their lands of Seabegs since the early seventeenth century. Walter Scott signed the Solemn League and Covenant on October 31, 1643 in Falkirk Parish Church. In February of 1640 he was entrusted to raise money for Seabegs, Castlecary, Carmures and Bogton to aid General Leslie's Scottish Army. His grandson, John Scott, was no doubt also of Covenanting sympathies as he was called before the Privy Council of Scotland on November 25, 1680 for "absence from the host and not coming out against the rebels" (Covenanters) at the Battle of Bothwell Brig.

The most romantic of the Scotts was Mary of Castlecary who may have been Janet's grandmother. Her story is told by James Love, in his 1908 book *Antiquarian Notes and Queries of Falkirk*. According to Love, she lived in the castle and one day to test her lover, James Scott of Seabegs, she disguised herself as a young man, wearing a wig, blue bonnet and belted plaid. Waylaying James she tells him that Mary of Castlecary has been untrue to him and so tests his love with good results. Hector McNeill (1746-1818), the poet, wrote the ballad "Mary of Castlecary" in her honour.

James, Mary's husband, erected the Family Burial Tomb on his lands near the village of Greenhill. Over the door is the inscription "Erected by James Scott, Owner of the Lands of Greenhill, Glenyards, Bogside, Lochdrum and Lochgreen 1756" and "The Burial Place of James Scott, Janet Scott, William Hannah and Mary of Castlecary and others." The burial ground is known locally as the Tomb of Mary of Castlecary and the custodian as of the late 20th century was the family of Thomas Hannah, Glenorchy, Head of Muir, Denny. The Scott Family endowed the School at Bonnybridge—"The teacher has £4 per annum, arising from £100 left by a Mr. Scott for that purpose, about sixty years ago (1770). He has also a school, dwellinghouse, and garden, rent free." This would be John Scott of Seabegs.

In October 1824, Thomas Stark, Grocer and Spirit Dealer, Parkfoot, is seized[291] in a piece of ground at Haggs of Bankier with the houses and

---

[291] given a lien on the property

others therein in security of £90 on bond and disposition.[292] by William Hannah, son of Thomas Hannah, workman, Thomastoun.

On March 20, 1840, Daniel Stark, sometime residing at Parkfoot now Merchant, Glasgow and heir to Thomas Stark, grocer and spirit dealer, Parkfoot, his father, seized[293] in a piece of ground at Haggs of Bankier with the houses etc., in security of £90 in bond and disposition by William Hannah, son of Thomas Hannah, Thomastoun to said Thomas Stark on October 9, 1824, by the said William Hannah on March 17, 1840.

These two entries tell a sorry tale: William followed his father as innkeeper. The Hannahs had not much money but William and his father Thomas stood surety for the debts of his brother-in-law Robert Scott of Glenyards who had succeeded his brother James Scott to Seabegs. Robert Scott is reputed to have been a hard drinker and was forced to sell piece by piece the lands of Seabegs, and when he got into debt he brought down with him his sister Janet and her family, the Hannahs. As a result of this disaster, Thomas was forced to return to the old Family Farm of Thomastoun and work as a labourer there, while his son, William, worked in the mines and became a coal contractor.

In the same year, the Hannahs lost the inn, and we see in the records the gradual dispersal of Seabegs.

Robert Scott died without any family and the guardianship of the Tomb passed to his sister Janet, who is buried in the Tomb with her husband William, who died in 1875. The guardianship then passed from Janet Scott to her son Robert Hannah. There are thought to be small pockets of land in the Barony of Seabegs which were not sold by the Scotts. The situation is now rather obscure as a result of William Hannah's death and his son Robert's emigration to Montreal, Canada.

When Robert Hannah emigrated he passed the guardianship of the Tomb to his father's cousin, William Hannah, of Glenorchy, Head of Muir, Denny, Falkirk, who in his turn passed it to his eldest son, William Hannah, Glenorchy. Born on November 7, 1894, the latter William died in 1959.

There has always been a tradition in the Hannah family that Robert Scott, although he disposed of the land, retained the mineral rights. These mineral rights are very valuable as the clay is used by a number of brick manufacturers. An attempt was made by Robert Hannah of

---

[292] **bond and disposition**: A Scots legal term meaning a bond and mortgage on a piece of land.

[293] took possession of.

Montreal[294] and William Hannah of Glenorchy to establish a claim to the mineral rights of Seabegs. This attempt was made at the end of the 1914/18 War and after a search of the titles at Register House, Edinburgh, it was decided not to pursue the claim. A previous attempt had been made prior to 1914 by William Hannah, Greenhill, and his brother, Alexander Hannah, sea captain of Leith.

The children of William and Janet Scott were:

- Thomas, born January 26, 1812, who married Helen Paton in Thomastoun on October 2, 1849, and had a son, William, who spent a number of years in Australia where he was very successful. He returned to Scotland and died in Glasgow having no family.

- James, born on March 13, 1814, with no issue.

- Robert, the third son, who was born on August 2, 1816, and married Ann Macinnes on June 27, 1838, in St. Andrews Parish Church, Glasgow. His family is described in more detail below.

- Jean (b. 1818) who married Robert Marshall of Bothkennar.

- Janet (b. 1821) who married William Ferguson, Carronshore, and had a daughter, Marion Hannah Ferguson, who married James Kerr whose son, William Kerr, was an officer in the Royal Artillery during the 1939/45 World War.

- Agnes (b. 1823)

- William (b. 1828)

- Margaret or Mary (b. 1826)

- John (b. 1832), whose family is described in more detail later in this chapter.

---

[294] presumably the son of the Robert who emigrated to Canada.

## 7.1. William Hannah (1828-1875), son of William

William Hannah and Janet Scott's son William, 1828-1875, married Agnes Todd.

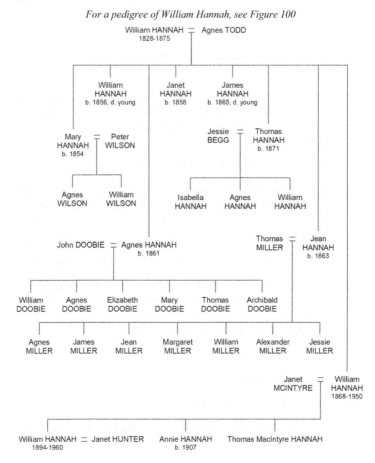

Figure 102: The Family of William Hannah and Agnes Todd

William and Agnes had eight children:

- Mary Hannah (b. 1854), who married Peter Wilson. Her two children were Agnes Wilson who married Malcolm MacDonald, and William Wilson, who married Margaret Wishart.

- William, born 1856, who died in infancy.

- Janet Hannah, who was born in 1858.

- Agnes Hannah (b. 1861), who married John Doobie. They had the following children: William, Agnes, Elizabeth, Mary, Thomas, and Archibald,.

- Jean Hannah (b. 1863), who married Thomas Miller. They had the following children: James, Jean, Margaret, William, Alexander, Jessie, and Agnes. Agnes married James Benson and had two children: James Benson (1913), and Thomas Benson (1915), who married Elizabeth Hannah on August 10, 1940. Elizabeth was the daughter of George Hannah and Helen Alexander, sister of Walter Alexander who founded Alexanders Ltd., Bus & Coach Proprietors of Falkirk. George Hannah was connected with Stirlingshire Hannahs but the exact relationship not established.

- James, born 1865, and died young.

- William (1868-1950), who married Janet Macintyre, granddaughter of Donald Macintyre of Glenorchy, a cousin of Duncan Ban MacIntyre the famous Highland Bard whose poems are to the Gaelic tongue what Robert Burns and his lyrics are to the Scots tongue. William lived at Glenorchy, Head of Muir, Denny, Stirlingshire, where he was a Parish councilor. On William Hannah of Greenhill's death he took over custodianship of the family burial grounds of the Hannahs and Scotts—The Tomb of Mary of Castlecary. William's family consisted of:

  - William Hannah (1894-1959), who lived at Glenorchy and married Janet Hunter. He was very interested in the Hannah Family History and compiled much information. He followed his father as custodian of the Tomb of Mary of Castlecary. He was a Parish councilor and a founding member of the Clan Hannay Society.

  - Annie Hannah.

  - Thomas Macintyre Hannah (born 1907), served in NW European Campaign during World War II with Inns of Court Regiment, Royal Tank Corps, 1944-45. He resided in Glenorchy, Head of Muir. Thomas succeeded his brother, William, as custodian of the Tomb of Mary of Castlecary. Thomas was also a founding member of the Clan Hannay Society.

- Thomas Hannah (b. 1871), who married Jessie Begg. Their children were:

  - Isabella (b. 1914) who married Robert Wright.

  - Agnes (b. 1917), who married Len Clements.

381

- William (b. 1912) who married Jean Cochran on November 16, 1938. Their children are Thomas Hannah; James Hannah; Isobel Hannah; Anne Hannah; Agnes Hannah and Eileen Hannah.

## 7.2. John Hannah (b. 1832), son of William

William Hanna and Janet Scott's son John Hannah was born in 1832.

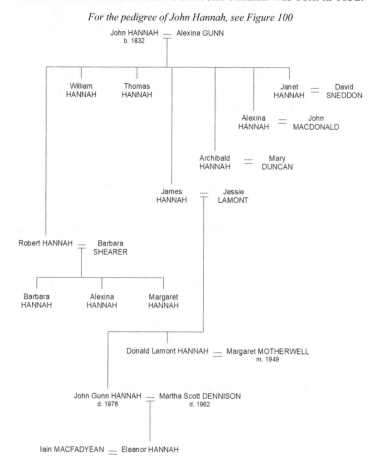

**Figure 103: The Family of John Hannah and Alexina Gunn**

John married Alexina Gunn from Sutherland. They had seven children:

- Robert Hannah, who married Barbara Shearer and had three daughters: Barbara, Alexina, and Margaret.

- William Hannah

- Thomas Hannah

- James Hannah, who married Jessie Lamont from Isle of lslay. This branch of the family is famous as pipers. James served in the 1914-

18 War as Pipe Sergeant in the 8$^{th}$ Battalion, The Argyle & Sutherland Highlanders. His children were:

- John Gunn Hannah who married, in 1939, Martha Scott Dennison. He was an excellent piper and served as an Honorary Piper to Musselburgh Highland Association. He composed a number of pipe tunes including "Eleanor Hannah's Gig" and "Robert Hannah's Welcome". He was also an Honorary Piper to the Clan Hannay Society and took part in the Lauriston Castle Gathering of the Clans in 1964 as Hannah Piper.

  He had one daughter, Eleanor Cameron Scott Hannah who was born in 1942. She was a well-known teacher of Highland Dancing and won the World's Championship for the best dressed Highland Dancer at the Cowal Highland Gathering in 1955. She married, in 1964, Iain MacFadyen of Mull, a teacher of piping for Ross-shire County Council and winner of many top piping awards. They had one child called Karen.

- Donald Lamont, who married Margaret Motherwell in 1949.

- Archibald Hannah, who married Mary Duncan of Braeface near Castlecary and died in U.S.A. aged 34

- Alexina Hannah, who married John MacDonald

- Janet Hannah, who married David Sneddon and had two children.

## 8. *Robert Hannah (1816-1882), son of William*

William and Janet's son Robert married Ann MacInnes, who came from Gilmerton near Crieff, Perthshire, where the MacInneses settled after the Jacobite Rising of 1745. For a family tree, see Figure 104.

*For pedigree of Robert Hannah, see Figure 100.*

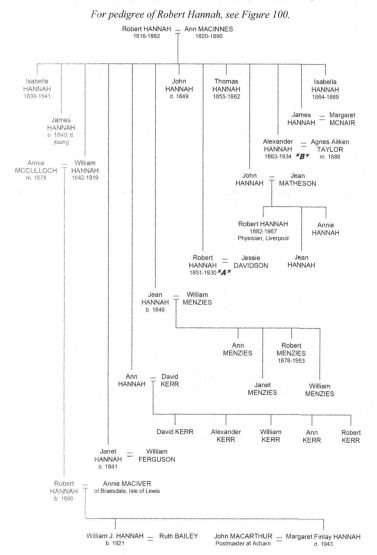

*A*: See Figure 105     *B*: See Figure 106

**Figure 104: Family of Robert Hannah and Ann MacInnes**

During that time the MacInnes Clan formed part of the Appin Regiment under command of Stewart of Ardshiel. The Appin Regiment fought with great gallantry for Prince Charles Edward Stuart and had the distinction of being the only Jacobite Regiment at the Battle of Culloden in 1746 to save their colours. These are today preserved in the museum of Edinburgh Castle. At Culloden a number of MacInneses appear among the killed and wounded. A nephew of Ann Macinnes, John Macinnes, was Inspector of Brakes with the Caledonian Railway. He invented an air brake called the Steel-MacInnes Brake from which the famous Westinghouse Brake was devised. He lived in Glasgow at the end of World War I.

Robert Hannah died in 1882 at Bothkennar, Stirlingshire, aged 66 years and is buried in the Parish Church there. There is a tombstone erected to his memory by his wife, Ann, who died aged 70 on June 26, 1890.

Their family was large: Isabella; James; William; Janet; Ann; Jean, who married William Menzies, Master Joiner of Falkirk, and owned property in Old Kirk Wynd, Falkirk; a John who died young in 1849; Thomas Hannah; Robert; a second John; Alexander; and James.

The sons William, Robert, the second John, and Alexander are described in more detail below.

### 8.1. John Hannah, son of Robert

The second John married Jean Matheson and founded the printing and stationery firm of Hannah & Co. of Charing Cross and Grange Street, Grangemouth. He is mentioned in Robert Porteous's book *Grangemouth's Modern History 1768- 1968* in connection with the founding of Kerse Church of Scotland in September 1897. There had been opposition to the Minister of the Parish Church, the matter was taken before the Presbytery of Linlithgow and John Hannah was one of the petitioners who spoke before the Presbytery. The petitioners carried the day and the ordination and induction of the Rev. M. Knowles, B.D., took place in the Town Hall of Grangemouth on September 2, 1897.

John and Jean had two daughters, Jean and Annie, and a son, Robert. Robert Hannah (1882-1967) graduated M.B. and Ch.B. at Edinburgh University in 1908, D.P.H. at Edinburgh in 1910, Member of the Royal College of Physicians and Surgeons of Glasgow 1918, registered as a doctor in Scotland on July 28, 1908. On the outbreak of World War I, he joined the Royal Army Medical Corps in September 1914. He went overseas to France with British Expeditionary Force, took part in the Retreat from Mons, and was decorated July 1917 with The Military Cross for bravery in the field. His name appears on the Grangemouth

Roll of Honour for the War. He was for many years attached to the Health Centre, Knowsley Road, Bootle, Liverpool 20. He resided at 171 Victoria Road, Wallasey, Cheshire, and never married. His two sisters, Jean and Annie, also died unmarried.

## 8.2. Robert Hannah, (1851-1930) son of Robert

Robert Hannah and Ann MacInnes' son Robert was born at Skinflats, near Falkirk. A family tree can be found in Figure 105.

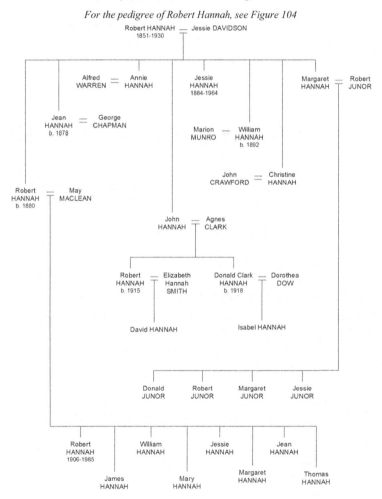

*For the pedigree of Robert Hannah, see Figure 104*

**Figure 105: Family of Robert Hannah and Jessie Davidson**

Robert married Jessie Davidson of Fort Rose in the Black Isle and had eight children:

387

- Jean, who married George Chapman and went to the U.S.A.

- Robert, who married May MacLean. They had eight children: Robert (1906-1985), James, William, Mary (1914-1931), Jessie, Margaret, Jean and Thomas.

- Annie, who married Alfred Warren and emigrated to Canada then to the U.S.A. They had three children.

- Jessie (1884-1964), who died unmarried.

- William, who married Marion Munro and emigrated to the U.S.A. They had a son and daughter.

- Christine, who married John Crawford.

- Margaret, who married Robert Junor of the Black Isle, and had four children.

- John, who married Agnes Clark. After World War I he emigrated to Canada and died there. There were two sons, Robert, born in 1915, who married Elizabeth Hannah Smith, and became a printer in Falkirk. They had a son, David, born in 1952. The second son, Donald Clark, born in 1918, married Dorothea Isabella Miller Dow. He served in the Royal Artillery and was a chartered surveyor in Edinburgh. He was an elder of Duddingston Kirk and was a founder member and honorary treasurer of the Clan Hannay Society. He had a daughter, Isabel, who earned a MA(Hon) at St. Andrews.

## 8.3. William Hannah (1842-1919), son of Robert

Robert and Ann's son William Hannah married Annie McCulloch in 1878. Annie had a brother, James McCulloch, who emigrated to Canada at the end of the nineteenth century, and whose family still resides in Hamilton, Ontario.

William spent part of his youth in Halifax, Nova Scotia, Canada. When he returned to Scotland he settled at Greenhill (formerly called Above-the-Wood of Seabegs), established a General Merchants Business and was appointed Postmaster. He was a Parish councilor and Chairman of the Falkirk Parish Council. He was guardian of the Tomb of Mary of Castlecary (described in more detail earlier in this chapter) and took a great interest in the history of the Hannah and Scott families. Unfortunately, his manuscripts have been lost.

A man of very distinguished appearance, possessing in his later years a close cropped beard after the style favoured by Edward VII, he was a great friend of James Love, in whose 1908 *Antiquarian Notes and*

388

*Queries of Falkirk, Volume 1*, appears a letter which tells us something of William Hannah's youth in Canada:

> "We have been favoured with the following interesting letter from Parish councilor William Hannah, Post Office, Greenhill, Bonnybridge, regarding Sir William Young, Prime Minister[295] of Nova Scotia. He says:
>
> 'Being a close reader of your Notes and Queries, I have been very much interested in your reference to the Young family. Being resident in Halifax, Nova Scotia, in the years 1868-1869, I had the pleasure of being acquainted with Sir William Young. He was then Chief Justice of the Province of Nova Scotia, and was reputed to be an able and upright judge. The honour of Knighthood was conferred on him, by the Governor, Sir Charles Hastings Doyle, in January 1869, I think.
>
> I was introduced to Sir William by Mr. John Scott, who was then gas manager at Halifax—also a native of Falkirk [one of the Scotts of Seabegs and a kinsman of William]. Mr. Scott is now back in his native town and is very well known. His sister is the wife of the Honourable William Kidston [A native of Falkirk who later became Premier of Queensland, Australia].
>
> After coming back to this district, I spoke to quite a number of aged men about Sir William, including the late Provost Keir and Mr. Beeby, but none of them knew anything about him. However, in talking to an old man at Bonnybridge, who was timekeeper to Messrs. Smith and Wellstood—his name was Alexander Higgins— I happened to mention the name of Sir William to him, when he told me he knew him, as he was a cousin of his. He further informed me that Sir William's father was a wood merchant in Falkirk; his shop is just close to the Red Lion Hotel.
>
> The picture in the *Herald* of Sir William is very like him. I don't think he had any family. His wife, Lady Young, was a Roman Catholic, and attended St. Mary's Roman Catholic Chapel: but Sir William belonged to the St. Matthew's Church of Scotland, of which the Reverend Dr. Grant was minister.'

Sir William visited William Hannah at Greenhill when on holiday in Scotland.

It was James Love who discovered that the Scotts of Seabegs endowed Bonnybridge with its first school about 1760.

William Hannah and Annie McCulloch had a son, Robert.

---

[295] i.e. Premier of the colony (at that time Nova Scotia was not yet part of Canada). Young held this office from 1854-1860, then was appointed Chief Justice of Nova Scotia from 1860 to 1881.

## 8.4. Robert Hannah (b. 1880), son of William

Robert Hannah was born on September 1, 1880 and married in 1917 to Annie Maciver of Braeschete, Stornoway, Isle of Lewis. Robert emigrated to Canada in 1904. During World War I he fought with the Black Watch of Canada in France. A very fine piper, he was Pipe Major of the Massed Pipes and Drums of the Canadian Army at the Vimy Ridge Memorial Unveiling in the 1930s.

Robert Hannah travelled greatly, in as far flung parts of the world as Australia, Canada and the Arctic. He was in Australia and Canada prior to 1914. On the outbreak of war he joined the Black Watch of Canada, accompanied them to Europe as Pipe Sergeant and became Pipe Major and carried the regimental Pipe Banner in action. After the war, he presented the banner to his Colonel's Lady. When Sir Ashby Cooper was Governor of the Hudson Bay Company he carried out a tour of inspection of the Company's posts in the Arctic and Robert Hannah accompanied him as his personal piper. Whilst on the trip, he flew over Hannah Bay and Sir Ashby pointed it out to him saying, "There must have been Hannahs here before you." On another occasion whilst playing at a Trading post, when he began to play a reel the Inuit formed a square and danced an Eightsome Reel. The dance was carried out perfectly and it was discovered afterwards that they had been taught Scots dances fifty years previously by Scots Whalers.

Robert and Annie Maciver, had two children, William J. Hannah and Margaret Finlay Hannah. William J. Hannah, in 1921. He married Ruth Bailey and they had no children. He too served with the Black Watch (Royal Highlanders) of Canada. He was wounded at Caen in France in 1944. He also was a distinguished piper and became Pipe Major of the Black Watch of Canada. He received tuition at the School of Piping at Edinburgh Castle under the famous piper, Major William Ross. He was in Scotland for Black Watch Memorial Celebration in 1952 when he was presented to Queen Elizabeth at Balmoral.

Robert and Annie's daughter Margaret Finlay Hannah married John MacArthur, Postmaster and General Merchant, Acharn by Aberfeldy. She died at Acharn on November 4, 1943. John MacArthur had learnt Gaelic and Margaret Finlay in time became a proficient Gaelic speaker.

## 9.  Alexander Hannah (1863-1934), son of Robert

The last son of Robert and Ann, Alexander Hannah, was born at Bothkennar, Stirlingshire on August 12, 1863. He was an indentured marine apprentice with James David Thomson, merchant and shipowner, Grangemouth, Stirlingshire.

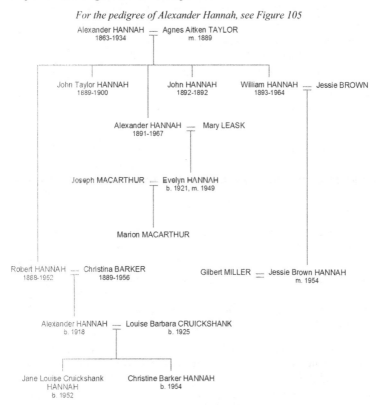

*For the pedigree of Alexander Hannah, see Figure 105*

**Figure 106: Family of Alexander Hannah and Agnes Taylor**

This indenture is an interesting social document. When young Alexander Hannah signed it in 1878 he had just left school, aged 14 years and 8 months. In 4 years, he earned £34, visited the Far East and 'rounded the Horn' as an apprentice on a full rigged sailing ship *The Earl of Zetland*. His first voyage was a long one, leaving Grangemouth in April 1878, and returning to London in March 1881, almost three years. He served his apprenticeship well, and in a letter home, his captain spoke highly of his ability. When Alexander left *The Earl of Zetland* the captain presented him with a gold U.S.A. dollar which Alexander retained as a luck piece. It is still preserved in the family along with the indenture agreement.

In those days an apprentice provided himself with "all sea bedding, wearing apparel, and necessaries," whilst the shipowner provided "sufficient meat, drink, lodging, washing, medicine, and medical and surgical assistance." Breach of contract by either party involved a penalty of £10.

From a photograph taken just before he sailed, young Hannah looked a well-turned-out boy in a navy reefer jacket and nautical cap, sporting a gold pin in his tie. The frame no doubt bought as a present for his mother, Ann Mcinnes, bears the legend, "East, West, Home's Best", and East he went by the Cape of Good Hope to Singapore and round the Horn home.

He served on four sailing ships but only two are known by name, *The Earl of Zetland* and the barque[296] *Staffordshire*.

Alexander Hannah served his apprenticeship in sail, but steam soon drove the picturesque tea and wool clippers from the seas, and after his period in sail we find him aboard one of those hybrid ships, the *Weimar* of Leith, powered by steam, but rigged for sail on her fore and main masts.

On December 26, 1888, he passed his Master Mariners Examination at Greenock and his certificate was issued at the Port of Grangemouth on December 31, 1888, "Whereas it has been reported to us that you have been found duly qualified to fulfil the duties of Master in the Merchant Service, we do hereby, in pursuance of the Merchant Shipping Act 1854, grant you this Certificate of Competency. By the Lord of the Committee of Privy Council for Trade etc."

By 1896 he was in command of the *S.S. Warsaw*; other vessels included the *Edina* and the *Olna*, etc. His ships in his early life took him round the world but in his later years he preferred the shorter continental runs out of the Forth to the Baltic, the low countries, France, Germany and Spain. An interesting relic of his voyage is a Black Postage Stamp, known as the Mourning Stamp of Finland, issued about 1900 by the Finnish Patriots during their struggles for Freedom from the Russians. The stamp was on a letter sent home by Alexander to his wife describing his visit to Finland.

During World War I he served at sea and qualified for the Mercantile Marine and the General Service Medals. He married Agnes Aitken Taylor in August 1889. She was the daughter of John Taylor (1834-1898) of Grangemouth whose family farmed Lochend near Restalrig, Leith. John Taylor took part in the Gold Strikes at Ballarat and Bendigo

---

[296] sailing vessel with at least three masts, the aft mast being rigged for fore-and-aft sails; the others being square-rigged.

near Melbourne, Australia, in the 1850s. He struck gold but had the bad luck to be held up by Bush Rangers when on his way back to Melbourne. He was robbed of his gold and lucky to escape with his life. He is believed to have taken part in the miners' fight at Eureka Stockade. Alexander's grandson Robert Hannah died in a somewhat similar situation in Sydney in 1916 when he and a shipmate were attacked by robbers in the dock area. Robert was armed and used his revolver.

After the War, Alexander retired from the sea to Leith, where he died on January 3, 1934, and was buried at Camelon Cemetery, Falkirk. His family consisted of: Robert (described below); John Taylor and John, who both died young; Alexander, and William. William Hannah (1893-1964) married Jessie Brown and was a Marine Engineer. He was Superintendent of Marine Engineering at Bombay for the Ministry of War Transport in World War II. He had one daughter, Jessie Brown Hannah, born at Leith in 1930 who became a Bachelor of Law and married Gilbert M. Miller of Stow in 1954.

## 9.1. Robert Hannah (1888-1952), son of Alexander

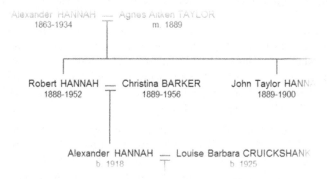

**Figure 107: Robert Hannah and Christine Barker**

Robert Hannah (1888-1952), born Grangemouth, Stirlingshire, eldest son of Alexander and Agnes Aitken Taylor, married on July 16, 1917, to Christina Barker, youngest daughter of George Barker of Leith and Isabella Duncan Davidson of Springwell, Coldingham, Berwickshire. George Barker, 1851-1935, was born in Buckhaven, Fife. He settled in Leith, where he originally started a small coopering business and later became a prominent herring and white fish merchant buying for the Midland and London Market. He took a keen interest in politics and for a time was agent for the Leith Tory Candidate. His wife was a cousin of Sir Michael Barker Nairn, Bart., of Rankeilour and Dysart, Fife.

393

Robert was indentured as an apprentice marine engineer with Cran & Sons of Leith, and educated at Leith Academy and Heriot-Watt College, Edinburgh. He served at sea during World War I, first on the *SS Clan Alpine*, of the Clan Line of Glasgow. When war broke out he was 3rd Engineer Officer on the *Clan Alpine* loading in Chittagong for London. She arrived safely, then sailed for South African ports and thence to Melbourne, Sydney, and Brisbane, whence she left for New York via the Panama Canal. After lying in Panama Bay for three weeks, because the Canal had been blocked by a fall, she was taken over by the British government; she discharged her cargo at Balboa and proceeded to Pisague, Junin and Iquiqui, loading nitrates, returning home, without incident, via the Magellan Straits, Montevideo and Tenerife in the Canary Islands, in all a voyage of ten months.

From 1916 to the end of the War he served on the *SS Clan Macintosh* and H.M. Transport *Clan Macaulay*. The *Macaulay* was requisitioned in September 1915, by the government as a transport, being continually employed running first to Bordeaux for the French Army, then as a store carrier for the British Expeditionary Force; she sailed from the Mersey, and later from Dublin, Belfast and Glasgow to Cherbourg, Le Havre, Dieppe, Calais and Boulogne. She made at least 116 passages, steamed 48,275 miles in the channel, carried 150,000 tons measurement of cargo, consisting of stores and war material, and averaged a speed of 12 knots mainly unescorted and without incident. On other occasions she acted as a commodore ship and earned a high reputation for entering ports of destination without escorts, pilots or assistance. During this period of his service, Robert Hannah sailed as 2nd and the Chief Engineer Officer.

Between the Wars, life for Robert was not without incident. His ship the *SS Clan Maciver* took part in the rescue of the passengers from the pilgrim ship, *SS Frangestan*, which caught fire in the Red Sea on April 2, 1924, while carrying pilgrims from Bombay to Jeddah. The *Frangestan* was carrying 1,200 Muslim Pilgrims on their way to Mecca; the rescue was carried out without loss of life.

During World War II, Robert had many close escapes. In October 1939 his ship, the *SS Clan Chisholm* was torpedoed and sunk by Nazi submarines off the Spanish Coast; she sank in eight minutes, and the survivors were four days in an open boat before being picked up by a neutral Swedish ship, the *Bardaland*.

At Dunkirk in 1940, he was Chief Engineer Officer of the transport *Clan MacAlister*, which was requisitioned by the Army to transport landing craft to the Dunkirk beaches to help rescue the British Army. She left the Downs at 3:30 a.m. on May 29 for Bray where she was attacked by dive bombers; the Stukas set her No. 5 hold ablaze and destroyed her gun platform. E. Keble Chatterton, in his 1940 history *The Epic of Dunkirk* describes the scene as follows:

> "The Clan MacAlister was alight, beams and other parts of the hatch twisted, a large hole on deck, and the crew's quarters just a mass of twisted woodwork. Moreover, the bomb penetrating through the side further aft had so burst that dead were lying about the decks."

The destroyer *HMS Malcolm* took off soldiers and injured crew, two lines were passed aboard and hoses directed at No.5 hold but could not reach the gun-platform already well alight. The German dive bombers attacked again and the *Malcolm* had to abandon her efforts of rescue. The *MacAlister* continued at slow speed, but all too certainly the conflagration gained; the ammunition on her decks kept exploding, but hardly was she underway when the Stukas attacked for a third time and damaged the gyro compass and the telemotor; unable to steer, she was a sitting duck. To try to save a complete disaster, Robert Hannah, with his 5th Engineer, went below to draw the fires. When they remustered, out of a crew of over 100 only 12 officers and 23 crewmen were left. They were rescued by the Minesweeper *HMS Panbourne* who, badly holed, managed to make Dover. The *MacAlister* was the largest vessel at Dunkirk. A third of her crew was killed and scores of soldiers who had boarded her in hopes of safety were dead and wounded. The Scots ship, although dead, proudly sat upright on an even keel in the shallow water, and Captain William Tennant, RN, in Bastion 32 counted no less than 27 dive-bombing attacks on the *Clan MacAlister*. Later Admiralty experts estimated her presence saved Britain £1,000,000 worth of shipping. For his services on the *Chisholm* and the *MacAlister*, Robert Hannah was awarded the O.B.E. which he received from the King at Buckingham Palace on June 2, 1943. He was also awarded after the war the *Médaille Dunkerque 1940*[297]. After Dunkirk he continued to serve at sea, taking part in the North Africa landings. He was a recipient of the following additional medals: Merchant Navy Medal 1914-9 ; Victory Medal 1919; 1939-43 Star; Africa Star with Clasp; Burma Star and the British War Medal.

Due to retire, in 1952 he died on his last voyage and was buried at Kanatte Cemetery, Colombo, Ceylon [now Sri Lanka].

Robert Hannah and Christina Barker had only one son, Alexander.

---

[297] A commemorative medal struck by the town of Dunkirk and given to Allied troops who participated in Operation Dynamo.

## 9.2. Alexander Hannah (born 1918), son of Robert

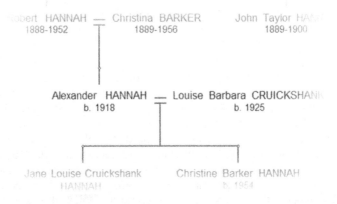

Figure 108: Alexander Hannah and Louise Cruickshank

Alexander Hannah was born in Leith on October 5, 1918. On leaving school in 1937, he joined the Head Office of the Caledonian Insurance Company as an apprentice. On the outbreak of war he enlisted at Glencorse Depot in the Royal Scots (The Royal Regiment), joined as Officer Cadet 168th Officer Cadet Training Unit, was commissioned August 1941 and posted to 5th (Dumfries and Galloway) Battalion, The King's Own Scottish Borderers. The 5th Battalion KOSB formed part of the 52 (L) Division, which was a Mountain Division and during the winters of 1942 and 1943 trained as ski troops. During August through October 1944, the 52 (Lowland) Division formed part of the 1st Airborne Army which included 1st Airborne Division, 82nd and 101st American Airborne Divisions. The 52nd Division were to reinforce the 1st Airborne at Arnheim. The 4th and 5th Battalions KOSB were briefed to land by glider but the operation was cancelled, and the 52nd Division was sent instead by sea to Belgium, and on November 1 the 5th Battalion took part in the assault landing at Flushing, having embarked at Breskins Harbour and crossed the River Scheldt in assault landing craft. Lieutenant Alexander Hannah commanded 10 platoon during the fighting in Flushing and was acting second-in-command of B Company (Wigtownshire) during the occupation of Oost-Souburg until the Battalion left Walcheren. He was slightly wounded by a grenade during an attack on a German Bunker in the Flushing Hook Area on morning of November 4, 1944.

During November and early December he saw service on the River Maas in Holland near 's-Hertogenbosch (Den Bosch); later he was with B Company in the line at Dorset Wood, Geilenkirken, in Germany,

Gangelt, and finally at Vintelen in Germany, where, commanding 10 Platoon, he was wounded in the chest by a machine gun bullet when a German company attacked his position in the early morning of December 28. The story of the battle is told in Captain E.V. Tullett's 1945 book *From Flushing to Bremen: The Campaign in Northwest Europe. A History of the 5th Battalion KOSB from 19th October 1944 until VE Day.*

As a result of his wounds at Vintelen, he spent eight months in hospital and relinquished his commission in August 1945. In the same months Alexander was mentioned in despatches in recognition of gallant and distinguished service in North and West Europe. On discharge from hospital, he rejoined the Caledonian Insurance Company and in 1950 qualified as a Fellow of the Chartered Insurance Institute and later Fellow of the Chartered Institute of Secretaries and Administrators. In 1955 he was appointed Manager at Inverness, in 1961 Stoke-on-Trent, and in 1965 West End Manager, London. On merger in 1967 with the Guardian Assurance Company he was appointed in 1969 Guardian Royal Exchange Assurance Regional Manager for the Midlands and moved to Birmingham, returning in 1971 on promotion to Regional Manager (Metropolitan) with responsibility for all London and Home Counties Branches of the Group.

Alexander Hannah was elected a Fellow of the Society of Antiquaries of Scotland in 1953. An expert and keen collector of Scottish Numismatics, he has contributed a number of articles to numismatic publications including one describing Sir Samuel Hannay's Token.[298] (see Figure 109).

---

[298] This bronze coin was used for advertising Sir Samuel 's patent medicine, the "only infallible preventive of a certain disease". This euphemistically referred to prophylactic treatment for venereal disease. Sir Samuel (d. 1790), as noted in Chapter VIII: The Hannays of Kirkdale, made and lost a fortune in the pharmaceutical business.

**Figure 109: Sir Samuel Hannay's Token**

He was one of the founding members of the Clan Hannay Society and was its first Secretary. Along with Major R.W. Rainsford-Hannay of Kirkdale and Donald Clark Hannah, he was one of the initial Trustees of Sorbie Tower.

On June 24, 1950, he married Louise Barbara Elizabeth Cruickshank, elder daughter of the late Robert Walker Cruickshank of Claymires, Turriff, Aberdeenshire and Mrs. Louise Jane Courie, Strathlea, Hilton Street, Aberdeen. The Cruickshank family were well known in the Turriff area: both Robert Walker Cruickshank and his father, Major Robert Cruickshank, being outstanding breeders of Aberdeen-Angus pedigree cattle.

They had two children, Jane Louise Cruickshank Hannah, born in Inverness on July 22, 1952, and Christine Barker Hannah, born in Inverness on June 1, 1954.

### 9.3. Alexander Hannah (1891-1967)

Alexander Hannah was born on June 5, 1891, in Leith. The second surviving son of Alexander Hannah, Ship Master in Leith, and Agnes Aitken Taylor, Alexander was educated at Leith Academy, and on leaving school entered the services of M.J. Ellingsen & Company, a Leith Shipping Firm, whose trading interests were with Iceland, Scandinavia, and, in particular, with Russia and Estonia, then part of the Russian Empire. In addition to shipping, Ellingsen had large timber interests with Russia.

Shortly after the outbreak of war, in 1914, Leith was raided by Zeppelins, and Ellingsen's office was damaged by German bombs. In the morning, after the raid, Alexander took his brother, Robert, to

398

inspect the damage; they found that the caretaker had been killed during the raid. History was to repeat itself in 1941 when German bombers raided Leith and shrapnel was found in the garden of Alexander's house at 2 Summerside Place. Luckily, this time no one was hurt, and only the building was damaged.

In 1916 Alexander joined the Army Service Corps and served in France with the newly formed transport section. After the war, he returned to Ellingsen to become cashier and office manager.

The Bolsheviks, however, had taken central control of the Russian economy after the Revolution in 1917, and the firm had lost forests in Russia estimated at one million pounds—nationalisation without compensation. This was a major disaster from which Ellingsen never recovered; it also became an important factor in the career of Alexander Hannah, Junior.

On July 16, 1920, he married Mary Leask, daughter of George Leask (1869-1936) and Mary Duncan (1874-1933). The Leasks were a Shetland family, and like the Hannahs had sea-faring interests.

In 1919, the Estonians revolted against the Russians, winning their independence and establishing their capital at Tallinn, the old Hanseatic town of Reval. The firm of Ellingsen rendered every possible help to their friends the Estonians, and one of their ships, the *Lembit*, was famous in Estonian history for running cargoes of guns and supplies from Leith to the Estonian army. This close association between the Estonians and Ellingsen was to have a great bearing not only on the fortunes of Alexander Hannah, but also on that of colleague Edward Neil. Neil was three months Alexander's junior; he had a distinguished war record, having won the Military Cross during World War I. The Estonian business became such an important part of Ellingsen's operations, that they became Estonian Consul at Leith, and it was decided that the department be expanded, and on Hannah's advice Neil was appointed the firm's representative in Tallinn, where he and his wife spent nine years. Neil already spoke German and during his stay in Tallinn he became a fluent speaker of Estonian, thus one of the few British people to speak the language.

In the late 1920's and early 30's shipping in Britain was in a bad way; old established shipping firms went to the wall, and Ellingsen, who had never recovered from their losses in Russia, were no exception. Hannah and Neil saw the crash coming; although young men, whose resources were only those of courage and a spirit of high adventure, they managed to acquire a few hundred shares in two ships, the *Koidula*, and the *Keila*.

A week before Christmas the crash came, and Ellingsen went into voluntary liquidation. Seven days' notice was all the staff received.

The Icelandic Department of Ellingsen was taken over by Robert Cairns & Company of Leith. The manager of the department was Mr. William McArthur, who was to become very active in Icelandic affairs, and was later in life to receive the Order of the Knight of the Falcon of Iceland. His nephew, Joseph Ewart McArthur, was later to marry Alexander Hannah's only daughter, Evelyn Mary Hannah. Although well aware of the impending crisis, and to a very small extent prepared for it, they founded a private limited company, Neil & Hannah Ltd. of Leith. Thus, with a capital of £300 divided equally between the two adventurers in commerce, it seemed appropriate that the motto of the Hannahs of Leith was "Per Laborem ad Alta" or "Through endeavour to the Highest Places".

With little money, no financial backing and the depression of the 30's, it needed courage to found a new firm; not even their bankers supplied them with financial backing. In fact, one of their guiding principles was to have no overdraft—and apart from £500 once for a few days their bankers were never required to help. It was not surprising that they had no backers, for the wiseacres in Leith shipping circles were saying, "Aye, they're daft—they'll be walking Commerical Street in a few weeks looking for a job." Commercial Street was the business street of Leith and walk it they did for forty years under the House Flag of Neil & Hannah Limited of Leith.

But although they had little financial resources, and most of that tied up in their ships, they had friends. Most of them were Estonians.

They rented an office in Commercial Street, from the Edinburgh & London Shipping Company Limited. It was in the heart of Leith opposite the Customs House, and close to the shore where Mary Queen of Scots landed from France in 1561.

Their brass plate was set up and stayed there until Alexander Hannah's death in 1967. Letterheads were printed, and a telephone installed; however they could not afford any office furniture or staff, so Mary, Hannah's wife, came back to work. She had managed Ellingsen's Estonian department during the war so she was not without experience. A typewriter had been bought and she typed the firm's letters with the machine balanced on a pile of books, seated on a wooden apple box!

Their first action was to telegraph those ships in which they owned an interest. The message was one of great optimism: "Old firm finished. Stop. Neil & Hannah Limited will look after you. Stop. End of message." Next day the masters were instructed to obtain any freight they could. The ownership of these Estonian vessels was in many ways

400

different to that of British ships. Many of the crew, such as the captain, chief engineer, steward, etc. were co-partners.

The masters, realising that Neil & Hannah would not have any spare cash, approached the crew and collected as much money as possible. This they used to pay the ship's way until they got back to home waters, when Neil & Hannah reimbursed them.

This friendship in difficult times was not to be forgotten by the directors and as we shall see later, Alexander Hannah and Edward Neil repaid the trust put in them by their Estonian friends.

The formative years to 1936 were difficult but exciting for Neil & Hannah. Ships were arrested in ports, the barrel was hastily scraped and money sent, the arrestment stopped and the ship put to sea.

To avoid arrestment for debts belonging to the old firm, the names of the ships were changed, mainly to Estonian names beginning with 'K': the *Ellind* became the *S.S. Kadri*, the *Lembit* became the *S.S. Kadli*. The house colours were also changed. The Ellingsen colours were a black funnel carrying three horizontal bands of blue, black and white. Neil & Hannah Ltd. adopted new house colours which commemorated Estonia's fight for freedom against the USSR in 1919, the new house flag being of equal horizontal bands of gold over red over silver and the colours on the ship's funnels being broad bands of gold, red and silver on black. These colours were symbolic: silver, the colour of the moon, represented the hope of Estonia emerging from the darkness of Russian oppression. Her successful fight against the Bolsheviks in 1919 was shown by the red of the dawn, while her freedom was signified by the gold of the sun at noon.

During the first few months times were very difficult. The Neil & Hannah wives had to run their homes on £2 10s. a week, not much even in the hungry 30's.

There were moments when all seemed lost; the *Kadri* (*Ellind*) was in the Tyne clearing for the sea when Alexander Hannah got a phone call from their agents advising that she had fouled a buoy, and her propeller and main-shaft were damaged. Repairs were £700 and they did not have the money. Their agents, however, had faith in the two Scots and persuaded Smith's Dockyard to put her on pontoons and anchor her in the river until the money was raised. Smith's repaired her and when they eventually sent their account no charge was made for the period the *Kadri* was on pontoons. Neil & Hannah never forgot this and during their lifetime whenever possible Smith's Dockyard repaired their ships.

Others also had faith in the firm. One day their banker met Alexander in the street and casually mentioned, "Oh, Mr. Hannah, I had a bank enquiry through the other day for you—I confirmed that you were all right." "How much?" asked Alexander hesitantly. "Oh, £20,000[299]," replied the banker, looking Alexander straight in the eye and adding, "They'll no need it all at once, I hope." And they didn't, which was just as well for all concerned.

The shipping section of the Leith Observer reports the firm as managing four ships in 1934, six in 1935, and seven in 1936.

A timber importing business was established, and when the Baltic ice melted in the spring, Neil & Hannah ships bearing the gold, red and silver bands could be seen beating up the Firth, laden with timber for Leith and the Forth ports. The ships were mainly well-decked so that they could carry a deck cargo of timber, and if the weather in the Kattegat, the Skagerack or North Sea had been bad, a ship would come up the Firth of Forth listing badly with half of her deck cargo gone.

The firm's trade was mainly with the Baltic and South America where their two largest ships, the *Koidula* and the *Keila*, both about 4,000 tons, carried coal from U.K. ports and brought back grain from the River Plate. The *Kaida*, their last acquisition, later to be famous in World War II, was mainly a coastal trader between U.K., Germany and the Low Countries.

The ships were manned by Estonian crews, flew the Estonian flag, and were registered at Tallinn. Most of the officers were members of the Estonian Naval Reserve.

Shortly after World War II broke out in 1939, the USSR occupied the Baltic Republics of Estonia, Latvia and Lithuania and overnight Neil & Hannah lost their valuable timber concessions, and what was worse, their Estonian Director in Tallinn was captured by the Russians and never heard of again.

The firm quickly suffered more losses—the *Koidula* was caught in Hamburg and badly damaged when the RAF bombed the German port in the early months of the war. The *Kadri* was also captured by the Germans and at the end of the war the British, thinking that she was Estonian, handed her over as reparation to Russia; Neil & Hannah fought this case in the British Courts, proved that the *Kadri* was mainly British owned, won their law suit, were awarded damages, and became one of the few firms to take the British Government to court. Compensation was received. No compensation, however, was received from our Russian allies for the *Liina* caught at Tallinn when the USSR invaded the Baltic Republic.

---

[299] Equivalent to roughly £1,750,000 in 2019.

After the experience of their Estonian friends, many of whom were never heard of again, Neil & Hannah had nothing good to say of Russia and her activities in Estonia. The initial months of the war cost the firm £200,000[300] in ships and timber concessions. Luckily, they had been more far-seeing than most, and remembering the Ellingsen losses in World War I, they had cut their Baltic land commitments to a minimum, but even so the day the Russians entered Estonia they lost £20,000[301].

Another ship, the *Kadli* (*Lembit*) was captured at Bergen in 1940 when the Germans invaded Norway. The *Kulda* had been trapped in Sweden at the beginning of the war and rather than chance running the German blockade of the Baltic she was sold to Swedish interests. This left only the *Keila* (renamed *Linda*), and the *Kaida*, which made British ports where their crews offered their services as Free Estonians to Britain and came under the Red Ensign.

Neil & Hannah were appointed Ship Managers for the Ministry of War Transport and given the management of other ships. The *Kaida*, the smallest of the ships, was used mainly on coastal trading round the Scots coast and twice she beat off attacks by German bombers and received two Admiralty Commendations.

The last ship Neil & Hannah bought was the *SS Lorna*. She was run under the Liberian flag. The reason for the Panamanian and Liberian registrations was that most of their crews were Free Estonians, and a British ship cannot be commanded by other than a British Master. Estonia no longer existed as a free country, having been overrun by Soviet Russia during World War II. To provide employment for their Estonian friends, Neil & Hannah registered their post-war ships in Panama and Liberia; they did, however, comply with British standards.

For political reasons, the names of the ships were changed and the house colours used by the *Lorna* after the war were: black funnel with St. Andrew's Cross of Scotland superimposed on their bands, red, white and red, representing the Liberian colours.

Alexander died at Leith on June 4, 1967. Amongst the mourners at the Cremation Service at Warriston Crematorium were the Estonian officers and crew of Neil & Hannah's last ship, *SS Lorna*. The ashes were buried at Gulberwick, the family's summer home near Lerwick. Alexander Hannah was a member of the Council of the Clan Hannay Society and acted as auditor from its inception until his death.

---

[300] £12,200,000 in 2018.

[301] £1,220,000 in 2018.

Mrs. Mary Hannah sold the family home in Leith in 1968 and returned to Shetland where she bought a house, Summerside, Lower Sound Road, Lerwick.

They had one daughter, Evelyn Mary Hannah, born Leith in 1921. She was a Licentiate of the Royal College of Music (LRCM) and music mistress at Cranley Girls' School, Edinburgh. She married Joseph Ewart McArthur, a descendant of Ensign Charles Ewart of the Royal Scots Greys, who captured the French Eagle of the 45th Regiment of France at Waterloo in 1815. They had one daughter, Marion, born in Edinburgh on October 14, 1956. Evelyn was the membership secretary of the Clan Hannay Society for many years, retiring in the early 2000s. She died in Edinburgh in October of 2014.

# XXIII: Tartan, Heraldry and the Clan Society

In early times our Celtic ancestors in Galloway, along with those in the Highlands, Ireland, and Celtic kingdoms of Cumbria, in all probability wore something in the nature of a kilt and went bare-legged. This resembled the "Breachen-faile" or belted plaid and was probably in some locally woven tweed. The design would not at this period represent any form of tartan sett that we should know today, and the dress would bear little resemblance to the highland dress of today.

From the 10th century onwards the people of the Lowlands tended to move from their Celtic traditions towards the more accepted English dress. By the fifteenth century the lairds of the Lowlands and Galloway were adopting the more sophisticated forms of dress of their French allies.

However, certainly by the end of the sixteenth century forms of tartan were being worn by Lowland lairds. Certainly, there were Lowland families, notably the Kennedys, Homes, and Leslies who have ancient tartans.

The Highland lairds adopted a form of dress for riding, the trews (trousers) of tartan material. Lowland gentlemen seem to have followed the fashion, particularly if they were attached to the Jacobite cause. At this time, it is doubtful if any specific family tartan existed. It should be remembered that until recently the setts have never been formally recorded and in ancient times the variations were great.

## 1. The Family Tartan

By background both the lordships of Galloway and the A'Hannas are Celtic and it is an interesting fact that it is in Galloway and Carrick that many of the first references in charters to clans appear. In the reign of David II, we have a number of charters of the office of "Capitaneus de Clan MacGowin, 1343; Clan of Clainconnan, 1344; Clan of Kenelman, 1344; Clan of Muntercasduff." In the time of Robert the Bruce, the Galloway clans—the MacDowalls, McCullochs, McClellans, McKies and A'hannas—all supported King John Baliol, who was the representative of the old Celtic lords of Galloway through his mother, the Lady Devorguila, daughter of Alan of Galloway, last Prince of Galloway. It is possible therefore that a form of tartan was worn in Galloway in early times. In William MacKenzie's 1841 book *The History of Galloway: Form the Earliest Period to the Present Time*, there is the following description of the dress of Gallovidians in the early 18th century:

> "The men wore kelts, or waulked plaiding coats, made of a mixture
> of black and white wool, in its natural state, which gave the cloth a

405

mottled appearance. Their hose were formed of pieces of white plading sewed together. Their bonnets or woolen caps, which they procured from Kilmarnock, were black or blue."

It is interesting to note that the family tartan is basically a black and white base with blue and yellow lines, although one version includes a red line.

Having glanced a little at the history of the tartan, let us record what we know of the Hannay tartans. A Hannay tartan in Galloway was confirmed by Sir Herbert Maxwell (author of *A History of Dumfries and Galloway*) to John Hannay, deputy Mayor of Chelsea. The Hannays of Kirkdale remember Hannay tartan being stocked in the local tailors shop in Newton Stewart at the end of the 19th century. In Stirlingshire, the Hannahs who lived in the Falkirk area wore, in the 19th century, a black, white and blue tartan, scarves, shawls and plaids. This was known locally as the Hannah Tartan.

A letter to Capt. T.S. Davidson of the Scottish Tartan Information centre from Alex Hannah, who was at that time secretary of the Clan Hannay Society, states:

> "At the request of one of our members, Miss Dorothy K. Hannay, Mountain Cottage, Braemar, I am enclosing some Hannay Tartan as she tells me that you require another piece.
>
> Since our correspondence in February last year The Society's Convener, councilor John Hannay of Chelsea, has died and his collection of Tartans has passed into my keeping. Among his papers I have discovered photographs of the paintings of Commander Alexander Hannay, 1788-1848 and his wife, Mary McKinnell, 1801- 1871; also a photograph of his Tombstone in Kirkcudbright Cemetery. He was the Commander of the East Indiaman, Duke of Lancaster, and died at Kirkcudbright on 10.7.1848, aged 60 years. It was from a dependant of this branch of the family that councilor Hannay obtained the old pattern.
>
> In the collection is an old scarf of Hannay Tartan and it is interesting to note that there is no yellow line. I am inclined to think that when it was redesigned by councilor Hannay he may have added the yellow line. I may be wrong about this, but there is an oral tradition of a similar pattern being worn by a branch of the Family - The Hannahs ~who lived in the Falkirk-Castlecary area from the 17th century. This pattern was in use as scarves, shawls, plaids etc., about the 1850's but the description handed down makes no mention of yellow, only black, white and blue. These colours are the Armorial Colours of the Chiefly House, The Hannays of Sorbie - Sable, Argent and Azure.
>
> The Tartan seems to have been in existence in both Galloway and Stirlingshire in the early 1800's but the yellow line may be a recent introduction."

Clan councilor John Hannay said:

"The origin of the A'Hannay Tartan etc. was brought to my notice many years ago by that well-known Gallovidian, the late Sir Herbert Maxwell, of Monreith. He pointed out that the design was a well-known weave in that part of Wigtownshire, the colour being in accordance with that displayed on our Crest, which was the custom in those far off days (the late Sixteens).

Years passed and one day Miss Meta Hannay from Washington, U.S.A., walked into my office here in London. She also produced our Crest in colour stating that somewhere there existed a Hannay Tartan. She toured Wigtownshire but without success in finding trace of this tartan. I told her I had evidence of it, but unless l could trace a branch of the family of Alexander Hannay of Kirkcudbright who are now living abroad, some in Australia, and some of that family also in the U.S.A., it would be a difficult job. I thought nothing more of it and several years elapsed until one day a Miss Anne Hannay on reading an article of mine on tartans in her home in Australia contacted me by letter stating that there existed an A'Hannay Tartan. I immediately replied and received no answer. Then one day months later she also walked into my office, and low and behold she produced the old scarf of A'Hannay Tartan which had been in an old family kist[302] belonging to Commander Alexander Hannay of Kirkcudbright 1788-1848.

As she was returning home to Australia via U.S.A. in two days I had to get busy, obtain wool of a similar colour (not an easy task) set it up on my hand loom in scarf form, thus was reborn the A'Hannay, Hannah, Hanna tartan.

Older Members of Family remember it being stocked by a Newton Stewart tailor in middle 1800's.

A Hannah Tartan was worn during the middle 19th century in Stirlingshire around Falkirk and Stirling. It was black and white with blue and described by Mrs. Agnes Aitken Hannah née Taylor (1864-1944) as being used for scarves and shawls. Bannockburn, south of Stirling, was the centre of the tartan weaving industry."

There are four versions of the Hannay tartan:

---

[302] clothes chest.

## 1.1. The Modern Tartan

The black, white, blue and yellow sett now adopted by the Clan Hannay Society was recorded in the Lyon Court Books (LCB 54) on December 19, 1984. Its Scottish Tartans Authority (STA) reference number is 1255. It is shown in Figure 110, and a colour version can be seen on the back cover of this book.

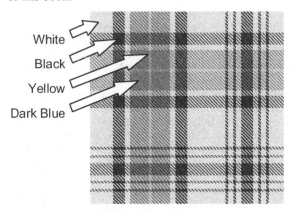

**Figure 110: The Modern Hannay Tartan**

## 1.2. The Old ("Hanna Bible") Tartan

Black and white with a blue line. A scarf of this sett was in the possession of the family of Alex Hannah, first secretary of the Clan Hannay Society. This may be the same as Scottish Tartans Authority (STA) reference 621, which was derived from a piece of tartan fabric discovered in a Hanna family Bible in America in the 19th century:

## 1.3. The Hannah of Leith Tartan

This tartan is the same as the sett in the Clan Hannay Society Tartan, but in old colours, brown for black, grey for white and faded blue and yellow. It is listed in the Scottish Registry of Tartans as Scottish Tartans Authority (STA) reference number 5144.

## 1.4. The Red Hannah Tartan

The Leith branch of the family also possess a piece of tartan which, whilst bearing the basic Hannah colours, includes red and is of a different sett from the other tartans. It seems to be of a modern tartan, but although similar to the Modern Clan Tartan, this Red Hannah does not have a narrow white stripe between the blue and black and the nearby white stripe is narrowed; and the red line is centred on the black. This tartan resembles the Hanna of Stirlingshire Tartan (Scottish Tartans Authority reference 5150):

The colours of the Hannay/Hannah Tartans are based on the heraldic colours of the Hannay Coat of Arms. *Argent* (white) field, 3 bucks' heads couped *azure* (blue) collared *or* (yellow) belled *gules* (red) and *sable* (black) for the crest, a cross-crosslet and crescent.

The original tartan (No. 1 above) was probably based on the Hannay of Sorbie Arms—white for the silver shield, blue for the bucks' heads, and black for the crest—and when rediscovered by councilor John Hannay, he redesigned the tartan and added the yellow line.

Of the two tartans used by the Leith Hannahs, No. 3 above was made specially for the family in the 1960s by A. & J. Scott, Kilt Makers, Aberdeen, and the colours adopted followed the Modern Clan Tartan (No. 2) sett but were 'Old and Faded Dyes'. No. 4 probably dates from about the 1880's and was part of a scarf or dress belonging to one of the Stirlingshire Hannahs. In a letter dated May 18, 1961, from Sir Thomas Innes of Learney, the Lord Lyon King of Arms, to Alexander Hannah, Sir Thomas suggested the 'white' may have been grey or that the clan tartan originally may have been red for white.

As the Hannay/Hannah Tartan (No. 2) is a restricted tartan, being made and worn by the family and is not commercialized, it is rarely found in the popular lists of tartans.

It is a tradition in the Kelso branch of the family and also of the Hannas of Newry, both cadet branches of the Kirkdale family, that the Stewart tartan—the tartan of the Stewarts of Garlies, Earls of Galloway—can be worn as a right granted through their friendship and loyalty.

However, relations were not always quite so cordial with the Galloways. Stewart Francis relates this undated incident whose source is unknown:

> It seems that the Earl of Galloway took advantage of the males at Sorbie being absent. The Earl of Galloway took Sorbie Tower by assault and with his followers set it on fire. When they were trying to take Mrs. Hannay out of one of the rooms, she clung to one of the bedsteads so much so that one of the Earl's followers cut off her hand with his sword and took her out of the Tower. Somehow, the bed was preserved and it was long kept in Whithorn with the mark of the bloody hand on it. A nice tale.

The official Modern Hannay tartan fabric is available for purchase (by members of the Clan Hannay Society) from the Clan Hannay Keeper of the Tartan. For more information, visit clanhannay.org.

409

## 2. Coat of Arms

The heraldry of the Clan is of considerable interest. Heraldry evolved in the first half of the 12th century, and by the 13th century it had become a scientific, hereditary system of identification.

In those early days, few could read or write, and heraldry supplied the people with an easy means of identifying their kings and chiefs.

The knights wore boldly coloured devices on their shields to identify them in tournament and battle.

**Figure 111: Arms of Hannay (or A'Hannay) of Sorbie**

**Note** that coats of arms are generally specific to heads of families, e.g. the arms of Hannay of Sorbie (Figure 111) technically can be worn only by the chief of the clan. Crests (described further below), on the other hand, can be used by any member of the clan. Furthermore, coats of arms belonging to an entity – for example, the Clan Hannay Society, – can be worn by any of its members (see Figure 112).

410

**Figure 112: Arms and Motto of the Clan Hannay Society**

A coat of arms is the general term applied to the whole armorial device and is technically called an *achievement*.

This consists of the following main parts:

1. **The Arms:** the shield and the *devices* or *charges* (badges and symbols) on it.

> **Hannay of Sorbie**: *Argent* three bucks' heads couped *azure*, collared *or*, with a bell pendent *gules*.

2. **The Helmet:** there are special types for royalty, peers, knights and baronets, feudal barons, esquires, gentlemen.

> **Hannay of Sorbie**: No helmet, aside from that above the arms of the Hannay baronets of Mochrum (descended from the Sorbie line, but dormant since the 18th century).

3. **The Mantling:** originally the cloth hanging down from the helmet. Its useful purpose was to insulate the Knight from the heat of the sun on his armour. The Mantling was of the principal colours of the Family.

> **Hannay of Sorbie**: *Argent* (silver) and *azure* (blue).

411

4. **The Wreath:** A skein of silk covers the join between the Crest and the Mantling and consists of six alternative twists of the livery of the family.

> **Hannay of Sorbie**: *Argent* (silver) and *azure* (blue).

5. **The Crest:** it is derived from the plume and the reinforcing ridge of the helmet. The Ridging was cut into shapes.

> **Hannay of Sorbie**: A cross crosslet *fitched* (pointed) arising out of a crescent, *sable* (black)

6. **The Motto:** originated on the standard and the seal.

> **Hannay of Sorbie**: *Per Ardua ad Alta* (Through Difficulties to the Highest Places).

7. **Supporters:** only granted to peers, knights grand cross, heirs, male and female of the minor barons of Scotland and chiefs of old families and clans.

> **Hannay of Sorbie**: None, however, the supporters for the arms of the Hannay baronets of Mochrum are two roebucks *proper* (natural colours).

Various branches of the Hannays have, during the centuries, registered arms. They mainly derive from those of the chief—A'hannay or Hannay of Sorbie—and we find their arms in the heraldic registers of Scotland, England, and Ireland.

## 3.   The Hannay Crest

The Hannay crest (see Figure 3) is a cross crosslet arising out of a crescent sable. Stewart Francis, in the 3rd and earlier editions of the book, believed this implied that a Hannay was engaged in or had been on a crusade to the Holy Land. It was thought that this crusade must have been the third one, in 1189-1192, and there is a tradition that a Hannay was at Acre with Richard *Coeur de Lion* and was knighted there.

Alexander Nisbet, in his 1722 book *A System of Heraldry,* gives the Motto and Crest a Crusader origin. The 1745 *Book of Galloway* by James Douglas states:

"A family which has dealt many blows in time of war from Flodden Field[303] to the Gates of Rhodes[304], and for some such service bore heraldic device of a crescent and a fitched cross."

During the Crusades for the recovery of the Holy Land, the troops of the various nations that joined in the Crusade displayed crosses on their banners and arms; every soldier bore a cross upon his dress. This was composed of two pieces of riband of equal length, crossing each other at right angles. The French Knights adopted the cross flory, which was a cross with their National Emblem, the *Fleur-de-Lis*, attached to the ends. The Crusaders from the Papal Dominions adopted the cross-crosslet.

In Galloway there is a tradition of 14 Knights fighting in the Holy Land, and it is true that, in addition to the Hannays, other Galloway families have a Crusader origin for their arms. The MacCairills, or, as they are now known, the McKerlies, who held the lands of Cruggleton, close to Sorbie, have a tradition that one of their Chiefs, along with other Galloway Knights, fought against the Infidel. He was made a Knight of the Imperial Constantinian Order of St. George and his descendants bear as the family crest a cross-crosslet, the sun and the motto of the order, *In Hoc Signo Vinces*.

E. Marianne H. McKerlie states in her 1916 book, *Pilgrim Spots of Galloway*, that the Crusade in question was the 4th Crusade (1201-1203) which never reached the Holy Land, winning, however, victories under the Doge of Venice, Dandalo, and resulting in reinstating the Emperor Isaac Angelus[305] on the throne of Constantinople with his son Alexis as Joint-Emperor. The McCullochs of Myrton nonetheless claim that one of their number fought in the 1st Crusade under Godfrey de Bouillon, who was King of Jerusalem in 1099.

If a Hannay participated in the Crusades, it would be an unusual distinction. Few Scottish knights took part in the Crusades. Perhaps the reason was the greater distance or the turbulent state of their own country. It does, however, point to the standing and security of the early Hannays, if they were able to dispatch one of their number on one of those long and unprofitable jaunts. In 1254, a Corps of Scots Guards

---

[303] The **Battle of Flodden Field**, between the Scots and the English, was fought in Northumberland in 1513.

[304] The citadel of **Rhodes** in Greece was a stronghold of the Order of the Knights of St. John during the Middle Ages.

[305] 1156-1204

was in attendance on Louis IX in the crusade in Egypt and Palestine[306]; no doubt the men of Galloway were represented.

Scots certainly took part in the Eighth or Ninth Crusade(1270-1272). In the reign of King Alexander III in Scotland, Ottoban de Frieschi, the Papal Legate in England of Pope Clement IV, tried to demand that the Scots should pay a tenth of their benefices to Henry III of England as aid for an approaching Crusade. This Alexander and the Scots clergy refused to do, but stated that they would send forth, at their own cost, a number of armed men to go with the Christian Army against the Turks. Alexander, with much wisdom, maintained that Scotland would not send money which might be stolen or wasted, but instead would send his own men to help the Pope. The 1577 book *Hollinshed's Chronicles of England, Scotland, and Ireland* states that Alexander despatched 1,000 men to St. Louis of France, under the command of the Earls of Carrick and Athole, John Steward, Alexander Cummin, Robert Keith, George Durward, John Quincy and William Gordon. They sailed with Louis to Tunis, where many died by sword and fever. Prince Edward of England, brother-in-law of Alexander III, in 1271 went on to Acre and no doubt many of the Scots accompanied him to the Holy Land.

As we have already seen, the Crusaders of the Papal Dominions bore the cross-crosslet and, as Alexander's force was sent to aid the Pope, they no doubt wore the cross-crosslet on their shields. The commander of the expedition, the Earl of Carrick, bore the cross-crosslet fitched on his coat of arms.

The presence of the crescent, under the cross-crosslet in the A'hanna Crest, was once thought to represent symbolically the triumph of Christian arms over the Infidel, or, possibly, some personal victory over a Saracen in battle. Most traditions are based on fact, but not always correct in detail. More recent research, particularly by Jett Hanna[307], has found strong circumstantial evidence that the early crescent motif is not related to the Middle East at all. It seems to have first appeared as an element in Islamic art only after the Crusades were long over. Before that, however, a crescent was being used in heraldry as a mark of cadency[308]. Following this line of thought, the crescent may have originally been used to differentiate the arms of a particular

---

[306] The 7th Crusade (1248-1254).

[307] Clan Hannay Society member and adjunct professor of law at the University of Texas at Austin. See his article *Are The Middle Eastern and Europeans Hannas Related?*, ClanHannay.org, June 3, 2017.

[308] an indicator of the junior status of a particular branch of a family. This is used to differentiate its coats of arms from that of the main or senior branch of the family.

Hannay who was not the eldest son, and then at some point became part of the family crest.

## 4. The Hannays and the Royal Air Force Motto

Several family members have served in the Royal Flying Corps or the Royal Air Force. The question of the RAF motto, *Per Ardua ad Astra* *("Through Adversity to the Stars")*, having been corrupted from that of our family, *Per Ardua ad Alta ("Through Adversity to the Heights")*, has been considered a serious possibility. The RAF adopted the motto in 1913, so it would appear that the earliest Hannay officers in the Royal Flying Corps—Lt. Col. George Daniel Hannay[309], who served from 1915 and Major William Andrew Hannay, who joined in 1916— had nothing to do with it. The RAF explanation, which they sent to the author Stewart Francis, is here reprinted for interest.

"Colonel Frederick Sykes, the first commanding officer of the Royal Flying Corps, asked his officers to suggest a motto for this newly formed flying service, which would foster esprit de corps. Soon afterwards, two subalterns, while walking from the officer's mess to Cody's shed on Laffan's plain at Farnborough were discussing the problem of a suitable motto, and one (J. S. Yule) suggested the Virgilian *Sic igitur ad astra* which, merely suggesting a journey to the stars, was rejected; then he proposed *Per ardua ad Astra*; this he interpreted as "Through struggles to the Stars" and it seemed eminently suitable. Colonel Sykes submitted it to the War Office and it was approved.

Where did it come from? At the time there was a very popular novel [*The People of the Mist*, 1893] in the Mess at Aldershot by Sir Rider Haggard and in the first chapter Yule had read, 'to his right were two stately gates of iron fantastically wrought, supported by stone pillars on whose summit stood griffins of black marble embracing coat of arms, and banners inscribed with the device *Per ardua ad astra*'.

But what of its origin? Did Sir Rider Haggard coin the words himself, or see them in some obscure book? Was it a coincidence that the motto had been that of the Irish family of Mulvany for hundreds of years?"

There is, however, no evidence that the Mulvany family ever had the motto *Per ardua ad Astra*, so why it is stated here is a mystery. Furthermore, there were several similar mottos in use at that time, any of which may have influenced the choice of motto, consciously or subconsciously. These include those of families such as MacIntyre ("Per Ardua"), O'Hearn ("Per Ardua Surgo")

---

[309] 1888-1941

and, of course, as noted in Chapter I: Origins of the Family: 9th to 14th Century, Vipont/Veterponte ("Per Aspera Ad Alta"), as well as those of schools, e.g. Colfe's School in Greenwich ("Ad Astra Per Aspera") and Dr. Challoner's Grammar School in Amersham (also "Ad Astra Per Aspera").

For further speculation on the origin of the RAF motto, see *Per Ardua Ad Astra*, Jack Dixon, New English Review, January 2012.

## 5. Historical References to Hannay Arms

There are a number of references to the Coats of Arms of the Hannays in R.R. Stodart's work *Scottish Arms of 1881*. He quotes from the following sources:

### 5.1. Workman's Manuscript

This is an illuminated heraldic manuscript completed about 1565-6 by an unknown hand. It became the property of James Workman, a herald painter, whose name, with the date 1623, it bears.

**Figure 113: Sample Page from Workman Manuscript**

416

It consists of two parts: the arms of foreign sovereigns and the Scottish monarch and the peers; also, seven hundred and forty-one shields of minor barons and gentlemen.

Three different Hannay Arms are given:

1) Hannay: Argent, a cross-crosslet fitched sable, issuing from a crescent gules between three stags' heads *cabossed* (cut off behind the ears).

2) Ahannay of Sorbie: Argent, three goats (more likely·bucks) erased sable, collared argent, *campaned* (belled) azure.

3) Hannay: *Argent*, three stags' heads *couped azure.*

To which branches the first and third coats belong is not known, but they are similar to Sorbie in the charges and may well belong to the old, but now extinct, branch of Ahanna of Capenoch, who received a grant of their lands in 1457 from King James II. Dougal Ahanna married Elizabeth Carlyle, a daughter of Sir John Carlyle the first Lord Carlyle, who was active in repelling the invasion of the banished Douglases in 1455. It was no doubt for the support that Dougal Hanna gave to his father-in-law that James II rewarded him with the grant of the lands of Capenoch and Culbrae, near Wigtown in 1457. An interesting side-light is that Elizabeth's ancestor, William Carlyle, married the Lady Margaret Bruce, daughter of the King Robert the Bruce, thus bringing the blood of the Bruces into the line of the Ahannas of Capenoch. Another possibility might be the Ahannas of Knockglass; while the Coat of Arms No. 3 is very similar to the arms of Hannay of Kirkdale.

## 5.2. The Manuscript of Sir James Balfour

The manuscript of Sir James Balfour, 1st Baronet, who was Lord Lyon from 1630-54, describes a coat of arms which is quite different from any of the Sorbie arms given in the Workman's Manuscript, or by later authorities. This coat of arms, with martens as charges instead of bucks, is a mystery. These arms date about 1450:

> **Hannay of Sorbie:** *Or*, a *saltire* between four Martens' heads *couped sable.*

## 5.3. Lindsay of the Mount Roll, 1542

Sir David Lindsay (c. 1490-c. 1555) held the post of Lord Lyon, the highest heraldic office in Scotland. He produced a work in 1542 illustrating 400 coats of arms, known today as *Lindsay of the Mount Roll*. These included:

**A'Hannay:** *Argent*, 3 bucks *azure*.

**Figure 114: A'Hannay of Sorbie (Sir David Lindsay, 1542)**


## 5.4.  Pont's Manuscript, 1624

James Pont's *An Alphabet of Arms of the Nobility and Gentry of Scotland* (1624) mentions the following arms for the family.

> **Hannay of Sorbie**: *Argent*, 3 bucks' heads, *azure*, collared *or* belled *gules*.

## 6.  *Arms of Various Hannays*

The arms of certain historical Hannays, as wells as certain groups of Hannays from particular regions, show different variations, as listed below.

### 6.1.  Sir Patrick Hannay

Patrick Hannay—Soldier, Poet and courtier, as described in Chapter XIX: The Hannay Poets—was the grandson or great-nephew of Donald Ahanna of Sorbie and was born in the latter half of the 16th century. He fought for Elizabeth, the Winter Queen of Bohemia, the high-spirited daughter of James VI of Scotland and the mother of Prince Rupert of the Rhine, Charles I's great cavalry leader.

He was a poet of some distinction and a great favourite of Anne of Denmark, the consort of James VI. One of his poems was dedicated to

418

her. His works were published in 1622 and contain an engraving of him by Crispijn de Passe (1554-1637), which depicts his arms and crest (see Figure 115).

**Figure 115: Arms and Crest of Patrick Hannay**

Arms are shown as Argent, 3 bucks couped azure, with a *mullet* (star) in the collar point for his difference; being possibly the third son of Donald Ahanna of Sorbie.

His crest is shown as a cross-crosslet fitched, issuing from a crescent, sable.

The engraving also includes the motto "Per Ardua ad Alta".

## 6.2.  Sir Robert Ahanna, 1st Bt of Mochrum (d. 1658)

Robert Ahanna (Hannay) was a son of Alexander Ahanna (Hannay) of Sorbie. He was popular with James VI, and in 1628 he was described as "one of the squires of our body", and granted the lands of Glencapp for sixty-one years for £30 Irish. In 1629, Charles I created him a Baronet of Nova Scotia, with a grant of the Dunbar Lands of Mochrum Park, Wigtownshire. From then on, he served in Ireland, where he was also granted lands in Longford Plantation of 500 acres. During the Civil War, he was Quartermaster-General to Sir Charles Coote.

His wife's death in 1662 is recorded in the Ulster Herald Records, and her arms are given as:

> lst and 4th quarter argent, three bucks' heads erased azure, horned or, and 2nd and 3rd quarters three cross-crosslets fitched issuing from as many crescents sable with the motto: "Per Ardua ad Alta".

These arms were no doubt registered by Sir Robert as a younger son of Sorbie, as, of course, the bucks and cross-crosslets fitched are the Family Charges.

419

The funeral entries contain two references to Hannay:

> (blank) Hannay departed this life the 8th day of January 1657 and
> was buried the 25th day of the same month.

Attached to this entry is a sketch of arms, Hannay impaling Stewart,
the Hannay blazon being Argent, three cross-crosslets fitched issuing
out of three crescents, thereon and escutcheon charged with the Royal
Arms of the Kingdom of Scotland.

### 6.3.   Sir Robert Hannay, 2nd Bt of Mochrum (d. 1689)

There are no particulars recorded as to death and burial, but the arms
are sketched thus:

> Quarterly, 1st and 4th, three cross-crosslets fitched issuing out of
> three crescents, 2nd and 3rd, three roebucks' heads, couped, thereon
> an escutcheon charged with the Royal Arms of the Kingdom of
> Scotland.

The Royal Arms of Scotland thus borne were used by certain Scottish
Baronets as an Addition of Honour.

### 6.4.   Samuel Hannay, 3rd Bt of Mochrum (d. 1790)

Sir Samuel was the eldest son of William Hannay of Kirkdale, and in
1783 served the male heir to Sir Robert Hanna, 2nd Baronet of
Mochrum.

He registered arms (See Figure 116) in 1784:

> *Argent* three bucks' heads *couped azure, collared or* with bells
> thereto *pendant gules.*

> Crest:  cross-crosslet *fitched* out of crescent *sable.*

> Motto: Per Ardua ad Alta.

> Supporters: 2 roebucks *proper.*

His descendants, the Rainsford-Hannays of Kirkdale, bear the same
arms without supporters. The carved stone bearing the arms of Hannay
of Sorbie, which was originally over the doorway of Sorbie Tower, is
now incorporated in Kirkdale House.

420

**Figure 116 - Coat of Arms of Sir Samuel Hannay**

## 6.5. Hannay of Kingsmuir - Fifeshire

The House of Kingsmuir descended from Robert Hannay(d. 1725), who married Margaret Livingstone of Baldamy[310], the widow of Colonel William Borthwick of Dechmont, and was first possessed of Kingsmuir about 1700. Their coat of arms is:

*Argent* 3 bucks *couped azure collared or.*

Crest: *Cross-crosslet fitched* out of a crescent *sable.*

Motto: *Cresco et Spero* ("I increase and I hope").

Captain William Hannay of Kingsmuir bore these arms as he states in his letter to Lady Ann Hannay. A grant is extant bearing the words "Defender of Sorbie" in addition to the motto.

---

[310] Probably Balhary or Balbinny.

## 6.6. The Hannas of Ulster

The arms derive from Sorbie, and the Irish Records quote the following crests:

> **Newry, Ireland**: Hands clasping couped at the wrist *sable*.

> **Dublin**: A lion *rampant, couped*, his *dexter* paw resting on a cross-crosslet *fitched*.

> **Newry**: A scallop shell.

There are a few different Irish mottoes:

> **Bellshoughton Branch**: *Per Ardua in Coelum* ("Through Hardship into Heaven")

> **Newry Branch**: *Ad Alta Virtute* ("To the Heights of Valour")

There is an interesting sketch representing the arms of **Hanna of Newry** from the papers of the late councilor John Hannay:

> *Azure* 3 bucks *erased* (heads cut off with a jagged edge) *or*.

> Crest: a lion *rampant couped proper*, *langued* (tongued) and *armed* (claws) *gules*, the *dexter* (right) paw holding a *cross-crosslet*.

> Motto: *Ad Alta Virtute*. ("To the Heights of Valour")

Stewart Francis mentions an old gravestone in County Clare which bears the Hanna Arms, but unfortunately, at present, its exact location is not known. As noted earlier, more research is required on the Irish Branches, and additional information on variations of Hannay arms will hopefully emerge in future editions.

## 7. *Other Crests*

### 7.1. Hanna (Australia)

From *Fairbairn's Book of Crests of the Families of Great Britain and Ireland*, 1905:

> **Crest:** A wolf's head *erased sable*.

This crest was used by Honourable Patrick Hanna, M.P., of Latrobe House, Melbourne, Australia, about 1863.

### 7.2. Hannay of England

From *Fairbairn's Book of Crests of the Families of Great Britain and Ireland*, 1905:

**Crest** -A stag's head *proper collared or*, between the satires a cross *pattée* (with flared arms) *gules*.

This shows somewhat similar charges to Sorbie: the stag and a cross, although not the cross-crosslet fitched.

## 8. Recent Arms

### 8.1. Scotland

#### 8.1.1. Robert Hannay, Merchant, Glasgow

Robert Hannay, circa 1760, carried as his arms, 3 bucks *couped*, *collared* and *belled*, which may be seen at Kelton[311] (no record in Lyon register).

#### 8.1.2. Hugh Hanna, Esquire, Paisley

Hugh was Clerk of the Kitchen to George III; he died in 1831. Arms and Crest as Hannay of Sorbie (Burkes General Armoury, 1884). (No record in Lyon Register - possibly unofficial use.)

#### 8.1.3. Peter Davies Hannay, 1863-1954

Peter Davies Hannay's arms were as Sorbie a *bordure* (band around the edge of the shield) *engrailed* (with circular arcs whose points face inward) quarter *gules* and *azure* for a cadet.

#### 8.1.4. Hannah of Leith

**Figure 117: Arms of Alexander Hannah of Leith**

---

[311] presumably a reference to the records of the parish of Kelton in Kirkudbrightshire.

The Coat of Arms of Hannah of Leith (see Figure 117) is as follows:

**Shield**: *Argent* 3 bucks' heads *couped azure collared or* with a bell *pendant gules*. On a *chief* (top horizontal band) of the last (*gules*) a tower of the first (*argent*) *masoned* (in a brick pattern) *sable* between two *lymphads* (galleys) *argent*.

**Liveries**: *Argent* and *Azure*.

**Crest**: A cross-crosslet *issuant* (depicting only the upper half) an open boat *sable*.

**Motto**: *Per Laborem ad Alta* (Through Suffering to the Heights).

**Pennon**: liveries *argent* and *azure* with arms in the *hoist* (half nearest the flagpole) bearing motto in the *fly* (half farthest from the flagpole) in two lines *counterchanged* (with colours reversed against the field).

## 8.2. Ireland

Sydney Hannah, M.B.E., gold and silversmith of 18 Arthur Street, Belfast, formerly wing-commander, commanding Northern Ireland Wing of the Air Training Corps 1939-45 War, and a pilot in the 1914-18 War.

**Crest**: Grant from Ulster King at Arms: A goldsmith's cup bearing the cross-crosslet thereon with insignia of M.B.E. (Military) below.

**Motto**: *Per Ardua ad Alta*. The charges on shield are Irish elks.

## 8.3. England

Rev. John Hannah, D.D., 1792-1867. Methodist Minister and Principal of Didsbury College. His family were settled for many generations in Lincolnshire and are now represented by the family of Canon John M.C. Hannah.

**Arms**: A Crane.

**Crest**: A Crane's head issuing from a ducal coronet.

**Motto**: *Memor et Fidelis* (Mindful and Faithful)

An interesting feature of this coat of arms is the similarity of the crest to that of the Veterponts, who bore a swan's head between two wings *proper* out of a ducal coronet, *or*.

## 9. The Hannay Plant Badge

As with other clans there is a plant badge.

Leaves or flowers have from time immemorial been the badge of various nations, e.g. the Thistle of Scotland, the Shamrock of Ireland and the Rose of England.

The use of plant badges has been common in Scotland, particularly amongst the Celtic Clans and Families, probably more in the Highlands than in the Lowlands. But such families as the Homes, the Kennedys, the Bruces, the Johnstons and the Stewarts all had their Plant Badge.

One of the most famous plant badges was the sprig of broom that the Plantagenets wore in their helmets.

It is perhaps unlikely that a man in armour would wear a plant in his helmet when a painted symbol would be a more practical form of identification. The Marquis of Montrose, however, at the battle of Aberdeen in 1642 instructed his men to wear oat stalks in their caps and helmets so that they could be identified from the Covenanting troops.

Some badges have historical origins; some are from heraldry, either the crest or the shield; and others because it was the local plant.

**Figure 118: The Periwinkle, the Hannay Plant Badge**

Not many families have documentation of plant badges before 1822, and it was at George IV's visit to Scotland that year that many of them made their appearance as part of a celebration of Scottish culture. It had been the first time a monarch of the United Kingdom had visited the country since the 17<sup>th</sup> century.

425

The Hannays have primarily regarded their Badge as the cross-crosslet and crescent—the crest of the Chief, the Laird of Sorbie. However, there are a number of sources which support a tradition in the family that the periwinkle is the plant badge of the family.

**Figure 119: Tombstone in Cruggleton Chapel**

It is interesting that the blue periwinkle, or as it is called in Latin *Vinca minor* and the Gaelic *Gille-Fionn*, when in flower, is the blue which is part of the livery colours of Hannay. That they should have a plant badge is likely because of their Celtic origin and the fact that Galloway was an old Celtic province where a form of Gaelic was spoken until the 16<sup>th</sup> Century. Sources which support the periwinkle as the plant badge are as follows:

1.  The heraldic tombstone (see Figure 119) bearing the Arms of Sorbie can be seen in Cruggleton Chapel where periwinkles surround the shield. It is the tombstone of James Hanna of Low Cults and his spouse, who must have been a "Lady of Charity" as the inscription shows:

    "Here lyes the Corps of Helen M'Credie spouse to James Hann, Tenant in Low Cults. She died April 23<sup>rd</sup>, 1796 aged 74 years. She

fed the hungary and clad the Poor and never let the Needy go
Empty from her door."

2.  The Chien-lung Armorial dinner service of Sir Samuel Hannay of
    Kirkdale bears the arms of Sorbie surrounded by periwinkles (see
    illustration in *Sotheby's Chinese Ceramics Sale* 1.6.1966).

3.  The book plate of Johnston Hannay of Torrs bears periwinkles
    around the shield. Johnston was the brother of Sir Samuel Hannay,
    3$^{rd}$ Bart. and 5$^{th}$ son of William Hannay of Kirkdale.

4.  The Hon. Patrick Hanna bought Latrobe House, Melbourne,
    Australia in 1863, and above the main door was a glass panel
    engraved with his arms, the crest of which was a Wolf Hound.
    Surrounding the arms are trailing plants which cannot be easily
    identified as periwinkles as the flowers are much larger but they
    may be a 'memory' of the plant badge.

These sources would help to vindicate the tradition that the periwinkle
is the Plant Badge of the Family.

## 10. The Clan Hannay Society

Without doubt the credit for the founding of the Clan Hannay Society
goes to George Patrick "Pat" Hanna (1888-1973), cartoonist, film star
and producer of Melbourne, Australia (though he was born in New
Zealand to an Irish father and an Australian mother). More can be
found about Pat in Chapter XXI: . It was his enthusiasm and untiring
efforts which made the Hannas, Hannahs and Hannays conscious of
the great tradition of their Family. In October 1959 he met in London
another enthusiast, John Hannay, Deputy Mayor of Chelsea—the first
Convener, and out of this meeting the Society was born.

Pat Hanna then contacted Donald C. Hannah, FRICS (Fellow of the
Royal Institution of Chartered Surveyors), of Edinburgh, and Alex
Hannah, FCII (Fellow of the Chartered Insurance Institute), of
Inverness, and exploratory meetings were held at the former's home in
Edinburgh on March 8, 1960, and at Sorbie Tower on June 28 when it
was decided to form the Hannay, Hanna, Hannah Clan Society, later
shortened to Clan Hannay Society, with the prime object of acquiring
the ancestral home of the Family, Sorbie Tower.

As a result of these meetings a world-wide council was formed with
John Hannay as Convener, Alex Hannah as Secretary and Donald C.
Hannah as Treasurer.

The first Council included Major R.W. Rainsford-Hannay of Kirkdale;
Pat Hanna, Melbourne; Mrs. M Playfair-Hannay, M.B.E., of
Kingsmuir; Sir Halter Fergusson Hannay, London; Judge G.B. Hanna,

Q.C., Belfast; Alex Hannah, Shipbroker, Leith; Dennis Hanna, Architect, Belfast; Rev. James A.M. Hanna, Ohio; John S. Hanna, Q.C., Winnipeg; Major Stewart Francis, Suffolk; Andrew Hannah, Sorbie Village; The Most Rev. Thomas Hannay, Bishop of Argyll and The Isles (Hon. Chaplain), and John Gunn Hannah, Musselburgh (Hon. Piper).

The first General Meeting was held on May 18,1962, at the Commonwealth Club, London, when coloured slides of Sorbie, Wigtown, Edinburgh, and The Tomb of Mary of Castlecary were shown and the history of their association with the Family was given by Alex Hannah. The Society took part in the Garden Party organised by the Council of Scottish Clan Societies at Lauriston Castle, Edinburgh, on September 8, 1962 (see Figure 120). This was one of the highlights of the Society's activities as various family heirlooms were on show such as: Armorial China and Miniatures from Kirkdale, prints from Kingsmuir, the Gustavus Adolphus Medal presented to James Godfrey Hanna for services to the Swedish King, at Lubeck; Sir Samuel Hannay's Token; a collection of Scottish coins illustrating the history of the Hannays from King William the Lion to Queen Anne; maps; coats of arms, etc.

**Figure 120: Hannay tent, Council of Scottish Clan Societies, 1962**

Each year thereafter a gathering has been held in Scotland, often including a talk on a subject related to the objects of interest of the Society. In 1966, for example, Nigel Tranter, a well-known Scottish author and lecturer, addressed the Society on the subject of the Scottish castles of which Sorbie is an example. In 1998, Clan Archaeologist Packard Harrington gave a lecture on his findings regarding the ancient motte that pre-dated the construction of Sorbie Tower. The annual gathering also includes a guided visit to the Sorbie grounds and tower as well as festivities such as a dinner and ceilidh. Some years, the gathering has been expanded to encompass tours to sites related to

428

Hannay history around Galloway as well as a day trip to Belfast to meet with Irish Hannas.

In addition, a yearly newsletter -- with updates on Hanna/h/e/ys from around the world and historical articles on the family and Sorbie Tower reconstruction -- is produced for members of the society.

More information about the Clan Hannay Society, including how to join, can be found online at **clanhannay.org**.

## *11. Sorbie Tower*

The castle of Sorbie (see Figure 126), or as it was called in the Middle Ages "The Place of Sorbie", is situated seven miles south of Wigtown. It is a single keep of four storeys, although currently in a ruinous state. Recent research indicates that the tower house was built in the sixteenth century, probably between 1550 and 1575.

**Figure 121: Sorbie Tower in the 1860s-1870s**

It was occupied until 1748 after which it was neglected (see Figure 121, the tower in probably its most decrepit condition). In its day it was a structure of considerable importance and may have been preceded by an earlier castle, as close by is a small hill which David MacGibbon and Thomas Ross in their 1887 work *The Castellated and Domestic Architecture of Scotland from the Twelfth to the Eighteenth Century*, mention as a "motte or artificial mound". This may be the remains of a wooden Norman castle once owned by the Viponts. The motte predates the tower house by perhaps three hundred years or more. Excavations performed on the motte by the Archaeological Department of Glasgow University in 1983 unearthed pottery dating from 1250.

The castle is "L" shaped and is typical of the period when, due to the marriage of the grim square Scots Tower with the graceful chateau architecture of France, many fine castles were erected. They present a combination of strength, vigour and grace unrivalled in Europe, with pepper-pot turrets, wheel stairs from first-floor level, crow-stepped gable-ends, corbelling and heraldic panels.

This was a tremendous building period in Scots history brought about by the Reformation which was responsible for the distribution of the church lands among the gentry: for example, it was at this time that the Laird of Sorbie acquired the Church and Lands of Kilfillan, and the King, in the fond hope of stabilising a country torn by feud and violence, insisted on the erection on each estate of a fortalice as a refuge for the common people. In practice, however, many a Laird used his tower to oppress his neighbours, and as we see from the Privy Council Records the Hannays, in their dealings with the Murrays of Broughton, were no exception in this respect.

The Tower was protected by a marsh, which in winter became a sheet of water extending from Sorbie Kirk to the Castle. In former times the Tower was not, as now, surrounded by a dense wood. James Douglas, in *The Book of Galloway* (1745), gives the following description, "looking eastward across the lake on the extreme verge, like a lonely sentinel, standing black against the sky on a treeless mound (surrounded by a fosse fed by a burn which issued from the Loch of Longcaster) a stronghold of the Hannays, a family who dealt heavy blows in times of war from Flodden Field to the Gates of Rhodes, and for some such service bore on their helmet the rare heraldic insignia of a Crescent and Fitched Cross."

The close approaches to the castle were covered by five corner turrets and gunloops. The entrance is in a re-entrant angle on the Northeast of the tower and opens on to the foot of the staircase. The door was secured by a drawbar housed in long slots in either jamb.

The ground floor (see Figure 122) is stone vaulted and consists of a kitchen 17' x 13'6" with a fireplace in the gable measuring 17' x 5' on either side of which is a small window, and a recess, possibly for storing salt.

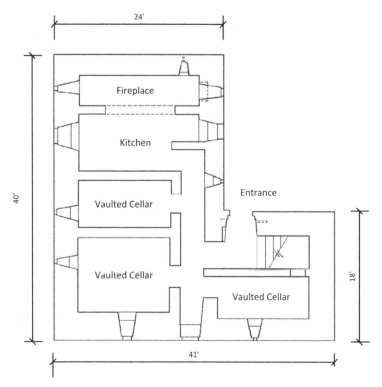

**Figure 122: Ground Plan of Sorbie Tower**

There are also two vaulted cellars in the main part of the building and a further cellar under the scale and platt staircase leading to the Great Hall. In times of trouble or siege, cattle would be driven into these apartments, and the stone vaulting was a precaution against raiders trying to burn out the defenders. One of these was usually the wine cellar and the records show that the Laird of Sorbie did not always pay duty on his wines. The well at Sorbie was likely to the East of the tower, connected to a cistern of sorts under the vaulted cellar of the Northeast wing (where the stairwell is located).

The Great Hall occupies the whole of the first floor (see Figure 123) and measures 27' x 16'6".

The second (see Figure 124) and third levels of the building are missing their actual floors and open to the sky. As such, the exact layout of the rooms is unknown, though the Laird's bedroom was for reasons of warmth probably above the Hall.

431

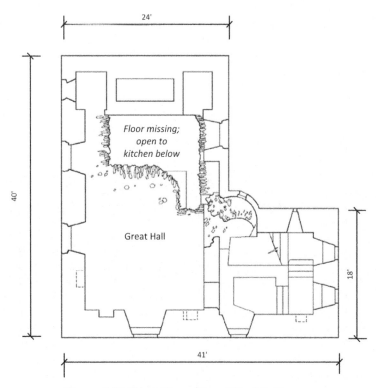

24'

40'

Floor missing;
open to
kitchen below

Great Hall

18'

41'

**Figure 123: First Floor Plan of Sorbie Tower**

The upper floors were approached by a turret stair corbelled out above the doorway in the re-entrant angle. The turret stair was deliberately built narrow so that if the castle was rushed in the night and the main hall reached, the staircase could be easily defended by a good swordsman until help came from the retainers who slept in the upper floor and attics. These stairs were built so that the turn of stairs made it difficult for the attackers to use their right or sword arm. Sometimes the stairway was built to include a trip-step slightly higher than the rest to make a stranger fall and give away his presence.

The external decorative features are a quaintly carved human head on the corbel termination above the door. Above and to the left of the doorway is an empty space which held the Heraldic Panel of the Hannays—Argent, three roebucks' heads couped azure, collared or, with a bell pendant thereof gules. According to *The Book of Galloway*, the motto *Per Ardua ad Alta* was carved above the doorway and on another architrave, the words *Cresco et Spero:* "I grow and I hope."

432

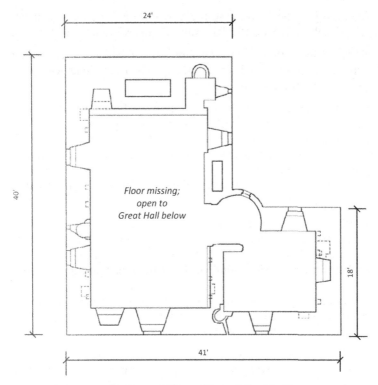

**Figure 124: Second Floor Plan of Sorbie Tower**

There is a local tradition of an underground passage leading from the Tower. Douglas refers to the "Pagan's Hole, a dungeon either bottomless according to general belief, or with an underground exit many miles away". He gives a very imaginative description of the Pagan's Hole. "From the Pagan's Hole, came the groans of prisoners, and above the clanking of doors, the rustling of silks, and the clatter of spoons." These traditions may be based on the right of a Baron to "Pit and Gallows" (royal privilege to inflict capital punishment), which the Hannays would have as tenants *in capite* of the King, i.e., in possession of the land through direct grant of the monarch.

The Tower was probably built by Alexander Ahanna (Hannay) of Sorbie, who succeeded his father, Patrick, after the latter's murder in 1543. At the time of the building of the Tower the Ahannas were at the height of their power. Their lands stretched right across the Machars of Galloway to such an extent that it was known as Machars-Hanna. It passed out of Hannay hands in 1626 and eventually into the possession of the Stewart family. Brigadier-General John Stewart was the last resident, dying there in 1748. It subsequently fell into ruin.

433

The history of the Tower is well covered in I.F. Macleod's pamphlet "The Old Place of Sorbie" (Galloway Gazette, Newton Stewart, 1969).

In November 1938, the structure was recognized as having archaeological merit, and was listed as a scheduled monument under the name "Sorbie, Old Tower of".

The Clan Hannay Society obtained "The Old Place of Sorbie" from Mrs. Jean Cummings in 1965, who generously presented the Tower and the ground surrounding it to the Clan Trust. Stabilization of walls and removal of ivy was performed by the Society over the next decade as initial steps to preserve the structure. In July 1972, the building was listed as a Category A monument, indicating that it was considered to be of national importance.

In 1983, a team from the University of Glasgow excavated the motte lying to the South of the tower. They found evidence that the site had been occupied as far back as the 12th century. The team also uncovered a cobblestone road which runs Northeast from the tower to a network of paths that crisscross the district, as well as the remains of a well and several buildings not far from the tower. Finally, they also noted the remnants of a ditch-and-bank system likely set up to protect the northern approach to the motte.

In 1996, archaeologist Packard Harrington carried out a geophysical survey of the site, finding traces of structures which had once been on top of the motte and in the area around the tower. Excavation uncovered household items from the 14th through 17th century. These collectively indicate that there was a settlement on the site comprising multiple buildings. This settlement either predated the tower or was contemporaneous with it, or both.

In the early 2000s, consolidation work was done on the walls and stair tower, including the addition of steel beams to brace unsupported portions of the structure.

In 2010, Historic Scotland declared the property suitable for restoration. The Clan Hannay Society subsequently commissioned architects to provide a scoping study and a conservation management plan. The latest of these was completed in 2013. The Clan Council decided in 2014 that the ultimate goal for Sorbie Tower should be a full restoration in which the structure could be used for short-term holiday lets, event rentals, community events, cultural re-enactments and school visits.

**Figure 125: The Sorbie Tower Charity**

In 2015, the assets of the Clan Hannay Trust were transferred to a new registered Scottish Charitable Incorporated Organisation, **The Sorbie Tower Charity**, and an international fundraising appeal was announced during a reception at the House of Lords in London. The goal of this ongoing fundraising effort is £2.2 million.

In 2017, new power lines were extended to the site. In 2019, a heated lavatory block, including shower facilities, was constructed on the grounds. Most recently, the Tower gained a temporary roof structure to speed the process of drying out the interior stonework, which has been exposed to the elements for over a century and a half.

> "Restoring Sorbie Tower is one worthwhile way… [to] unite
> Hannays, Hannahs, Hannas and Hanneys across the world."
>
> - *Lord David Hannay of Chiswick, former British*
>   *Ambassador to the United Nations*

The Clan Hannay Society invites members of the global Hannay family to be a part of this historical endeavour.

> "This is your heritage. Please help us to restore Sorbie Tower for
> future generations."
>
> - *Stephen Hanna, Clan Convenor*

More information on contributing to the reconstruction of Sorbie Tower can be found at clanhannay.org.

**Figure 126: Sorbie Tower in 2003**

# Appendix A: Currencies

The Scottish Pound was valued separately from the English Pound Sterling until the Act of Union (1707) merged the currencies of England and Scotland. From its first minting in the 1100s until 1373, the Scottish pound held roughly the same value as the English Pound (From the time of King David I, in the late 1100s, the crown mint actually issued 5% less silver weight than face value, which is taken into account in the graphs below). From 1373 to 1603, its value increasingly devalued in relation to its English equivalent, due to a rise in the cost of minting the Scottish currency and the Scottish government's corresponding reduction of precious metal content in the coinage. From 1603 to 1707, its exchange rate with the Pound Sterling was fixed at 12 to 1. Since 1707, Scottish and English Pounds have been equivalent.

The two following graphs represent the present-day equivalent values of the Scottish Pound from 1250 to 2016.

The *purchasing power* graph indicates the value of purchased goods over time. It reflects both the above-mentioned devaluation as well as the growing inflation rate in order to give an approximate idea of the buying power of the amounts referenced in this book. Note that the forces of inflation are offset more markedly in some date ranges than others by the rate of devaluation of the currency.

The *wages* graph reflects, on average, what people were paid for labour and services. It is difficult to compare historical wages directly, since the economic state of Scotland changed greatly over the decades. Present-day equivalent of wages is more accurately calculated from the per capita gross domestic product (GDP) at the time, rather than from the purchasing power of the money.

This data is interpolated from the following sources: The Scottish Archive Network, Economic History Service, the Bank of England and *MeasuringWorth.com*.

## 1. *Purchasing Power in Scotland*

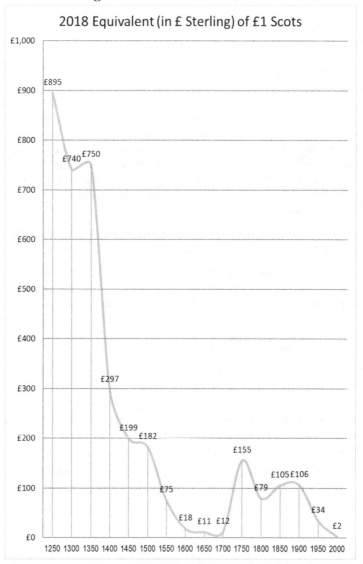

The above shows the average buying power of one Scottish pound over time.

**Example**: £1 in 1750 would be worth approximately £155 in 2018 (find 1750 on the timeline and see where the vertical line extending from it meets the gray line). Note that the relative value of specific categories of goods—e.g., food versus manufactured goods—can vary widely over time, depending on the cost of labor and materials.

438

## 2. *Wages in Scotland*

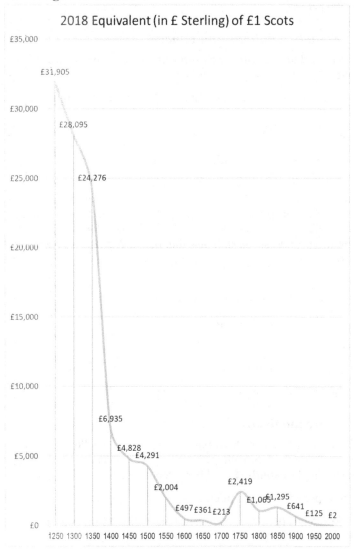

2018 Equivalent (in £ Sterling) of £1 Scots

The above chart follows average wages from 1250 through 2000.

**Example**: To get an idea of the 2018 equivalent of one pound (£) of income in 1800, find where the vertical line extending from the date on the horizontal axis, 1800, crosses the gray line. The result, on the vertical axis, is £1,065. Putting this particular example in context, in the late 18ᵗʰ century, a farm servant's salary was one shilling (1/-) per day or £15/12/- per year[312]. In 2018 currency, this is equivalent to about £26,790 per year.

## 3. *Pounds, Shillings and Pence*

If you are unfamiliar with the British system of currency which existed prior to 1971, it is described as follows:

There were three basic denominations: **Pounds (£)**, **Shillings (s)** and **Pence (d)**

12 **pence** made one **shilling**, or 12d = 1s

20 **shillings** made one **pound**, or 20s = £1

Note that shillings and pence were often written **s/d**; for example, **7/6** meant seven shillings, sixpence. Pounds and shillings were sometimes listed as **£.s**; for example, **8.10** denoted eight pounds, ten shillings. Figures after a second decimal place denoted pence; for example, **2.7.4** meant two pounds, seven shillings, four pence. A dash ("-") represents zero (nought); for example, 10 shillings, 0 pence would be written **10/-**.

Some other denominations were as follows:

A **merk** was 13 **shillings**, 4 **pence** or 13/4

A **crown** was 5 shillings

A **guinea** was 21 **shillings** (equivalent to 1 **pound**, 1 **shilling**)

A **ha'penny** (half penny) was 0.5 pence or ½d

### 3.1. Decimalisation

In February 1971, British currency was altered to follow a decimal format. From then through the present day, the denominations have become simply **Pounds (£)** and **New Pence (p)**:

100 **new pence** made one **pound**.

The New Penny (**p**) was a brand-new coin, worth 2.4 times the existing penny (**d**). The "New" designation has since been dropped, as there are no longer any pre-decimal pence in active circulation.

---

[312] Source: Clan Historian Emeritus Tony Lowe

# Appendix B: Timelines

## 1. *6000 BC – 1000 AD*

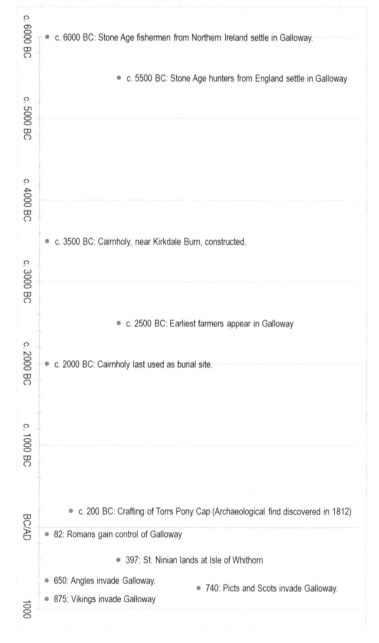

c. 6000 BC | c. 5000 BC | c. 4000 BC | c. 3000 BC | c. 2000 BC | c. 1000 BC | BC/AD | 1000

- c. 6000 BC: Stone Age fishermen from Northern Ireland settle in Galloway.

- c. 5500 BC: Stone Age hunters from England settle in Galloway

- c. 3500 BC: Cairnholy, near Kirkdale Burn, constructed.

- c. 2500 BC: Earliest farmers appear in Galloway

- c. 2000 BC: Cairnholy last used as burial site.

- c. 200 BC: Crafting of Torrs Pony Cap (Archaeological find discovered in 1812)
- 82: Romans gain control of Galloway

- 397: St. Ninian lands at Isle of Whithorn

- 650: Angles invade Galloway.
- 740: Picts and Scots invade Galloway.
- 875: Vikings invade Galloway

## 2. 1000 – 1400

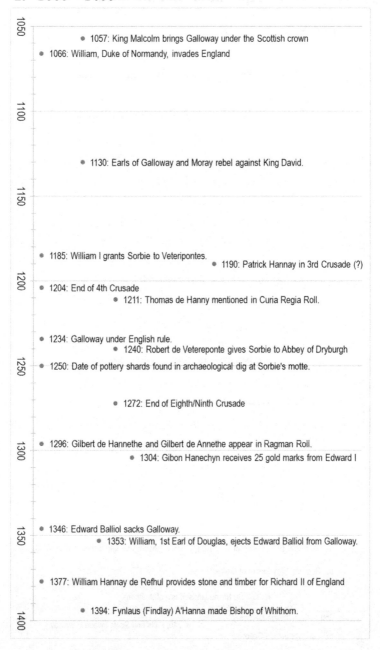

- 1050
- 1057: King Malcolm brings Galloway under the Scottish crown
- 1066: William, Duke of Normandy, invades England
- 1100
- 1130: Earls of Galloway and Moray rebel against King David.
- 1150
- 1185: William I grants Sorbie to Veteripontes.
- 1190: Patrick Hannay in 3rd Crusade (?)
- 1200
- 1204: End of 4th Crusade
- 1211: Thomas de Hanny mentioned in Curia Regia Roll.
- 1234: Galloway under English rule.
- 1240: Robert de Vetereponte gives Sorbie to Abbey of Dryburgh
- 1250: Date of pottery shards found in archaeological dig at Sorbie's motte.
- 1272: End of Eighth/Ninth Crusade
- 1296: Gilbert de Hannethe and Gilbert de Annethe appear in Ragman Roll.
- 1300
- 1304: Gibon Hanechyn receives 25 gold marks from Edward I
- 1346: Edward Balliol sacks Galloway.
- 1350
- 1353: William, 1st Earl of Douglas, ejects Edward Balliol from Galloway.
- 1377: William Hannay de Refhul provides stone and timber for Richard II of England
- 1394: Fynlaus (Findlay) A'Hanna made Bishop of Whithorn.
- 1400

## 3. 1400 – 1500

- 1412: Archibald, 4th Earl of Douglas, forges an alliance with the French nobility.

- 1416: Andrew Hannay of the Earl of Wigton's Royal Archers is in France.

- 1424: John Hannay first appears as shipmaster to King James of Scotland.

- 1438: John Hannay, shipmaster, sails the King's Barge to La Rochelle.

- 1448: Gilbert Hannay, Wigtown official, mentioned in assize.

- 1453: End of Hundred Years' War.

- 1457: Dougall Hannay receives Capenoch and Culbrae from James II.
- 1459: First mention of Ethe Hannay of Sorbie.

- 1463: Nicholas Hannay appears as a judge in Edinburgh

- 1466: Gilbert Hannay becomes chaplain to the Parliament of Scotland.

- 1477: John Hannay of Glasgow appears as a witness in a burgh court case.

- 1480: Thomas Hannay granted property in Perth.

- 1490: Dougal Hannay appointed Royal Falconer.

- 1498: Mariote Hannay, daughter of Odo, sells land North of Wigtown.

443

1500

1503: Wardship of Sorby granted to Alexander Hannay.

1510

1513: Donald Hannay fights in battle of Flodden Field.

1520

1522: John Hannay of Sorbie signs the Charter of Monuments in Glasgow Diocese.

1527: Ninian Hannay is Prior of Whithorn

1529: James Hannay is Master Gunner to the King.

1530

1532: Alexander Hannay acquires land at Kirkdale

1535: Thomas Hannay is Tailor to the King in Edinburgh.

1540

1543: Patrick Hannay of Sorbie murdered.

1547: John Hannay is keeper of the artillery at Edinburgh Castle

1550: Earliest estimated date of construction of Sorbie Tower

1550

1554: William Hannay purchases land expanding Kirkdale property.

1560

1561: Mary Queen of Scots arrives in Leith from France

1566: John Hannay is Royal Baker to Mary Queen of Scots

1570

1575: Latest estimated date of construction of Sorbie Tower

1580

1589: John Hannay becomes Member of Parliament for Wigtown

1590

1595: Birth of James Hannay, later to become Dean of St. Giles in Edinburgh.

1600

1600

* 1603: Union of the Scottish and English crowns under James VI/I

1610

* 1618: Start of the Thirty Years' War

1620

* 1623: James Hannay appointed Dean of Edinburgh
  * 1625: Sir Patrick Hannay commended by King Charles I.

1630

* 1630: Robert Hannay created first Baronet of Mochrum

  * 1635: James Hannay becomes Dean of St. Giles, Edinburgh

1640

* 1640: John Hannay becomes last Hannay owner of Sorbie

1650

  * 1650: George Hannay taken prisoner, transported to Barbados

* 1658: Death of Robert Hannay, 1st Baronet Mochrum

1660

  * 1661: Death of James Hannay, Dean of Edinburgh

* 1667: Robert Hannay succeeds his father as 2nd Baronet of Mochrum

1670

  * 1672: George Hannay is Deputy Provost Marshal of the Barbados

* 1677: Sale of Sorbie lands to Alexander, Earl of Galloway

1680

  * 1681: Test Act declares supremacy of the king in civil and church matters
* 1684: The "Killing Times" - slaughter of dissidents across Galloway.

1690

  * 1690: Start of lengthy economic depression in Galloway from the religious wars.

* 1695: James Hannay is made Provost Marshal of Barbados.

1700

## 6. *1700 – 1850*

1700

1707: Union of Scotland & England. Southern trade impoverishes Galloway.

1710

• 1714: Death of Queen Anne of Great Britain

1720

• 1722: Alexander Nisbet publishes A System of Heraldry

1730

• 1736: Death of Ann Hannay of Kingsmuir

1740

• 1743: Death of William Hannay of Kingsmuir

1750

• 1750: Manufacturing and agricultural boom begins in Galloway.

1760

• 1763: End of Seven Years' War

1770

• 1776: American Declaration of Independence

1780

• 1783: Samuel Hannay served heir to Mochrum title as 3rd Baronet

1790

• 1790: Samuel Hannay the younger becomes 4th Baronet.

1800

• 1800: Ramsay Hannay purchases property of Carsluith

1810

• 1812: Start of British-American War (ends 1815)

1820

1830

• 1827: Birth of James Hannay, future British Consul in Barcelona

• 1836: Merchant firm of Hannay and Coltart founded in Antigua

1840

• 1841: Death of Samuel Hannay, 4th Baronet Mochrum

1850

# 7. *1850 – 2018*

1850
1860
1870
1880
1890
1900
1910
1920
1930
1940
1950
1960
1970
1980
1990
2000
2010
2020

- 1851: Peak of population in Galloway; subsequent decline lasts to present day.

- 1865: Birth of James Owen Hannay (the author George A. Birmingham)

- 1875: First modern reprint of Patrick Hannay's 1622 collection of poetry

- 1888: James Hannay editor of the St. John (New Brunswick) Gazette
- 1892: Death of Northern Irish firebrand Hugh Hanna

- 1901: Robert Kerr Hannay, Historiographer Royal, teaches at U. of St. Andrews

- 1914: First World War (through 1918)

- 1928: Birth of Arthur Dion Hanna, future Governor-General of the Bahamas

- 1939: Second World War (through 1945)

- 1951: Dr. Walter Fergusson Hannay knighted

- 1960: Clan Hannay Society formed

- 1973: Death of "Pat" Hanna, founder of the Clan Hannay Society

- 1983: Archaeologists conduct "dig" of Sorbie Tower grounds

- 1996: Geophysical survey performed on site of Sorbie motte

- 2004: Death of Major Ramsay Rainsford Hannay, First Chief of Clan Hannay

- 2014: Conservation Management Plan for Sorbie Tower completed.

# Appendix C: Monarchs

## 1. Monarchs of Scotland, 1058-1603

| | |
|---|---|
| Malcolm III | 1058-1093 |
| Donald III | 1093-1097 |
| Duncan II | 1094* |
| Edgar | 1097-1107 |
| Alexander I | 1107-1124 |
| David I | 1124-1153 |
| William I (the Lion) | 1165–1214 |
| Alexander II | 1214–1249 |
| Alexander III | 1249–1286 |
| Margaret (the Maid of Norway) | 1286–1290 |
| (interregnum) | 1290–1292 |
| John Balliol | 1292–1296 |
| (interregnum) | 1296–1306 |
| Robert I (Robert the Bruce) | 1306–1329 |
| David II | 1329–1371 |
| Robert II | 1371–1390 |
| Robert III | 1390–1406 |
| James I | 1406–1437 |
| James II | 1437–1460 |
| James III | 1460–1488 |
| James IV | 1488–1513 |
| James V | 1513–1542 |
| Mary, Queen of Scots | 1542–1567 |
| James VI (James I of the United Kingdom) | 1567–1603 (1625) |

*Reigned 7 months before his predecessor resumed the throne

## 2. Monarchs of the United Kingdom, 1603-present

The English and Scottish crowns were united in 1603 when James VI of Scotland became James I of Great Britain.

| | |
|---|---|
| James I (James VI of Scotland) | 1603-1625 |
| Charles I | 1625-1649 |
| Interregnum: Charles I executed; Charles II in exile overseas | 1649-1660 |
| Charles II | 1660-1685 |
| James II | 1685-1688 |
| William III and Mary II[313] | 1689-1702 |
| Anne | 1702-1714 |
| George I | 1714-1727 |
| George II | 1727-1760 |
| George III | 1760-1820 |
| George IV | 1820-1830 |
| William IV | 1830-1837 |
| Victoria | 1837-1901 |
| Edward VII | 1901-1910 |

---

[313] Ruled jointly.

| George V | 1910-1936 |
| Edward VIII | 1936-1936[314] |
| George VI | 1936-1952 |
| Elizabeth II | 1952- present |

---

[314] Abdicated.

# Appendix D: Baronets of Mochrum

The official title of the Hannay Baronetcy was **Baronet Hannay of Mochrum, Kirkcudbrightshire** (created March 31, 1630 and currently dormant). It is not to be confused with Baronet Dunbar of Mochrum, Wigtownshire (created March 29, 1694 and as of 2019 represented by Sir James Michael Dunbar, 14$^{th}$ Bt.).

| Name | Years Held |
|---|---|
| Robert, 1$^{st}$ Baronet | 1630 - 1667/68 |
| Robert, 2$^{nd}$ Baronet | 1667/68 - 1689 |
| *Title dormant* | 1689 - 1783 |
| Samuel, 3$^{rd}$ Baronet | 1783 - 1790 |
| Samuel, 4$^{th}$ Baronet | 1790 - 1847 |
| *Title dormant* | 1847 - present |

# Appendix E: Dates and Calendar Differences

The methods by which dates are calculated have differed over time from country to country. In general, they have been uniform since 1752. The two main differences before that year were:

- **The date when a year number changed** (e.g. 1389 to 1390). For centuries, the first day of the year in Britain was held to be March 25th ("Old Style"). Gradually, this changed to January 1st ("New Style"). When referring to dates prior to the change from "Old Style" to "New Style", historians generally use the format *OS/NS*: *OS* represents the year which would have included dates prior to March 25th but after December 31st, whereas *NS* represents the year as calculated with the present-day calendar that begins January 1st. For example, March 1st, 1599/1600 means March 1st in the year when every day after March 24th was considered the year 1600.

- **The adoption of the Gregorian Calendar**, which was more precise than the old Julian Calendar at calculating leap years. The adoption also required the addition of a few days gradually lost since the time of Julius Caesar due to the seasons getting out of sync with the calendar.

The following diagram (Figure 127: Date Calculation over the Centuries) illustrates the differences during the transitional period between 1522 and the present day for dates in **Scotland** and **England**.

France has been added as an example of a typical continental Catholic nation for comparison. Before 1564, the new year started on Easter Day (whose exact date varies from year to year). Countries loyal to the Pope (including France) generally adopted the Gregorian Calendar in 1582, although many had still not chosen January 1st as the first day of the new year.

| | | Pre-1522 | 1522-1563 | 1564-1581 | 1582-1599 | 1600-1751 | 1752-Present |
|---|---|---|---|---|---|---|---|
| **Scotland** | First Day of the New Year | March 25 | | | | | January 1 |
| | # of days out of sync* | 11 | | | | | 0 |
| | Sample Date | March 13, 1520 | March 13, 1564 | March 13, 1564 | March 13, 1582 | March 13, 1751 | March 24, 1753 |
| **England** | First Day of the New Year | March 25 | | | | | January 1 |
| | # of days out of sync* | 11 | | | | | 0 |
| | Sample Date | March 13, 1520 | March 13, 1564 | March 13, 1564 | March 13, 1582 | March 13, 1750 | March 24, 1753 |
| **France** | First Day of the New Year | Easter | | | January 1 | | |
| | # of days out of sync* | 11 | | | 0 | | |
| | Sample Date | March 13, 1520 | March 13, 1564 | March 13, 1565 | March 24, 1583 | March 24, 1751 | March 24, 1753 |

| Sample Date Present-Day System (Gregorian) | March 24, 1521 | March 24, 1565 | March 24, 1565 | March 24, 1583 | March 24, 1751 | March 24, 1753 |
|---|---|---|---|---|---|---|

*compared to Gregorian Calendar

**Figure 127: Date Calculation over the Centuries**

To see how the period 1522-1752 must have been a rather confusing era of international correspondence, consider the **Sample Date** in Figure 127. If someone in **France** wrote a diary entry on **March 24th, 1751** according to the **French** calendar, it would have been dated **March 13th, 1750** in **England,** but **March 13th, 1751** in **Scotland.**

# Appendix F: Maps

## *1. Great Britain*

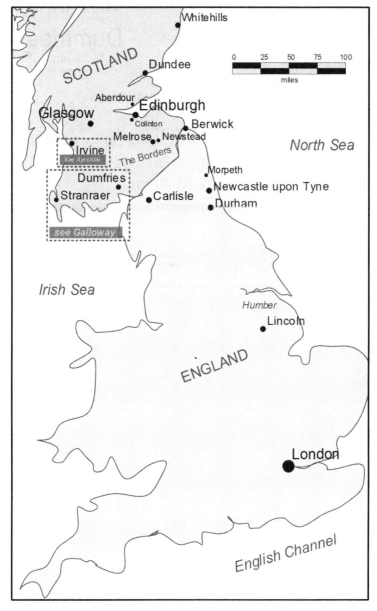

## 2. *Dumfries and Galloway*

Knockdaw
Glenlee
Dumfries
Mochrum
(Kirkcudbrightshire)
Cree River
Minnigaff
Larg
Castle Douglas
Leswalt
Stranraer
Newton Stewart
Torrs
Craigton
Lochnaw
Castle Kennedy
Saulset
Rusko
Gelston
Craigley
Wigtown
Glenluce
Knockglass
Auchinree
Kirkdale
Balcarry
Bladnoch River
Twynholm
Kirkcudbright
Portpatrick
Mochrum
(Wigtownshire)
Ardwell
Luce Bay
Whithorn
see Wigtownshire
Solway Firth
Irish Sea
0
5
10
15
20
miles

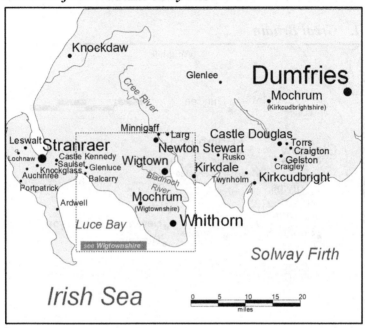

## 3. Wigtownshire

Minnigaff • • Larg

**Newton Stewart**

Kirkcowan • Kilsture •

**Glenluce**

Gass •

Spittal (Spital) •

Kirkmabreck •

Barquhill • • Mochrum Park

*Bladnoch*

**Wigtown** • Kirkbride •

Kilfillan •

Bladnoch •

**Kirkdale**

Old Place of Mochrum

**Culmalzie**

Clauchrie • • Baldoon

Barnbarroch

**Ravenshall**

Capenoch
(Kippinach) •

• Kirkinner

Slewhibert
(Sloehabbert) •

Orchardton

Culbrae
(Culbae) • Longcastle **Sorbie**

Mochrum •

*Wigtown
Bay*

Killantrae •

*see Sorbie and
Environs*

**Port William**

• Outon

*Luce Bay*

**Monreith**

**Whithorn**

• Gararrie

Knock •

• Balnab

0  1  2  3  4
miles

*Burrow
Head*

*Solway
Firth*

## *4. Sorbie and Environs*

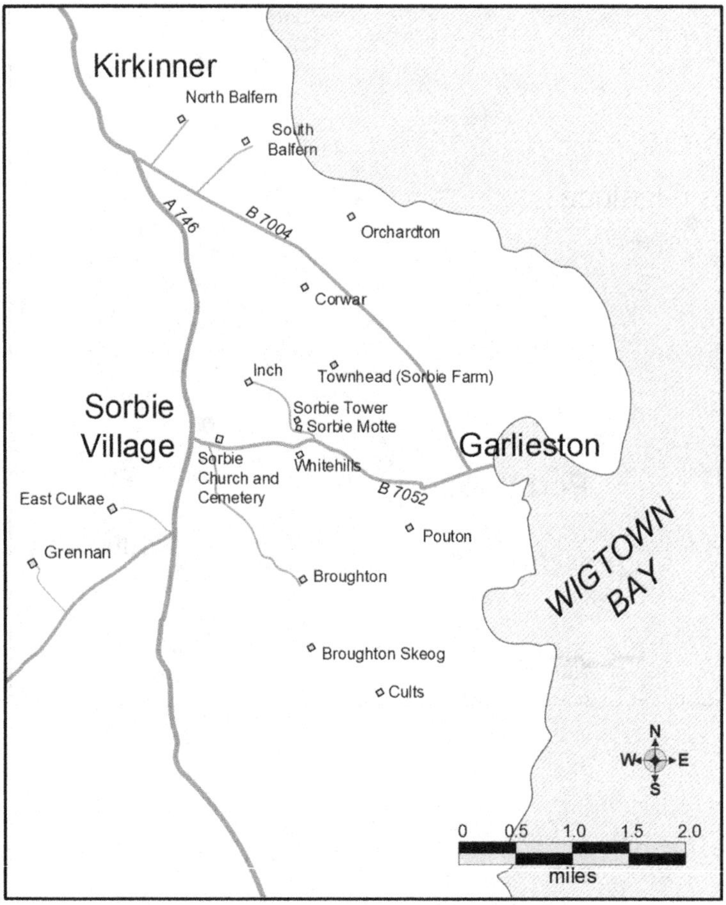

Kirkinner
North Balfern
South Balfern
A 746
B 7004
Orchardton
Corwar
Inch
Townhead (Sorbie Farm)
Sorbie Village
Sorbie Tower
Sorbie Motte
Garlieston
Sorbie Church and Cemetery
Whitehills
B 7052
East Culkae
Pouton
Grennan
Broughton
WIGTOWN BAY
Broughton Skeog
Cults
N
W
E
S
0
0.5
1.0
1.5
2.0
miles

## 5. *Ayrshire*

Irvine
A77
Firth of Clyde
River Ayr
A76
Auchinleck
Trabeauch
Logan
Ayr
Cumnock
0 1 2 3 4
miles
Dalrymple
Cassilis

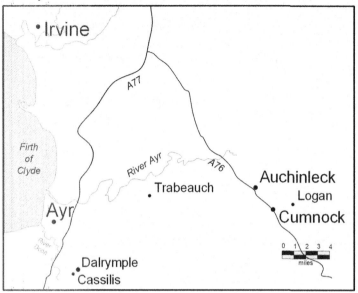

## 6. *Ireland*

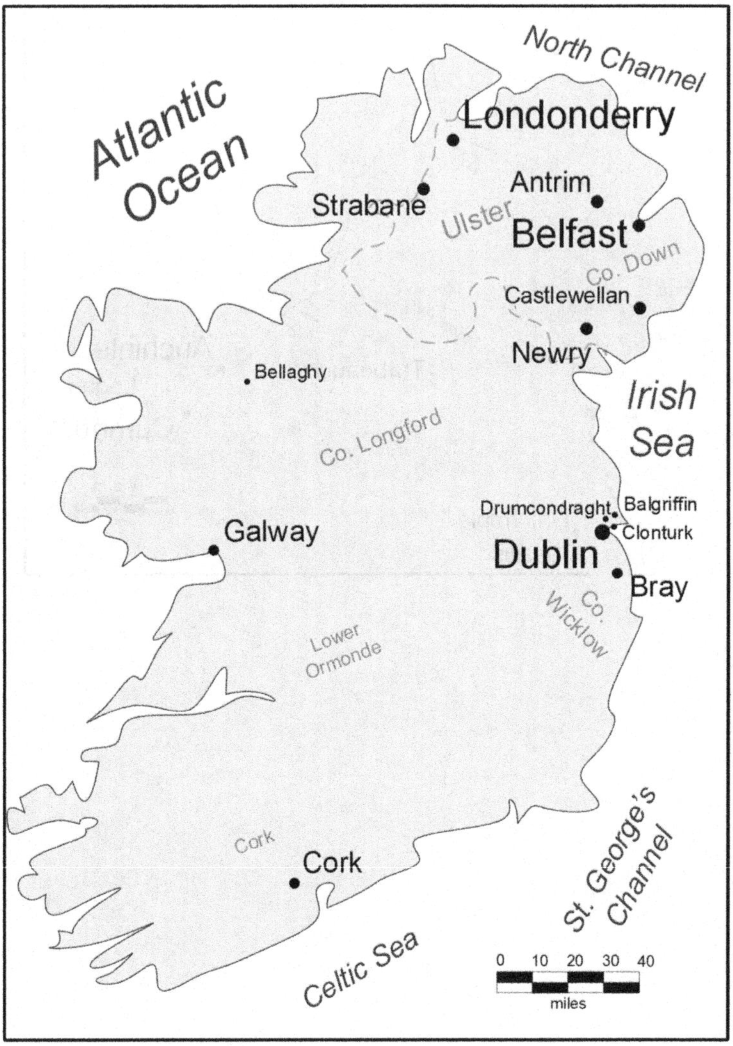
North Channel
Atlantic Ocean
Londonderry
Strabane
Antrim
Ulster
Belfast
Co. Down
Castlewellan
Newry
Bellaghy
Irish Sea
Co. Longford
Drumcondraght
Balgriffin
Clonturk
Galway
Dublin
Bray
Co. Wicklow
Lower Ormonde
St. George's Channel
Cork
Cork
Celtic Sea
0 10 20 30 40
miles

# Glossary

**a:**

1. (*preposition*) of

2. (*preposition*) on

**achievement:** (*heraldic noun*) The entirety of a coat of arms including crest, supporters, escutcheon, etc...

**acre, Scots:** (*noun*) a measure of land area equivalent to 1.3 imperial acres or 0.51 hectares.

**airt and pairt:** (*phrase*) aiding and abetting, instigation and actual assistance (in a crime).

**amercement:** (*noun*) fine assessed as an alternative to imprisonment.

**ane:**

1. (*ordinal number*) one

2. (*adjective*) own

**ANZAC:** Australia and New Zealand Army Corps, initially formed in 1914. It has since disbanded and reformed multiple times for various deployments in WWII, the Vietnam War and the East Timor Crisis.

**A.R.C.M.:** Associate of the Royal Conservatory of Music

**assize(s):** (*noun*)

1. superior court.

2. judicial inquest.

**attainder, bill of:** (*noun*) legislative act that stripped an individual of civil rights, of any title of nobility, and, in many cases, of life.

**attaint:** (*verb*) make subject to a **bill of attainder**.

**aucht:**

1. (*cardinal number*) eight.

2. (*ordinal number*) eighth.

3. (*pronoun*) anything.

459

**4.** (*verb*) owe, be owing.

**baillie:** (*noun*)

1. municipal officer or magistrate. Town councils had a **provost,** and next in line came the **baillies** as members of the council and magistrates. The provost was elected from the ranks of the baillies by his peers.

2. farm manager on a large farm.

**beir**: (*noun*) barley.

**boll**: (*noun*) a dry measure roughly equivalent to six imperial bushels or 218 litres.

**brokin**: (*adjective*) lawless.

**Broughton:** (*place name*) an estate in the parish of Whithorn, located on the road between Sorbie and the hamlet of Cults. – *Tony Lowe*

**burgess:** (*noun*) **1.** free citizen of a burgh (town/city), as opposed to a peasant owing allegiance to a lord. **2.** trader licensed by a burgh to carry out his trade.

**Burgess Roll:** (*noun*) census list of sorts used for determining the civic duties of various townsmen (e.g. taxation and military service). In some cases, membership in a tradesman's guild required listing on a burgess roll.

**burgh:** (*noun*) officially incorporated town, usually established through royal charter.

**burn**: (*noun*) stream.

**Calendar of Documents:** *(noun)* collection of published abstracts of the affairs of state executed by the Secretary of State under the direction of the royal council.

**Canongate**: (*place name*) part of the old town of Edinburgh; in the 1700s, it was apparently a rather dodgy area of the city.

**cartulary**: (*noun*) church record or registry.

**carvel-built:** (*adjective*) in boatbuilding, constructed so that the planks abut each other, rather than overlap.

**caution, stand**: (*verb*) act as bail/guarantee/surety. One standing caution would act as either a 'backer' or 'character witness'.

**charge**: (*heraldic noun*) an emblem on a shield. It can be an object, person, animal or plant.

**choir**: (*noun*) part of a church or cathedral between the altar and the nave.

**clerkship**: (*noun*) office or position of clerk.

**C. B.**: (*order of knighthood*) Companion of the Most Honourable Order of the Bath.

**C. O.**: Commanding Officer. An officer in charge of a unit of battalion size or larger. Compare with **O. C.** (Officer Commanding).

**collared**: (*heraldic adjective*) bearing a collar, when referring to a charge on a shield.

**compare**: (*verb*) appear in court.

**conform [to]**: (*adjective*) corresponding [to].

**constitute**: (*verb*) appoint.

**cordine**: (*noun*) shoemaker.

**couped**: (*heraldic adjective*) cut off at the ears, when referring to a charge.

**Craigilton** (*place name*) possibly a variant of Craigton, near Gelston, or, alternatively, a variant of Crugilton.

**cross-crosslet**: (*heraldic charge*) cross whose arms each comprise smaller crosses.

**Crugilton**: (*place name*) also called Cruggleton, this castle near Sorbie stood on the cliffs, but little now remains of what was once a place of strength. – *Tony Lowe*

**culverin**: (*noun*) medieval cannon.

**curator**: (*noun*) guardian or administrator of affairs (e.g. to a legal minor).

**customer**: (*noun*) customs officer.

**decreet**: (*noun*) a judgment in a (Scottish) court of law.

**denarius**: (*noun*) a Scottish coin, usually a penny, but depending on context, could apply to a mark, shilling or pound.

**devyid**: (*verb*) part, separate, depart.

**dilection**: (*noun*) love, affection.

**dispone**: (*verb*) grant, convey.

**dittay**: (*noun*) indictment.

**Dryburgh**: (*place name*) a town and abbey (now in ruins) on the banks of the Tweed, in the Borders (Southeast Scotland).

**ell**: (*noun*) unit of fabric measurement, usually 45 inches (1.143 metres), but variations as small as a yard and as large as 48 inches were known. The measurement was originally defined as the length of the arm from shoulder to wrist, and so could change regionally. In particular, a Scots ell was approximately 37.2 inches.

**entail**: (*noun*) inheritance restriction that ensures property remains in the family and cannot be sold.

**erased**: (*heraldic adjective*) referring to an animal charge, whose head has been cut off in a jagged fashion (versus *couped*, meaning cut off in a straight line).

**escheat**: (*verb*) revert the possession of a piece of land to a feudal lord under certain legal circumstances, for example on the owner dying without heir, or as punishment for a crime.

**escutcheon**: (*heraldic noun*) area on an achievement on which arms are placed. Usually a shield, though sometimes a lozenge (for female heraldry).

**factor**: (*noun*) agent or business representative.

**factorage**: (*noun*) commission paid to an agent or business representative.

**F.R.S.A:** (*post-nominal title*) initials signifying Fellow of the Royal Society of Arts, an honour bestowed on individuals who have made significant contributions to the fields of art, manufacturing or commerce.

**galcoit (galcolt):** (*noun*) jacket or coat.

**Galdus:** (*proper noun*) a Caledonian chief, also known as Cobredus, who fought the Romans in the 1$^{st}$ Century A.D. Legend has it that he is buried beneath Cairnholy II, a standing stone located near Kirkdale.

**Gallovidian:** (*noun*) a person from Galloway. See also **Galwegian.**

**Galwegian:** (*noun*) a person from either Galway (Ireland) or, less commonly, Galloway (Scotland). See also **Gallovidian.**

**Gelston:** (*place name*) a town in the parish of Kelton, Kirkcudbright – The name is derived from "Gavil's" or "Giles'" dwelling. – *Tony Lowe*

**german(e):** (*adjective*) for siblings, having the same parents, as in *brother german* or *sister germane*; for cousins, being first cousins, as in *cousin german*.

**glebe:** (*noun*) land assigned to a clergyman as part of his compensation (in addition to salary).

**goodman:** (*noun*) head of household.

**Great Seal Register:** The collection of official records of charters issued under the king's name. These include royal land grants, commissions, patents of nobility, letters of legitimisation and naturalisation, official pardons, articles of incorporation, patents and licenses to print money.

**gules:** (*heraldic colour*) red.

**hagbut:** (*noun*) *arquebus*, or archaic rifle-like firearm.

**halbrown:** (*noun*) armoured vest.

**handsense:** (*noun*) banner.

**heritor:** (*noun*) major landowner, functioning in many ways as a member of the gentry, appointing judges, hiring schoolmasters and clergy, maintaining roads, and levying taxes to pay for it all.

**horn, put to the:** (*verb*) denounce as a rebel or outlaw, derived from a herald's horn blast preceding the announcement.

**horning:** (*noun*) the act of being put to the horn (see above).

**hundredweight:** (*noun*) a British unit of mass equivalent to 112 pounds or 50.8 kilograms. Note that in the United States, a hundredweight means 100 pounds.

**ilk:**

1. (*adjective*) each.

2. (*adjective*) same.

3. (*noun*[315]) family, kind.

**impale:** (*heraldic verb*): combine side-by-side with another set of arms, usually due to a marriage (for persons) or a merger (for organizations or political entities)

**in hac parte:** (*Legal Latin*) in this matter.

**Inch:** (*place name*) settlement about 1km to the northeast of Sorbie village, and 500m to the northwest of Sorbie tower.

**infeft:** (*verb*) to invest a new owner with legal possession of inheritable property.

**ische:** (*noun*) exit, egress.

**item:** (*adverb*) likewise.

**jak:** (*noun*) armoured doublet

**kail-wife:** (*noun*) a (female) seller of herbs.

**kelt:** (*noun*) rough mixture of black and white wool in its natural state.

**Kilfillan:** *(place name)* most likely identified with **Kilphillan**, the site of a church or chapel on the farm of Millisle near the junction of the Sorbie and Wigtown roads. It may also refer to a chapel dedicated to St. Fillian in the parish of Old Luce. – *Tony Lowe*

**kirk:** (*noun*) church.

**kist:** (*noun*) chest for storing clothes.

**knaiffschieppes:** (*noun*) knaveship.

---

[315] This definition is fairly common today, but it is technically an inaccurate use of the adjectival form. For example, "John Hannay of Sorbie and that **ilk**", is really a contraction of "John Hannay of Sorbie and that **ilk** (same) **family**"

**knave**: (*noun*) (1) boy; (2) serving man.

**knaveship**: (*noun*) a fee paid in grain to the servants running a mill.

**Knight Bachelor**: (*rank of English knighthood*) The oldest form of knight in England. Knights Bachelor are not members of a particular order (e.g., Order of the Bath or Order of the Garter).

**Knockglass**: (*place name*) a village southwest of Stranraer.

**kye**: (*plural noun*) cattle.

**lozenge**: (*heraldic noun*) diamond-shaped escutcheon.

**L.R.A.M.**: (*post-nominal title*) Licentiate of the Royal Academy of Music.

**Machars**: (*noun*) low lying coastal land.

**mae**: (*adjective*) more.

**mailes**: (*noun*) rents.

**march with**: (*verb*) border, as in "his land marched with mine" = "his land bordered mine".

**M.P.**: (*post-nominative title*) Member of Parliament.

**merk**: (*noun*) an amount of money equal to Scots 13s, 4d.

**merkland**: (*noun*) Originally a merkland was a measure of land assessed as yielding a specified number of merks in rent. Nowadays this is found as the name of a farm in several areas. There are several farms with 'money' names such as Poundland in Dunscore Parish, Tenshillingland in Ayrshire and Sixpence in the Carrick division of Ayrshire. – *Tony Lowe*

**moorland**: (*noun*) field of peaty soil covered with moss, bracken and heather.

**mora**: (*noun*) (a) "moor" or "heath"; (b) delay in fulfilling a contract or in filing a claim. "**Keeper of the Mora**", a title given to the Kingsmuir Hannays, may have implied either the guardianship of a piece of land or (less likely) a notarial position that kept records of contractual infractions.

**morrioun**: (*noun*) helmet.

465

**motte**: (*noun*) mound or embankment upon which a castle and/or fortification were built.

**mullet**: *(heraldic charge)* star.

**natural**: (*adjective*) as in "natural child" or "natural son", illegitimate, bastard.

**nonentre**: (*noun*) state into which a property fell when no heir claimed possession after the previous owner had died. Until an heir claimed possession, the feudal lord to whom the owner was subject retained any income from the land.

**O. C.**: (*military rank*) Officer Commanding. An officer in charge of a unit smaller than a battalion. Compare with **C. O.**

**OCTU**: (*British military training facility*) Officer Cadet Training Unit.

**oxgang**: (*noun*) Scottish measurement of land approximately equivalent to 13 acres (on average, as the exact size varied from between 10 and 18 acres from region to region). It is supposed to be the amount of land ploughable by a single ox in one year.

**Owtoun [Outon]**: (*place name*) group of farms just outside Whithorn burgh. Also, an area of the same name formed a portion of the Broughton estate in Kelton parish of Kirkcudbright. – *Tony Lowe*

**oistellar**: (*noun*) inn keeper. Variants include **oislair**, **oisllar**, **ostler** and **oisler**.

**or**: (*heraldic colour*) yellow.

**oulk**: (*noun*) week.

**oulkly**: (*adverb*) weekly.

**particate**: (*noun*) an area of land equal to 13,690 square feet (0.314 acres) or 1,272 square metres (0.1272 hectares).

**pendent**: (*heraldic adjective*) suspended, hanging.

**perfyt**: (*adjective*) complete, entire, perfect. In legal documents, often used to describe age of majority, e.g. "perfyt age."

**persewair [-war]**: (*noun*) plaintiff in a legal suit.

466

**Picts**: (*noun*) Ancient Celtic people of the British Isles.

**portioner**: (*noun*) owner of a small part of an original, larger estate which had been subdivided, perhaps among the original owner's heirs.

**Powton**: (*place name*) also called Powtoun, Pouton or Powstoun, this was a hamlet in the parish of Sorbie. The name is derived from the "tun" (dwelling) beside the burn (stream) named Pow. – *Tony Lowe*

**precept**: (*noun*) order, command, mandate.

**pretendit**: (*adjective*) alleged, supposed.

**procurator**: (*noun*) agent or attorney.

**proper:** (*heraldic adjective*) in natural colours.

**protocol book**: (*noun*) notary register.

**provost**: (*title*) head of Scottish local government, roughly equivalent to a mayor.

**provost marshal**: (*title*) head of the military police.

**puncheon**: (*noun*) liquid measure equivalent to 84 gallons.

**quhair**: (*adverb*) where, in what place.

**quidnam**: (*adjective, pronoun*) what.

**quhile**: (*adverb*) (1) sometimes, from time to time; (2) at an earlier time; (3) for a time.

**quihilk**: (*adjective, pronoun*) which.

**relict**: (*noun*) widow.

**retour**: (*noun*) record of the passing of a right, estate or office to a successor.

**reversion:** (*noun*) right to future possession (of an estate or title). If party A were granted the reversion of a piece of land currently owned by B, then the property would pass to party A upon the death of party B.

**RAF:** Royal Air Force.

**RAOC:** Royal Army Ordnance Corps.

**RCA**: Royal Canadian Army.

**RCAF**: Royal Canadian Air Force.

**RMA**: Royal Military Academy. The RMA trained officers for the Royal Artillery and Royal Engineers from 1741 until the Second World War. In 1947, it was merged with the Royal Military College to form the Royal Military Academy Sandhurst (RMAS).

**sable**: (*heraldic colour*): black.

**saltire**: (*heraldic charge*) An x-shaped cross, as in the Cross of St. Andrew found on the Scottish flag.

**samen**: (*adjective, adverb*) same.

**sasine**: (*noun*) the act of taking possession of land by an heir or the transfer to a grantee.

**seize**: (*verb*) put in legal possession of (land).

**servander**: (*noun*) servant.

**shew**: (*verb*) display, put forward, submit for inspection.

**skeoch**: (*noun*) a small cave; cleft or crevice in rocks.

**smith**: (*noun*) craftsman who works with metals; e.g. a *black*smith (iron), a *gold*smith (gold).

**solidus**: (*Legal Latin*) shilling.

**stemmet**: (*noun*) A woolen fabric used to make hose (stockings).

**stent**: (*noun*) tax assessment.

**swerdslipper**: (*noun*) armourer, craftsman who sharpens swords.

**taburner**: (*noun*) drummer.

**tak**: (*noun*) agreement defining the terms of a lease or tenancy; also, can refer to the land in question which was leased.

**terce**: (*noun*) life-rent to widows, usually a third of the income and/or lands of the estate until the death of the surviving spouse.

**Test, the**: a law that required proof of adherence to the established (i.e. Anglican) church for anyone seeking public office.

**threave:** (*noun*) measure of approximately 24 sheaves (bundles) of cut grain.

**tiend:** (*noun*) tithe.

**toft**: (*noun*) homestead or croft.

**tollbooth, tolbooth:** (*noun*) a combined town prison or jail, the latter frequently consisting of cells under the town hall. The term comes from the stalls (booths) where taxes (tolls) were collected.

**totting:** (*noun*) sum, total, as in a bill of sale.

**trone:** (*noun*)

1. public scales in the market.

2. the market square itself.

**tutor**: (*noun*) legal guardian.

**twa**: (*number*) two.

**ult**: (*adjective*) past, of the previous month.

**umquhile:**

1. (*adjective*) late, deceased.

2. (*adverb*) sometimes, from time to time.

**umquhile...quhile:** (*adverbial construct*) at one time...at another time.

**V. C.**: Victoria Cross, The highest military award in the United Kingdom.

**vennel**: (*noun*) small street, narrow alley or lane. – *Tony Lowe*.

**wadset:** (*noun*) an early form of mortgage. The mortgagee paid over an agreed sum of money in return for custody of the land and the rents it provided. If the landowner did not redeem the wadset within seven years, the territory was forfeit to the lender. Wadset payments were recorded in a protocol book (notary register). Many landowners, or would-be landowners, made use of the wadset to increase their own land holdings.

**wark lume:** (*noun*) tool, workbench.

469

**wright**: (*noun*) a craftsman who makes and repairs things generally made of wood; e.g. *ship*wright, *plough*wright.

**writ**: (*noun*) letter, memorandum, written paper or account; usually a formal document of some sort having legal force.

**W. S.**: (*post-nominative title*) Member of the Society of Writers to Her Majesty's Signet, a Scottish professional society for solicitors.

# Index

### *A*

***B***

### *C*

***D***

***E***

482

484

489

491

***I***

# J

# K

493

***L***

***M***

### *O*



### *P*

## R

*S*

***T***

*U*



*V*



*W*

***Y***



***Z***

# Sources

- Agnew, Andrew, *Hereditary Sheriffs of Galloway*, Edinburgh, 1893
- Agnew, Robert Vaus, *Correspondence of Sir Patrick Vaus of Barnbarroch, Knight*, Ayr and Galloway Archaeological Association, 1887
- Amery, L.S., editor, *The Times History of the War in South Africa*, Sampson Low, Marston and Co., Ltd, London, 1909
- Anderson, William, *Scottish Nation*, Edinburgh, 1861.
- Anglo-Norman Dictionary, The - http://www.anglo-norman.net
- Balfour, James, editor, *The Register of The Great Seal of Scotland*, Volume II, Edinburgh, 1882
- Black, George Fraser, *The Surnames of Scotland, their origin, meaning and history*, New York: New York Public Library & Readex Books, 1962.
- Bank of England, www.bankofengland.co.uk (inflation calculator)
- British Monarchy official website, www.royal.gov.uk
- Burke's Peerage & Gentry website, www.burkes-peerage.net
- Burke, Ashworth P., *Family Records*, Harrison and Sons, London, 1897
- Canadian Oxford Dictionary [1998 Edition]
- Canmore, the National Record of the Historic Environment, Historic Environment Scotland, canmore.org.uk
- Chalmers, George, *Caledonia: or, a historical and topographical account of North Britain, from the most ancient to the present times with a dictionary of places chorographical & philological*, Alexander Gardner, Paisley, 1887
- Clay, Jane, *The Old Hannay Bible*, The Journal of the Northumberland and Durham Family History Society, Vol 22, No. 4., Autumn, 1997
- Cokayne, George E. (George Edward), *Complete Baronetage*, Volumes II and IV, William Pollard and Company, Exeter, 1902.
- Commission of His Majesty's Works, *Certificate of Service of Notice Affecting the Old Tower or Place of Sorbie in the Parish of Sorbie and County of Wigtown*, No. A.M./15/64556, Edinburgh, 28 November 1938
- Crisp, Richard, *Posthumous Rhymes by John Hannah, Beccles (private printing), 1854.*

- Croly, Herbert David, *Marcus Alonzo Hanna*, MacMillan, New York, 1912.
- National Library of Scotland and the University of Edinburgh Library– www.catalogue.lib.ed.ac.uk
- Dictionary of Scottish Architects, 1840-1980: www.scottisharchitects.org.uk
- Dictionary of the Scots Language, www.dsl.ac.uk
- Dobson, David, *Barbados and Scotland, Links 1627-1877*, Baltimore, Maryland, 2005.
- Douglas, James, *The Book of Galloway*, 1745, reprinted 1912 (Newton Stewart)
- Dumfries and Galloway Family History Society, www.dgfhs.org.uk
- Dumfries and Galloway Natural History and Antiquarian Society website: www.dgnhas.org.uk
- Egan, Simon and Edwards, David, *The Scots in Early Stuart Ireland: Union and Separation in Two Kingdoms*, Manchester University Press, 2016
- Fairbairn, James, *Fairbairn's Crests*, Edinburgh, 1905
- FamilySearch, www.familysearch.org
- Federation of Family History Societies website: www.genfair.com
- Forces War Records, https://www.forces-war-records.co.uk
- Fraser, Antonia, *Faith and Treason: The Story of the Gunpowder Plot*, Anchor Press, 1996
- Fraser, Marie - Electric Scotland – Baronets of Nova Scotia - www.electricscotland.com/canada/fraser/baronets_novascotia.htm
- Gillies, Marge, *Army Wives: From Crimea to Afghanistan: The Real Lives of the Women Behind the Men in Uniform*, Aurum Press, 2017
- Google calculator (Google.com) *for measure conversion*
- Hanna, Flora A., *Book of Benjamin Hanna*, Cleveland, Ohio, 1925
- Hanna, Rev. James A. M., *Hanna of Castle Sorbie, Scotland and Descendants*, Fourth Impression, Edwards Brothers, Ann Arbor, 1959
- Hanna, Sarah A., *The House of Hanna*, Brookville, Indiana, 1906.
- Hanna, William S., *The Hanna Family*, Cleveland, Ohio, 1930.
- Hannay, William Vanderpoel (b. 1896), *Genealogy of the Hannay Family*, Albany, New York, U.S.A., 1913

507

- Hannay, William Vanderpoel (b. 1896), *The Hannay Family*, 2nd Edition, U.S.A., 1969
- Historic Environment Scotland, *Cairn Holy Cairns 1 and 2 Statement of Significance*, Edinburgh, 2013
- Institution of Civil Engineers, Minutes of the Proceedings of, Volume 109 (1892), p 403-405
- Laing, David (editor), *Poems of Patrick Hannay*, Hunterian Club, 1875
- Lees, Sir James Cameron, *St. Giles, Edinburgh: Church, College and Cathedral, from the earliest times to the present day, W & R Chambers, Edinburgh/London*, 1889
- Library Ireland – www.libraryireland.com
- Lundy, Darryl – the Peerage Dot Com – www.thepeerage.com
- MacGibbon, David and Ross, Thomas, *The Castellated and Domestic Architecture of Scotland From the Twelfth to Eighteenth Century*, David Douglas, Edinburgh, 1887.
- Macleod, J. F., *The Old Place of Sorbie*, Galloway Gazette, Newton Stewart, 1969
- MacKay, W., *The Mediaeval Castle in Scotland*, Methuen, London, 1927
- MacKenzie, William, *History of Galloway from the Earliest Period to the Present Time*, John Nicholson, Kirkcudbright, 1861
- Macleod, J. F., *Gatehouse of Fleet and Ferry Town of Cree – ancient monuments – historic sites*, 1970
- MacNeill, Duncan Harald, *The Scottish Realm*, A. J. Donaldson, Glasgow, 1947
- Maxwell, *A History of Dumfries and Galloway*, Blackwood and Sons, Edinburgh and London, 1896
- McKerlie, Peter Handyside, *History of the Lands and their Owners in Galloway*, William Paterson, Edinburgh, 1877
- Measuringworth.com
- Microsoft Encarta 2004
- Morris & Co., Hong Kong, *Morris' Directory for China, Japan and the Philippines, Etc.*, 1870
- National Archives of Scotland - http://www.nas.gov.uk
- Nicolson, Joseph and Burn, Richard, *The History and Antiquities of the Counties of Westmorland and Cumberland*, Strahan and Cadell, London, 1777
- Nisbet, Alexander, *A System of Heraldry*, Volume I, Plate 23, Page 335, published 1722
- O'Hart, John, *Irish Pedigrees*, Dublin, 1888, Part VII, Chapter 1.

- Ordnance Survey (national mapping agency), www.ordnancesurvey.co.uk
- Paton, Henry, editor, *The Register of Marriages for the Parish of Edinburgh, 1595-1700*, Edinburgh, 1905
- Pont, James, *An Alphabet of Arms of the Nobility and Gentry of Scotland*, 1624
- Rice, Charles Elmer, *A History of the Hanna Family*, Pim and Son, Damascus, Ohio, 1905
- Robertson, John F., *The Story of Galloway*, Lang Syne Publishers, Ltd., Glasgow, 1985.
- Romanes, Charles S., Editor, *Selections from the Records of the Regality of Melrose*, Vol. III, University Press, Edinburgh, 1917
- Royal Commission on the Ancient and Historical Monuments of Scotland, *Fifth Report and Inventory of Monuments and Constructions in Galloway, 1: County of Wigtown* (1912)
- Royal Commission on the Ancient and Historical Monuments of Scotland, *Fourth Report and Inventory of Monuments and Constructions in Galloway, 2: County of the Stewartry of Kirkcudbright* (1914)
- Russell, James Anderson, *The Book of Galloway: History and Lore, Names and Places, Abbeys and Antiquities, Greater and Lesser Worthies*, Blacklock Farries And Sons, Dumfries, 1962
- Scotland's Places, scotlandsplaces.gov.uk
- Scottish Archive Network, www.scan.org.uk
- Scottish Register of Tartans, www.tartanregister.gov.uk
- Jeaffreson, J. Cordy, *A Book of Recollections*, Hurst & Blackett, Ltd., London, 1894
- Sizes.com
- Sorbie Family Website, www.sorbie.net
- Stodart, R. R., *Scottish Arms: being a collection of armorial bearings, A.D. 1370-1678*, William Paterson, Edinburgh, 1881
- Temperley, Alan, *Tales of Galloway,* Mainstream Publishing, Edinburgh, 1979
- Tranter, Nigel, *The Fortified House in Scotland* (Volume 5, Pages 230-232), Mercat Press, Edinburgh, 1986
- Trevelyan, G.M., *England Under the Stuarts*, Putnam, New York, 1922.
- University of Edinburgh School of Geosciences website - www.geo.ed.ac.uk
- Yahata, Masahiko, *A Novelist, George A. Birmingham*, geo-birmin.com

# Image Credits

Unless noted below, images included in this work are from the public domain.

Cover picture of Sorbie Tower: David Hannah

Figure 1: The Galloway Coast, Southwestern Scotland: Frank Lawler

Figure 2: The Wigtownshire Coast (Machars Peninsula): Frank Lawler

Figure 3: The Clan Crest: Frank Lawler

Figure 4: The Yellow Caravel: Kim Traynor / CC BY-SA 3.0Figure 5: Early Hannays: Frank Lawler

Figure 6: The Knockglass Family: Frank Lawler

Figure 7: The Descendants of Robert of Sorbie: Frank Lawler

Figure 8: Hannays of Culbrae and Capenoch: Frank Lawler

Figure 11: James IV with Falcon: National Gallery of Scotland / CC-BY-NC 3.0

Figure 12: The Hannays of Kilfillane: Frank Lawler

Figure 14: Descendants of John Hannay, MP for Wigtown: Frank Lawler

Figure 15: The uproar at St. Giles: Unknown / CC-PD-Mark

Figure 16: 18th C. engraving of the famous stool: National Library of Scotland / CC-PD-Mark

Figure 17: The Hannay and Coltart Farthing: Clan Hannay Society

Figure 19: Origins of the Kirkdale Hannays: Frank Lawler

Figure 20: The Hannays of Kirkdale: Frank Lawler

Figure 21: William Hannay of Kirkdale (died 1759): Clan Hannay Society

Figure 22: Margaret Johnston (married William Hannay in 1740): Clan Hannay Society

Figure 23: John Hannay of Ruscoe (died 1797): Clan Hannay Society

Figure 24: Ramsay Hannay: Clan Hannay Society

Figure 25: Johnston Hannay: Clan Hannay Society

Figure 26: Jane Johnston (2nd wife of Johnston Hannay of Torrs): Clan Hannay Society

511

512

513

# About the Author

Stewart Francis was born in 1920. He was educated at Forest School and entered the 5th Battalion, the Royal Berkshire Regiment in 1938, later serving in the 7th·Battalion, and during World War II at Headquarters, 78th Division, on the General Staff and in the 1st Battalion of the East Surrey Regiment in North Africa and Italy, and for a short time as an A.D.C. at General Alexander's Headquarters, and finally in the Greek Army 1947-8. During the war he became a regular officer in the Royal Berkshire Regiment and was mentioned in despatches.

Subsequently he served in the Arab Army of South Arabia and took part in the Radfan and South Arabia campaigns between 1964 and 1967. These campaigns were part of the Aden Emergency, an insurgency which eventually led to the independence of Yemen, in 1967, which had been under British rule since 1839. He finally served as a Lieutenant Colonel in the Zambia Regiments. In 1960 whilst serving in Nigeria he rode two Nigerian polo ponies from Nigeria to England, a journey of 7000 miles. He was a well-known polo player in Nigeria and played for the British Army touring Team in 1966 in Aden. He was a Fellow of the Royal Society of Arts.

Until his death in June, 1996, Stewart Francis resided at Armathwaite Castle in Cumberland.

# About the Editor and Co-Author

Frank Andrew Lawler was born in Ottawa, Ontario, Canada; he is a graduate of Trinity College School and Harvard University. He designed and managed software development projects for Cambridge Technology Group in Cambridge, Massachusetts, before concentrating on multimedia design and production, first at the Chedd-Angier Production Company in Boston, then with Microsoft's Interactive Television Group and the Microsoft Network in Redmond, Washington. In the early 2000s, he changed careers to focus on theater, primarily as an actor. He is the co-author of two plays, *The Elsinore*

514

*Diaries* and *Holiday of Errors,* and is a past president of the board of directors of Theatre Puget Sound and Strawberry Theatre Workshop. He resides with his family in Seattle. Mr. Lawler has been an active member of the Clan Hannay Society since 1998 and currently serves as an officer of the clan council.

rev.: 2020.10.20

Made in the USA
Monee, IL
07 April 2024

56562257R00292